THE IDG BOOKS STRATEGIES ADVANTAGE

We at IDG Books Worldwide created *Computer Telephony Strategies* to meet your growing need for access to the most complete and accurate computer information available. Our books work the way you do: They focus on accomplishing specific goals — not learning random functions. Our books are not long-winded manuals or dry reference tomes. In each book, expert authors help you understand new technology and teach you how to evaluate its usefulness for your needs. Easy-to-follow, comprehensive coverage and clear language and design — it's all here.

The authors of IDG books are uniquely qualified to give you expert advice as well as to provide insightful tips and techniques not found anywhere else. Our authors maintain close contact with end users through feedback from articles, training sessions, e-mail exchanges, user group participation, and consulting work. Because our authors know the realities of daily computer use and are directly tied to the reader, our books have a strategic advantage.

Our authors have the experience to approach a topic in the most efficient manner, and we know that you, the reader, will benefit from a "one-on-one" relationship with the author. Our research shows that readers make computer book purchases because they want expert advice. Because readers want to benefit from the author's experience, the author's voice is always present in an IDG book.

You will find what you need in this book whether you read it from cover to cover, section by section, or simply one topic at a time. As a computer user, you deserve a comprehensive resource of answers. We at IDG Books Worldwide are proud to deliver that resource with *Computer Telephony Strategies.*

Brenda McLaughlin
Senior Vice President and Group Publisher
Internet: YouTellUs@idgbooks.com

COMPUTER
TELEPHONY
STRATEGIES™

Jeffrey R. Shapiro

IDG
BOOKS
WORLDWIDE

IDG Books Worldwide, Inc.
An International Data Group Company

Foster City, CA ♦ Chicago, IL ♦ Indianapolis, IN ♦ Southlake, TX

Computer Telephony Strategies™

Published by
IDG Books Worldwide, Inc.
An International Data Group Company
919 E. Hillsdale Blvd.
Suite 400
Foster City, CA 94404
http://www.dummies.com

Library of Congress Catalog Card No.: 96-77079

ISBN: 0-7645-3013-5

Printed in the United States of America

10 9 8 7 6 5 4 3 2 1

1B/QS/QY/ZW/IN

Distributed in the United States by IDG Books Worldwide, Inc.

Distributed by Macmillan Canada for Canada; by Contemporanea de Ediciones for Venezuela; by Distribuidora Cuspide for Argentina; by CITEC for Brazil; by Ediciones ZETA S.C.R. Ltda. for Peru; by Editorial Limusa SA for Mexico; by Transworld Publishers Limited in the United Kingdom and Europe; by Academic Bookshop for Egypt; by Levant Distributors S.A.R.L. for Lebanon; by Al Jassim for Saudi Arabia; by Simron Pty. Ltd. for South Africa; by Pustak Mahal for India; by The Computer Bookshop for India; by Toppan Company Ltd. for Japan; by Addison Wesley Publishing Company for Korea; by Longman Singapore Publishers Ltd. for Singapore, Malaysia, Thailand, and Indonesia; by Unalis Corporation for Taiwan; by WS Computer Publishing Company, Inc. for the Philippines; by WoodsLane Pty. Ltd. for Australia; by WoodsLane Enterprises Ltd. for New Zealand. Authorized Sales Agent: Anthony Rudkin Associates for the Middle East and North Africa.

For general information on IDG Books Worldwide's books in the U.S., please call our Consumer Customer Service department at 800-762-2974. For reseller information, including discounts and premium sales, please call our Reseller Customer Service department at 800-434-3422.

For information on where to purchase IDG Books Worldwide's books outside the U.S., contact IDG Books Worldwide's International Sales department at 415-655-3172 or fax 415-655-3295.

For information on foreign language translations, contact IDG Books Worldwide's Foreign & Subsidiary Rights department at 415-655-3021 or fax 415-655-3281.

For sales inquiries and special prices for bulk quantities, contact IDG Books Worldwide's Sales department at 415-655-3200 or write to the address above.

For information on using IDG Books Worldwide's books in the classroom or for ordering examination copies, contact IDG Books Worldwide's Educational Sales department at 800-434-2086 or fax 817-251-8174.

For authorization to photocopy items for corporate, personal, or educational use, please contact Copyright Clearance Center, 222 Rosewood Drive, Danvers, MA 01923, or fax 508-750-4470.

 is a trademark under exclusive license to IDG Books Worldwide, Inc., from International Data Group, Inc.

ABOUT THE AUTHOR

Jeffrey R. Shapiro divides his time between consulting in IT and computer telephony, heading a software development company, and working as the editor for two electronic newsletters, *Online Business Today* and *Online Business Consultant,* which are read in more than 45 countries.

Welcome to the world of IDG Books Worldwide.

IDG Books Worldwide, Inc., is a subsidiary of International Data Group, the world's largest publisher of computer-related information and the leading global provider of information services on information technology. IDG was founded more than 25 years ago and now employs more than 8,500 people worldwide. IDG publishes more than 270 computer publications in over 75 countries (see listing below). More than 90 million people read one or more IDG publications each month.

Launched in 1990, IDG Books Worldwide is today the #1 publisher of best-selling computer books in the United States. We are proud to have received eight awards from the Computer Press Association in recognition of editorial excellence and three from *Computer Currents'* First Annual Readers' Choice Awards, and our best-selling *...For Dummies*® series has more than 25 million copies in print with translations in 28 languages. IDG Books Worldwide, through a joint venture with IDG's Hi-Tech Beijing, became the first U.S. publisher to publish a computer book in the People's Republic of China. In record time, IDG Books Worldwide has become the first choice for millions of readers around the world who want to learn how to better manage their businesses.

Our mission is simple: Every one of our books is designed to bring extra value and skill-building instructions to the reader. Our books are written by experts who understand and care about our readers. The knowledge base of our editorial staff comes from years of experience in publishing, education, and journalism — experience which we use to produce books for the '90s. In short, we care about books, so we attract the best people. We devote special attention to details such as audience, interior design, use of icons, and illustrations. And because we use an efficient process of authoring, editing, and desktop publishing our books electronically, we can spend more time ensuring superior content and spend less time on the technicalities of making books.

You can count on our commitment to deliver high-quality books at competitive prices on topics you want to read about. At IDG Books Worldwide, we continue in the IDG tradition of delivering quality for more than 25 years. You'll find no better book on a subject than one from IDG Books Worldwide.

John J. Kilcullen

John Kilcullen
President and CEO
IDG Books Worldwide, Inc.

IDG Books Worldwide, Inc., is a subsidiary of International Data Group, the world's largest publisher of computer-related information and the leading global provider of information services on information technology. International Data Group publishes over 270 computer publications in over 75 countries. Ninety million people read one or more International Data Group publications each month. International Data Group's publications include: **ARGENTINA:** Annuario de Informatica, Computerworld Argentina, Infoworld, PC World Argentina; **AUSTRALIA:** Australian Macworld, au.World, Client/Server Journal, Computer Living, Computerworld, Computerworld 100, Digital News, Network World, PC World, Publishing Essentials, Reseller, WebMaster; **AUSTRIA:** Computerwelt Osterreich, Networks Austria, PC Tip; **BELARUS:** PC World Belarus; **BELGIUM:** Data News; **BRAZIL:** Annuário de Informática, Computerworld Brazil, Connections, Super Game Power, Macworld, PC World Brazil, Publish Brazil, SUPERGAME; **BULGARIA:** Computerworld Bulgaria, Networkworld/Bulgaria, PC & MacWorld Bulgaria; **CANADA:** CIO Canada, Client/Server World, ComputerWorld Canada, InfoCanada, Network World Canada; **CHILE:** Computerworld Chile, PC World Chile; **COLOMBIA:** Computerworld Colombia, PC World Colombia; **COSTA RICA:** PC World Costa Rica/Nicaragua; **THE CZECH AND SLOVAK REPUBLICS:** Computerworld Czechoslovakia, Elektronika Czechoslovakia, PC World Czechoslovakia; **DENMARK:** Communications World, Computerworld Danmark, Macworld Danmark, PC Privat Danmark, PC World Danmark, PC World Danmark Supplements, TECH World; **DOMINICAN REPUBLIC:** PC World Republica Dominicana; **ECUADOR:** PC World Ecuador; **EGYPT:** Computerworld Middle East, PC World Middle East; **EL SALVADOR:** PC World Centro America; **FINLAND:** MikroPC, Tietoverkko, Tietoviikko; **FRANCE:** Distributique, Golden, Hebdo-Distributique, Info PC, Le Guide du Monde Informatique, Le Monde Informatique, Reseaux & Telecoms; **GERMANY:** Computer Partner, Computerwoche, Computerwoche Extra, Computerwoche Focus, Electronic Entertainment, GamePro, I/M Information Management, Macwelt, PC Welt; **GREECE:** GamePro, Multimedia World; **GUATEMALA:** PC World Centro America; **HONDURAS:** PC World Centro America; **HONG KONG:** Computerworld Hong Kong, PCWorld Hong Kong, Publish in Asia; **HUNGARY:** ABCD CD-ROM, Computerworld Szamitastechnika, PC & Mac World Hungary, PC-X Magazine; **ICELAND:** Tolvuheimur/PC World Island; **INDIA:** Computerworld India, PC World India, Publish in Asia; **INDONESIA:** InfoKomputer PC World, Komputek Computerworld, Publish in Asia; **IRELAND:** ComputerScope, PC Live!; **ISRAEL:** People & Computers; **ITALY:** Computerworld Italia, Computerworld Italia Special Editions, Macworld Italia, Networking Italia, PC Shopping, PC World Italia, PC World/Walt Disney; **JAPAN:** Macworld Japan, Nikkei Personal Computing, SunWorld Japan, Windows World Japan; **KENYA:** East African Computer News; **KOREA:** Hi-Tech Information/Computerworld, Macworld Korea, PC World Korea; **MACEDONIA:** PC World Macedonia; **MALAYSIA:** Computerworld Malaysia, PC World Malaysia, Publish in Asia; **MEXICO:** Computerworld Mexico, Macworld, PC World Mexico; **MYANMAR:** PC World Myanmar; **NETHERLANDS:** Computable, Computer! Totaal, LAN Magazine, LanWorld Buyers Guide, Macworld, Net Magazine, Totaal! Beurskrant; **NEW ZEALAND:** Absolute Beginner's Guide, Computer Buyer, Computer Industry Directory, Computerworld New Zealand, Electronic Entertainment, MTB, Network World, PC World New Zealand; **NICARAGUA:** PC World Costa Rica/Nicaragua; **NIGERIA:** PC World Nigeria; **NORWAY:** CAD/CAM World Norge, Computerworld Norge, Computerworld Privat (Datamagasinet), CW Rapport Norge, IDG's KURSGUIDE, Macworld Norge, Multimediaworld, PC World Ekspress, PC World Nettverk, PC World Norge, PC World's Produktguide; **PAKISTAN:** Computerworld Pakistan, PC World Pakistan; **PANAMA:** PC World Panama; **P. R. OF CHINA:** China Computer Users, China Computerworld, China Infoworld, Computer & Communication, Electronic Design China, Electronics Today, Electronics Weekly, Game Camp, PC World China, Popular Computer Weekly, Software Weekly, Software World, Telecom World; **PERU:** Computerworld Peru, PC World Profesional Peru, PC World Peru; **PHILIPPINES:** Computerworld Philippines, PC World Philippines, Publish in Asia; **POLAND:** Computerworld Poland, Computerworld Special Report, Macworld, Networld, PC World Komputer; **PORTUGAL:** Cerebro/PC World, Computerworld/Correio Informático, MacIn/PCIn, Multimedia World Portugal; **PUERTO RICO:** PC World Puerto Rico; **ROMANIA:** Computerworld Romania, PC World Romania, Telecom Romania; **RUSSIA:** Computerworld Russia, Mir PK, Sety; **SINGAPORE:** Computerworld Singapore, PC World Singapore, Publish in Asia; **SLOVENIA:** MONITOR; **SOUTH AFRICA:** Computing S.A., InfoWorld S.A., Network World S.A., Software World; **SPAIN:** Computerworld España, COMUNICACIONES WORLD, Dealer World, Macworld España, PC World España; **SWEDEN:** CAP&Design, Computer Sweden, Corporate Computing, MacWorld, Maxi Data, MikroDatorn, Nätverk & Kommunikation, PC/Aktiv, PC World, Windows World; **SWITZERLAND:** Computerworld Schweiz, Macworld Schweiz, PCtip; **TAIWAN:** Computerworld Taiwan, Macworld Taiwan, PC World Taiwan, Publish Taiwan, Windows World; **THAILAND:** Thai Computerworld, PC World Thailand, Publish in Asia; **TURKEY:** Computerworld Monitör, MACWORLD Turkiye, PC Games, PC WORLD Turkiye; **UKRAINE:** Computerworld Kiev, Computers & Software, Multimedia World Ukraine, PC World Ukraine; **UNITED KINGDOM:** Acorn User, Amiga Action, Amiga Computing, Appletalk, CD-ROM Now, Computing, GamePro, Macaction, Macworld, Network News, Parents and Computers, PC Home, PSX Pro UK, The WEB; **UNITED STATES:** Cable in the Classroom, CD Review, CIO Magazine, Computerworld, Computerworld Client/Server Journal, Digital Video Magazine, DOS World, Electronic Entertainment, Federal Computer Week, GamePro, InfoWorld, I+Way, JavaWorld, Macworld, Maximize, Multimedia World, Netscape World, Network World, PC World, Publish, SunWorld Online, SWATPro Magazine, Video Event, WebMaster; **URUGUAY:** PC World Uruguay; **VENEZUELA:** Computerworld Venezuela, PC World Venezuela; and **VIETNAM:** PC World Vietnam.   6/24/96

DEDICATION

To my mother, with all my love.

CREDITS

**Senior Vice President
and Group Publisher**
Brenda McLaughlin

Acquisitions Manager
Gregory Croy

Acquisitions Editor
Ellen L. Camm

Software Acquisitions Editor
Tracy Lehman Cramer

Brand Manager
Melisa M. Duffy

Managing Editor
Andy Cummings

Administrative Assistant
Laura J. Moss

Editorial Assistant
Timothy Borek

Production Director
Beth Jenkins

Production Assistant
Jacalyn L. Pennywell

**Supervisor of
Project Coordination**
Cindy L. Phipps

Supervisor of Page Layout
Kathie S. Schutte

Supervisor of Graphics and Design
Shelley Lea

Reprint Coordination
Tony Augsburger
Theresa Sánchez-Baker
Todd Klemme

Blueline Coordinator
Patricia R. Reynolds

Senior Development Editor
Erik Dafforn

Development Editor
Susan Pines

Copy Editor
Kerrie Klein

Editor
Gary Garcia

Technical Reviewer
Ron Nutter

Project Coordinator
Sherry Gomoll

Media/Archive Coordination
Leslie Popplewell
Melissa Stauffer
Jason Marcuson

Graphics Coordination
Angela F. Hunckler
Brent Savage
Gina Scott

Production Page Layout
E. Shawn Aylsworth
Brett Black
Linda M. Boyer
J. Tyler Connor
Dominique DeFelice
Maridee V. Ennis
Jane E. Martin
Drew R. Moore
Mark C. Owens
M. Anne Sipahimalani
Kate Snell
Michael Sullivan

Proofreaders
Michael Bolinger
Sandra Profant
Nancy Price
Dwight Ramsey
Robert Springer
Carrie Voorhis
Karen York

Indexer
David Heiret

Book Design
IDG Production Staff

ACKNOWLEDGMENTS

Writing a book is like driving in a grand prix. The author races around like a lunatic. The only thing on his or her mind is the checkered flag. But without the racing team to pump the gas, change the tires, wipe the sweat, tune the engine, check the nuts and bolts, and provide the nourishment, where would the driver be?

I had many wonderful people on my team, without whom this book would not have seen its checkered flag. It's hard to find the right words to thank them all.

Thanks go to my publisher, IDG Books Worldwide, Inc., for providing me with an outstanding editorial team. In particular, thanks go to Ellen Camm for her initial support and faith in my ability to deliver this work. Keeping me on my toes with excellent editing, continual insight, and worthwhile suggestions was my copy editor Kerrie Klein. And indispensable help came from my development editors Erik Dafforn, who coordinated the whole process, put all the pieces together for me, and made the tasks easier with his great sense of humor, and Sue Pines, who kept the book on the straight and narrow until the final words had been penned. Thanks . . . dream team.

I am also thankful to cartoonist Randy Glasbergen for the contribution his cartoons have made to the treatment of the subject.

Besides those directly involved with the book, I want to thank the other people who stood by me in my effort. First, I owe many thanks to my wife, Kim. Thank you for your understanding, your patience, and your unfaltering support during the times I locked myself away in front of a computer or simply "vanished" into another world.

Thanks go in particular to my friend and partner, Karl Slatner, publisher of *Online Business Today,* who made the resources (computers, networks, software, and more) of Home Page Press, Inc. available to me for this work. I would also like to thank Karl for pulling me away from the PC for regular coffee walks (220 to be precise) and donuts, for his vision, upbeat and colorful manner, and for his wise advice.

The book also owes a lot to my agents, David Fugate and Matt Wagner of Waterside Productions, Inc. David especially deserves accolades for his invaluable support, encouragement, and commitment.

Many people supported me from a distance. Although their thoughts were constantly with me, without their loyalty, commitment, and friendship, I would not have had the strength to put the words to paper herein.

Firstly, there is my mother, Elaine Shapiro, the world's best fiction editor, my harshest critic, most loyal friend, and anchor in my life. She has stood by me in every endeavor, hoping that one day I would write a book. This one's for you, Ma, and for all sacrifices you have made in the past years. I will not let you down.

Special thanks must go to the Azrael family, Ellen, Jake, and their daughter Rose, for their support over the years. This book was conceived in their home, and the first pages were written in their basement, amid probably the world's largest collection of piano rolls and some of the oldest rotary dial telephones which should be in the Smithsonian.

A primary source of support and encouragement (especially during a dark hour in my life) came from my good friend Gil Caplan, of Voicematix, Cape Town, South Africa. Gil is one the world's leading computer telephony vendors and consultants. Much of this book is based on consulting for several of Gil's longest established clients, such as Novell and Microsoft. I especially owe Gil and his wife, Margaret, a special thanks for flying me and my family down to Cape Town for an all-expenses-paid vacation that I definitely needed.

Special mentions go to Hugo Truter, senior editor for Tafelberg Publishers (Cape Town, South Africa), for his long-term friendship and support, and, for her faith, belief in me, and support, to my friend Margaret von Tresckow.

I also owe thanks to my partners and friends at Home Page Press, Inc., Dr. Wayne Kearney, and at Nortech Software, Inc., Erik Rosaen, for their help and encouragement. And for patiently waiting for me to return to work.

During the writing of this book, I spent much of my time "getting my hands dirty" with some of the latest in computer telephony hardware and software products. For this opportunity, I thank Rhetorex, Inc. — especially CEO Al Wokas, marketing director Mike Ross, and marketing executive, Treysi Hefling — for the loan of their TAPI-compliant voice-processing development kits for Windows 95.

I also received a great deal of help in the form of a continuous stream of the Visual Voice computer telephony software toolkits, from the Computer Telephony Products Group of Artisoft, Inc.(formerly Stylus Innovation, Inc.), and in particular, from Vice President of Marketing David Krupinsky. Several other computer telephony companies provided me with support and material, including Applied Voice Technology, Inc., Plantronics (whose marvelous headsets enabled me to take calls and still have both hands on the keyboard), Spectrum Signal Processing, Dialogic Corporation, Natural MicroSystems, and the Voice Messaging Educational Committee (VMEC), which you can access on the World Wide Web at http://www.vmec.com.

Special mention goes to Shane Mattaway, Chief Technical Officer of NetSpeak Corporation, for allowing me to burn up his valuable time delving into the "biology" of intranets and Internet telephony.

Finally, the computer telephony industry would not be what it is today without the evangelizing of Harry Newton, the Publisher and Editor-in-Chief of *Computer Telephony Magazine*. I would like to thank Harry for inviting me to participate as a moderator and Judge in the Computer Telephony Expo that his organization sponsors.

(The Publisher would like to give special thanks to Patrick J. McGovern, without whom this book would not have been possible.)

Contents at a Glance

Table of Contents

PART II: COMPUTER TELEPHONY SERVICES 134

FOREWORD

The telephone is ubiquitous but dumb. If I dial a wrong number, I have to hang up and re-dial. Even my $3 calculator has a backspace erase key. And 75 percent of my calls end up in "voice-mail jail." That scenario drives me ballistic because every un-completed call represents an irritated customer and a lost sale. What good is your phone if you can never reach anyone?

Soon, my laptop PC will be a phone. It will have intelligence. My PC will be able to dial my calls, find people, leave messages, transcribe my calls, chase me down when the call is urgent, set up my conference calls automatically, never put any of my callers into voice mail but tell them what they are calling for, and generally handle my calls like a 24-hour a day, never-tiring, super-smart secretary. My PC will be able to handle all my messages — paper, e-mail, voice, fax, and images. And my computer will let me manipulate and manage these messages off-line.

I wanted a way to describe this great new world. I came up with the term *computer telephony*. I define computer telephony as the adding of computer intelligence to the making, receiving, and managing of telephone calls.

Computer telephony encompasses four broad elements:

1. **Messaging.** Voice, fax, and electronic mail; fax blasters, fax servers and fax routers; paging and unified messaging (also called integrated messaging); and Internet Web-vectored phones, fax, and video messaging.

2. **Real-time connectivity.** Inbound and outbound call handling, *predictive* and *preview* dialing, automated attendants, LAN/screen-based call routing, one number calling, "follow me" numbers, video, audio and text-based conferencing, PBX systems in PCs, and collaborative computing.

3. **Transaction processing and information access via the phone.** Interactive voice response, audiotext, customer access to enterprise data, "giving data a voice," fax-on-demand, and shopping on the World Wide Web.

4. **Adding intelligence (and thus value) to phone calls.** Screen pops of cus-tomer records coinciding with inbound and outbound phone calls, mirrored Web page "pops," smart agents, skills-based call routing, virtual (geographi-cally distributed) call centers, computer telephony groupware, intelligent help desks, and *Advanced Intelligent Network* (AIN) computer telephony services.

I see computer telephony as having two basic goals or benefits: (1) to enhance one's personal productivity by making it easier to make and receive phone calls, and (2) to please one's customers who call in or who are called for information, service, help, and so on.

To attain these goals, you add computer intelligence to the desktop, to the office phone system, and to the public switched telephone network. The next few years will see an explosion in adding computer intelligence to the world's phone networks.

The best news: We now have the technology, the resources, the computer power, the new standards and the muscle to deliver on the promises of computer telephony. We also have many new players who are, thankfully, not burdened by the assumptions of yesteryear's telecommunications industry. We also have legions of developers and systems and integrators who are grabbing these computer telephony tools and cranking out hundreds of customer-pleasing, productivity-enhancing solutions for your business.

Computer telephony delivers. And fortunately, the industry now wants it.

But where do you start? That's where *Computer Telephony Strategies* comes in. Jeffrey Shapiro has written a book to help you realize the benefits to your business from adopting computer telephony. Check it out.

Once a year (typically in March), industry leaders meet at a trade show called the Computer Telephony Conference and Exposition. A monthly magazine covering the industry is also available called *Computer Telephony Magazine*. I'm proud to say I'm associated with both of them. If you'd like to learn more, drop me an e-mail: `harrynewton@mcimail.com` or snail mail me at:

Harry Newton
Publisher, *Computer Telephony Magazine*
12 West 21 Street
New York, NY 10010

INTRODUCTION

In March 1993, I attended the Computer Telephony Conference and Exposition in Dallas as an exhibitor. My company was boasting a computer telephony product that offered a number of Microsoft Windows applets that enabled the user to access voice mail and manage personal computer telephony resources from the desktop.

During the show, several colleagues and friends noticed a solitary man dressed in a dark gray business suit wandering around the pavilion. He would come by our booth, peek at the applications, and then walk away. This game of "hide and seek" went unnoticed by me for quite a few days. He was so quiet while I demonstrated the product's features to attendees that I never noticed him staring over my shoulder. As the days went by and the end of the show drew nearer, our friend's appearance at the demos became as regular as the sun. I was convinced that this guy either worked for the KGB or had been hired by a competitor as a spy.

On the last day, our "Spy in Gray," as he became known to us, finally approached me. It was probably the first break I'd had from the attendees in four days.

"I'm from Microsoft," he said, sounding almost nonplussed. "I have been watching your booth for a few days, but I could never get a chance to talk to you." With that, he pressed a package of disks into the palm of my hand.

"What's this?" I asked.

"It's Version 1 of the software development kit for TAPI."

A week or two later — after having studied the hundreds of pages of documentation — I knew that in several years, the likes of Microsoft would change the face of computer-telephone integration and that a new era would emerge. I envisioned a new age in which software developers would be able to write applications that conformed to a standard telephony API (applications programming interface), when a PBX could be treated like a printer or a scanner. I became very excited, and my company began to work towards the time when the hardware vendors would emerge with drivers to support the new standards.

That age is now upon us: 1996 is going to see some major shifts in the computer telephony industry, consolidation in some areas, new alliances, newer and better technology, and the inevitable industry shakedowns. This new age also has brought with it a kaleidoscope of applications and products that can make a prospective CT user's head spin.

The purpose of *Computer Telephony Strategies* is to help you make sense of the whirl-wind computer telephony industry and the applications that exist in this new age.

Since 1993, I've observed with much interest the increasing media coverage of the new standards, the advent of Novell's Telephony Services API (TSAPI), continuous reports about which standard would prevail, and the war between camps led by Microsoft and IBM and Apple. As a result of all this publicity, the overall awareness of computer telephony and its benefits rocketed. The clients I visited would immediately ask me about TAPI and TSAPI at a time when the PBX (private branch exchange) industry's support for the two standards was still two years out.

But computer telephony is not only about the new API standards. It's also about trying to "blend" two disparate technologies (PC systems and telephony) into a unified system. I began to notice during extensive consulting in 1994 that my clients were keen and ready but did not fully understand what computer telephony entails. It was then that I began to recognize the need for a book that looks at computer telephony from a holistic point of view. Computer telephony has many issues that cannot be solved by using these standards alone. These problems have to do with how the makeup of every enterprise works with computer telephony: its management, its staff, its IT systems and IT staff, and so on. I discuss all these issues and more in this book.

The first time I considered writing *Computer Telephony Strategies* was while I was consulting for a number of companies that were considering installing call-processing and voice-mail systems. I later concluded that these companies had decided they needed such systems without clearly understanding what the benefits of these systems would be, what resources would be needed, and what would be required of them for successful implementation. As you'll learn in this book, lacking that knowledge can kill your computer telephony project before it even gets off the ground.

I'm always impressed at how thoroughly and completely my consulting clients have downsized or "rightsized" since the beginning of the decade. In spaces where monster-size mainframe systems once stood, you now find hundreds of servers connected together by local area networks, enabling thousands of personal computers to converse with each other.

However, this practice resulted in a trait that was common to all my clients: The people there are concerned about staying on the cutting edge of technology, almost to the point of paranoia. Yet that admirable attention is rarely extended to the telephone systems. Few IT executives spend more than five minutes a week on communications and technology problems related to their firm's telephone system.

In 1993, for example, I did some consulting work for a busy hospital. After monitoring the telephone system, my colleagues and I discovered that 30 percent of the daily calls to the hospital were callers who had to retry their calls because they were unsuccessfully connected or routed to extensions on the first try. The installed PBX was 15 years old, yet management had decided that not one dime of the technology and IS budget would be allocated to upgrading the telephony system or integrating it with the enterprise-wide information network.

Even after we advised them that a huge hole in their information system setup was burning a similar hole in the hospital's budget, they still remained unmoved. The hospital lost thousands of dollars a day as a result, as well as the respect of some of the callers; only after the telephone system collapsed and patients and doctors started migrating to other hospitals did management wake up and take our advice.

Today, many companies are talking about computer telephony. Several magazines are published on the subject. The excuses for depriving your organization of a computer telephony system that can be fully integrated with the enterprise-wide information network are quickly dwindling to nothing.

The information technology industry currently is witnessing the emergence and the growth to maturity of computer telephony. The new telephony age is certain to be explosive. That huge, cabinet-like PBX attached to the wall behind the door in the men's room or in a basement somewhere will shrink in size until it can be mounted on an interface card that can be plugged into a PC.

Thanks to technology, people are no longer out of touch. You can reach people anywhere at any time — that is, if they want to be reached. People can get messages to us via e-mail, voice mail, fax mail, over the air, via pagers, and so on. Whereas you once picked up the pink message slips when you arrived at the office, read them, and tossed them away, you now have the option of using the mailboxes that software companies are selling, which present all of your message types in a uniform list and enable you to view and manage them from your PC. There's a trade-off, however: Our lives are being swamped with a variety of electronic message types that sometimes can end up being more difficult to manage than they are worth.

So, do you need all this? Do you need computer-telephone integration and computer telephony? Ask yourself what would happen to your business if you disconnected your telephone lines for the day: Does your telephonist tell you that he or she has no time to go to the rest room? Did your assistant "notify" you of the amount of telephone calls with which he or she has dealt? Can you, with relative ease, manually work out what your telephone system costs you, how many calls were successful, and how many callers turned to your competition?

If you can't readily answer yes to these questions, then you may indeed have the need for computer telephony.

WHO THIS BOOK IS FOR

This book provides a holistic overview of computer telephony and the elements that comprise this technology. It introduces IT and management information system people, network managers, network engineers, PC technicians, telephone technicians, power users, small businesses, and all serious PC owners to the wonders of computer telephony. Any business that considers the telephone as the life-blood of its company needs to invest in CT education.

Many sections of this book are aimed at IT specialists, information officers, systems integrators, and network engineers. A major objective of mine in writing this book is to create a place for the computer telephony guru (a hybrid species of network/telephony engineer) in the workforce of the IT department. This book also provides IT staff with an understanding of some of the business issues (such as customer satisfaction and staff acceptance of the CT system) of which they need to be aware.

Many issues in the text relate to the business activities of executive officers, business planners, entrepreneurs, and small business owners. Besides the gain in productivity, computer telephony can tremendously empower the enterprise. Computer telephony can mean the difference between success and failure of your business because you are dealing with a technology that directly touches customers. Computer telephony systems reside on the front line of your business dealings: They manage the phones and they keep the calls coming. They provide the buffer you need to ward off competitive threats.

In late 1995, the Internet phenomenon began to rock the computer telephony boat. By mid-1996, both industries had collided head-on. The result, however, was not wreckage but rather the birth of new service domains known as *Internet telephony* and *Intranet computer telephony*. These domains put humans firmly on the road to deploying single enterprise networks carrying both voice and data. I introduce this subject in Chapter 12.

THE STRUCTURE OF THE BOOK

Part I provides an overview of computer telephony, the enabling technologies in it, and how computer telephony fits in the overall information technology picture. Part I also provides an overview of telephony and computer-telephone integration.

Part II discusses, in detail, the various computer telephony service domains: call processing, voice processing, audiotext, IVR, and more. If you look at the Table of Contents, you'll note that I also discuss the Internet and the World Wide Web as they relate to computer telephony.

If you are quite new to the whole subject, you'll need to read Chapters 1 and 2 and then the chapters in Part II. If you are one of the many people who hate voice mail or can't stand to call your bank, you may want to start with Chapter 13.

In Part III, I deal with strategies for effectively implementing and using computer telephony. This part looks at computer telephony as a part of the business planning process. These chapters also deal with deploying computer telephony as part of that plan for your enterprise. If you have a basic understanding of computer telephony, you can start with these chapters and then go back to Part II.

HOW TO CONTACT THE AUTHOR

If you find any problems with the text, concepts, examples, or case histories or if you have anything specific that you want to ask of me, I would be happy to receive your mail. As a caveat, I am not an electrical engineer; I majored in communications and spent a great deal of time studying psychology, philosophy, business, and journalism — and in the past ten years, studying information technology and software development. So, if you want to convey some ideas or point out issues related to purely technical or engineering subjects, go ahead — I would definitely like to hear from you.

Many of my examples are drawn from the work I have done in Africa and North America. I also managed the South African approval process for the international versions of Rhetorex, Inc.'s voice-processing boards (which we gained in 1992), so I know just how complex the world of electrical engineering — and telephony in particular — can be. I value your unbiased opinion about these issues so I can improve the technical treatise for future editions.

You are also welcome to send for the shareware software mentioned in the book. Drop me a note, and I will have them sent to you via e-mail.

You can reach me on CompuServe at 73353,2444 or via the Internet at 73353.2444@compuserve.com.

You also can reach me on the Internet at jeffs@hpp.com or at my Nortech Software, Inc. Internet address, at js@wizzkids.com. You also are invited to drop into the computer telephony lounge located on the Internet at http://www.wizzkids.com/ctlounge. Someone will always be around whom you can ask a question or who may be able to help with a computer telephony problem.

I hope you enjoy reading this book as much as I have enjoyed writing it!

Part I

Understanding
Computer Telephony

"As promised, you'll have free use of the company golf course during your lunch hour. Just double-click on the icon labeled 'GOLF'."

IN THIS CHAPTER

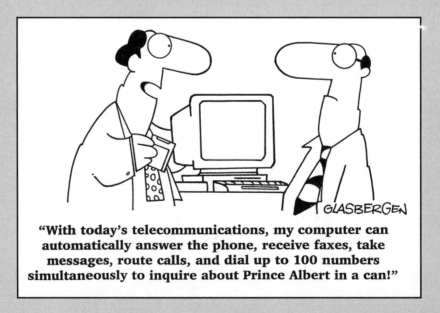

"With today's telecommunications, my computer can automatically answer the phone, receive faxes, take messages, route calls, and dial up to 100 numbers simultaneously to inquire about Prince Albert in a can!"

CHAPTER 1

Understanding Computer Telephony

This chapter provides a holistic overview of computer telephony, starting with definitions. Computer telephony services, such as voice mail and audiotext, have been around in various forms since the 1970s. Today, computer telephony is a full-blown service domain of information technology, a means of empowering the enterprise for competitive advantage.

This chapter also helps you to understand what the term *computer telephony* means. Before diving in, let's try to clear up a small semantics problem that has everyone scratching their heads. The terms in question are

✦ Computer telephony

✦ Computer-telephone integration

✦ Computer telephony integration

COMPUTER TELEPHONY

The person who coined the phrase *computer telephony* (circa 1992) is Harry Newton, a telecommunications expert and the publisher of several magazines and books covering telecommunications, including the leading magazine to serve the industry, *Computer Telephony*. Harry also is the man behind the world's most important Computer Telephony Exposition and Conference, "Computer Telephony Expo," held every Spring in Los Angeles. The following description is Harry Newton's definition of computer telephony, as it reads in his 1,300-page tome, *Newton's Telecom Dictionary:*

Computer telephony is the term used to describe the industry that concerns itself with applying computer intelligence to telecommunications devices, especially switches and phones. The term covers many technologies, including computer-telephone integration via the *local area network* (LAN), interactive voice processing, voice mail, auto attendant, voice recognition, text-to-speech, facsimile, simultaneous voice data, signal processing, video conferencing, predictive dialing, audiotext, "giving data a voice," call centers, help desks, collaborative computing, and traditional telephone call switching and call control.

Computer telephony has, however, evolved to represent a great deal more than a term used to describe an industry and its plethora of service technologies and domains. As you will learn from this book, computer telephony is an exhaustive, multi-faceted science that has many divergent issues, disciplines, and services.

COMPUTER-TELEPHONE INTEGRATION (CTI)

Some industry people call it art, others call it engineering, but essentially, *computer-telephone integration* (CTI) is the process of integrating external networked or stand-alone computer systems with the telephone network and the switch. The switch can be the device or network of devices used to connect and route telephone users on the public telephone networks, the central exchange, or devices used in private telephone networks. The private switch is known as the *private branch exchange,* or PBX (which I discuss in more detail in forthcoming chapters).

The actual integration can take many forms, but the ultimate goal is the same: to merge data networks with the telephone network and extend the capability of telephony devices and computer systems to communicate with each other. By the end of the decade, experts foresee a situation in which many enterprise networks will consist of one fast, digital, high-bandwidth network carrying voice, data, information, and video.

In 1996, it became all too clear that Internet technologies will facilitate this model. Although TCP/IP-facilitated network communications (the Internet protocols) have been around for decades, the critical emergence of the Internet in the public domain has provided the computer telephony industry with many new options for advancing the concept of voice-data digital networks. Technology enabling humans to converse in real-time over wide-area digital networks now exists.

The technology also is available to switch voice calls made over the public switched telephone network (PSTN) to the Internet. Humans can use computers and connections to the Internet to call any telephone in the world for free. Companies are deploying Internet technology on their enterprise information networks at an incredible rate. These new extensions to the corporate intelligence network are becoming increasingly known as intranets, and I tackle this subject in Chapter 12.

The link between a computer telephony system (a computer stuffed with computer telephony hardware and software) and the PBX is referred to as the *CTI link*. I refer to *CTI* and *CTI links* throughout this book.

COMPUTER TELEPHONY INTEGRATION

The term *computer telephony integration* can mean several things. Many people confuse it with CTI, but it's *not* the same thing. As this chapter shows, computer telephony has exploded into a major service domain of information technology (IT). As a service domain of IT, computer telephony systems have to be carefully and meaningfully integrated into the existing or complimentary computer and telephone systems of the enterprise. Hence, I use the term computer-telephony integration throughout this book to describe the integration process. The computer telephony industry knows the difference between computer telephony integration and computer-telephone integration, so this explanation is aimed primarily at the general IT industry — and at LAN and system integrators in particular, who need to be aware of the difference to fully understand the technology.

As a computer telephony consultant, I strive to paint the entire picture for my clients. The jobs of computer telephony gurus — and of the people they train to oversee a computer telephony project — encompass more than how to best make disparate computer technologies and telephone systems talk to each other. Yes, computer telephony is mainly about computers and telephony or telecommunications, but I make sure that my clients understand that it is also about people, information technology, information engineering, information and data processing, customer satisfaction, corporate culture, and more.

To fully understand computer telephony, you have to look at this subject holistically. On the one hand, the various services of computer telephony, such as voice messaging and audiotext, have outstanding capabilities and features; but on the other hand — like all technology — they can cause problems if they are misused or abused. The Japanese, for example, are very particular about how they address each other (as they have been for centuries); thus it has taken the Japanese some time to feel comfortable with human-computer dialog, especially voice mail.

Human capacity for using technology is a factor in computer science that is often overlooked. You also have to consider the resistance to technology that exists with older generations. These people still find computers scary and confusing; you can imagine how they feel about a computer that calls you up and talks to you. This problem exists for both the internal and external environments of a business. Without considering all the possible effects that the technology will have in areas such as corporate culture, human habit, and practice, and without strategic planning, your ambitious computer telephony project may be heading for certain disaster without you even knowing it.

MORE THAN JUST LINKING COMPUTERS AND TELEPHONES

Before 1992, a standard term to describe the emerging computer telephony industry was not available. I felt that the term *computer-telephone integration,* or CTI, aptly described it, because at the core of this "science" lies the integration of computers and telephones. The worlds of data communications, computing, and voice communications remained separate and often mutually hostile to one other because they have been viewed as separate entities for so long — especially in the minds of the people who work in these industries.

Telephony people are very different from computer or IT people. In the past, telephony people typically took a great deal longer to understand the needs of business than the computer professionals did. Perhaps business is partially to blame for this fault because telephony has never been brought under the authority of IT (I'll explain why this is important later). In 1994, a senior engineer from one of the world's largest PBX companies presented me with an incredible suggestion for fixing a massive bug in my client's 3,000-extension PBX: "Cut down on the number of telephone calls you receive."

Finally, in 1992, the term *computer telephony* became official. As computers become part of telephony systems and vice versa, the term will become more applicable and widely understood. For now, however, the term does not convey the intensive — and often frustrating — integration effort that a business has to endure to reap the benefits of the technology.

So, what is this greater definition of computer telephony to which I have alluded? Here is *my* academic definition: Computer telephony is a broad spectrum of computer and telecommunications technologies (the elements) integrated into a unified system (consisting of various service domains) to empower the enterprise by facilitating and enhancing the processing of telephonic communications. (I am always searching for something better, however, so see my e-mail address in the Introduction if you have a suggestion.)

But my definition does not end here because the integration of computer telephony systems into the enterprise is, like the other service domains of IT, a continuing process. The following variations help bring computer telephony into focus:

✦ Computer telephony is about computers "using" telephones and telephone systems in the same way that humans do (or once did) — and then some.

✦ Computer telephony is about computers helping humans to better use the telephone (and use it less) and thus be more productive.

✦ Computer telephony is about humans interacting with computers on the phone.

✦ Computer telephony is about integrating computers and the enterprise network (the LAN) with the telephone system — computer-telephone integration.

COMPUTERS THAT USE TELEPHONES AND TELEPHONE SYSTEMS LIKE HUMANS

Can you imagine office life without the telephone? Have you ever gone to the office on a Sunday morning and stood there in the silence, marveling at how different the scene was from the weekdays? No phones ringing, everything so perfectly quiet. Imagine if every workday were like that. I've know first-hand what it's like, but in this case it wasn't a pretty picture.

Several years ago, I witnessed the head of a company almost strangle a telephone technician who powered down a PBX while hundreds of telephone conversations were taking place — and caused the telephone system to collapse. The ripple-effect was devastating. Some clients said they even noticed the effect at the stock exchange.

Although you may not always appreciate it, the telephone is the life-blood of the enterprise, its life-support system. This fact still holds true even in the age of cyberspace in which we now live and work. Today, the telephone system is the reason why many of us are in business. Rather than just being a technology that supports the enterprise, the telephone is the enterprise in many cases or the reason for the enterprise's existence and survival.

The telephone system was originally built by humans for use by humans. This resource enables people to communicate with each other in real-time, without having to be in the same place. Today, the telephone system — or rather, the telecommunications system — may be a telephone at the end of a twisted-pair wire or a 10 Mbps connection to the Internet. Even using computers to access data in on-line databases — via bulletin board systems, the Internet's World Wide Web, an interactive voice response system, or a fax-on-demand system — is basically human-to-human communication. Humans put data in, humans get data out, or they manipulate it for further human consumption and use. Whatever the technology or scope of the system, however, the bottom line is people communicating with people.

Before the advent of the personal computer and the enterprise communications network (better known as the LAN), almost all activity between two points on a telephone network was between two or more people. People seemed to have more time to talk to each other on the telephone. (Ironically, computers seem to have created more of a workload rather than lessened it.) If you needed your account balance, you simply called the bank and a friendly representative read you the data. If you wanted to check the status of an order, you called the order clerk. At this time, the only devices using telephone and data networks, other than huge mainframes, were modems, telex, and teletext machines.

As the Information Age came about, however, Human Resources specialists realized, through the research efforts of companies like Octel and VMX, that more than 60 percent of time spent on the telephone is wasted, unproductive time. Other people also realized that the time and effort spent on the telephone often could be delegated to a CPU, allowing them to devote more time to other tasks. Their rationale? Let the computers waste time on the phone. After all, they're bought and paid for — they don't earn salaries.

Think about it: Do you need a person to sit at a console all day simply to route thousands of calls to extensions? Do you need a worker whose sole job is to take down messages? Do you need a person who just reads repetitive information to callers? A computer can do these tasks for you, frequently much more effectively. I, for one, would rather rely on a computer to take a message for me than a human. (I have yet to find someone who can take down a message that doesn't require me to return the call just to find out what the person wanted from me in the first place.)

Computer telephony enables users to be more productive in the office and less stressed. Consider the following:

✦ The average telephone call lasts about four minutes. More than three minutes of that call is time wasted on idle chatter. After the call ends, the parties require several minutes of "settle back" time, getting back to what they were doing before the call.

✦ The content of about 75 percent of business-to-business calls could be conveyed without both parties present. In other words, the information can be conveyed to or by a computer.

When people delegate some of their time spent on the phone to computers, they can spend more time away from the telephone (not just on it) without the worry of missing calls. These people have more time to go out to meet with clients, brainstorm with other employees, go to the health club, and so on. Computer telephony can result in a great gain in productivity because it snaps the chain that binds us to our desks, both mentally (such as when you're worrying about whose calls you missed while you were out) and physically, waiting for calls. Over the years, I have dug up the following statistics about my clients:

✦ About 45 percent of their workdays are spent away from their desks (or out of the office).

✦ About 10 percent of their workdays are spent on breaks and other timeouts (a 10-minute jog, for example). For many, the allotted time is much less because they sacrifice this time to make up for time lost.

✦ About 25 percent of their workdays are spent on the telephone (a lot of it wasted as described above).

✦ About 20 percent of their workdays are spent doing work that cannot be interrupted.

Computer telephony was thus born to facilitate the use of telephone systems by computers. This is the essence of the CTI process: Get computers and telephone systems to work together. The goal is to make life easier for people, not to complicate it. This CTI process will keep getting better as telephony and computer people begin to cooperate and merge their efforts, as well as agree on standards and open architectures.

Although computers are supplementing people on the phone, the primary concern of telephone manufacturers will always be on how people use their products, not computers, and it had better be. Their products must still allow humans to communicate as quickly and easily as possible. A human can, without much thinking, grab a telephone handset and communicate a critical piece of information to another human. If you see a person in need of medical assistance, you grab the handset to dial 911. Another human grabs the call and gets the emergency people moving.

If a human finds a computer on the other end, the call-processing and communication flow has to be transparent to the parties. In other words, the computer, like a human, detects the ringing on the telephone line. It answers the call, and the first thing that the computer does is assume a human is on the other end; then it speaks. If the computer is the only resource left to take the call, it needs to work like a human, by taking down the information as a voice message or data input ("Press 1 to raise hell") and trying every possible means to transfer either the call or the message to the emergency team. This process is known as cascading notification, as shown in Figure 1-1.

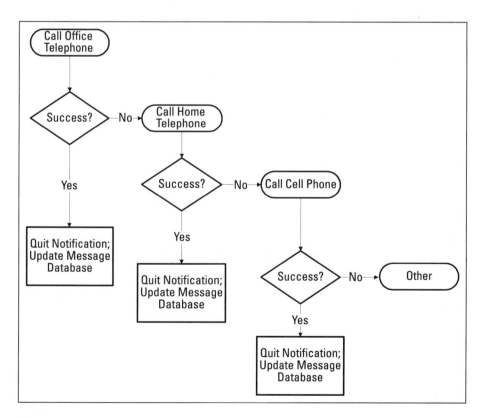

Figure 1-1: A good messaging system enables the mailbox user to decide how best to be notified.

If you want to replace (or, better yet, supplement) humans with computers at the telephone, the computers must be able to emulate the human senses of speech and hearing. In other words, the human-computer dialog needs to be as close to human-human dialog as possible. The computer needs to listen to a human voice over the phone and respond with a human voice. The computing power needed to perform this task and to make the conversation between a human and a computer as lucid as possible is enormous. However, such computing power has arrived. It's cheap, and it's getting more and more powerful every day. (This technology is discussed in Chapters 4, 5, 6, and 15.)

COMPUTERS THAT HELP HUMANS USE THE TELEPHONE MORE PRODUCTIVELY

Telephony has been around for more than a century. The plain old telephone — fondly known as the POT, a derivative of *Plain Old Telephone Service* (POTS) — has not changed much since its rotary dial was replaced with touch pads for pulse dialing, and later, touch pads for DTMF (dual-tone multifrequency signals, or touch tone) dialing. In other words, the process of making and receiving calls is the same (see Chapter 4). It's what you can now *do* with the calls that has changed. More buttons are available, but they conceal features that are both difficult to access and use. Telephone-switching systems are more sophisticated today and the switching equipment has many more features. So what can you do from your phone? Here are some of the tasks you can now perform:

✦ Park a caller at an extension or in PBX "orbit," thus allowing another employee to seize the call or receive the call as soon as the extension is free.

✦ Conference the call with other parties, local and remote.

✦ Override the extensions settings and get your PBX to follow you around the office or the world.

✦ Program the keys on multi-button phones to perform different tasks; for example, to dial the voice mail system and enter your password for you automatically.

✦ Dial a call pick-up code and seize a call ringing at another extension.

✦ Program the PBX to transfer your calls to a monitored extension (coverage) so that another attendant, whether computer or human, can answer calls in your absence.

How do you use these features? By entering cryptic codes on your telephone set. To forward calls on a phone, you may have to key in something like *83 to invoke the feature and #83 to cancel it. How do you know whether you've entered the right code?

Some PBXs go berserk if you do the wrong thing — that's one way to find out. Usually, however, the dial tone uses an alternative cadence when you enter the code that activates the feature. Almost every PBX works this way.

The interface to PBX features is mostly nonexistent or consists of a very limited liquid-crystal display (LCD) screen. Most people do not really need many of the offered features in their day-to-day, hectic schedules. But the computer-telephony system does.

Imagine how much easier it would be if you could load software on your PC that can do all these tasks for you without making you enter the codes (see Chapter 5). A dialer does exactly that. With your mouse, you can click on a button that can transfer your call. You can enter the extension in the available field or pop up a dialog box and select from a list of extensions (or better still, a list of office associates). As described in the forthcoming chapters, such software can enable the computer telephony manager to view the entire call-forwarding layout of the telephone system from any computer on the network. At a glance, this person can see the coverage provided for every extension, such as which extensions forward calls to voice mail and which extensions forward calls to other employees.

A system such as this one would help prevent mishaps. For example, I had a client who accidentally diverted his calls to his boss rather than voice mail by entering 9 instead of 6 on the key pad. How different his life would be now had he been able to select the call-forwarding extension from a pull-down or pop-up menu. . . .

This software does not work in isolation. It must be integrated with the PBX. This integration is achieved through a digital connection over the LAN or by connecting the PC to a desktop telephone. Such an integration is what CTI is all about; you can accomplish it by using smart software engineering and the new telephony service interfaces that major software and telephony vendors have recently released. I discuss these interfaces in more detail throughout the book.

Many office workers still battle to use the PBX and its call-processing features. Some PBX companies assume that humans have the ability to interface with the inner workings of their equipment. These companies have consistently failed to realize that the average office user finds it difficult to activate the features of a PBX from the telephone. But the attitudes of these companies are changing, thanks in particular to the evangelizing of Harry Newton, who referred to such narrow-mindedness as being like "teaching pigs to fly."

PBX companies have never really seen or taken advantage of the burgeoning need for computer telephony systems. Instead, they sat back and watched how the gurus in the software business were able to create computer telephony products that interfaced, albeit in a limited way, with their equipment. Then it suddenly dawned on them that money could be made here.

This computer telephony market has been growing at a steady rate for years. Many software companies (mine included) built functions into software programs running under desktop operating systems such as Windows and DOS to make it easier for the users to control and use the hidden features of a PBX. With new operating systems, more powerful computers, and the advent of significant enabling technology, this industry is now set to boom.

In 1992, I headed a team of engineers that designed software that could pick up a caller on hold and transfer the caller to another extension; the software accomplished this task through the interface of a Rhetorex voice-processing card. To activate this feature, the user simply had to enter the park or hold number via the keyboard and click on an icon. The software then instructed the voice processing card to snatch the caller from hold; dial an extension; listen for ring, busy signal, or answer; and then act accordingly. If the destination party was not available, the software could transfer the caller to the voice mail facility for that extension.

My team created this design because the PBX offered no means of telling the voice-mail system which user needed voice mail services. A voice-mail system has hundreds of users, all of whom have private mailboxes. When the voice mail system picks up a call diverted from a busy or unanswered extension, it needs to know which mailbox to open and which greeting to play.

The only device that can do this is the PBX. If the PBX cannot communicate this information (as explained in later chapters), then the call has to be tracked by the voice mail system from the moment it arrives at the enterprise. In other words, like the human telephonist, the voice mail system has to transfer the call *on consultation,* which means it has to perform call-progress analysis to determine whether the call was answered or the extension was busy. (During this time, the caller is on hold.) If the call cannot be completed, the voice mail system has to abort the transfer (bring the caller back from hold) and present the caller with the opportunity to leave a message in the correct mailbox.

My client employed a work force that needed to pick up voice mail from the field. Thus, we had to direct the call flow from a PC. From the monitor, the user could watch the voice-processing card process the entire call, resulting in successful transfer of the call to another extension or to voice mail. The product was years ahead of its time, but it worked; the PBX product manager nearly fell off his chair when he saw it. At the time, the number of enterprises using this particular model of PBX was more than 10,000, so it presented a lucrative opportunity for my company. I guess you could say we were one of the first — if the not the first — to invent desktop computer telephony.

It took a few more years for the PC operating systems to become stable enough to accommodate desktop computer telephony in a true multitasking environment, however. The old Windows "Unexplainable Application Errors" rendered the technology too unreliable. Today, all operating systems are responding to the demand for computer telephony rising to meet the needs of desktop and server-based call control.

The TSAPI and TAPI standards (see Chapters 3 and 5) are the best efforts to date for providing standards that all parties in the computer telephony industry can adopt in turning computer telephony into a pervasive computing service.

Today, most office workers are captive at their computer monitors, so it makes sense to enable users to open up the telephony interface within Windows or as part of running applications. This way, it then can be integrated and merged with the other, everyday applications, such as order processing and customer service.

HUMANS INTERACTING WITH COMPUTERS ON THE PHONE

Another name for computer telephony is *interactive telecommunications*. Computer telephony was often referred to by this name in the late '80s and early '90s. Interactive telecommunications is about humans interacting with computers over the telephone — having a human-computer dialog, so to speak. (I deal with this subject and the respective services that use it in Chapters 8–11 and 13.)

Let me give you an example of the usefulness of interactive telecommunications. Several years ago, my company was approached to build an application for Philips, the giant electronics company headquartered in Belgium and the Netherlands. It planned to run a contest with its prime-time TV advertising. Whenever its ad ran, a question would be posed and the viewer could dial a number on the screen to answer the question. However, Philips' problem was how to answer and record the flood of calls in the five minutes allotted for responses. On the first night of the competition, more than 30,000 people called the competition number. If Philips had hired humans to process the calls, the first cases of operator death syndrome might have been reported.

Although Philips had wanted to use humans to process the calls, the company instead followed my company's advice by using a system of Rhetorex voice-processing cards to answer the phones when the ad appeared on TV and record the callers' reactions to the prompts. (Rhetorex, Inc. is one of the industry leaders, and its components are known for their quality of "voice.") If someone called in too early, he or she would hear, "You're too early; call back in two minutes."

During the allotted time span, callers were prompted for the correct answers as well as their names and addresses. The information was saved onto a cassette tape and then taken to the competition moderators for processing. By using a computer system, the company was able to process at least six times more calls than live operators would have been able to process.

Interactive telecommunications has many applications in the Information Age. Interactive voice response (IVR) systems enable callers to query and enter information in databases over the telephone. I discuss IVR systems in further detail in Chapter 11.

INTEGRATING THE DESKTOP COMPUTER AND THE ENTERPRISE NETWORK WITH THE TELEPHONE SYSTEM

Understanding computer telephony means understanding that, for the foreseeable future, the transmission of data and voice will not be totally achieved on a unitary enterprise network. In other words, the LAN and the telephone network will remain separate entities (the reasons for this fact are discussed later in the book).

Understanding computer telephony also means understanding that the installed base of telephones in the world far outweighs the installed base of computers. Although the number of installed personal computers is climbing everyday, telephone systems are not as dispensable as computers.

Consider the following: Most businesses that use computers extensively replace or upgrade their computer equipment every six to nine months. A great deal of software is upgraded, or goes through a maintenance release, at least once a year.

The telephone system, on the other hand, is unlikely to be replaced or junked for several years. In some countries, the purchase price of PBX equipment was so expensive that the owners are locked into lengthy lease contracts extending past the year 2010. To upgrade their PBX equipment, these businesses either have to renegotiate their PBX leases or live with PBX equipment they have. (The chance that these systems have of becoming part of the enterprise information network is as good as the chance of a bat adapting to daylight.) The majority of these systems will not be upgraded to make them easier to integrate into the enterprise's corporate computer telephony systems. These systems were not designed for that. They were designed to switch calls and connect humans.

Despite the limited user interface on most PBX systems, PBXs do the job they were designed to do, and they do it well. You can rely on the POT and the switching network to do its job — switch calls without any significant downtime. A good PBX can last decades. For example, a bank that I consult for had to replace its entire network of computers and software within a year (the server software changed three times in one year), whereas its PBX (two nodes serving over 1,000 extensions) had been around since the sixties. Replacing PBXs also involves a great deal more than just money (as discussed in Chapters 7 and 17), so the bank wanted to install computer telephony without changing the PBX.

COMPUTER TELEPHONY AND INFORMATION TECHNOLOGY

If you're a pundit in any of the computer telephony services and technologies, you may raise your eyebrows when you see that I've included e-mail and the Internet services in this book. E-mail and the World Wide Web are not computer telephony systems, you may say.

You would be correct if you're considering the computer telephony industry pre-1996. But you will encounter many technologies from the other service domains of information technology (IT) that belong in the computer telephony models, or at least alongside them. These technologies are part and parcel of information technology. Figure 1-2 represents an organizational chart of IT and its various (not all) service domains.

The CIOs (Chief Information Officers) and IS (information systems) engineers need to know about a great deal more than computers and telephony to make sound implementation decisions. A large computer telephony project requires the combined expertise of several IT experts to achieve successful implementation. Even the experts supplying the switching and PBX technology to the project must have their butts firmly seated on the IT chair.

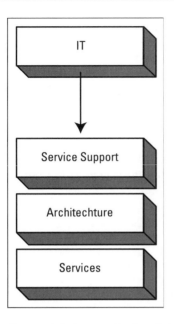

Figure 1-2: IT organizational chart and service domains.

Remember, too, that I'm talking strategy here. If fax-on-demand is part of computer telephony, then you can argue that hypertext is also — because both serve electronically based information to the user over the telephone network. Both services are sewn into the fabric of the enterprise information network and the IT layers that support it. Callers now can access documents on the Internet from their fax machines. Many IT people who embraced fax technology as recently as a year or two ago never spared a thought for the Internet. Now the services are as intertwined as a plate of steaming-hot fettucine noodles.

Some companies are already exploring having callers enter an e-mail address over the telephone so that a computer telephony system can e-mail information to the caller rather than fax it. Why? Because it cuts out the need for character recognition on moribund fax documents. These services are really variations of the same idea (electronic messaging), like apples and oranges are variations of fruit. Therefore, I prefer to discuss these technologies as siblings (service domains) of the same parent, information technology.

Thus, e-mail, v-mail (voice mail), and f-mail (fax mail) are quickly morphing into a unified messaging paradigm and are no longer considered to be in separate worlds. For example, I cannot recommend fax-on-demand to my new clients in the fervent manner I did before the World Wide Web took off like a firecracker. For many companies (especially the ones located in North America), hypertext on the Internet has left fax-on-demand standing in the dust as a customer satisfaction tool. It's a cheaper and more accessible method of disseminating or providing information. However, fax-on-demand is still very useful and will have its place in IT and computer telephony strategy for many years.

For these reasons, the more that you understand computer telephony and the strategies to use it, the better off you will be when you implement it. So, let's begin without further delay.

HOUR-GLASS SYNDROME

The primary reason that drives almost every computer telephony project is an attempt to overcome the *hour-glass syndrome,* or bottleneck, at the PBX. This classic telephony nightmare is usually one of the first (human) telephony problems that computer telephony addresses. One problem consequence is illustrated by the cartoon shown in Figure 1-3.

"Our Mrs. Phelps is one heck of a woman. Today she routed 2,000 phone calls and still had enough time left over to guzzle 43 cups of coffee and sneak in a quick nervous breakdown!"

Figure 1-3: A human can process only one call at a time. If two calls arrive at the same time, one call has to be put on hold.

To understand how this problem occurs, you first must understand how your PBX works.

Your PBX essentially is a miniature telephone exchange operating inside a cabinet or your computer. For now, think of the PBX as a train station for telephone calls. When trains (phone calls) arrive at the station, the station master (the human telephonist) operates the switching gear (the processor and switching matrix of the PBX) to switch the trains (calls) to different tracks (extensions) and sends them to other destinations (such as phone sets or ports where the calls are processed). But what would happen if several more trains appeared out of nowhere and all demanded to be immediately processed? The station master has to hold these trains on their tracks until platforms can be cleared. And train drivers have a great deal more patience than telephone callers. Chapters 4, 5, and 7 discuss PBXs and switching systems in more detail.

Now that you understand what the hour-glass syndrome is, let me show you how this problem can sneak up on a company in a real-world example. The case of one of my first consulting clients, Motor Vehicle Insurance Services, Inc. (MVIS), provides a perfect example of a computer telephony project that a company started to solve the hour-glass syndrome.

In case you're wondering, this firm really does exist. You won't find it listed in the business section of your phone book, however — I've changed the name of the firm because I want to discuss some astounding events that took place there during a year with this project. A lot of mistakes were made, and I want you to learn from them in the chapters to follow. So, let's launch right into the case history with some information to set the scene.

My consulting firm inherited MVIS as a client when the chief IT consultant for MVIS, the late Dr. Michael Edwards, joined our firm. MVIS had been in the insurance business for many years before the company decided to merge with another firm. Since its start, MVIS had experienced steady growth. But MVIS had decided it was time to take action to increase the pace of growth and, hence, the value of the business. MVIS bought and took control of its former strategic partner, a smaller insurance company that had rock-solid contracts with banks and leasing companies. (MVIS needed those contracts to grow.) After the two firms merged, MVIS assumed all the staff and operations of the smaller firm and moved all new employees to MVIS corporate headquarters.

Prior to the merger, MVIS employed two telephonists to handle its telecommunications. (I choose to call these people telephonists rather than operators. To me, the word "operator" implies being only machine-oriented, whereas telephonists frequently deal with people and are public relations experts.) Before the merger, these telephonists processed a substantial, but manageable, number of calls to MVIS — about 700 calls a day. Rarely was the MVIS main number not answered in the first three rings by a friendly, pleasant voice. The company's PBX, about 18 months old, capably served around 100 extensions and provided the capacity for 300. There were 30 trunks (a telephone line between the facility and the telephone company) running into the facility, mostly unused.

This telecommunications system had worked fine for MVIS because most of its client base was composed of several large banks, fleet owners, and a host of fleet-management firms. Individual policy owners rarely needed to call the company.

However, two weeks after the merger was completed, the situation was drastically different. It now took more than 30 rings to reach the telephonists at MVIS; if the caller was lucky enough to get through, often he or she would hear "MVIS, please hold." With so many callers on hold, the previously-unused 30 trunks soon maxed out, and dialing the MVIS main number finally resulted only in busy signals.

Warning: The first words heard by a caller when the telephonist or computer answers the phone creates an immediate and lasting impression. (See Chapter 8 to learn about answering message strategies, particularly if your computer telephony system is the first "voice" a caller hears.)

The problems began when the telephone company re-routed all calls from the former location of the smaller partner to MVIS headquarters. By rapidly integrating several large accounts into its existing operations and by winning a huge contract from a leasing bank that required MVIS to manage small insurance policies and warranties numbering in the hundreds of thousands, MVIS increased its call volume by several thousand percent practically overnight. Although MVIS had anticipated a large increase in calls from individual owners calling in claims, no one had expected the suddenness with which it would take place.

How could the problem be solved? MVIS's first thought was that it needed more telephone lines. We pointed out that although that may be the case, the problem at hand was a human one. There were too many calls for two people to handle (humans have only two hands, two ears and — thank God — one mouth). The job of the telephonists was to answer the calls, determine the services required by the callers, and then route the calls to the correct extensions. That's not too much of a problem if you only get a call every 45 to 60 seconds. But when the call volume began to increase to the point where several calls were coming in every few seconds, many of them at the same time, the telephonists were forced to put the callers on hold. The callers simply could not be processed by humans alone.

MVIS added two telephonists to the staff, to little avail. By the time Dr. Edwards and I were called in to fix the situation, the telecommunications fiasco was having a serious impact on the business. Adding more telephonists and lines to process calls would not solve the problems down the line. Computers were needed to step in and assist the process of getting callers to the correct departments and extensions. MVIS (and perhaps you also) needed to adopt a computer telephony strategy to handle and process the calls more effectively. (Chapters 7 and 8 explore this subject more fully.)

In a meeting with the CEO, the PBX company offered to take out the 18-month-old switch and put in a larger unit that allowed *direct inward dialing* (DID); this process would allow callers to directly dial an extension (DID is the subject of a chapter later in this book). The PBX guy threw out the classic line for hour-glass syndrome cases. "You have a problem at the switchboard (the console)? We have a simple solution. Just bypass the operators and have people dial the extensions directly."

Luckily, Dr. Edwards and I were there to interject. We knew what DID can do if used incorrectly — it can double or triple the load on the telephonists and cause more telecommunications chaos. DID often needs a "safety net" (computer telephony) to back it up. (I cover this technology in Chapters 7, 8, and 13.)

Instead, we recommended the use of an *automated attendant*. An automated attendant is a computer that emulates the telephonist (see Chapter 8). This robot can answer the telephone, prompt the callers for information, and route calls to the desired extension. Automated attendants do these tasks a lot quicker than humans do, and they don't need coffee breaks, smoke breaks, salaries, food, sex, shrinks, and sleep. One computer can typically answer and process 16 calls at the same time. That's 16 fewer callers to put on hold. A few decades ago, we would have shot anyone who suggested such a machine. Today, we thank Heaven for this technology.

Within two weeks, an automated attendant facility was installed at MVIS. With this installation, MVIS increased the number of telephonists from 4 to 16: 4 human telephonists, and 12 voice-processing ports in a single, 486-class personal computer. The hour-glass syndrome at the MVIS PBX was solved. But the fun of solving the overall telecommunications problem was just about to begin, as you learn in later chapters.

COMPUTER TELEPHONY AND THE ENTERPRISE INFORMATION NETWORK

You can effectively employ computer telephony as an enterprise communications tool. By using the technology in the right places, you can increase your company's productivity. For example, rather than send paper memos when you can't reach someone by phone, you can send e-mail or leave a voice mail message.

You may be wondering whether to use e-mail or voice mail. One factor to consider is that not everyone has access to their e-mail all the time. Voice mail is easier to use than e-mail for digital memos on the fly. By "hanging" a voice mailbox on the end of an extension, you provide the caller with an immediate facility to leave a message without taking much further action. Today, when you want to drop someone a line, typically you grab for the phone before you "grab" for the e-mail. This may have something to do with the human nature of "hoping" for an immediate live response: the chance that the person will be available and that you will be able to interact with him or her in real time. When you discover the person is not available, you can immediately leave a message for them (a non-interactive communication). With e-mail, on the other hand, the communication is non-interactive from the outset.

There are several things that you cannot say in e-mail, whereas using the telephone provides more opportunities to leave a message. By providing a call-processing or voice-mail facility, the calling party can immediately leave a message without having to hang up; the caller also can try another extension or check his or her own voice mail.

Voice mail and e-mail now coexist in the same mailbox, along with fax. An important strategy is to ensure that all electronic messaging interfaces provide message notification. Later in this book, I talk about incorporating beepers and fax into the messaging mix and discuss cascading message notification, internal help desks, company distribution lists, voice directories, and more.

It's possible to take the idea of computer telephony too far. Some people are fanatical about ensuring that their employees get back to customers right away or can be reached all the time. For example, one successful software retailer told me about his idea of implanting transponders into his employees' buttocks, so that when they walked into the office, their voice-mail systems would immediately deliver their messages to the telephone nearest to them. When I started laughing, he asked, "Why are you laughing at me?"

One client in Georgia came up with a slightly less fanatical use for the technology. He instructed the PBX people to install phone extensions in the restrooms. Mounted above the toilet-paper dispensers, the phones were reachable from the sitting position. This way, his people could check their voice mail from that location and get back to people "on the spot," if necessary. If someone called this manager's office while he was away from his desk, the voice-processing system would first call the men's restroom to deliver the message.

The telephone interface to data and information has become the means by which customers and associates can gain access to information residing on the enterprise information network. Interactive voice response (IVR), often described as giving data a voice, enables callers to access data in corporate database management systems over the phone (see Chapter 11).

Banking systems that provide callers with account data are good examples of IVR systems. IVR systems allow the caller to access accounts and pay for goods, services, or outstanding debts. Another good example involves traffic citation and fine management IVR systems. Callers can find out how much their citations are and then can use their credit cards to settle the debt during the same call. These systems save time and money by replacing the operators who would provide clients with order status data. Instead, the caller is prompted to enter certain information, and the IVR systems "speak" this information back to the caller.

Other information flow and access systems include audiotext and fax-on-demand. I discuss the strategic implementation and uses of these systems and technology in detail in Part II.

You may have noticed that I included the Internet and World Wide Web (WWW) as the subject of Chapter 12 (see also Chapter 3). I consider cyberspace to be a service domain of computer telephony; thus, it has strategically important considerations for the implementation of computer telephony projects. In that respect, I discuss whether various applications employing the services of IVR, fax-on-demand, and audiotext are served better by Internet access or whether they should be augmented or integrated with it. I also go into the new Internet telephony technologies that have emerged.

WHO SHOULD BE THINKING ABOUT COMPUTER TELEPHONY

Acquiring and implementing computer telephony technology should be on the agenda of all managers, from the CEO downwards, but I will stress throughout this book the importance of bringing this technology to the business plan. As a developer and reseller of computer telephony systems, and later as a consultant, I have stressed this idea for years. Technology plays an important part in all aspects of a corporation or business, no matter how big or small — especially with the recent advancements made in caller-identification technology and services.

In the past, the technology cost a bundle (voice-mail systems once boasted million-dollar price tags); many said computer telephony was only for large corporations or high-volume call centers. But in every business, customer service is catered to almost entirely over the telephone. A dated telecommunications system can result in slower and less effective customer service and, in turn, can cost a corporation millions in lost sales. Computer telephony can play a vital role in marketing and advertising strategy sales (as with the Philips example), workforce and personnel management, and more.

Computer telephony projects can fail, however, without the full understanding and *support* of senior management. For example, in 1992, one executive at a South African pension company failed to see how voice messaging could solve her company's messaging problems (the human operators were unreliable for taking accurate messages and delivering them). For some reason, she was dead set against using voice mail, so the company did not take advantage of it.

Several months later, my colleague set up a temporary voice-mail system for the same company's Managing Director while the executive was visiting the United States. The Managing Director was so impressed with the system that when he returned from his trip, he ordered his staff to take a crash course on computer telephony so that the company could pursue installing it.

DELEGATING THE COMPUTER TELEPHONY TASK

Computer telephony systems require intensive management and upkeep. If you neglect the systems after you integrate them into your company's structure, serious consequences can result. To avoid this problem, it's important to hire a person to become the computer telephony guru or champion of your company. This employee should be good with computers, understand LANs and telephone systems, be able to work with people and lend a good ear, have strong mathematical skills, and be able to think, reason, and apply logic. Sounds like the perfect employee, right? This strategy is probably *the* most important one you can implement for using computer telephony, and I will bring it up again. Find this person and give him or her this book now, before you call in the consultant.

You may wonder why this step is so important. Consultants and vendors cannot be at every customer site every day of the week. Computer telephony systems need to (mostly) be maintained by staff on site. When these systems crash, the result can be even more damaging than the crash of a LAN. For example, imagine the scene when an automated attendant that was cheerfully processing a thousand calls an hour suddenly dies because some wacko yanked out its LAN connection (this should not happen, but it does). Not even a wormhole in space can get staff to that site fast enough. Everyone will know when voice mail is down.

Another good reason for having this guru is that many companies install computer telephony systems, whether they are voice mail systems or automated attendants, but never use them because no one showed them how. Without this guru, the company may continue being miserably inefficient until a champion comes along to take care of the computer telephony project.

For example, I once had a client (a huge legal firm) who had just partnered with a firm in the United Kingdom and now needed a voice mail system to communicate information about clients during different working hours. When I visited the site and asked to a look at the PBX, I was taken down to a dark room next to the elevator shaft. There, buried under tons of dust and old telephone directories, stood a voice mail system, its LEDs still blinking. I located its ports, identified the corresponding extensions on the PBX, and called in. The system was still working like a dream. My voice was the first human voice it had heard in five years.

Upon further investigation, I learned that few people had been shown how to use the system, and because no specific person was given the responsibility of its upkeep and maintenance, the firm forgot about the voice-mail system and thought it had been removed.

It is remarkable how people who do not know how to use a system automatically consider it to be a waste of time and money. When the results start to bear fruit, however, these same people will admit that they don't know how they survived without it.

Today, it's unlikely that an enterprise will install a computer telephony system and forget about it. The use of the telephone has exploded to such an extent that an enterprise that chooses not to integrate its computer systems with its telephone network may just burn out.

SUMMARY

This chapter defined computer telephony and illustrated how the practice of integrating the computer and the telephone has exploded into a full blown service domain of information technology. I also showed how computer telephony steps in to take care of the explosion of telephone calls to the enterprise, by taking over the (once human) tasks of answering the telephone and routing callers.

Where do you want to go from here?

✦ If you're not sure how computer telephony can empower your enterprise, turn to Chapter 2.

✦ If you need to look at computer telephony (especially voice mail) from a fresh perspective, you can skip Chapter 2 for now and go directly to Chapter 3. After Chapter 3, you can jump to Part II and read Chapters 7–13.

✦ Chapter 15 helps you establish where computer telephony fits into your IT scheme.

IN THIS CHAPTER

✦ Establishing the need

✦ Customer satisfaction

✦ Determining whether you're ready for computer telephony

"How shall I torture you today?
Put you on the rack? Boil you in oil?
Make you call a technical support line?"

DO YOU NEED COMPUTER TELEPHONY?

Computer telephony needs to be applied to many situations that exist 24 hours a day in an enterprise. This chapter highlights some of the important areas that you should empower with the service domains of computer telephony. Perhaps the most important function to facilitate is *customer satisfaction*. Keeping customers satisfied is of paramount importance, and to do it, you need the tools for the job. This chapter briefly discusses this topic, and provides some case histories and anecdotes of real-world situations where computer telephony worked — and where it failed.

ESTABLISHING THE NEED

Have you ever had the opportunity to say to a computer telephony consultant: "Give me ten good reasons why I need computer telephony?" Now's your chance.

I can give you more than ten reasons. I can give you 25, 100, even 200 reasons why you should use computer telephony — and I also can give you reasons not to use it. A lot of people have asked me this question, so I'll give you enough food for thought later in this chapter. But, as we race towards the year 2000, it should be plain to you that computers (and software) empower business, computers empower people, and computers increase productivity. Telephones also empower business. You may be able to argue that the telephone *is* your business (as it is mine). Telephones let you communicate. So, when you integrate computers and telephony systems, you communicate with power.

COMPUTER TELEPHONY = POWER BUSINESS

Dare I say now that if you have a telephone or a computer (or both) on your desk, or in your briefcase, you need computer telephony? More than likely, you're already using computer telephony in some form or another; you just don't know it. You're bound to have stumbled into computer telephony at least once in your busy workday. After all, voice mail is as common as toothpaste.

Before I proceed, I want to emphasize again that computer telephony is not a means of simply replacing or cutting down on staff. Nor is it a technology that you should force onto your organization and the people related to it just because you heard it will save time and lots of money.

CUSTOMER SATISFACTION

My friend, Karl Slatner, is a customer satisfaction expert and consults for hundred-million dollar companies. He allowed me to use the following lines from one of his reports on this fascinating subject:

Unquestionably, your greatest business asset is your list of satisfied customers. It's not your building; you can move. It's not your staff; no one is indispensable. Holdings such as land, equipment, and patents can be bought, sold, and replaced, but *customers* are what really drive your business. Gaining new customers is one subject, but *keeping* customers is what customer satisfaction is all about.

The market is changing fast as competition intensifies in all products and services. Product quality is becoming more equal. Price is becoming more equal. Consumers are more fickle — less loyal. With everything else being about equal, your competitive edge lies in *service.*

Service is the area in a business that benefits the most from computer telephony technology. The faster, more easily, and more professionally you can respond to your customers' needs, the better; computer telephony empowers you in this way.

Any one of the many service domains of computer telephony can provide the enterprise with a competitive advantage. Not every aspect of computer telephony touches the caller directly. ANI (automatic number identification) or DNIS (dialed number identification services) do not touch the caller directly. But they enable your representatives to answer the telephone more professionally and to treat the call as a resource which can be acted on to best serve a particular customer. ACD (automatic call distribution) does not touch the caller directly, but it get callers to available (and appropriate) stations (monitored by a representative) more quickly.

Other aspects of computer telephony touch the caller directly, such as messaging, voice processing, voice response, fax-on-demand, audiotext, and so on. Voice recognition is now so powerful and processes calls so quickly that many humans don't even have time to realize that the polite telephonist was a machine. And frequently, the digitized speech, or the voice of computers, is so clear and human-like that it fools many, so you may have to edit the prompts to alert people that they're talking to a machine.

For example, I get fooled every time I call Citibank to use the IVR system to check the bank account. The system says, "Hello, Citibank," and pauses just long enough for me to say "Hi, how're you doing," before I realize that I'm talking to a machine.

Computer telephony helps you be more effective in your customer service efforts; it helps you keep a high customer-satisfaction profile — or as my friend Karl says, *customer satisfaction index, or CSI rating.* Being the anywhere, anytime enterprise is what customer satisfaction is all about.

Software companies are good examples of situations that cry out for CT. If you've had reason to call the likes of Microsoft, you know that they employ on-hold jockeys that give you live commentary regarding your position on hold ("We have five people on hold for Windows 3.0 and 10 million on hold for Windows 95 . . . "). When people call for help and have their registration or license numbers ready, you can prompt them to enter this information before transferring them to live helpers. This way, the help-desk representative can retrieve a screen of information on a caller before taking the call.

If a license, for example, is not valid or was entered incorrectly, you can switch those callers to other departments. Using this method, you're routing and filtering calls at the same time, saving time for both you and the customer. All the reasons for employing CT that I discuss in this chapter serve the customer-service commitment of a business and help you increase the customer satisfaction index, if the right strategies are used (I talk statistics and numbers in Parts II and III).

ARE YOU READY FOR COMPUTER TELEPHONY?

YOU ARE IF YOU HAVE A TELEPHONE ON YOUR DESK

Many consultants go as far as to say that if you have a telephone on your desk, that fact alone is reason enough to implement CT. I, on the other hand, will go as far as to say that you already have access to some form of computer telephony; you just need to know how to invoke it and use it wisely. The voice-mail service that your telephone company offers you is an example. But I know some very busy professionals who tell me that they just don't need computer telephony. Or they say, "I know about voice mail. I don't want to use it — it will give me a bad name."

At least, these professionals don't *think* that they need CT. But if you're frequently not in a position to talk to a party in real time (technical jargon meaning now), you need a voice messaging facility. Voice messaging enables the other party to start the conversation and enables you to reply later. There's nothing worse than having to say to someone, "Not now, I'm busy." A better method is to transfer them to another representative or to voice messaging and then call back as soon as you can. If you're finding the telephone more of a hindrance than a service or tool, you're ready for computer telephony. Computer telephony can help turn these hindrances back into tools and enhance them to work better for you.

If you are busy but not busy enough to hire a telephonist, a small, PC-based computer telephony system may be exactly what you need. (If this description seems to fit you, then go directly to Chapter 16, which touches on computer telephony in the small office/home office setting. Chapter 5, which discusses Windows Telephony, also touches on the SOHO (small office/home office) setting.) On the other hand, many professionals, such as my son's pediatrician, feel that taking a call, even while consulting, builds a good reputation of always being there when you're needed. I disagree, however — what about the patient he's consulting with? I get peeved when the doctor is interrupted while looking at my son's tonsils. The last time this happened, the wrecked surgery convinced the doctor that he needed voice messaging (you don't mess with the terrible-twos). The strategies for using computer telephony that follow show you why you need it.

Personal computer (including the Mac) operating systems dated 1995 and later already have computer telephony built in to them to some extent. In Chapter 5, I tell you about some free dialer software that can put you on the road to computer telephony empowerment. All you need to do is buy hardware that is TAPI (Telephony Application Programming Interface)-compliant and your computer will be dialing away.

The big debate since the early '80s has been whether PC technology makes the worker more productive or not. From around 1985 through 1992, PCs just were not powerful enough or easy enough to operate to be helpful to many people, and workers had to go through extensive training to learn how to use these PCs because they were different from anything they had previously used (I discuss this in more detail in Chapter 3). Today, however, there is no arguing that computer telephony can make you really productive.

YOU ARE IF YOU HAVE BOTH A COMPUTER AND A TELEPHONE ON YOUR DESK

I do some work for the City Hall of a beach community in south Florida. It employs just over 100 people, and I was impressed at how computer-savvy City Hall was. It has a client/server Windows NT network interfaced into government-services host mainframes and connected to terminals in every department in the city. It also has an IT and IS crew that most companies dream about. But it doesn't have computer telephony.

City Hall was a perfect candidate for computer telephony services at the desktop. Each worker there has a desk and a computer work-center (mostly a credenza, but often a separate platform that, due to layout of the offices, ended up more than six feet away from the telephone). With this setup, telephones were either a full 180 degrees behind employees while they were working at the computer, or the computers were 180 degrees behind them while they were on the phone. One device always had to be abandoned in favor of the other. Employees were shocked at the number of times they were going around in circles to use the two devices. I advised City Hall that it needed to look into using computer telephony at the desktop or station. This solution would be a better one than the alternative of providing two telephones for every employee.

Workers who spent a great deal of time on the telephone and at the computer could be equipped, for example, with headsets that can be connected to either their desk phones or their computers. (In Chapter 4, I talk about the emergence of a new standard in connecting peripheral devices to the computer known as Universal Serial Bus (USB); it enables the worker to move around with headset equipment and plug into any computer without having to reboot or power down.)

You may think that the workers could have moved their phones or computers to make their workstations ergonomically sound, but that alternative is not always possible. For example, the chief architect/town planner at City Hall gets a great deal of visitors and takes a lot of calls. When he's not in meetings, he's working in front of a 21-inch monitor and digitizing tablet located outside his office. Every time the phone rings, he has to get up and go back to his desk.

But even just having the computer and the telephone placed alongside one another does not push the proverbial computer telephony envelope far enough, in many cases. For example, I have abandoned my physical telephone set in favor of a computer-telephony-enabled headset and the dialer software described earlier. Coupled with a dialing device like Comdial's PATI (PC and Telephone Interface; see Chapter 5), which connects to the parallel port of my computer, this saves me valuable time.

When I receive calls or need to make a call, I don't have to waste time looking for telephone numbers written down on pieces of paper or turning around in circles to use the phone, nor do I have to take my eyes off the monitor. Computer telephony allows me to highlight any string of numbers on the screen and then click on the dial button. (See Chapter 5.)

I have even installed voice recognition on my computer so that, when calls ring in the earpiece, I just say "answer" to retrieve the call. The time saved by using this feature earns me another ten words per phone call. I calculated that I can write an extra five pages a day based on that feature alone because I can process calls without taking any time away from the computer.

YOU ARE IF YOU HAVE A TEENAGE DAUGHTER

In April 1994, I received a call from the top gun at a well-known company. He started the conversation by immediately spilling out his problem: "I've installed more lines and the problem just gets worse. No one can reach us, the lines are always busy, and people complain they're on hold too long."

I said, "Let me come and see you. I'll bring our top engineer along. Where are your offices?"

"The problem's not at work. It's at home."

This poor guy's problem was his teenage daughter. She had many friends, and the flood of calls during the early evening hours was driving the family nuts. Even his business associates were being told to call back in the morning.

When I asked him why he didn't just bar his daughter from the phone, he told me that the solution wasn't that easy because his daughter was the leader of several school projects, and some callers had a genuine need to reach her. Instead, he wanted me to set up a system to screen calls, enable people to leave messages, and route calls to other family members — because, as he said, "We're all getting sick of playing the operator for her."

The installation of the system was easy; there were few people to train. I installed the system on an old 386 machine. I was able to obtain the call-processing card and a 4×4 (four trunks; four extensions) switch from the secondary market for approximately $500. The son in the family maintains the system, although he was warned not to listen in on his sister's voice messages. Now when you call this house, you hear the following:

> Thank you for calling the Harrisons. If you know your party's extension, enter it now. For Mindy, press 1. For Shaun, press 2. For Sam, press 3. For Elaine, press 4. If you do not know the party with whom you wish to speak, please leave a message at the beep.

Warning: Never record a reception message that tells the caller something like "We've gone to Hawaii on vacation." What the caller may hear is "No one will get in your way if you want to come and clean us out." The same holds true, more urgently, for a business. In 1992, one of my first clients added the following message to the system which kicked in after-hours. "Thank you for calling ABC Company. Our offices are closed, and there is no one in the building who can take your call. . . ."

YOU ARE IF YOU EMPLOY PEOPLE WHO ARE DIRECTLY INVOLVED IN CUSTOMER RELATIONS

I've encountered companies that use computer telephony for customer relations, but not to the extent that they could. For example, have you ever had to call your typical utilities company? I recently had a question regarding my utility bill. I wanted to know how much power my air conditioner was using and how much it was costing me to run it. So, I called up the company that supplies our volts.

Before transferring callers to the help desk, this company uses an impressive computer telephony system that prompts you with choices to determine what information you need. Almost every option requires that you have your account number ready; however, the system doesn't tell you this on the phone (research has shown that many callers do not have this information ready). When you finally reach a human representative, you are asked for your account number. The representatives must then confirm your name before they can process your query any further.

To get a rough estimate of how long the verification process takes after a caller reaches a representative, I timed a call. The time it takes from when the representative asks you for your account number to when you're asked to verify your name can range from 14 to 80 seconds, according to my calculations. (That's assuming that that you have a bill handy from which to read your account number and that your last name isn't Kennedy, in which case you'll lose another two minutes explaining that you're not related.) But to simplify the next example, let's say that 30 seconds is the average time it takes to go through the verification process.

The company's system was smart enough to tell me that another 24 people were on hold during the five minutes I was on hold. I called the company and asked how many callers this particular office gets on an average day. The answer was 1,500, which is relatively small. If you do the math, this means it receives around 547,500 calls a year. Now multiply this by 30 seconds (the average processing time), and the company has lost more than 4,500 work hours a year by not using computer telephony effectively.

How can this company recoup the loss? By using a CT server on the LAN. A voice-processing or voice-response system can collect this additional information from callers before they are transferred to the agents. If you have to put callers on hold before you can process their calls, use the time to fish out the information you need from them. You can have your integration and IT gurus create a method for transporting this information directly to the customer service representative's computer, so that when the representative takes the customer's call, information about that customer and his or her account pops up on the screen. (I talk about some of the considerations for implementing a similar system later in this book.)

The rule is that if you employ people involved in customer relations, or in fact are involved in any customer relations activity, you should employ the services of computer telephony. You need it. CT will save you money. It will make you more effective at what you're doing. CT will pay for itself over and over. Here's a script I would have liked to have heard from the utility company's system while I was on hold:

"If you want to find out how to save money or conserve energy, press 7."

After you make your choice, the system could prompt you for your account number.

"Please enter your account number."

After processing the information, the system can verify your name:

"Is your last name spelled S-H-A-P-I-R-O? Say yes or no (or press 1 for yes, 2 for no)."

After the system verifies that the name is correct, you may then hear something like this:

"Thank you. While you're holding, we would like to offer you some energy-saving tips that can put money back in your pocket."

Then, when the call goes through to the representative, you may hear something like this:

"Good evening, Mr. Shapiro. How can we help you?"

The main point here is not so much that the computer telephony model was missing some pieces; rather, the point is the loss in time and productivity the utility company would experience if it had not used computer telephony at all. The company would have a hard time projecting a respectable image otherwise. Industry surveys have found that at least 50 percent of the callers would have dropped the line had the computer telephony system not told them where they stood in the call queue. The new paradigms and emerging standards, such as those discussed in Chapters 4 and 5, will enable corporations to better handle customer-satisfaction calls.

YOU ARE IF YOU EMPLOY PEOPLE WHO WORK IN GROUPS

Computer telephony is groupware. It helps people who work in groups or special project teams to communicate effectively. Team leaders can leave messages for all members of the groups by using distribution lists. Messages that another group member can handle more effectively can be forwarded or replied to easily by using a computer telephony system.

As I mention in Chapter 1, when you want to bounce something off a person or get an immediate response to a question or a problem, you will probably grab the phone rather than use another communication method. Voice messaging provides the first opportunity to leave a message. If what you want to communicate requires more than a few words of explanation, you may resort to e-mail and send a long memo, perhaps with an embedded worksheet. To express the urgency of a matter, CT-literate humans send e-mail and leave a voice message that instructs the colleague to check his or her e-mail. Some CT systems can communicate e-mail over the phone, so users do not have to leave an additional voice message. Isn't that great? You write out one e-mail memo that takes care of the voice message as well.

Using computer telephony to empower people working in groups is important. It helps them communicate more effectively and saves a great deal of time (assuming that the group members use computer telephony correctly). But using CT for groups provides strong support in more than the messaging area. CT products also provide support for a group's call-processing abilities. For example: By having a CTI link (see Chapter 5), workgroup members can pick up advance information about an inbound call before having to answer the telephone. The call can then be redirected to another member of the workgroup without having to inconvenience the caller. Nothing is more irritating to the customer than being shunted around the office, going on and off hold, until the correct person can be located.

YOU ARE IF YOU HAVE A HELP DESK, OR YOU'RE PLANNING ONE

Help desks are ideal candidates for computer telephony. A burgeoning help-desk industry exists and is closely allied to the computer telephony industry. The internal technical support people in a company move around a lot, so they're rarely at their desks to take calls. A voice-processing and -messaging system can beep them when a caller leaves a message. Computer telephony enables support personnel to call in and listen to their e-mail and respond to people who need help from any location in the company.

In the preceding customer relations example, the computer telephony system of the help desk can prompt callers to enter an identification number or an account number or perhaps their telephone numbers in case they get disconnected.

YOU ARE IF YOU HAVE A LAN

Suppose that you've been using your network and a huge array of hard disks to store and maintain information that was once stored on paper. Now, instead of moving paper from office to office in trays (using tons of Post-it Notes — Hey Jim, read this, Ed), you move information around the company by using the LAN and the file server, from desktop to desktop to desktop. Okay, so you're helping to save the rain forests and saving costs by keeping the information in binary form in the company's information network, but how many saplings are you axing by printing information to a laser printer and then faxing it to your customer?

You could use computer telephony to send all information that you extract from the LAN directly to the customer's computer screen (assuming that your customer has a computer, of course). Many companies transmit as many as 400 documents a day using this method. You need computer telephony to perform this task, whether you transmit the information by fax server, fax-on-demand, or the World Wide Web. Then you can add the following line to the bottom of every document in the LAN: "ABC Corp. saves trees by storing, retrieving, and transmitting documents electronically." Talk about your good PR!

Computer telephony is a must if you have a great deal of corporate literature or information that people request from you every day, especially when you have repetitive requests for the same company information.

YOU ARE IF YOUR COMPANY IS IN THE PUBLIC EYE

If you publish your company's telephone numbers—whether they are main numbers or department numbers (such as customer support)—then you're losing huge sums of potential customer dollars if you don't use computer telephony technology. People will see your ads, take down your numbers, and call. These potential customers may be located several time zones away from you or they may be located next door. You need to be the anywhere, anytime enterprise.

I am surprised at the number of times I get a RNA (Ring-No-Answer) when I call people after spotting their ads in the press or at expos. What a waste of time, money, and opportunity! If a person makes an impulse call, even over lunch, and gets nothing but ringing, he or she may think that you've closed down or that he or she has dialed the wrong number. A CEO once offered me this excuse for this situation: "If we are not around to take the call, why should we go off-hook and incur telephone charges for the call?"

Let me tell you why: Some callers will try again at another time, but most will try another company. You need to take the call, even if you're paying for it, and offer a dozen ways to keep the customer link by using computer telephony.

Computer telephony empowers business to remain open, albeit unstaffed, 24 hours a day. If no one is available to take a call, invite the caller to leave a message that will be responded to at the first opportunity. Invite the caller to send a fax, fill-in a voice form, or probe information residing on your network; give him or her your e-mail addresses and trumpet your Web page.

Did I say Web page? You bet. More than 100,000 companies have home pages on the World Wide Web. Now these companies are paying millions to tell everyone about them. But call a company's main telephone number, and does it tell you about its Web page in the greeting (or while you're on hold)? *No.* These companies are wasting a prime opportunity to promote their Web pages.

In a few years, however, you'll see voice-over data used more frequently. As a result, many callers will be able to access you via the Internet and talk to you at the same time. For more on computer telephony strategies and the Internet, see Part II, especially Chapter 12.

YOU ARE IF YOUR ORGANIZATION IS GEOGRAPHICALLY DISPERSED

Company-wide computer telephony systems can easily span multiple offices, even if some offices are located on other continents. E-mail via the Internet or other on-line services, such as MCI Mail or CompuServe, works well for communicating data over long distances. But voice messages also can traverse time zones and distance.

For example, a consulting group in the United Kingdom asked me to set up a voice-messaging facility in its South African office so that traveling employees could retrieve voice messages recorded in their mailboxes in England by transferring the messages to their mailboxes in Johannesburg. Using this method, the company (a heavy user of voice messaging) could forward the messages to the remote sites without incurring heavy long-distance charges and also avoid duplicating messages at the two sites. This problem is easy to fix by using common systems at each location or standards like AMIS (audio messaging interchange specification), which enables two voice mail systems to interchange messages. (See discussions on voice messaging in Chapter 13.)

That few voice-mail systems can share and understand each other's messages is a good example of how a lack of standards, or ignorance of available ones, limits the user. A recent amusing story in the *Wall Street Journal* told of how a friendly lady recalled an amorous night out with a co-worker in a lengthy, steamy voice message. The message has found its way to thousands of voice mail installations around the world. But how? Voice mail systems do not inter-network like the many computers on the Internet. Users shared the message by calling up friends and conferencing the calls with their voice mail systems.

Global companies also can install call-processing systems that switch callers who dial a branch that has closed for the day to a branch that's still open. For example, one aggressive software company I know takes calls at its main office in California, at a site in Florida, and then at a location in Ireland, all 24 hours a day. This way, a user who dials technical support in Ireland in the late evening can be switched to a live agent in Florida or California.

YOU ARE IF YOU HAVE TO PUT PEOPLE ON HOLD FOR ANY AMOUNT OF TIME

Making the most out of on-hold time is a favorite subject of mine, and I devote an entire chapter to it later in this book. In two out of every three calls I make, I get nothing but silence when I go on hold — even at my literary agent. Okay, so maybe these companies don't have much to say to me while I wait patiently to get through, but after three minutes or more, I begin to wonder whether the PBX has slipped into a coma, and often I forget who I called.

Computer telephony extends to the on-hold service of a PBX switch and all call-sequencing equipment. If you have several people on hold, you can use computer telephony during this time to grab the attention of as many as five million people over a year and transmit information to them using a method that can be many times more effective than a publicity campaign costing thousands of dollars. (See Chapter 14 for more on-hold computer telephony strategies.)

YOU ARE IF YOU EMPLOY SOMEONE TO ANSWER YOUR PHONES, ROUTE CALLS, AND TAKE MESSAGES

No situation is more aggravating than visiting a company in the flesh and being ignored by the telephonist for 15 minutes while the poor soul takes call after call after call.

In addition to cases where the hour-glass syndrome applies, a company with a high number of repeat callers (from regular customers, users, and schmoozers) can ease a telephonist's workload by as much as 75 percent by installing a call-processing system on departmental trunks. This strategy should be a priority if your customers have reason to call you at the same time, such as to make inquiries to an electric company during a power outage or to share an opinion on whether O.J. is guilty.

The telephonist's time is wasted further if you expect him or her to take down messages. The illegibility level of a message increases with the number of callers on hold, trunk indicator lights (on the PBX console) flashing, and ugly faces in the reception area. Pink slips are a waste of paper and time and should be abolished once and for all. Let your computer telephony system handle the load so that your telephonist can pay attention to those customers standing in line (like me).

The telephonist's load increases if members of the company spend a large portion of their time away from the office or if you employ a sales force that's always on the move. Human personal assistants spend more time relaying information to field agents and staff rather than preparing critical reports, typing sales letters, helping clients, and more — which, in turn, affects your profit margins. Field staff should be able to call in to CT services to get voice mail, e-mail, and fax mail.

You Are If Your Telephone System Is Used Mostly for Outbound Calls

Computer telephony plays an important role in collections and paying bills. By integrating telephony into the LAN and the accounts database (or at least the reports generated from it), a computer telephony system can determine when to call an account holder, proceed to tell the person about his or her overdue bill, and then turn the call over to a live operator. These systems are called *predictive dialers,* and work in the telemarketing arena. The dialers work on algorithms that enable the telephony system to dial people and transfer a live call immediately to a customer relations person for processing.

What about using computer telephony for telemarketing? If you're fortunate enough to be in a position to keep reselling to your installed base, the same technology applies.

You Are If You Do Market Research

To compile market research in the past, companies had people standing on a street corner with forms and a pencil, irritating every passerby who may or may not be interested in its product or service. Forget this practice — you can better spend this money on free gifts for people who call your computer telephony system and do a survey over the phone. With carefully scripted prompts of yes/no answers and multiple-choice lists, you have a highly effective market research tool in your computer telephony system.

You can use computer telephony (such as IVR service) for gathering information about your market share, what your company's doing right or wrong, and what the public wants you to do. Other companies have used CT for these tasks very successfully. Have you noticed how television talk shows and radio stations can rapidly drum up public-opinion statistics? They get viewers and listeners to dial a number and press 1 for a yes vote or 2 for a no vote. Others get you to dial a premium rate number (900 numbers and pay-per-call) that can cost around a buck for a vote. Dialing one number chalks up a vote for issue A, whereas dialing another number chalks up a vote for issue B.

Why don't we elect the next U.S. president into office this way? If we bring in the votes on premium-rate lines, maybe we can pay off a large chunk of the national debt!

You should store the gathered information in a database where you can access and manipulate it on the fly. You can listen to the caller's answers to important questions on fill-in voice forms to obtain valuable input that is seldom obtained by harassing people in malls.

YOU ARE IF EVERYONE, INCLUDING YOUR SPOUSE, HATES YOUR VOICE MAIL

Computer telephony has been around for more than a decade, most auspiciously in the form of voice mail systems. Many outdated voice mail systems are still used — these systems are complicated for users and callers alike and make using them unattractive. Now is the time to get rid of these old timers. Few, if any, of these systems can be integrated with the LAN and the desktop.

Modern voice mail systems are easy to configure from graphical user interfaces. Sophisticated design tools are available to help you plot the entire call path through a system, all the way into a mailbox and out again.

A word of warning for those of you about to update your voice mail systems, however. You want to be careful of who you hire to install your system. Because of the added features of new voice mail systems, some techno-freaks can get carried away when they install it.

For example, in 1994, while I was evangelizing computer telephony for four days at Comdex Spring in Atlanta, I met the CEO of an interior design firm who had a bad experience with her voice mail consultant. When I brought up the term voice mail in our conversation, all hell broke loose. "Voice mail! We hate voice mail, no thanks."

Later I learned the reason for her reaction. Some whacko had sold her firm, which thrived on personal service, a voice mail system that nearly destroyed the company — and lost two $50,000 clients.

The firm had a dozen or so clients that managed large properties. They all called the company on a regular basis and knew exactly with whom they wanted to speak. An automated attendant facility would have worked well for this situation — after all, if your customers know the extension of the party they're calling (it's almost always on the business card), why take up the valuable time of a human to route the call?

The consultant, however, installed a complicated voice mail system without any advance warning to the firm's customers. In fact, several employees did not know about the transition either — including the CEO. The "expert" went live with the system without orders from the CEO. So, when two regular clients called in and were faced with several menus that led to nowhere, they took their business elsewhere. The CEO related a few more horror stories, like the time the system was accidentally switched off, providing clients with nothing but RNA for two hours.

A *needs synthesis* would have prevented a great deal of these problems. A needs synthesis is a research project that helps determine the strategies for implementing new technology in a company or organization. (I discuss this topic in depth in Part II.) After the study was complete, a proper plan for deployment should have been drawn up and followed.

After a free consultation, the CEO and her accompanying group of executives agreed to stop by the pavilion and look at some of the CT products that I was exhibiting for Rhetorex. When you call the firm today, you are greeted by a warm and friendly, yet very human, telephonist because the firm still believes that a human should answer the telephone in keeping with the personal service philosophy. But backing up this person is a very effective computer telephony system that kicks in when the call load gets too heavy. And when a caller finds an account executive unavailable, the call is forwarded directly into voice mail.

SUMMARY

This chapter highlighted the many situations in the enterprise that can be empowered by computer telephony. The lives of your service- and knowledge-workers can be made much easier, and these workers can be more productive with the right tools. Convinced? Then where to next?

Chapter 3 discusses how computer telephony is making the transition to a new era in information technology.

You can proceed directly to Chapter 6 to find out more about the elements of computer telephony — those slices of techno-heaven that will make life easier for you.

IN THIS CHAPTER

✦ Why enterprises were repulsive in the old frontier of information technology

✦ Why voice mail became and remains Public Enemy Number One

✦ The new frontier of information technology

✦ Computer telephony in the new frontier

✦ New enabling technologies for computer telephony

✦ How your enterprise can use computer telephony to become a global, 24-hour operation

Employees at Digimax Industries are expected to speak at least one foreign language.

COMPUTER TELEPHONY AND THE NEW FRONTIER IN INFORMATION TECHNOLOGY

Computer telephony has a colorful and somewhat notorious history. IT also has had its legacy era, during which it was unfriendly and threat-ening to both users and customers. To achieve a measure of suc-cess when requisitioning and integrating computer telephony, it is impor-tant to recognize that a fundamental shift has taken place in the world of information technology in general and computer telephony in particular. New technologies are creating these paradigm shifts. The new tech-nologies will change how you view and use computer telephony services.

But first, let's take a look at the road on which computer telephony has traveled.

THE REPULSIVE ENTERPRISE IN THE OLD FRONTIER OF INFORMATION TECHNOLOGY

Peter Drucker, in one of his most popular books, *Managing in Turbulent Times,* argued that "the first task of management is to make sure of the institution's capacity for survival, to make sure of its structural strength and soundness, of its capacity to survive a blow, to adapt to sudden change and to avail itself of new opportunities." He argued quite rightly that the profits of the present were nothing but the deferred costs of stay-ing in business.

Company managers thus welcomed the age of information technology. IT arrived with the hope and promise of corporate survival, with the tools to maintain company strength and soundness. IT was the weapon of survival.

But, as history has shown, technology is often misused. Many managers, pressed hard by board members and shareholders to cut costs, used IT to save money by cutting jobs. Computers and software were acquired with the blind motive to replace people and save salaries and resources. As the cartoon in Figure 3-1 illustrates, few organizations saw IT as the ultimate worker-enabling, empowering tool — a means of pushing productivity to new, untold heights. Many tried to resist the shift into the age of enterprise computing and networking.

"I refuse to bring a single computer into this office until they invent one that will tremble at the sound of my voice and wince when I shoot it one of my menacing glances!"

Figure 3-1: IT was often enlisted as a means of cutting back on staff. Workers believed that they did not need computers and thus saw the new machines only as a threat to their jobs.

For this reason, the arrival of IT and information systems in every company brought with it fear of worker obsolescence. In many cases, computers replaced entire divisions of people overnight. Lost jobs were the price of automation and information technology.

The typical relationship that existed between management and their staffs during this era did not help ease the tension that IT instilled in workers. Management often was a remote entity on the top floor, navigating the company battleship in a sea of corporate wars, raids, and takeovers; seldom did it address the concerns or needs of the crew directly. IT was the battleship's smart bomb that got things done faster, cheaper, and better, with less people. It was both evolutionary and revolutionary.

I witnessed the dark side of the IT age as a cub reporter. While working at one of the world's largest daily newspapers in 1980, I was shaken by the hundreds of jobs axed in the layout, paste-up, typesetting, and typography departments to make way for the installation of the huge Atex systems (the doyen of electronic publishing technology, owned by Kodak). The publisher had no doubt that this system was going to make life easier and save hundreds of thousands of dollars in salaries and materials. But it wasn't until a few years later, as a financial reporter, that I began to understand the management decisions that left many people bitter at IT for more than a decade.

As the job-eating era of IT rolled into the '80s, IT carried with it a reputation of worker replacement. Many workers rebelled. The most notable rebellion took place in the newspaper-press unions in the United Kingdom, which had managed for years to prevent management from installing the miraculous electronic typesetting equipment. The workers were so vociferous in their stance that riots threatened, and the unions held out for years. Although rebellions like these saved many existing jobs, people were not replaced as older workers retired. Thus the IT age installed a master-slave mentality in many companies. It made employees feel more temporary than they already were.

These were the days of the so-called legacy host computer systems — workers slaving away at dedicated terminals. The relationship between the host computers and employees reminds me of the repulsive creature Jabba the Hut in *Return of the Jedi,* the third film in the Star Wars trilogy. This huge, fat, worm-like beast (the host mainframe) ruled over his subjects (the workers at terminals) without mercy, chaining many of them to his inhuman form so that he could summon them at his bidding. The lives of his subjects were tenuous — when they stepped out of line or became expendable, they were sentenced to be consumed (their jobs terminated) by a monster (IT) that lurked in a cavern. And there are many enterprises today that still continue to do business in this fashion.

The early days of the Information Age also were the days of cryptic and unfriendly computer user interfaces that only a handful of people in an enterprise were able to use. The colorful GUI (graphical user interface) and the charismatic mouse did not yet exist. Locked into stifling closed systems, architectures, and proprietary technology, the enterprise succeeded in turning valuable employees into captive slaves. This supposedly liberating and empowering technology turned the enterprise into a repulsive organization (see Figure 3-2).

"Please press 1 to transfer your call.
If you're calling from a rotary phone,
hang up and go buy a new telephone for Pete's sake!"

Figure 3-2: The IT dream was to empower the enterprise and give it a competitive advantage, but its misuse often turned the enterprise into a repulsive entity.

This repulsive appearance often was projected toward the external environment of an enterprise. Organizations and corporations transformed from well-meaning enterprises into economic dictatorships. Their information systems often repelled their customers rather than assisted them and brought them back. Often, when the computer system crashed, the event was treated with disinterest by workers, and this attitude led to a culture of cynicism that rubbed off on customers.

How Voice Mail Became Public Enemy Number One

Although the IT era started with the dream of increased productivity, the narrow-minded strategy, mismanagement, and greed with which it was applied turned it into a nightmare. Because of this attitude, voice mail and automated attendant systems were seen, and sadly still are, as Public Enemy Number One (after John Dillinger relinquished the honor) by the computer users of corporations and their customers.

Of course, other important factors played a part in creating the bad name that voice mail still carries around, which I get into later in this chapter. (For a full discussion on voice mail, see Chapter 13.)

PROBLEM 1: USING VOICE MAIL TO REPLACE WORKERS

Not only were these early systems hard to use and annoying to the customers, but they were installed without thought, and — most importantly — they were installed as a means of *replacing* people rather than empowering them. As such, many people refused to use voice mail and no longer trusted the technology.

Unfortunately, this attitude still lingers today among corporate business and IT planners. Companies still look at voice processing initially as a means of cutting staff. As recently as January 1995, I was approached by one of the world's largest pharmaceutical companies to investigate the feasibility of using computer telephony on a company-wide scale. In my first meeting with the management team, I was disappointed to discover that the prime objective of acquiring computer telephony was to cut jobs. The management team shot at me straight from the hip: "Can the system help us cut jobs?"

I explained that computer telephony should be seen as an employee-empowering tool, a means of saving time, of making people more productive, of letting the computer work the phone while people get meaningful work done. Installing it only as a means of cutting staff is trouble, I told them. (I once learned from a well-known conservationist that you cannot shoot just a few elephants in a culling operation and not expect the surviving elephants in the herd to go berserk, take out their anger on the environment, and even have nervous breakdowns. The collateral damage can be devastating.) I explained that many employees would view the sudden installation of computer telephony as a threat to their livelihood, not as increased support from management.

The reply from management was this: "That's great, but we've got orders that the first priority is to get rid of those bodies in the reception who do nothing all day but route calls and give people directions to the facility."

Warning: The primary objective of computer telephony is to empower the enterprise by allowing its workers to be more productive and helping to maintain a competitive advantage. Computer telephony should not be viewed only as a means of downsizing the staff.

Although computer telephony *can* be used to get rid of people, that attitude is outmoded and outdated. There's bound to be some redundancies between the jobs that humans and the technology perform; but you should view that as a payoff — not as a sign that the worker is no longer needed.

PROBLEM 2: USING DIFFICULT, LIMITING VOICE-MAIL SYSTEMS

Another problem that helped voice mail earn its bad rep stemmed from the manufacturers of these systems. A "bolt-on" mentality in the PBX and telephony industries still exists that refuses to change. Many PBX companies looked for ways to milk their clients — locked in with long-term leases — for more money, luring them with the promise of voice-mail bolt-ons (voice-recording units that attach to proprietary ports of a PBX; these bolt-ons belong with a LAN as much as fish do on land; see Figure 3-3.) These companies trapped their customers with fairy tales of how much money could be saved by using the bolt-on. In reality, however, the bolt-ons only served to further lock in the customer to vendors who rarely were able to extend the device as needed by the enterprise.

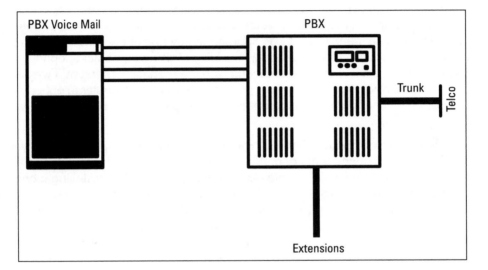

Figure 3-3: The PBX voice mail bolt-on is a proprietary box connected to the analog or digital ports of a PBX. It's isolated from the LAN and can only be accessed from the telephone.

The limitations of these systems and the equipment produced by the emerging computer telephony industry turned customers and employees against voice mail. Instead of using the technology, they abused it. Employees, frustrated with the difficulty of managing voice messages, began to adopt evasive tactics to using it. When customers called and left messages, they were seldom called back within an hour, if at all. Soon, when customers encountered voice mail, they would simply terminate the call and go elsewhere because they held the impression that voice mail did not work. (See Chapter 13.)

When MVIS, Inc. introduced voice mail at their company, Michael Edwards and I were seen by many in the office as the technology Gestapo. We were met with incredible hostility because the workers, most of them attached to their desks with headsets and taking thousands of calls from claimants, were never consulted about the decision. Not fully understanding how voice mail was supposed to help them, the employees suspected it to be a tool that management could use to monitor and spy on people. Absurd stories began to circulate about the system's capability to help managers eavesdrop on calls.

The stress of learning the new technology was insurmountable for several workers. One claims manager (I'll call him Henry) headed for retirement was unable — and unwilling — to navigate the voice-mail system to retrieve his messages. The CEO was unsympathetic; the managerial attitude was that it was time for Henry to retire any-way, so this was the final call. Other employees began to spread rumors that if you can't use the voice-mail system, you'll get the ax.

Henry caved in from the stress. One morning, the IT manager marched over to his desk and told him that he had to listen to all his voice-mail messages before taking any calls. Michael sat with Henry and walked him through the menus. Unfortunately, a configuration error in the voice-mail software caused a dozen mailboxes to regurgitate their messages into several other mailboxes, which, in turn, dumped all their messages into Henry's mailbox. When the quaint female voice of the voice-mail system said, "You have six thousand messages," Henry flew into a rage, swept all the stationery off his desk, and stormed over to the CEO's office, where he handed in his resignation. (We later learned that he had almost suffered a nervous breakdown and was confined to bed by his doctor.)

Today, it is not uncommon for busy professionals to legitimately accumulate thou-sands of messages. One technical support person I know arrived back from several weeks' leave to find almost a thousand messages in his mailbox. He was powerless to do anything with the messages but delete them.

This problem still pops up today because thousands of the voice mail systems in use are survivors of the old IT era, making telecommunications repulsive to some users. As a result, "I hate voice mail" became the motto of many people. The computer tele-phony industry, frustrated by the lack of available computing power and standards, was powerless to do anything about it. No amount of PR would help. As a result, many IT companies went to work developing new technologies that would bring about the new paradigms discussed in Chapters 4 and 5 and in Part II.

Automated attendants have also repelled customers by the millions. The problem was that early versions of automated attendants capitalized on a great idea — grab those calls within three rings — but failed to follow through on it (we've answered the phone — now what?). In Canada, for example, one organization forces people to wade through more than 200 menu options before obtaining the service that they want. (The critical need for this organization is the only reason why it still survives today.)

As a result, people often tell me that when they hear a voice-processing system, they "just hit the 0 key" to get a live operator. If these customers hear something like "Invalid selection" or "The operator is not available at this time," they drop the line and take their business elsewhere. This trend became so bad at one company that callers were still hitting the 0 key weeks after the system had been fixed.

This situation is partly the fault of the early voice mail installers but mostly the fault of the old era of IT. Computer telephony requires a great deal of computer-processing power to make it truly interactive and helpful. Can you blame users for hating voice mail if they have to wade through hundreds of messages of silence or disconnect tones because the system is unable to recognize that the caller had hung up? Can you blame callers for hating voice mail after they end up in "voice mail jail," unable to back out of the message trap into which they've fallen? Many people would say that the idea of voice mail and voice processing is a good one, but that in practice, it stinks.

As the new era of IT rolls around, however, the way that you use and think about computer telephony and related technologies will change. Let's take a look.

COMPUTER TELEPHONY IN THE NEW FRONTIER OF IT

The new frontier in information technology is upon us, and it brings with it a new age in the world of computer-telephone integration. This new IT age consists of visual programming, open systems, client/server systems, accepted standards, workgroup computing, incredible processing power, plug-and-play software and hardware components, and a host of other enterprise- and worker-enabling technologies and integration capabilities (these factors are key to successful CT implementation strategies and are discussed at length in Chapter 15).

With today's technology, I (and you also) can quickly create a computer telephony application that several years ago would've taken me, a colleague, and three engineers as long as six months to do. All this can be accomplished with the aid of a PC in a matter of hours. The difference lies in cheap computing power and object-oriented programming.

The new IT era brought forth software that enables workers to manage and control their environments, empowers them to interact and communicate on a peer-to-peer basis, and converts the fear of replacement into increased worker productivity and pride. Workers are now adopting the computer with confidence.

The modern graphical user interface (GUI) made the computer easier to use and bolstered a worker's ability to produce; it helped eliminate the urge to run and hide that many workers experienced when they saw a computer. Today, the computer has become an extension of the employee, a tool that can help a worker advance at one's will and pace or even help someone find and keep a job.

For example, a librarian at the main Broward County library in Ft. Lauderdale, Florida, recently told me how computer telephony helped him land his job. After noticing an ad for the job in a Manhattan newspaper, he called the number and navigated his way around the automated attendant, taking note of all the options presented by the attendant. Then he used his home computer and a modem to access and peruse the library's catalog (he received the information about it from the library's audiotext service). Satisfied that he was now familiar with the library's collection, he applied for the job, hoping that his prospective employers would be impressed with his knowledge of the library's collection. Within days, he was packing his belongings and heading for the sunshine state.

IT is advancing so rapidly now that few people are impressed with the new products that arrive from the software and hardware vendors every day. Even the ability to have almost free, two-way, long-distance telephone conversations over the Internet is ho-hum. Thanks to technological advancements, the service domains of computer telephony have received a major shot in the arm. You could say that recent advancements in IT are the steroids that have enabled the technology. These advancements include

✦ Stand-alone computing to GUI-based workgroup computing

✦ Open systems and standards

✦ Incredible and cheap computing power

✦ Dumb computing to artificial intelligence

STAND-ALONE COMPUTING TO GUI-BASED WORKGROUP COMPUTING

Before the new frontier, people worked as individuals. Even in the early days of the LAN, work mentality was singular and narrow-minded because few resources could be easily shared. We had to make copies of everything. For example, we would copy a word-processing file onto a diskette and then mail it to a colleague who also needed to work on the file. The colleague then would return it with his or her changes, and the process would repeat until we found ourselves juggling a dozen versions of the same project. This setup made it virtually impossible to keep track of the chronology of the work and who was responsible for which changes.

Today, several people can work on one document concurrently, and you only need to have one working version of the file. The software automatically keeps track of all the changes, who made them, and when they were made for you.

We also had to clone our physical resources before the new IT age came along. The fax machine is a good example. The typical enterprise had to invest in one machine for each department, which sometimes resulted in several machines on one floor. My sister sold fax machines and made a nice living on this clone syndrome; in one case, she sold more than a thousand fax machines to a single corporation. Today, that same corporation, though still needing fax machines, channels 75 percent of its faxing through the LAN and a fax server — an example of the new workgroup architecture and related systems at work.

With the advent of the peer-to-peer and client/server networks, humans can work and communicate with each other from one side of an enterprise to another. The modern LAN set the scene for workgroup computing and groupware. The advancements in LAN technology, communications software such as e-mail, and groupware such as Microsoft Office, WordPerfect Office, and Lotus Notes have enabled users to share and exchange information (not just text messages), have virtual meetings, correspond with one another, and share applications and ideas. Similarly, computer telephony systems can be easily accessed over the LAN and integrated with the workgroup computing environment.

But the real clincher for using computer telephony was (as mentioned earlier) the graphical user interface. By interfacing with the complex world of binary data via familiar symbols and icons, users have returned to the very computers they once abandoned in disdain. This new attitude holds true for computer telephony as well. Voice mail is no longer a media accessible just from the confined POT, but also from a graphical user interface that enables users to manage the messages more easily — as well as *visually*. Computer telephony software is now easy to use, not scary and complicated (see Chapter 13 for more details).

OPEN SYSTEMS AND STANDARDS

Product standards have helped transform shackled enterprises into efficient business operations. The telecommunications industry supports international standards that all telecommunications manufacturers, PTTs (public post, telephone, and telegraph administrations), telephone companies (telcos), value-added service providers, and so on must also support. The truly global support of the telephony standards is the reason why we find it so easy to make a call to any location on earth that is connected to a PSTN (public-switched telephone network).

As a result, many firms are shedding their restrictive relationships with vendors touting proprietary technology (closed systems) instead of open systems that adhere to established, supported standards. The telephony and PBX industries will have to depart from their old ways as users demand products that comply with standards that enable users to integrate their systems. Users don't want to be stuck with products that are difficult to change, upgrade, or extend.

Such standards are developed by international public-standards-making bodies. All public standards are open to scrutiny and debate during the formulation process. Such standards are referred to as *de jure* standards. Perhaps the most important of these public bodies is the International Standards Organization (ISO).

But other "international" standards exist that, despite enjoying widespread use, are not truly international public standards. These standards usually include the protocols and procedures that a product uses as defined by the product's manufacturer, such as Microsoft or IBM. Through the definitions and interfaces they publish, the products become so widely adopted that, in essence, they become a standard. Such standards are called *de facto* standards because they have not been universally adopted.

De facto standards present a problem in that you often end up with battling standards. Two good examples of *de facto* standards wars are the Beta versus VHS standard and the IBM PC versus the Apple Macintosh wars. Remember how frustrating you found it when you had VHS-format tapes in one hand and a Beta video machine in the other? Or, try running Windows on a Mac and see how far you get.

However, many *de facto* standards have made significant contributions to the IT industry. One of the best efforts that you can find is the Transmission Control Protocol/Internet Protocol (TCP/IP), a protocol connecting thousands of different computers via a global network of networks (otherwise known as the Internet).

In the computer telephony domain, two such emerging standards are the Telephony Services Application Programming Interface from Novell, Inc., and the Telephony Applications Programming Interface from Microsoft Corp. — TSAPI and TAPI, respectively. Users want computer telephony systems and telephone systems that can be integrated with existing information systems, and these APIs cater to this need. Since their introduction in 1993, these APIs have become cohesive factors in the computer telephony industry. I discuss them in detail in Chapter 5.

INCREDIBLE AND CHEAP COMPUTING POWER

The personal desktop computers of today wield hundreds of times more power than the host or mainframe systems of the old IT age, and the microprocessor-based machine is increasing in power daily. Soon, the term MIPS (millions of instructions per second) will become ZIPS (zillions of instructions per second), and BOPS (billions of operations per second) will become ZOPS (zillions of operations per second). After that happens, the power of personal computing will be astonishing.

Voice processing is becoming as pervasive as word processing. Although you can trace the history of CT (and voice-processing technology in particular) back to the late '70s, the technology has, generally, been too expensive to be worth the investment for medium to small enterprises. (That situation is changing rapidly, however.)

In the early IT era, the cost of acquiring advanced computing power was out of the stratosphere. Only a few years ago, a computer that could tell the difference between *yes* and *no* and single-digit numbers over the telephone cost more than $100,000. Now, corporations buy computers with cash and do not have to wait for the financial officers to take several months to approve a budget.

Today, computer telephony is mostly DSP- and microprocessor-based and has been built for PC, workstation, and even notebook architectures. Thanks to the incredible economies of scale in the PC industry, the IBM-compatible computer has become the platform of choice for computer telephony. Thus, computer telephony is ready and affordable for nearly every enterprise, from a one-person show to a giant conglomerate that employs 10,000 souls.

In the computer telephony industry you'll want to watch two important technologies: digital signal processing (DSP) and the universal serial bus (USB). Both items are set to take computer telephony to new heights not believed possible a few years ago. The technologies are discussed in more detail in Chapters 4 and 5.

DUMB COMPUTING TO ARTIFICIAL INTELLIGENCE

With the advent of artificial intelligence, expert systems, and fuzzy logic, computers are beginning to take on personalities. Soon, these software wizards will adapt to a user's behavior and to the environments in which they work — computers will be able to recognize your voice, manners, and practices.

This advance has important ramifications for the security issue. One of the most frustrating things about computer telephony systems is that you have to identify yourself to the computer whenever you call in to get your messages or other sensitive information, such as bank balances. By using the new technologies now available (especially DSP), a CT system can recognize a user's voice by voice print analysis and verify who is calling. Of course, the systems may still be required to perform an extra security check to make sure that it's really you and not a clone calling, but the inquisition will be more friendly and less time-consuming than ever before.

The Alluring Enterprise

With the new frontier in IT, today's companies have no excuse for being repulsive, not to their employees and certainly not to their customers and strategic partners. IT makes today's firms accessible. Customers should be able to reach into a company's database and gain easy access to information that can solve their problems and provide them with solutions. I'm not saying that customers should be able to penetrate to every level of a company — that's why we have firewalls. But they should find the company accessible.

The Internet is providing this quality for business (although some words about security in Chapter 12 are worth heeding). The Internet enables customers in the external environment to gain easy access to information owned or provided by the company. Nothing is more frustrating than having to pry information from a company over the telephone. Just entering a calling-card number and passwords can be lunacy at times. Conversely, nothing is more satisfying than clicking on a few icons and watching as the World Wide Web opens the windows to the information you were seeking.

For example, while writing this book, I called a cartoonist who used a fax-on-demand (FOD) system to send examples of his work. When the system answered, the computer told me that the FOD service had been discontinued and that I could see examples of the cartoonist's work on the World Wide Web instead. Or, I could leave my e-mail address and the computer telephony system would make sure that the examples were e-mailed to me. Fancy that — a cartoonist has a computer for a sales rep!

Companies need to use computer telephony to become more accessible to their customers at times that fit the customer's needs. The telephone is still the fastest way to connect individuals with corporations, and you cannot afford to answer the telephone with statements like "Our hours of business are . . . ." That's like saying "Sorry, we do not want your business right now, call back some other time." You need to be doing business all the time, even while you are asleep.

IT and computer telephony in particular can make your enterprise the anywhere, anytime company. Callers can place orders, check company records, access information, leave messages, pay accounts, fill out forms, and even create their own invoices and statements for processing without human intervention. Some customers will do this task via your home page on the World Wide Web; others will choose to use your computer telephony services. With these services, you can become a truly global, 24-hour operation.

Computer telephony also empowers a company by making it more responsive to customers. Customers should be able to get results fast. Nowadays, you need information in minutes, not hours. Take Federal Express, for example. Customers no longer need to interface with a human just to keep track of shipments and delivery times. Instead, they can access this information themselves by using the company's computer telephony services and the Internet. You simply enter your tracking number into the system, and you get a real-time update of the location of your parcel. Citibank is another prime example: Its most important slogan is "The CITI never sleeps." That's because computer telephony keeps the bank running when most of the human tellers go home to sleep.

The new frontier of IT — and computer telephony in particular — has enabled the corporation to shed its repulsive, lizard-like skin to become a responsive, responsible, integrated enterprise. It makes your company easy to do business with.

The power strategies that you learn here and later in the book will help you best use computer telephony. Implementing these new strategies is now possible, thanks to the new frontier of information technology. This new frontier has arrived to sweep away the repulsive enterprise — like the timely arrival of Luke Skywalker to save Princess Leia and Han Solo from Jabba the Hut.

SUMMARY

In this chapter, I discussed the transformation of computer telephony from the old IT frontier, where it was viewed mostly as a way to cut jobs, to the new IT frontier, where computer telephony empowers the firm and its workers. I discussed how advancements such as those in computing power and workgroup-based computing helped bring about this transformation and led customers and workers to view the technology with more than a jaundiced eye.

A great deal still exists to learn, however. From here, you may want to try the following chapters:

✦ To learn more about computer telephony as it stands today, turn to Chapter 4.

✦ If you're more interested in learning about audiotext, a particular computer telephony service, read Chapter 9.

✦ If you want to learn how computer telephony fits in with your firm's overall business plan, turn to Chapter 16.

IN THIS CHAPTER

✦ The public switched telephone network

✦ How do you make a call?

✦ Key computer telephony hardware

GLASBERGEN

"Thank you for calling technical
support. All lines are busy now,
they have always been and they
always will be. Get a life."

UNDERSTANDING TELEPHONY

I use the computer to do things with the telephone that I don't have the time to do myself. It answers my calls, takes messages, and dials for me. When I open my notebook, I expect it to become my alter ego, to perform at my beck and call, whether I ask it to retrieve a fancy quote or download a sexy calendar photograph from the World Wide Web and display it on the desktop when I get to work.

But you have to teach the machine how to make and take calls, how to send and receive messages, how to do what *you* typically do on the telephone. Essentially, you have to teach the machine "how" to use the telephone, just as you would teach your children.

Of course, the computer does not learn how to do things quite the same way as humans do. Humans, especially in First World countries, learn how to use the phone before the age of two; they know how to pick up the handset and that the device will help them indulge in some form of communication. Children learn this by observing and mimicking other humans who use the phone.

You cannot hope to make a computer use the telephone, or even to be a telephone, simply by placing it next to the telephone and hoping it will "observe" how you make the call. You have to know a little more about telephony and the enabling technologies of computer-telephone integration to achieve your computer telephony objectives. This chapter thus serves as an introduction to telephony, the enabling technologies of computer-telephone integration discussed in Chapter 5, and computer telephony.

THE PUBLIC SWITCHED TELEPHONE NETWORK (PSTN)

The *public switched telephone network,* or PSTN, is a complex machine. People involved in computer telephony integration and CTI will have many occasions to rub shoulders with this animal. For the purposes of the discussion in this chapter and in the chapters ahead, here is a basic overview.

The telephone network can be divided into the following four groups:

1. Devices and instruments

2. Switching facilities and equipment

3. Local loops

4. Telephone (trunk) circuits

DEVICES AND INSTRUMENTS

This group consists of the telephones, modems, fax machines, and other devices that you attach to your telephone line. Today, the network is strong enough to withstand the attachment of any product you buy at your local electronics store. In the past, the AT&Ts of the world freaked if you attached anything to the line not approved by them. Many people saw this as a means for AT&T to own and control the market for telephone devices; but the privatization of the world's telephone companies changed all that.

In some countries, however, inspectors can still stroll up to your home and seize anything that is not "approved" by the "department" because it fears (with some merit in the less-advanced regions of the world) that the network will collapse. Generally speaking, however (especially in the U.S.), if you want to connect your toaster to the telephone network, go ahead.

Multiline telephones can be fully digital telephones or analog feature phones that have additional wires for sending and receiving control data. These phones are often known as multibutton phones. The dual-tone multifrequency (DTMF) and rotary/pulse-dial telephone connected to the switch by one twisted pair are nothing more than "plain old telephones," better known as POTs.

SWITCHING FACILITIES AND EQUIPMENT

This group represents the switches and computers that connect devices and instruments to each other. These objects are housed in an elaborate and complex network of central offices (COs) around the world. Companies such as Northern Telecom, AT&T, and Siemens make this equipment.

LOCAL LOOPS

Local loops are the wires that connect your phones to the COs. The following section talks more about COs and the transmission media used.

TELEPHONE (TRUNK) CIRCUITS

This group encompasses the lines and other transmission media that connect the COs. (The term *trunk* is slowly becoming redundant, so I will not use it much in this book.) These circuits can carry one telephone conversation between two villages in a rural area or they can carry thousands of calls between cities.

The circuits nowadays employ a variety of transmission media, such as copper wires (still the most common transmission medium), coaxial cables, microwave radio, and fiber optics. Here's an interesting related fact: The world record for the longest fiber-optic link was broken by South Africa in March 1995. It runs from Cape Town to Pretoria, covering a distance of more than 1,600 kilometers. The 622 Mbps link carries 7,560 simultaneous channels. (Now, who says the Information Superhighway is a pipe dream?)

HOW DO YOU MAKE A CALL?

Whether in the office connected to a private switch or at home connected to a bigger public switch, when you want to call someone, typically you pick up the handset and listen for a dial tone. This task has become such a common practice in human life that you don't really have to teach anyone how to start or complete the telephone call process. But you *do* have to teach your machines to do this.

But let's go behind the scenes, because making a call happen is not as simple as it looks. Let's say that your office extension is 400. When you want to call your assistant on extension 405, you pick up the handset and wait for a dial tone, which you will get 99.999 percent of the time. But remember, your phone is attached to a private branch exchange (PBX); thus, the dial tone you hear comes from your office's PBX, not from the public switched telephone network (PSTN). The dial tone you hear when calling from your home telephone is the tone sent by the telephone exchange. To get *that* tone behind your PBX's tone, you first need to dial the [network] access digit. In the U.S., the access digit is the 9 you dial before the area code and telephone number.

But before getting too deep into that subject, let's look at what took place when you lifted the handset. The CPU recognized that you went "off hook." (Translation: you requested a service from the telephone.) The CPU knows this fact because the extension's activity scanning electronics and signaling analysis told it so (see Figure 7-2 in Chapter 7). In techie jargon, this point is where the user's phone sends the switch's CPU a "supervisory" signal. Your phone generates this supervisory signal by "seizing" the phone line either through a loop start or a ground start signal. In other words, you are starting the line — it's sort of like turning an ignition key.

SEIZING A LINE

As you may have learned in science lab, you only need two wires to have a conversation. The wires that connect the telephone to the switch are known as the *loop* (especially when you bridge them to form a circuit). Your connection to the telephone exchange is referred to as the *local loop* (see Figure 4-1).

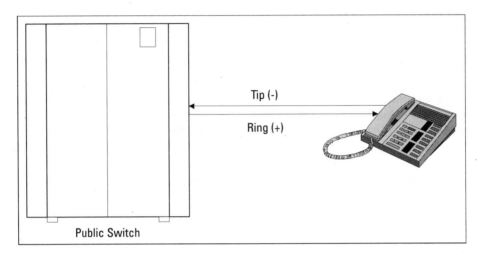

Public Switch

Tip (-)

Ring (+)

Figure 4-1: The local loop connects your telephone to the public switch.

But you also need a current to carry the signal — and, in turn, your conversation — through the loop. Figure 4-2 illustrates the wave form of an analog conversation (I discuss digital telecommunications later in this chapter). For analog telecommunications, the telephone company provides current in the form of a DC voltage across the loop. This voltage is called the *loop current*. This setup forms your plain old telephone service (POTS).

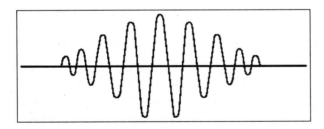

Figure 4-2: The analog transmission of a conversation.

When you take the telephone off-hook (that is, when you remove the handset from the cradle), the lever in the cradle, known as the *switch-hook*, springs back to complete the circuit (bridging the loop wires).The loop wire that carries the signal consists of two copper strands twisted together. This wire is generally known as *unshielded twisted pair* (UTP). Twisting the wires protects the signals carried by the current against electrical interference from other electronic devices. These two wires are basically all you need to have a POT conversation. Any additional wires that you see running through the cable casing or alongside the UTP are used to transmit data between the telephone set and the PBX.

As mentioned earlier, you have two ways to seize a line. With the *loop start* method of seizing a line, you start the line basically by bridging the end of the wires. This action takes place when you lift the handset out of the cradle and release the switch-hook. The negative end is called the *tip,* and the positive end is called the *ring* (refer to Figure 4-1).

The other method of starting a line is known as *ground start.* With this method, one of the wires is briefly grounded to an earth connection. PBXs usually work on ground-start lines, whereas telephones and small switches work on loop-start lines. The difference is transparent to the caller. When installing new telephone equipment, you must know what type of lines you need. The telephone company and PBX supplier can determine this easily.

Whether you request telephone service via loop start or ground start, the switch or exchange acknowledges the request by providing you with a dial tone. It then makes a connection between your telephone set and a digit (the DTMF tones that represent the numbers you dial) receiver, which waits for you to dial. When you hear the dial tone, you know that you can now dial the digits 405. (Remember that assistant you wanted to call?)

Dial-tone cadences and frequencies are not consistent throughout the PBX or telephone industry. The frequency and cadence varies remarkably from device to device. Humans have been taught to dial when they hear a dial tone, any dial tone. When you don't hear a dial tone, you probably deduce that either the PBX broke, temporarily crashed, or that the phone company shut off your service because you forgot to pay the telephone bills. Sometimes you hear a reorder tone, which means that the telephone circuits are *blocked.* (I discuss blocking in more detail a little later in this chapter and in Chapter 17.)

Often you can dial as soon as you lift the handset, just as my three-year-old does, assuming that a dial tone exists or that you can dial without it. Many devices that make telephone calls are programmed to enable you to do just that. (Of course, the drawback is that if you can't reach your three-year-old in time, you may get some strange long-distance charges on your phone bill.) Some voice-processing systems, for example, go off-hook, hope for the best, and then perform some form of call-progress analysis, such as waiting for an answer (call-progress analysis is discussed at length in Chapter 5).

Some modems refuse to dial when they hear a different dial tone such as the different cadence (mine sounds like water running through the telephone line) that the central office or PBX uses to signal that you have messages waiting somewhere. This quirk can be a real nuisance. And you wonder why we have to take four steps back for every two technological steps forward we make?

DIALING

Let's get back to your plain old telephone call: At this point, it may be a good idea to examine the two technologies used in the dialing process. More than likely, most of you reading this book are familiar with DTMF tones, commonly referred to as touch tone in the U.S. But many parts of the world, the U.S. included, require you to use pulse or rotary-dial telephones.

In fact, the total world population of pulse- or rotary-phone users is about 85 percent. In the U.S., about 30 percent of the population still uses rotary phones.

So, what's the difference between pulse- and tone-dial technology? Before touch tone, a caller advised the switch of the number he or she wanted to call by opening and closing the loop current provided by the switch, thus switching the current on and off. The techie term for this process is called *loop current disconnect* or, more commonly, *loop disconnect.*

The process generates *pulses* of loop current (hence the name). In other words, to indicate *1,* your phone stops the DC current flow by breaking the circuit once. To signify *9,* the phone switches the current on and off nine times; for *0* (zero), the phone interrupts the current ten times. Of course, you can use the switch-hook to break the circuit as well. But flashing the switch-hook *x* number of times to represent a digit to the switch is an effort requiring intense concentration and coordination, not unlike sending Morse code. If you keep your finger down for a millisecond too long, you risk permanently disconnecting the call.

The rotary dial was invented to automate this circuit making-and-breaking exercise. The frequency of the pulses varies from telephone network to telephone network. It can be anywhere from around 9 pulses per second (pps) to around 22 pps.

As technology improved, the rotary dial was replaced by a push-button dial. But the only difference here was fancier electronics. Under the phone's "hood" (or in this case, under the switch-hook), it's still loop disconnect dialing.

You may have the unfortunate fate of working with a fully computerized, digital PBX only to discover that the telephone service beyond the walls of the enterprise is loop disconnect or rotary dial. I have worked on many sites connected to these older exchanges, and I have no doubt that many still exist in the world out there, so be prepared for them. They turn up in the most unexpected cases. For example, Swaziland's PSTN consists of full-blown ISDN, yet if you arrive in London with a notebook computer and modem equipped to start World War III, chances are that you will have to connect to a pulse-dial exchange.

In the situation of a PBX connected to a pulse-dial exchange, the telephone instruments of the PBX may be rotary or push-button loop disconnect dialers; the reason is that, to dial an outside telephone number, you have to transmit loop disconnect signals because the exchange only accepts that type of signal. Later, as users demanded touch tone for faster internal dialing, the PBX manufacturers had to install tone-to-pulse conversion circuitry in the PBX to make the external call to the exchange. The user could merrily dial with touch tones and enjoy the speed of tone dialing. But to make an outside call, the PBX had to trap those tones and convert them into pulses for the benefit of the old, clunky, rotary-dial exchange beyond the wall of the enterprise.

If your exchange is still loop disconnecting away, you need to make sure that your computer telephony system can switch between the two methods of dialing. If not, you may have to forego some features, such as delivering messages to the home telephones. I caution you about using rotary/pulse dialing in several chapters to follow.

Warning: If you plan to install a computer telephony system that offers interactive services such as audiotext and interactive voice response (IVR) but your target audience is still saddled with pulse-dial technology, then pulse recognition or pulse-to-tone conversion technology may not be sufficient to make the service work. You need to find out what type of telephones your callers are using.

Many modern pulse-dial phones, like their tone-dial cousins, have small memories to buffer the digits for automatic redial. When this memory fills up, the phone will not be able to dial any more digits, and your audience will have no choice but to abandon the call. Older rotary-dial phones do not "run out of pulses" like the more modern versions, so they work, but the chance of your audience switching to older rotary phones is approximately zero.

COMPLETING THE CALL

Now that you have a dial tone, and the PBX has commissioned a digit receiver, you can dial 405. As soon as the PBX detects the first digit, it discontinues the dial tone, and the digit receiver collects the string of digits 4-0-5. Now the PBX checks the number 405 for validity. In other words, it checks to see whether 405 is an actual extension — and verifies whether it's in service or has some condition attached to it.

The verification process is important because the extension may not exist or perhaps can only be dialed under certain conditions. Maybe the extension you dialed is a "phantom" extension; perhaps it's a pool of several extensions; or perhaps it's a service and not an extension at all, like a night or after-hours bell. In such cases, if your extension is not authorized to make the call, the PBX will send back a tone that basically tells you "extension not available; please reorder the dial tone."

In the U.S., this tone is called the *reorder tone,* whereas elsewhere in the world, it's referred to as the *service unavailable tone.* This tone often sounds like a busy tone, only it's much faster and is often known as, you guessed it, *fast busy.* Sometimes, however, the PBX just goes "click" on you. If this happens while you're trying to integrate a computer telephony system, your next step will be to see whether the PBX can defy gravity from seven stories up.

The fast busy signal, or reorder tone, relates to a concept in telephony known as *blocking*. Blocking is a condition that occurs when a telephone network is unable to connect two parties because all available paths between them are in use. Both blocking and non-blocking networks are available. The public switched telephone network is a blocking network. Dedicated data networks are built around non-blocking architectures. (You'll run into this term in several parts of this book.)

In the past, blocking on a voice communications network was considered acceptable because telephone conversations were generally short. However, that's not always the case anymore. With the surge in telephone traffic and the incredible popularity of the Internet and on-line communications, a level of blocking now exists on the telephone network that our telephony forefathers would never have dreamed possible. It takes just one nutcase on the Internet to circulate a rumor or point everyone on the World Wide Web to some "jewel" of information or graphic, thus creating an Internet "hysteria" that can block a whole country.

Smarter PBXs can send you a digitized voice message stored on the PBX itself instead of a reorder tone to indicate a problem. You may hear "extension unavailable, please confirm the number and try again." The central office switch does this task, telling you that the "number has been disconnected." In the U.S., if you hear this message, more than likely it means that the person you are calling has not paid the telephone bill. (I don't know of anyone in the U.S. who temporarily disconnects a service voluntarily; after all, many people depend on voice mail if they're not home.) However, this rather embarrassing announcement gets the job done: it gets bills paid. Most telephone exchanges just return the ring-back signal though (which, in a sense, doesn't help either because you don't know whether the person is dead or alive).

If extension 405 is a valid extension and you have authority to dial it from your extension, the PBX will send back ringing tones (or *ring-back signals*) if the extension is not busy. If the extension is in use, the PBX will send a busy tone. When the party on 405 answers, the switch sets up a connection between 400 and 405 (see Chapter 7). The process of establishing the connection is so fast that it seems like you were directly connected to the person's telephone in the first place, that they had only to lift the handset. But all during the time you hear ringing, no such connection exists.

You go through the same process if you want to make a call across the PSTN. When you lift the handset on the telephone connected to a PBX, you first get the local dial tone — that is, the dial tone provided by the PBX. But you don't want to dial an extension there, so to get the PSTN dial tone, you need to access the public switch through your local private switch. To do this, you press the *access digit,* which is typically 0 (zero) in Europe and 8 or 9 in North America.

By pressing the access digit, you tell the PBX to connect you to an external line. If all the outside lines are busy, the PBX sends you a reorder tone. If a line is available, you hear the dial tone from the PSTN.

If you are on the receiving end of the call, you know that someone is trying to call you because the PBX or PSTN prompts the telephone to ring. It does this task by sending A/C voltage along the line to the telephone. The electronics of the telephone device can detect this voltage, which is what causes the bell to ring. Of course, the caller does not hear this ringing; the caller hears the ring-back signal — a confirmation that the remote set is ringing. When the called party answers, the ringing process terminates.

DISCONNECTING

After one of the parties replaces the handset, that party's phone is back *on hook*. On hook means that the switch-hook is depressed and the circuit is broken. The broken circuit terminates the loop current and, in turn, the connection. Although either party can disconnect the call in most cases, many exchanges require the calling party to disconnect before tearing down the connection.

Some countries have laws that govern calling-party disconnect. In North America, the central office alerts the PBX or remote device to call termination or abandonment with a drop in the loop current. Almost everywhere else in the world, at least in places where I have worked, the central office informs the connected device of the other party's abandonment by transmitting a control signal. This tone is often called a *disconnect* or *hang-up* tone. (This control signaling is known as *in-band* signaling; I talk about it in more detail in Chapter 5.)

In North America, many PBXs do not extend the disconnect information (the drop in the loop current, for example) to the answering device at the extension (usually the computer telephony system). Because you do not get a tone there, the only way that you can determine that the call is over is by silence. Humans may be able to quickly deduce that silence means the call is over, but a computer telephony system attached to the analog extension will have to work on a time-out scheme to recognize that the line is "dead."

In Europe and South Africa, the PTT (Post, Telephone, and Telegraph administration) approval process requires the computer telephony systems to release the line when the person called hangs up on them. The computer telephony system must be able to detect a called-party disconnect signal in order to release the line. If it does not detect the disconnect, then when the called party tries to make a call, the computer telephony system will still be holding the line. This situation can lead to a serious problem if the called party wants to make an emergency call and finds the line still open to a telemarketing machine. In the final chapter, I discuss strategies for using disconnect and hang-up detection in more detail so that you can avoid this problem.

FLASHING THE SWITCH-HOOK

When you want to signal to the switch that you need service, you typically "flash the switch-hook." (And you didn't even know it, right?) *Flashing* is the process of depressing the switch-hook long enough to send a signal to the switch but not long enough to disconnect the call. This flashing is the reason why people often refer to the switch-hook as the flash-hook. You flash the switch-hook to put someone on hold and take them off hold.

The duration of the flash varies from switch to switch. The flash time is measured in milliseconds. If the duration of the flash is too short, the switch will not receive the signal. If the duration of the flash is too long, you may disconnect the caller or terminate the call, essentially signaling the PBX that you want to go on-hook.

Flashing the switch-hook for service is also known as recalling the switch. To prevent an accidental disconnect, many telephones include a *recall* button. When you depress the button, you flash for the exact duration needed to recall the switch for service.

When you flash the switch-hook, the PBX places the passive party on hold while the controlling party (which can be a device such as the voice processing system) dials a service access code. This code, usually tone dialed, can signal the PBX to transfer the passive party, recall the passive party, or engage additional parties in a conference. The process is virtually the same when working with the central office switch. It's essentially how Centrex, described in Chapter 7, works.

TRANSFERRING A CALL

You can transfer a call in two ways: *transfer blind* or *transfer-on-consultation.*

TRANSFER BLIND

When you transfer blind, you simply put the caller on hold, dial an extension number, and hang up the receiver (depress the switch-hook). The caller on hold is transferred to the extension, and the receiving party has no prior knowledge of the call. In this situation, the transferring party does not care about who will answer or where the call ends up; the call could end up at a human, an ACD system, or a computer telephony system.

TRANSFER-ON-CONSULTATION

When you transfer a call *on-consultation,* you wait for the called party to answer while the caller is still on hold. You then *consult* the called party to (a) verify if the extension is the correct one, (b) identify the caller to the called party, and (c) check if the called party can take the call.

CT systems should be able to transfer blind and on-consultation.

COVERAGE

Calls that are not answered after a given time (usually after three rings) need to be diverted because you don't want the caller to abandon the call. This diversion or forwarding process is known as *coverage* in North America, but it's also known as *call-forwarding.*

Coverage can be activated on all inbound calls to an extension; it makes no difference whether the call was dialed directly to the station as a direct inward dial call (DID) or "put-through" by a human telephonist or a computer telephony system. Every enterprise has a policy and set of rules governing the coverage process. Calls can be (a) diverted back to the live telephonist for a decision or (b) diverted to another extension or (c) diverted to a CT system, such as voice mail or messaging services.

Callers enable voice mail facilities at their extensions by sending control signals to the switch, telling it to divert any calls not answered after a certain number of rings to an extension used by a CT system port.

At home, you can use coverage by requesting a diversion service to be activated on your telephone line. The call can be diverted to any other telephone in the nation or even to an international location. Naturally, the telephone company will charge you accordingly for the diversion; the caller only has to pay for the call up to the line diverting off the switch. If the diversion is long distance, then you (the called party) will have to pay long-distance charges for the diversion.

MAKING THE CALL . . . BIT BY BIT

Digital transmission technology has the capability to carry several simultaneous conversations over the same twisted pairs (X2s) used in analog transmission. In North America, Hong Kong, and Japan, the digital transmission standard is known as T-1, which provides for 24 64-kilobits-per-second (Kbps) connections.

In the rest of the world, the digital transmission standard is the European E-1, which provides 30 simultaneous conversations. E-1 provides data transmission rates of 2.048 megabits per second. The 2.048 megabits per second (Mbps) provides for 32 64-Kbps channels — 30 channels that carry conversations and 2 that carry signaling and supervision data.

The principles of the signaling process are essentially the same as analog signaling, except that the signaling information and substance of the communication is represented in binary data (1s and 0s) rather than as the analog audio signals that travel on loop current (see Figure 4-3 later in this chapter).

Both T-1 and E-1 have been enhanced over the years to provide the now popular Integrated Services Digital Network, better known as ISDN.

Many variations exist for the call-completion processes described earlier. Some PBXs and central office switches incorporate fancy features into the process to assist telephone users. Remembering how to use some of these features is easy, such as putting a party on hold. But as the features become more complex and numerous, they become more difficult to invoke through the telephone handset alone. This is where CTI comes in.

KEY COMPUTER TELEPHONY HARDWARE

Had it not been for the invention of the voice-processing card, I doubt that computer telephony would have turned into the industry it is today. This small, and usually rather expensive, PC-based interface card is at the center of it all. You may hear talk about PBXs and switching gear, telephones, and fax boards and fax machines, but without the voice-processing board, you have no interactive service, no human-computer telephone conversation.

VOICE PROCESSING

The voice-processing board is many things to the computer telephony system. Let's look at its anatomy. Its essential components are the following:

+ Electronics that interface with the telephone line (usually through the RJ11 modular plug system)

+ Analog/digital converting electronics (known as the codec)

+ DTMF and MF tone detection, generation electronics, and hardware for loop disconnect (pulse) dialing

+ Digital-signal-processing chips

+ Memory used to load firmware and the DSP operating system

By using these key electronics, the voice-processing card makes possible all the human-computer dialog services described in Part II, that is, voice processing (computer telephonist), audiotext, fax-on-demand, and IVR. It can also handle call processing, initiating and receiving calls, transferring, and so forth.

Without going into an involved discussion of voice-processing technology (a book in itself), here are the essential duties that the voice-processing card can perform:

+ Go on and off hook

+ Detect and generate tones with ease

+ Perform loop disconnect (pulse/rotary) dialing with ease

+ Perform call-progress analysis and monitoring (see Chapter 5)

+ Flash the switch-hook

+ Record and playback audio (at which it excels)

+ Perform text-to-speech, or TTS

✦ Detect pulse digits (with effort)

✦ Recognize voice (but it needs another hardware component to which it can offload this effort: the voice-recognition board)

✦ Switch calls (although this task is better left to a dedicated switching device)

Whereas the voice-processing card is at the center of the computer telephony system, the DSP chip lies at the heart of the voice-processing industry. Because of the important role that the DSP chip plays here, I'll give it some special treatment.

THE DSP CHIP

One could argue that voice-processing components make it possible for humans to interact and have conversations with computers over the telephone. After all, the most natural form of communication between human parties on the telephone is voice. It only seems fitting then that humans converse with computers in the style to which humans are accustomed.

Enter the DSP chip. It tries to make sense of analog-turned-digital information that emanates from the world around it and then communicates this info, as binary code, to the computer for a response. (See Figure 4-3.)

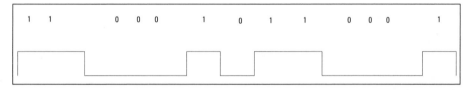

Figure 4-3: Digital language, represented by 1s and 0s (binary code), is the language of computers. To make sense of the human language, computers have to convert analog speech patterns to binary information.

For the purposes of this book, here is a very rudimentary description of DSP technology. Figure 4-4 illustrates the course of action: When an analog signal arrives at the voice-processing port (the telephone connection on the voice-processing card), the port feeds it to a coding/decoding device (the codec). The codec changes the analog wave form into digital data (a collection of 1s and 0s), which is the language that computers speak and understand. By being able to perform mathematical calculations at incredible speeds (billions of calculations per second), the DSP chip is able to digitize and compress analog audio into digital information.

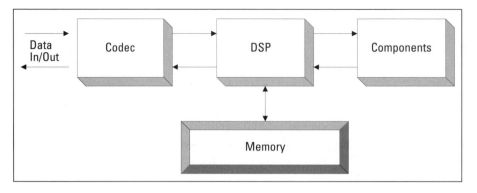

Figure 4-4: Digital signal processing (DSP) lies at the heart of all information processing and computer telephony.

After the analog information comes out digital from the codec, the DSP chip "looks" at this digital data and attempts to make sense of what it represents, in a process similar to the way living beings use their senses to process information. The DSP chip "processes" the signal by blazing through billions of mathematical operations per second. This processing is controlled by the DSP operating system that loads onto the telephony card at run-time. (The fact that the DSP chip has its own operating system is another great attribute of this marvelous invention.)

Just recognizing that a human, rather than an answering machine, said "hello" involves countless calculations. If you had to sit down with a calculator and try to duplicate the effort manually, it would take you years to finish. But the DSP does this task in a sliver of time (it gives the software something to match against information). After the DSP finishes processing the signal, the computer telephony software picks up the result and determines whether it should say "hello" back or hang up.

The processing power of these components is astonishing: Currently, they can handle approximately two billion operations per second (2 BOPS); by the end of the decade, you may be plugging in devices that can process twice this amount in the same time. Already, interactions between computers and humans are becoming so lucid that it's sometimes hard to tell whether you're talking to a machine or a human. DSP is the technology that will make the dream of having conversations with computers, a la *Star Trek* style, a reality.

Think about the reasons why voice mail and automated attendants have been so repulsive. Don't you hate having to wade through menu after menu? You may not know it, but all you're doing is changing around some 1s and 0s on the system's hard disk. DSP will make the following telephone conversation a real alternative:

Computer: "Thank you for calling Most Important Bank, did you know tha—"

Human: "Shut up and give me my balance."

Computer: "Call back later, sir, after you've learned some manners."

One of the leading manufacturers of DSP chips is Texas Instruments. You can find its technological touch on all leading computer telephony components. As of this writing, Texas Instruments is rolling out an incredible component called the *MVP.* MVP stands for *Multimedia Video Processor,* but the chip is better known in DSP programming and computer telephony circles as the TMS320C80. (Quite a mouthful, huh?) I won't go into the technical underpinnings of this chip, except to say that it can process 2 BOPS and run cool without constantly needing a fan on its back, unlike some of the high-end microprocessors on motherboards. One of the important applications that this chip will enable is real-time video.

Thus, the DSP chip has been the chief enabling technology in the voice-processing industry. By using this chip, you can stick all this techno-wizardry onto cards that plug into PCs. You could say that the DSP chip has been the driving force behind computer telephony.

UNIVERSAL SERIAL BUS (USB)

Another technology, in this case a standard, moving to the center of the CT industry is Universal Serial Bus (USB). It is a standard that, among a number of objectives, makes it easier to connect a telephone to a computer. Here is how it works:

One of the limiting factors of the new era in information technology, especially in the realm of breakneck developments in the PC industry, has been the dearth of peripheral devices that can be attached to the computer. These devices include modems, keyboards, mice, printers, scanners, joysticks, and more.

To connect these devices to the computer so that data can move to and from the device, you have to insert adapter cards into the interface slots on the computer's motherboard. A motherboard typically has eight slots. With so many interface cards being manufactured, such as voice-processing boards, the external peripherals have been finding life on the PC bus rather crowded lately.

The PC industry also is trying to squeeze all the PC innards into smaller cases so that notebook computers can keep getting smaller while becoming more powerful. Enter the new age in computer telephony and the PC-telephone connection (not CTI) craze ignited by Microsoft's TAPI (the subject of Chapter 5). Now there's another device that users will want to connect to their computers: It's called the telephone.

USB is emerging as a computer telephony standard for connecting the telephone to the computer. It employs *Plug and Play* capability and hot attach/detach (hot docking) technology that empower you to configure your computer according to the wildest inventions of your imagination. You can attach and remove a device from the computer at any time without having to power down or reboot the computer. And you can connect all kinds of devices to the computer wherever you can locate a USB port. (See Figure 4-5.)

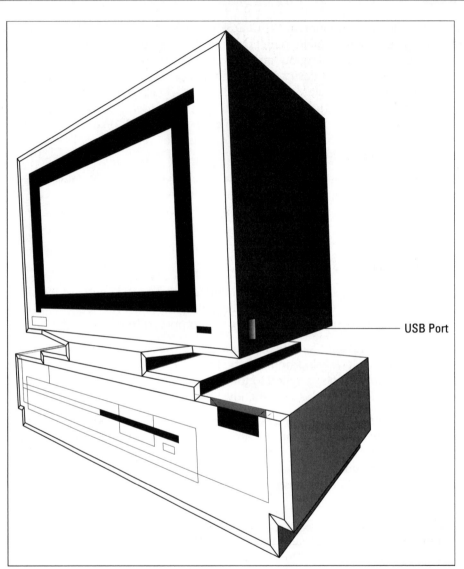

USB Port

Figure 4-5: The USB port connects telephones to computers.

For example, if a port is located on the monitor, then you can plug in a device such as a headset there. If the port is on your keyboard, then you can attach your headset there. You also can detach your headset and attach it to another computer without interrupting the computing environment. Because of the functionality that USB provides, companies will soon be installing USB hubs on their LANs.

Here are some of the important specifications of USB:

✦ USB supports up to 127 devices, including gaming devices and virtual-reality goggles.

✦ It has a 12 Mbps design and can transfer data isochronously and asynchronously. (See the following sidebar for the definitions of isochronous and asynchronous data transmission.)

✦ It supports up to five meters of cable.

✦ It supports daisy chaining through a tiered, star, multidrop topology.

Isochronous, asynchronous — what's the difference?

Isochronous transmission is an important aspect of voice communications. The term *isochronous* comes from the Greek words "iso" for equal and "chronous" for time and has to do with the time-sensitive transmission of data. Voice and video transmission equipment need isochronous transmission because this method enables the communication to happen in real-time. Isochronous transmission delivers voice and video data without detracting from the natural style of conversation taking place between several parties.

Asynchronous transmission, on the other hand, is a method of data transmission that enables data characters to be sent at irregular intervals. Fax mail and e-mail clearly do not need isochronous transmission and can be delivered via asynchronous transmission.

Why is USB so important for CT, you ask? For starters, you can create a CTI link without specialized add-in cards by using USB. Second, this bus supports high-speed digital interfaces like ISDN, T1, and E1 (T1 and E1 are the North American and European digital standards, respectively, and are discussed in Chapter 14). Third, you can unplug telephony devices from your desktop computers and connect them to your portables, further eliminating the cloning syndrome. Thus, you will finally be able to call up the coffee machine and have a fresh pot of Colombian waiting for you when you get to work.

SUMMARY

That's our crash course in telephony and the enabling technologies of computer telephony. For information covering the integration of telephone networks with Internet technology, turn to Chapter 12. Many good books are available that can take you deeper into this complex world of engineering. I refer you to the Bibliography for a short list of them. For some short definitions and explanations of computer telephony enabling technologies, you should turn to the Lexicon.

Now the fun and games start: computer-telephone integration (CTI), Chapter 5.

IN THIS CHAPTER

"Peter, you never *talk* to me anymore.
All you ever do is point and click!"

CTI

Several years ago, I demonstrated an MS-DOS-based, call-processing application running on a Rhetorex voice-processing board to a client. It was one of the first (or, most likely, *the* first) true, object-oriented (C++), multitasking computer telephony schedulers ever invented. In fact, it was actually adapted from sample code published in *Computer Language* magazine. The application used the Phar Lap DOS extender to get the additional memory needed to perform the tasks required of it: third-party call control. Our clients had various applications that needed to be integrated to get this setup to work (I won't go into which ones).

The application's purpose was to signal to the computer telephony server to automatically handle call conferencing. We established a client/server connection to the computer telephony server over the network. The process involved sending a message to the server, which would then call the PBX and establish some sort of influence over a conversation, such as barging in or conferencing in another caller.

We had many difficulties to resolve. Each PBX worked differently: Some PBX software needed upgrading to get around problems such as third-party privileges, rights to intrude, and so forth. The only CTI-link was the in-band call control commands that the Rhetorex board could "pipe" to the PBX.

When the engineers were finally able to get this caller conferencing application to work on a large Philips PABX, I remember saying this: "One day, all telephony equipment and switches will be like printers — you'll be able to connect the PBX to the server via the RS-232 ports or to plug an Ethernet card into the PBX. Then you will only need to select the relevant PBX driver from the Windows Control Panel, and all the computer telephony applications on the network will be able to drive the device."

These days have arrived. Facilitating this new age is the AT&T/Novell Telephony Services API (TSAPI) and Microsoft Windows Telephony Services (TAPI). This new age also brought with it new models in computer telephony. But before discussing the new paradigms and the new age in CTI — which has been riding on the wave of much publicity — let's first look at the important objectives of CTI, how first-generation CTI works, and how it set out to achieve some of these objectives. In this chapter, I also briefly sketch the two new models for integrating the PC with the telephone network. You should strive to implement these models for your own systems.

With the arrival of the NetWare Telephony Services (NTS) and Windows Telephony Services (WTS), I find it necessary to talk about two categories of CTI. The first generation of CTI encompasses the CTI practices of the past decade or so — the practices that leave bald patches of skin on most computer telephony consultants and vendors from pulling their hair out.

The second generation of CTI, which represents a fundamental shift from the old era, is being driven by the heavyweight software and computer companies now present on the CT scene, such as IBM, Microsoft, Novell, and Intel, and by the support for open standards (finally) in the PBX community. But let's discuss CTI in general first, so that you can appreciate why I consider the new era to be Heaven-sent.

CTI

All modern PBXs and telephone equipment incorporate some form of computer control or processing. Don't forget that modern PBXs have a built-in computer, although its processing power is nothing compared to that of a workstation or a PC. But when you consider the alternative available before these computers came along — that is, switches manually controlled by humans — you'll be glad to have any computer that can help out.

In addition to these smart, sophisticated, (yet often hard to use) PBX systems controlled by a CPU, you can "integrate" external computer equipment with the services of a PBX to achieve powerful computer control over the telephone call. This integration enables you to automate and empower your telecommunications service. This integration also brings to life the services of computer telephony described in Part II.

From an engineering perspective, the objective of CTI essentially is to provide two divisions of service:

✦ Computer control of the call and the ability to take and make a call

✦ Human-computer dialog over the telephone

The call-control side empowers the enterprise by liberating the human from the call answering, routing, filtering, and dialing process; whereas the human-computer dialog side obviates the need to have two or more humans involved in a telephone conversation. Figure 5-1 summarizes the CTI objectives.

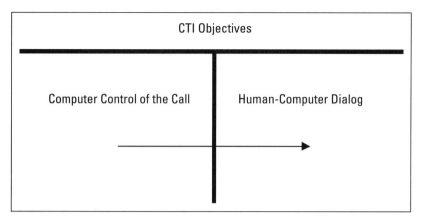

Figure 5-1: CTI objectives are: (1) computer control of the call, and (2) human-computer dialog. (The arrow highlights that division 1 is the essential service.)

If all you need to do is route and process calls to representatives or automatically dial out to colleagues or the external environment, then you do not really need a computer telephony system that includes the capability to have a dialog with a caller. A division 1 only system is likely to be an ACD, a predictive dialing service, a personal dialer, or a sequencing system that (at the most) plays a digital recording pleading for you to stay on hold. All other computer telephony services require both services, as depicted in Figure 5-2, to do both call processing and to have a *meaningful* human-computer dialog.

Computer Control of the Call	Human-Computer Dialog
Initiate calls	Computer telephonist
Receive calls	Audiotext
Transfer calls	Fax-on-demand
Park calls	IVR
Conference calls	Messaging
Tear down calls	
Perform CPA/CPM	
Report	

Figure 5-2: The two divisions in CTI objectives enable several services.

It is important to note here that in the past decade, computer telephony systems did not provide a user interface at the user's PC. The only interface was via the telephone. So you had two interfaces: one for the owner of a mailbox or service, and one for the customers or callers. Today, the desktop represents the third interface into the world of computer telephony.

I devote much of this chapter to the enabling technology of the first division, CTI. The services that enable human-computer dialog are discussed in Chapters 7 through13.

To qualify as a computer telephony system, the product first must, for myriad reasons, be able to automatically *and* manually perform one of the following functions (in no particular order):

✦ Initiate or set up calls

✦ Receive calls

✦ Transfer calls

✦ Park calls

✦ Conference calls

✦ Tear down calls and conferences

✦ Perform call-progress analysis (CPA)

✦ Perform call-progress monitoring (CPM)

✦ Provide real-time reports (data) on the aforementioned functions

Secondly, although not as important, the system should be able to perform these functions one call at a time or concurrently. A powerful computer telephony system can perform any of these functions concurrently on multiple telephone lines. In other words, it should be able to receive and make calls at the same time.

How do you make a computer do this? Just because the telephone and the PBX were designed for human usage, why can't someone just create software that makes a PC behave in the same way? In other words, let's get the PC to lift the handset (go off-hook), listen for dial-tone (perform CPA), dial some numbers, and then wait for (a) ringing or (b) a busy signal (again, perform CPA). When either of the tones are received, the computer should be able to decide what course of action to take. This decision process is illustrated by Figure 5-3.

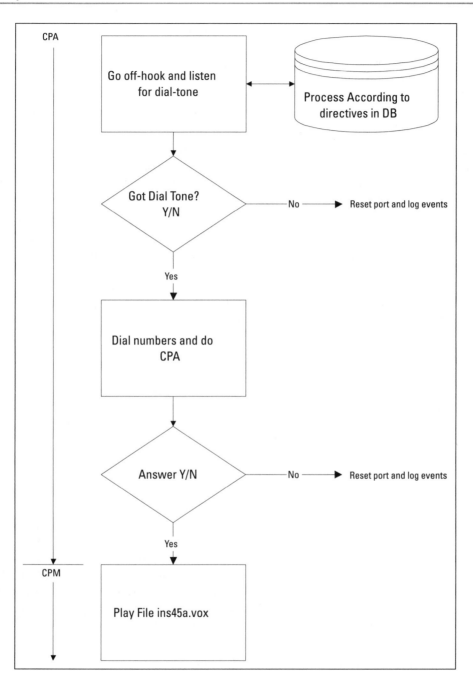

Figure 5-3: Here, the CT port goes off-hook, listens for dial-tone (CPA), and after dial-tone has been determined, dials the numbers. Then it attempts to detect rings or busy signals to determine the next action.

Sounds easy enough, right? Not really. Some years back, just writing the software to perform the actions illustrated by Figure 5-3 took an engineer, albeit new in telephony, several weeks to complete. (This time also was before the advent of computer-aided software engineering tools and toolkits that strip away some of the complexity of the task.) If the software had to work with a number of PBXs, the development cycle for such a program exploded into several months, causing the poor engineer to work many late hours.

But it doesn't end there. The systems integrator then had to attach the systems to the customer's PBX. (This process sometimes is an easy one; other times, however, it becomes a nightmare.) Then came the task of integrating the modified setup into the existing information systems architecture and the LAN.

Granted, the awareness of computer telephony has risen at an astounding pace, thanks to the involvement of industry-leading computer and telephony companies. such as Microsoft, Novell, AT&T, Intel, IBM, and others too numerous to mention. But as Chapter 1 explained, you also must understand the difference between *computer-telephone integration (CTI)* and *computer telephony integration*. These terms are not interchangeable, as is often practiced by the popular computer press and some culprit technology companies that should know better.

CTI is possible with one small PC and a 2×4 switch (two lines; four extensions). Computer telephony integration means taking the PC integrated with the switch and putting it on the LAN. Depending on the enterprise and the application, that may mean a trivial addition of a PC to a network served by a single server or a not-so-simple integration into a highly complex collection of internetworking LANs and telecommunications services, consisting of many different types of servers, network operating systems, protocols, topology, and more. Thus the systems integrator or network engineer may have to perform two tasks: (1) get the CT system and the PBX on talking terms (CTI) and (2) integrate the CT system into the IT architecture without turning the enterprise upside down.

While writing this book, I was astonished at how the Computer Press oversimplified the process of integrating computers and telephones or invented things that don't exist. For one, integrating the PCs, servers, LAN, and more with the telephone network requires a more than cursory understanding of both data and telephone networks and the enabling technologies. As a result of a lack of understanding of the telephony side, few IT executives have commissioned extensive computer telephony integration until their network engineers better understand the implications. LANs are hard enough to manage and maintain as it is, so few want to mess with what's working as is.

This factor also has a great deal to do with wiring up a business to the Internet. The press have fallen in love with the Internet and management loves it, but IT says "Wait a minute . . . who's the chump who has to integrate all this and make it work?" With regard to our subject, many still question the reliability of the new models of CTI, an issue I expand on in Chapter 17.

Thus, out in the real world, the integration of customer premise (CPE) telephony equipment with computer telephony systems is a ongoing battle being fought by tough, hard-skinned soldiers. Their weapons are not only an exceptional knowledge of computer systems, software, and data networking, but also a more than basic understanding of wide-area telecommunications, telephony, and telephone systems.

As an example, Applied Voice Technologies (AVT), one of the leading vendors of CT systems, requires that its resellers carry and know how to use a *butt set*. A butt set, once the tool only of telephone engineers, is a device that enables the engineer to "butt-in" on a telephone call and monitor and perform computerized tests on the line. A butt set looks like a huge telephone with a mini-computer built into it. The computer telephony engineer is hard to come by, so the the demand for people who understand the CTI process will rocket in the next few years as everyone appreciates the need for computer telephony and what it can do for productivity — and learn how difficult it can sometimes be to integrate computer telephony systems.

FIRST GENERATION CTI

Thanks to the invention of the voice-processing card, a measure of computer-telephone integration has been possible for some time. The principle means of "coupling" a voice-processing or voice-mail system has been via the analog channel on the wire that connects the telephone to the switch. This practice is known as in-band integration.

IN-BAND INTEGRATION

What do I mean by *in-band*? As you can see from Figure 5-4, an analog channel's bandwidth supports a 300 to 3100 Hz frequency range sufficient to transmit voice communications and sound. Telephone equipment, however, uses this same frequency range for control signaling. *Control signaling* is the process of using multifrequency tones to signal to the PBX CPU equipment the requests for dial tone, disconnect, conference, station busy, and so on (all the services discussed earlier).

Thus, when you pick up a handset and enter some tones to transfer a call or put a call on hold, you're using the audio bandwidth of the analog channel to signal the PBX. With digital services, your telephone system delivers the control signals on channels outside of the voice channels, or *out-of-band*. A digital (data/RS-232) connection between the switch and the computer telephony system usually provides the medium for out-of-band integration.

Many PBX systems are quasi-digital devices that use digital electronics for switching and signaling tasks and analog transmission electronics for transmitting voice. These devices typically have several wires traveling between the telephone sets and the PBX. You will also notice that the telephonist's console can send and receive signals to and from the PBX CPU by using an external data connection, such as an RS-232 interface.

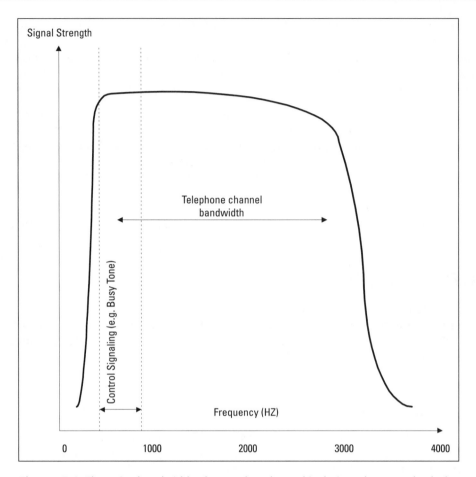

Figure 5-4: The voice bandwidth of an analog channel is designed to carry both the conversation and control signals.

Although it is possible to communicate with the PBX by dropping and loading loop current, almost all control communication is done by sending control signals along the voice channel. Computer telephony systems thus integrate with PBX and telephone systems by sending and listening to in-band signaling. Almost all call-progress monitoring done by computer telephony systems is done in-band. When a computer telephony system works with a PBX by detecting, sending, and analyzing in-band signals, the process is called *in-band integration.*

In-band analog signaling is achieved by connecting the analog device at the end of the twisted pair to an analog interface card plugged into the PBX. In the U.S., these ports are called *2500 ports,* AT&T's code name for a DTMF (touch tone) analog device. The old rotary- or pulse-dial phones were called *500 port* devices.

CALL-PROGRESS ANALYSIS AND CALL-PROGRESS MONITORING

Call-progress analysis (CPA) is the capability of CT telephony systems and telephony devices (such as modems) to analyze the signals on the telephone line in the process of setting up or tearing down calls. For example, your modem performs CPA when it goes off hook and listens for dial tone. If it detects the (correct) dial tone, it dials the string of digits to set up the call and then listens for either busy or ringing tones coming from the network. A busy tone tells the modem to try later, and a ringing tone tells the modem to wait for an answer or to time out after a period of ringing cycles.

If the remote device or network connection dies for some reason, the modem will re-analyze the signal coming back from the network to decide if it should go back on-hook. Some years back, the modems would remain on-hook long after a connection died and had to be powered down to put them back on-hook.

Call-progress monitoring (CPM) is the capability of the CT system to monitor the progress of a telephone call between connection and abandonment. In other words, the detection and analysis of signals is active during the conversation. Although CPA and CPM may appear to be the same, they are not. A CT system may use CPM, for example, to listen for a period of silence on the line. It then has to decide if a period of silence is the result of caller abandonment (when no other advisory signal is present) or a long period of breath-holding by the parties on the line (something the Cousteau family might do during a conversation).

Today, signal analysis is becoming so powerful that the device can detect and determine that although no one is talking, the background noise suggests that the party put the telephone down (perhaps to look for something) but did not go off-hook. CPM is most often used in human-computer dialog.

In many cases, the PBX does not send any signals back for call-progress monitoring. The CT system essentially has to guess at what's happening by using other information, such as a "hello" on the other end of the line. Often, it can detect call status by monitoring changes in the loop current. When a systems integrator encounters a PBX that doesn't have a loop current signal and that offers no in-band control signaling during a call, a computer telephony integration is almost impossible. Or, at the least, the integration will be featureless — getting nothing more than an answering machine on steroids.

CPA and CPM are made possible by technology such as digital-signal processing (described in the the previous chapter). Without CPA and CPM, many of the services described in Part II would not be possible.

USING IN-BAND SIGNALING WITH CPA AND CPM

When a computer telephony system tries to place a call, the digital signal processor and supporting electronics on the computer telephony or voice-processing equipment (usually the voice-processing board) performs signal analysis. To do the analysis, the devices use in-band signaling. The results of the computation are then handed to software control, which then compares the characteristics of the call, such as cadence and frequency, with signal information in a tone- or signal database. The value ascribed to the result enables the CT software to switch to certain functions in the software, such as playing a file or beginning a recording process.

How does a computer telephony system know that a phone is ringing and that it should abandon after, say, three rings? As the decision tree in Figure 5-5 illustrates, when the CT system receives a tone, it compares the tone to the information in the tone table or database. The system can rapidly determine whether the tone is a ringing signal, busy signal, reorder tone, and so on. Then it checks the computer telephony application database to figure out what to do if it gets a ringing signal. The database may, for example, wait three rings and then transfer the call to the next extension.

In-band signaling (integration) is the chief means by which CT systems enable the caller to leave a voice message in the correct mailbox. Without an open partnership between PBX manufacturers and set standards to control how PBXs should work, the only way to do CTI with many switches has been by analyzing and acting on the divergent control signals.

Even when a PBX company has been hostile to the integration of computer telephony with their product, it still has been possible to do CTI. Some form of CTI is possible if the PBX uses the voice channel for control signaling — and every PBX does, even the 100 percent digital systems.

Modern PBX architecture enables the mixing of digital and analog phone cards on the PBX data bus. I have worked with a few companies that installed massive iSDX systems catering to more than 1,000 extensions. The iSDX is an ISDN switch. You can connect both ISDN and analog phones to this switch. At $500 to $1,000 a pop for an ISDN or digital phone, few companies want to hang a digital telephone off every extension. Without the voice channel and the control signal, the users would not be able to use the switch features — in fact, they would not be able to communicate with the switch, let alone make calls.

So, the rule for integration (in whatever form it takes) is that if you can find a analog extension somewhere, some form of CTI is possible. You also have to remember that digital or ISDN PBXs and telephones do not operate in a world devoid of analog telecommunications. If an ISDN PBX requires a voice mail system, it should enable a caller on the PSTN to use an analog telephone to receive messages, even from a rotary-dial telephone.

As far as CTI goes, anything that a user can do, the CT system doing call processing can do (often better); it just automates the process and clones the processing on every port available to it. The following process describes an automated attendant in action: When the caller connects and hears the greeting, he or she enters the extension number which the CT system, using signal recognition (DTMF/MF detection), matches against a database of extension numbers and users. The CT system then puts the caller on hold and calls the desired extension. While it's calling the extension,

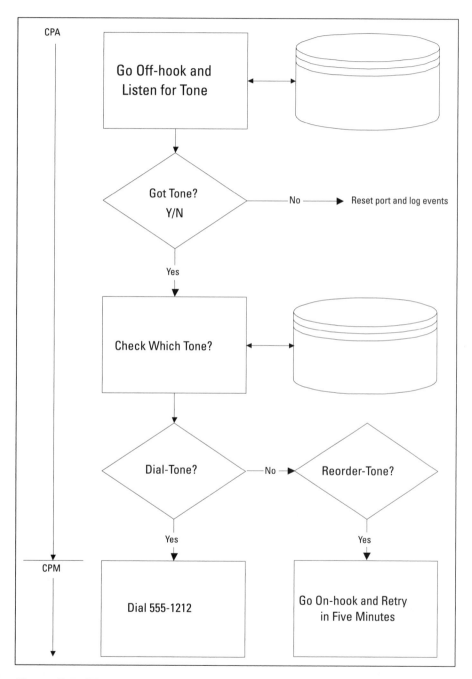

Figure 5-5: CT systems compare the tones they receive to program or databased information to determine how to process the call.

the system listens for the call control or call progress (in-band) signals, thus performing CPA. A short, fast tone means that the extension or station is busy or that service is not available. A ring-back signal tells the CT system that the station is free but not being answered. If the system detects a busy signal, it will check its database to decide what to do next.

The next step may be to try another extension or to transfer the caller to a voice mailbox. Allowing the extension to ring continuously may provide the same result. The path that the call takes now is determined by the system administrator and the user — the information is kept in database tables for fast lookup. If the call is answered, the system goes off-hook, which connects the caller to extension.

No two PBXs are the same; with all the different models available from the dozens of manufacturers around the world, the integration process can be a nightmare. Computer-telephone integration can thus be very tricky and time-consuming for the systems integrator. The best of computer telephony consultants became as good as they are only after years of bashing their heads against PBX cabinets, screaming "Why, why, why?" The following list is just a few of the control signal requirements that need to be taken into account when doing in-band integration:

✦ The amount of time before loop current off is considered to be caller abandon

✦ Flash duration

✦ Tones to dial before a transfer is made

✦ Tones to dial after a transfer is made, before replacing the handset

✦ Tones to dial after a transfer is made, but the call must be retrieved

✦ Tones to dial before a blind transfer is made

✦ Tones to dial to recall a failed transfer to a busy extension

✦ Tones to dial before setting up a conference

In one case, my colleagues and I even had to attach an oscilloscope to the telephone line to figure out why the CT system was detecting "call answer" during CPA, when, in fact, the extension was still ringing. We called this the "case of the lying PBX." You can imagine the problem this caused. The CT system thought the calls had been answered; it flashed the switch-hook and said "buh-bye" to the callers it put on hold. Meanwhile, the calls had not been answered, and the call-process objective collapsed like a star going to supernova. We, the computer telephony people (not the PBX engineers), finally discovered a flaw in the PBX's ring generator and a software bug that was suddenly causing the cadence of the ringing signal to change.

The problem was that compensating for the flaw and the bug was impossible because the change occurred spontaneously and sporadically. And this wasn't any crackerjack system, either — it was a huge Siemens system, one of several nodes and worth several hundred-thousand dollars. Without going into the details, the ring generator had to be replaced and some PBX software had to be rewritten, all of which was going to take time that the client didn't really have.

The client was furious; the company had just spent six figures on a computer telephony system that had to be put on light duty. Until Siemens could replace the offending electronics and software, the CT system could not deliver messages to users' telephones and, more importantly, it could not transfer callers and perform reliable CPM.

But in-band signaling for CTI does not end there. Because some calls are diverted or forwarded to a CT system for coverage (see Chapter 4), the system first has to obtain prior information about the inbound call ringing at one of its ports, so that when it answers, the system can present the caller with the appropriate services. Why is this important? If a CT system does not have this information, it will simply go off-hook and default to the company or service's main greeting. This may not be a problem for, say, an audiotext voice response or ACD service, but it will be a problem for a voice mail service.

Without such information available to the CT system, the enterprise will have to rely on the human telephonist to connect a calling party to a specific mailbox just to leave voice mail. In other words, when coverage brings the call back to a live attendant, the attendant has to put the caller on hold, call the CT system, manually enter the correct mailbox number, and then replace the receiver. Only then would the caller hear the right mailbox greeting.

Of course, no person in his or her right mind wants to force callers to re-enter extension numbers at the message desk, especially if he or she is at all concerned about customer satisfaction. What a waste of human resources to have to do this manually! Most humans do not have time to engage in such exercises of upside-down technology. Without this vital CTI, a voice mail system is useless.

How do you get this information to the CT system? One way is through in-band signaling. In this scenario, you have the PBX forward a string of tones to the CT system port as the CT system goes off-hook. It does this automatically by using a method known as *repeat dialing* (or *digit echo*, as it is known in Europe and English-speaking countries.) This enables the CT system to form an association with the call in order to identify it and link the call to a mailbox or a service. The process is as follows: When the CT system detects the ringing signal at the port, it goes off hook and listens for signals before playing a greeting. The PBX then transmits (repeat dials) the tones that represent the extension number dialed by the caller to the voice port. Using this method, the CT system knows which mailbox to drop the caller into and which personal greeting to play.

Repeat dialing is often used to enable users to depress a single, programmable key that calls the voice-mail system, repeat-dials the extension number, and even transmits the passcode.

Are you beginning to see how complex CTI can be? It doesn't get easier. What if the PBX cannot perform repeat dialing, and a CT system does not have access to real-time station status information (digital) provided by the PBX? Then the only way to provide a voice mail service is to use voice mail in conjunction with a computer telephonist (automated attendant; see Chapter 8).

A computer telephonist can perform this process because *it* handled the transferring process from the start, from the time the caller first connected to the enterprise. After the caller enters the digits corresponding to the extension required, he or she is put on hold and the system calls the extension. The computer telephonist now performs CPA (call-progress analysis) to detect an answer or busy signal. At this stage, the system is able to perform CPA because it is attempting to transfer on-consultation (remember "The Case of the Lying PBX"). Naturally, you have to disengage coverage on the extension; otherwise, the CT system will be merrily performing CPA when the PBX suddenly decides to send the call bolting off down the hall to another extension.

All in all, however, in-band integration is not the best way to connect a computer telephony system to a PBX. Often, using in-band integration is like having two people communicate in a common language that is the native tongue of only one of the parties. The receiving party may not understand 100 percent of the conversation because of differences in inflections and other idiosyncrasies that are not part of his or her culture.

The CT systems integrator has to remember that the integration method being used, in-band, was not designed for computer telephony. Many frustrating problems can arise as a result. For example: What if the CT system takes a message and then attempts to deliver it to a user? If the PBX has been signaled to divert the call into voice messaging, the CT system essentially ends up calling itself. Though in-band integration will always be needed, we also have to look for alternative methods of integration.

Perhaps one of the biggest drawbacks to in-band integration is due to the critical nature of computer telephony in these mad-house days of call centers and the dearth of messages. A great deal of time is wasted when a CT system has to put a caller on hold and "test" an extension to see if the party is available. If the extension is busy, then a few seconds have been wasted while the system gets the tone back, compares it to tone or signal information, and then transfers the caller into voice mail. Multiply a few seconds by thousands of messages a day, and the seconds turn into minutes, which turn into hours. Wouldn't it be great if the CT system were cognizant of the extension's status before or as soon as the call arrives? The caller then would go straight to voice mail.

DIGITAL INTEGRATION

Digital integration implies integrating or interfacing computer telephony with the PBX at the PBX's available data receptacle, which usually is an RS-232 interface. Two data streams of information are available that the PBX can provide at this port: (1) *Station Message Detail Recording (SMDR)* and (2) *Station Message Desk Interface (SMDI)*.

The SMDR feed provides data on every call made by a user to the outside world and the duration of the calls. It provides this information for call accounting purposes. The SMDI feed provides the computer telephony system with information needed to present the caller with the correct mailbox. The objective of repeat dialing and SMDI integration is the same: to tell the CT system who the message is for. The only difference is that the former information is delivered in the voice bandwidth of the audio channel, whereas the latter is delivered via an external digital link.

Several PBX companies have assisted the computer telephony process by enabling the ports to send more than rudimentary data to the SMDI or SMDR port. This data enables the CT system to determine who is calling whom. It tells the CT system that the call ringing on its port (associated with a PBX extension) was diverted from extension X.

Both in-band and digital integration have been used for years, often very extensively and to a great degree of success. In some cases, the PBX's in-band signaling has been sufficient enough to enable some nifty CT features.

But both in-band and digital integration are much like the process a neurologist-psychologist goes through to study the electrical signals of the brain. Using an electroencephalograph, the neurologist can study the brain as an outside observer. But it is a limited study, because God did not think that His creation needed a data port for external investigation. We humans have not "grown" a special interface where the neurologist can just plug in a device into the "main stream" of our thought processes. It has to be crudely attached.

The second generation of CTI — the new wave of CTI — has provided a comparable interface to enable computer telephony services. I discuss this interface as part of the following section on the new CT paradigms.

THE NEW COMPUTER TELEPHONY PARADIGMS

This section is about the important, emerging standards in CTI and computer telephony, NetWare Telephony Services (NTS) and Windows Telephony Services (WTS) — TSAPI and TAPI, respectively. But it goes much further than providing a loose description of the two dominant APIs, because these standards will bring about new models and the advent of new applications and empowerment . . . the second generation of CTI.

In computer telephony circles, the idea of a telephone standing unintegrated next to a computer is an abhorrent concept. The two should either be logically or physically integrated. A great deal of power goes untapped and much productivity is lost if you don't integrate these devices. You already have the two devices; all you have to do is connect them. Think of it as owning a fast sports car and never driving it above 90 mph. You may as well sell the engine and keep the body.

This setup describes the old model of computer telephony, where the user's workstation was excluded from the integration effort (the first generation CTI). Here, computer-telephone integration only concerned a PC stuffed with voice-processing cards that talked to the PBX via the analog extension like a human.

The advent of the workstation provided a combination of POT and PC, but the two have never been connected to the point where you can take advantage of all the wonderful things that a PBX can do . . . via the graphical user interface. (Here, the workstation is a place in an office where a human uses the telephone and the computer that live side-by-side.)

CALL CONTROL

Before discussing the two models, I want to introduce you to two buzzwords with which you should be familiar: first-party call control and third-party call control.

FIRST-PARTY CALL CONTROL

First-party call control implies that you have direct control over a call that has arrived at your telephone (which you may have snatched from another extension). Both parties on either end of a call (human or computer) have such control over a call, which is what call control refers to. The controlling party can put the caller on hold, park the call, and transfer the call. After the call is transferred (and is connected to another party), the control is lost.

Understanding that you still have control over a call after you transfer it is important, but only until another party receives the call. If the station to which you transferred the call does not take the call, you can dial a code to the PBX CPU and snatch the caller back. Even conferencing in another caller is first-party call control, because the first caller is temporarily suspended or put on hold while you call another person. To conference a group, one person needs the capability to control all calls and connect all three participants in a conversation.

First-party call control can also be achieved from your computer by having a physical connection between the PC and the telephone. Or, perhaps your PC is the telephone for your office.

THIRD-PARTY CALL CONTROL

Third-party call control implies control over calls that have not arrived at your telephone. You also can gain control over a call from your telephone, from your computer, or by connecting (via the LAN) to another device, such as the telephony server, ACD unit, or PBX. Call pick-up is a form of third-party call control because you can seize a call ringing at another extension or hanging out in hold, park, or queuing services. Telephonists perform third-party call control because they can manipulate and seize calls ringing at various extensions in the enterprise. They can easily retrieve a call that is not being answered and offer the caller a range of alternatives, such as leaving a message or trying another party.

DESKTOP COMPUTER TELEPHONY

Let's elaborate a little more and then talk turkey. To understand the desktop computer telephony model, you must view the workstation as a PC that is connected, logically or physically, to the telephone set. You gain access to telephony services through telephony-enabled applications like the one shown in Figure 5-6. With such a connection, four important concepts come to life:

1. You can access and take direct control of the telephone through a graphical user interface (GUI) on the workstation. Such first-party control empowers you to automate time-consuming and unproductive call-control actions in the telephone process, such as making repeat calls, answering numerous calls, putting callers on hold, transferring, conferencing, and more.

2. You provide an alternate user interface (when you can call it an interface) to the services that exist in the world of telephony, such as ANI (automatic number identification) and Caller ID. The telephone service and PBX comes loaded with many wonderful features hidden away from users, because these features are difficult to enable or access from the simple telephone.

3. You can use the telephony information that you extract to drive applications on the PC, which further helps to save time and makes you more productive. A good example is linking ANI information (if it exists) with a database record. The application then can automatically launch the database and call up a record associated with the Caller ID information.

4. You can do away with the need to invest in an expensive feature-phone. The screen-based dialer can do everything a fancy feature phone can do and then some.

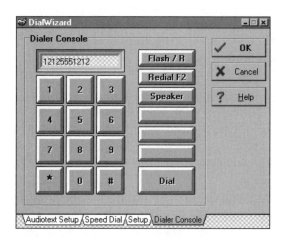

Figure 5-6: This GUI dialer can be programmed and setup to suit the user. Keys are programmable and can be changed to comply with the model of PBX. It can essentially replace the expensive feature (3D) phone.

You may wonder: "Why do I need the desktop telephone? If I can put a dialer into the PC, which is essentially a telephone on a card, couldn't I scrap this extra body that clutters my desk?" You get ten stars if you asked this question, but there is something you have to consider in all this techno-euphoria: Habit.

The telephone service started before the Chattanooga Choo Choo belched out its first puff of smoke in the late 1870s. The dial telephone goes way back to 1919, years before television became popular. Children learn how to use the telephone before they learn about computers; even my grandmother's African Grey parrot used to take calls. Hey, we've been using the telephone for decades — you can't just chop it out of the picture.

Although the GUI is great for opening up windows to all the fancy features of a PBX, only powerful voice recognition (and even that has limitations) beats the telephone keypad for dialing (at least *I* think so). Using a mouse to dial digits from the screen is like using chopsticks to pick up grains of rice. It takes me five to tens times longer to do it. And don't forget the handset, or receiver, because if you're not in a call center (wearing a headset), then how do you expect to have a telephone conversation? It will take some years and some getting used to before the telephone set fades away completely.

Figure 5-7 is a schematic of a CT-enabled enterprise information network (EIN; both LAN and telephone network). The illustration depicts a station that is (a) logically integrated, and (b) physically integrated with the computer. The CT-enabled desktop, or just desktop, is the GUI to the software that you use to access telephony services. These services and features may reside in the station, in the telephone standing next to it, or in a computer telephony server on the LAN. Wherever they reside, all telephony roads in an enterprise lead to a switch: either the PBX or the central exchange.

The desktop computer telephony model empowers the user by integrating both telephone and telephony services into the PC. Besides doing call control, this setup enables the user to continue working at a keyboard while receiving, processing, and initiating calls. For example, suppose that the telephone rings while I am typing this paragraph. In the desktop computer telephony model, the CT applet pops up a window that appears over my work and reads: "You have a call from the editor. Should I take a message, or do you want to answer?"

Now I can choose from a variety of options to respond to this call: I can press G on my keyboard for "grab caller" and use the microphone attached to the monitor to speak to the caller, or I can press "Z" for "zap caller" and have the applet fire the call straight into voice mail. Of course, I would never think of doing that to my editor, but I would not hesitate to do it if the caller is on my "zap" list.

Is your imagination running wild with ways that you can use this technology yet? With such power, I can tell the applet to take all future calls and tell the caller that I am "working at my computer and cannot be disturbed" instead of "I am either on the phone or away from my desk," which never impresses anyone. Or, I can click on a

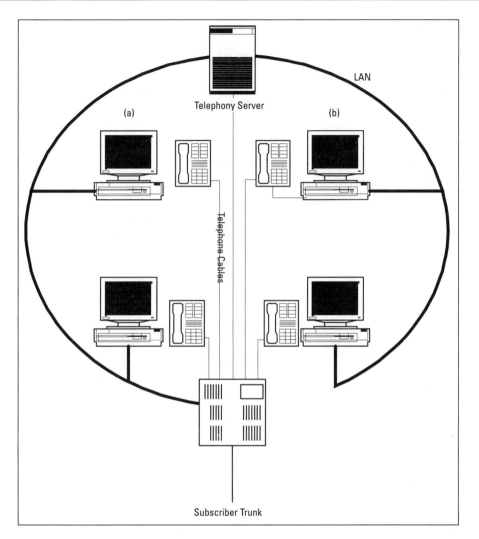

Figure 5-7: Desktop computer telephony. The workstation in A is logically integrated with the PC, while in B, it is physically integrated with the PC.

Transfer To option, which tells the applet to talk analog to the PBX or central office (as a recall or hookflash for services, which I discussed in Chapter 4) to activate the transfer. I also can have it digitally talk directly to the PBX, if telephony services are available on the company's LAN or intranet. You, too, can do all this stuff and more.

Note: The dialer depicted in Figure 5-6 is shareware and was created by my company. If you would like a copy, just drop me a note at the e-mail address shown in the Introduction and I will forward you a copy. It is also a TAPI-compliant application.

COMPUTER TELEPHONY SERVER

Suppose that you got the wild idea to stick PBX components, faxes, modems, LAN cards, digital interfaces, call-, voice-, and speech-processing cards, and more into a PC. Next, you loaded an array of enabling software, network operating systems, protocols, databases, and so on. The result? You have yourself a computer telephony server.

The computer telephony server (client/server) model differs from the desktop computer telephony model in two important ways:

1. It provides telephony services to all callers and users throughout the enterprise. One computer is often dedicated to computer telephony services. A computer telephony server, for example, can provide voice mail facilities to hundreds, even thousands, of users. Although the desktop telephony model can provide a voice mail service, it is not suitable for many users.

2. The server *logically* connects all telephones to the computer via the CTI-link to the PBX.

This type of logical connection is discussed further in the section on NetWare Telephony Services that follows, so I won't delve further into the concept here, except to say that many enterprises may prefer this method of connecting the desktop workstation to the telephone. What you do and how you do it in your business determines whether you go for a logical connection, physical connection, or a mix of both when considering call control. A factor you need to consider is cost. Many IT budgets don't allow for the additional expense of a physical connection between the PC and phone in the desktop model, especially if they employ hundreds or thousands of people. Others, however, do have the funds and not only fork out cash for the connection but also buy TAPI-compliant feature phones that can do anything short of launching the space shuttle.

Both computer telephony models can provide extensive telephony services to an enterprise. The desktop model is ideal for small offices/home offices (SOHOs) because it is cost effective. But some of the newer SOHO systems match or exceed the capabilities of older systems costing a thousand times more. I should also reinforce that the server model can do some fancy desktop telephony stuff as well.

The server model interfaces with the PBX via analog communications (in-band signaling) and can also interface directly with digital ports of a modern PBX (called the digital CTI-link). It can operate "behind" PBX; this means that the calls pass through the PBX before they are processed by the server. This model also can operate "in front of" PBX, which means that calls arrive for processing at the telephony interface cards in the server without passing though a PBX first. The telephony server itself can be a PBX; it can switch calls, process calls, take messages, and so on over its own, self-contained digital highway — all within the confines of a small computer case.

In the realm of client/server technology, this computer telephony server (which may also be the LAN server) can function as a station complete with desktop software for work and server management. But for robust or critical services, it should be left alone to serve computer telephony needs throughout the company. When it's not processing calls and taking messages, the server should be performing housekeeping, which may include removing unwanted messages, compacting the hard disk, backing up databases, and archiving.

An enterprise's computer telephony services are always mission critical (crash the LAN and you'll get kicked in the butt; crash the telephony server and you'll get a one-way ticket off the planet). It's not wise to risk downtime by putting a human at this server to, for example, edit a huge document, compile software, or play a game of pinball — especially if the server is performing the work of a PBX. Crash this server and you'll have a potential disaster, not only on the LAN but on the telephone as well.

You have to carefully consider the operating system's strengths and weaknesses, hardware and architecture, and more for your computer telephony server. Plain ol' DOS will not do, because it is not an ideal operating system for multitasking. It also does not provide enough memory for the processing-intensive computer telephony applications — although I have been involved in projects where DOS was extended and expanded beyond recognition. My computer telephony OS of choice is Windows NT, and the reasons are explained in the sections that follow.

THE NEW STANDARDS FOR CTI

Over the years, Novell and Microsoft witnessed the burgeoning need for computer telephony and CTI and, in their genius, recognized the great market opportunity. Today, they cater to these needs and have introduced extensions to their operating systems so that telephony devices can be attached to the computer or network. As a result, Microsoft Windows and NetWare can treat a PBX or a telephone just like any other device, such as a printer or a monitor.

What Novell and Microsoft have essentially done is create *applications programming interfaces* (APIs) for developers of computer telephony products. These APIs have the dual role of providing standards for computer-telephone integration (see Chapter 3, where I have included a section on Open Systems and Standards). But since the advent of these APIs, I have found end users, telephony people, and IT executives rather puzzled about these products and what they set out to achieve.

It serves no purpose really to debate the pros and cons of each API, the approach and philosophies of the groups, and even to fully explore each API, because this book is not about programming or software engineering. A detailed description of the two APIs/standards would, in any event, run to more than 500 pages each and would only interest a software developer and the service provider/vendor. As a systems integrator and software developer, I am just too happy to have a standard at all, even if it is a *de facto* standard. In any event, the war is not between TSAPI and TAPI: it's between Novell and Microsoft.

You, the end user, consultant, or IT executive, should not concern yourself with API wars; only the applications that you need to empower the enterprise. As a result, you may have to use one application conforming to one API over another that conforms to a different API. And you may have to mix and match your products to achieve your computer telephony integration objectives. Without writing a book on the basics of software engineering, we need to take a crash course in computer science to cover a few fundamentals before taking a brief look at the philosophies behind the two products. If you know what an API is, you can skip the next part.

A CRASH COURSE IN SOFTWARE ENGINEERING

What is an API? Funny you should ask. Basically, the API is the interface between the application — in this case, the CT software that the end user works with — and the environment in which it runs and with which it communicates.

A major component of the environment is the *operating system* (OS). An operating system is a complex piece of software (machine code) that runs the computer and controls the various components of the machine. When a software developer builds an application that requires access to or control over the physical components of the computer, such as the hard disk, modem, input/output devices (I/O devices), he or she writes some code that, when compiled, calls on the operating system for service.

The services required by an application — be they generated by the application itself as part of its logic or by an event initiated by the user — can be any of a broad range of services. On the instant of a key press, the service requested may be moving data from one device to another (even across a network) or sending messages, such as datagrams, across a network that will activate certain processes and functions on remote machines.

When you want to access or initiate functions on the remotes machine (server), you make (from the client) what is known as a *remote procedure call* (RPC). Making RPCs is really client/server technology in action. And client/server technology is the dream of distributed computing. I discuss client/server computing in a little more depth in Chapter 15.

Making calls to an operating system is complex and time consuming. Just displaying a message or calculating some figures can require a programmer to write a great deal of code. The task gets more difficult when you add network support to the operating system. What if you need to display a message on the remote machine or run some routines there? Now the application needs to call on the operating system to pass information to the physical layer of the network to, say, send the message or make an RPC to a remote machine.

The design and creation of software is highly complex. The effort it takes to build a significant piece of software requires similar brain power to build a huge bridge, such as San Francisco's Golden Gate, or a building, such as the Empire State building in New York City. Debugging software is no fun, either. A popular belief is that ridding a program completely of bugs (errors in the code) can take many millions of years — in other words, it never happens. It is also very difficult for one engineer to inherit and continue working with another engineer's code.

To reduce the complexity and to speed up development, we work through application programming interfaces (APIs). One of the best examples of an API is the Windows API. When Microsoft Windows first debuted in the 1980s, it was an extremely complex operating system to write applications for. Without the API, software developers would have found it nearly impossible to write any application that could run on the operating system.

Microsoft's strategy, however, was to get as many people as possible to write applications for Windows, (a strategy that resulted in over 80 percent of the world's personal computers running Windows today). Hence, it published the Windows API, a layer residing above the operating system that made it easier for programmers to write Windows applications. Instead of hundreds of lines of code required to open a dialog box and say "Hello Bill," the programmer now only needed only several lines. I guess you could compare this practice to a seance: To talk to the spirit you have to go through the medium or psychic.

Basically, the API insulates and shields the application from the environment's components and the underlying technology. Therefore, software engineers no longer need to worry about the intricacies of the operating system and how it interacts and supports the physical components — or how it makes the monitor display a message. They only have to pay attention to the APIs and what they do. As a result, the underlying complexity becomes transparent to the developer.

However, even writing applications that make calls directly to the API is not a simple matter. Many software engineering firms nowadays publish tools that add another layer above the Windows API to further speed up the creation of applications. These layers include visual programming environments like Visual Basic from Microsoft and Delphi from Borland. The equivalent layer in the computer telephony world is Visual Voice, from Stylus Innovation, which adds telephony features to Visual Basic. Visual Voice is further discussed in Chapter 17.

In computer telephony, the application enables the user, through a graphical user interface (usually Windows), to access the features and functions of the telephony environment connected to the enterprise information network (which is the integrated telephone and data network). The telephony environment includes devices that have a physical interface to the telephone network, such as telephones, modems, fax machines, voice-processing cards, switches, and so on, and devices that have a physical interface to the data network, such as interface cards and routers that connect the networks.

But there's more. An API also ensures a uniform, controlled approach to the development of the applications. Through the API, the publisher ensures, as far as it can in a world of adventurous individuals, that applications do not violate operating system integrity or access regions of the operating system/architecture that have not been documented or are not supported. This reminds me of a joke that did the rounds of software companies some years back: Question: How many software engineers do you need to change a lightbulb? Answer: None . . . Microsoft changed the industry standard to darkness.

The device manufacturer's responsibility to conform to the API is often referred to as the service provider domain. The manufacturer has to write device drivers that conform to the API, so that when the application makes a call to the API, the request will be correctly translated all the way down to the physical device that the user wants to control or enable. The device interface side of the API is usually known as the *service provider interface*, or SPI. The manufacturer needs only to conform its product to the SPI, knowing that any application that conforms to the API will function as intended.

With this quick crash course under your belt, I can now turn to the discussion of computer telephony APIs and standards.

NETWARE TELEPHONY SERVICES AND TSAPI

NetWare Telephony Services (NTS) is Novell's solution to providing a standard for the integration of computers and telephones (server-based call control in client/server architectures) on the enterprise information network.

The Novell network operating system (NOS), NetWare, is used by millions of enterprises to network their computers. It is believed that as many as 50 million computers are connected by the NetWare operating system. This product fundamentally changed the way people view and use computers. Introduced in the mid-1980s, NetWare started the transformation of the PC into a critical communications device. By the sheer weight in numbers of NetWare users, any API Novell introduces for NetWare automatically becomes a de facto standard. It thus made no sense for PBX manufacturers to continue sinking money and time into proprietary CTI efforts when Novell *et al* came along with TSAPI in 1993.

Novell emphasizes that the key definition of NTS is the so-called logical connection (as opposed to a physical connection) that the service can provide between the telephones residing on the desktop and the switch *and* the computer telephony applications running on the clients or servers on the EIN.

A Novell Telephony Server, or *TServer* (I coined this exact phrase, uppercase S included, in 1992 and then forgot to trademark it), and client software work together to create and maintain this logical connection. You do not need any special telephones or telephone interface cards or connectors, PC boards with telephony interfaces, and so on at the server or the desktop. The TServer running NTS provides the physical CTI link between the LAN and the switch by way of the RS-232 port, an Ethernet adapter, or network interface card (NIC). (Several ACDs and PBXs are available into which you can plug a NIC, just as several printers are available that can take a NIC.) This point, between server and switch (see Figure 5-8), is where the LAN and the telephone network integrate.

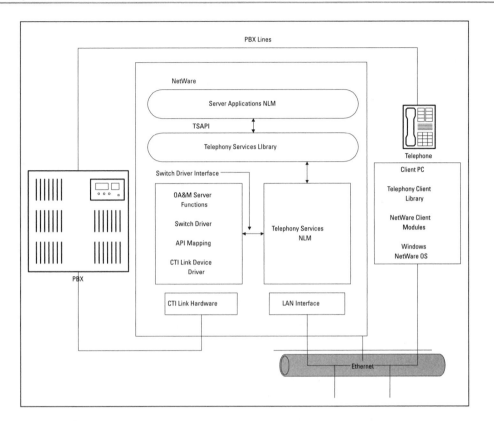

Figure 5-8: NTS provides a link between the server and the switch.

After Novell embarked on creating TSAPI, it conformed the API to the definitions for computer telephony already established by the European Computer Manufacturers Association (ECMA) in 1992. These definitions are known as the CTI standard definition of Computer-Supported Telecommunications Applications (CSTA). A number of computer and switch manufacturers support the CSTA standard, including IBM and Siemens/Rolm. CSTA is a *de jure* standard.

Naturally, the PBX companies could have come along with their own CSTA-compliant products. But as discussed already, application development would have been hampered because every computer telephony software developer, including corporate developers, would have to write applications according to product-specific APIs, which would not be standard.

The CSTA standard defines call control services, call and device monitoring services, and query services, among other services. More importantly, the CSTA standard defines the logical connection between the telephone and the personal computer. Some of these definitions are referred to in the Lexicon at the end of the book.

The NTS environment, as documented by Novell for the API, consists of the following components:

✦ **CTI link.** This link supports the Computer Telephony Integration (CTI) protocol that logically integrates the telephone and the client workstation at the users' desktop. A CTI link connects link-specific hardware in the server and the switch. It provides sessions between TSAPI applications and the call-processing software within the switch. The CTI link is PBX-specific.

✦ **CTI link hardware.** This hardware is any server hardware that terminates the CTI link to a switch. This hardware is PBX vendor-specific.

✦ **Switch driver.** The switch driver is a set of software modules (NLMs). A *NLM* (NetWare Loadable Module; see following definition) is a network service, utility, or application that runs on top of the NetWare operating system. A key feature of the NLM is that you can load and unload it without bringing down the server. Thus, NTS can be supported on any server on the LAN running NetWare.

The NTS NLMs support and terminate the switch-specific CTI link and protocol, map the CTI protocol to the TSAPI (if required), support any administration and maintenance capabilities of the switch driver (if any), and support a driver interface to the CTI link hardware. The Switch Driver modules are PBX-vendor-specific.

✦ **Switch driver interface.** This component is a software interface between the switch driver and the NetWare Telephony Services NLM that passes messages between applications and the switch driver. Typically, the messages consist of CSTA service requests, responses, and events for TSAPI clients. The messages may also be administration and maintenance requests, responses, and events for an application performing PBX driver administration or maintenance. The switch driver interface is PBX-independent and supports any Telephony Services-compliant driver.

✦ **Telephony Services NLM.** This software module provides communication between multiple, telephony-enabled applications and the switch driver. The Telephony Services NLM routes messages from the switch driver to the applications waiting for telephony events and passes the messages received from applications (TSAPI service requests) to the switch driver. All messages between client applications and a PBX switch driver pass across the switch driver interface. The Telephony Services NLM enforces user restrictions administered in the Telephony Server's security database. This module is switch independent and supports any Telephony Services-compliant driver

✦ **Telephony Server.** The TServer is merely a situation with the NetWare Telephony Services NLM software running on a particular server.

+ **Telephony Services API (TSAPI).** TSAPI is the CSTA-based, C-language definition of the functions (services), data types (parameters and structures), and event messages that telephony-enabled applications use to access Telephony Services.

+ **Telephony Server Library.** This library is used by the server-based applications to access TSAPI functions. The library accepts TSAPI service requests and delivers responses and events to server applications. This library can run on the same physical server as Telephony Services or on any NetWare server in the network.

+ **Telephony Client Library.** Client-based applications use this software module to access TSAPI functions. This library accepts TSAPI service requests and delivers responses and events to client applications.

The schematic in Figure 5-8 illustrates how NTS works and the concept of the logical connection. It all comes together as follows: First, you connect the PBX to the server running NetWare. You do this task via the CTI link as explained earlier. But no two switches are the same, and the hundreds of devices installed in the world each have differing protocols and architectures. (This often happens with products made by the same company. For example, a huge difference exists between Siemens switches manufactured by different subsidiaries of this monolithic company.) So the PBX maker has to provide a driver in the form of a NLM.

An NLM is defined by Novell as a program that executes at the NetWare Server (atop of the NOS). These programs can be loaded at the command line, by a configuration program, or by another NLM. NLMs do several things. The important functions that they provide are client support, management, and applications for the network users — you, me, and the PC.

Besides the switch driver, everything in the server is independent of the PBX. The applications need only conform to the TSAPI. Now when a TSAPI compliant applications requires services, such as the placing of a call, it makes a call to the API. The API, in turn, makes a remote procedure call to the NetWare server, which loads the necessary applications in the NLM. The NLM interfaces with the switch driver via the switch driver interface, which hands the request for services to the PBX. The PBX then "gets the message" and carries out the user's request.

If all goes well, and the PBX is truly TSAPI-compliant, the telephone rings at the user's desk and a logical connection is made between the PC and the telephone.

The preceding actions appear to happen instantaneously to a caller. But many people worry about network reliability in mission-critical computer telephony applications. Let me put some of your worries to rest. First, if the network crashes, it won't cause the switch to explode. The worst possible case is that you'll have to roll back to the way you used to process calls for however long it takes the lunatic that brought the LAN down to get it back up. (Six months ago I was assisting with an integration project for a sizeable client in West Palm Beach, Florida. We brought the LAN down with a thud because the integrator had inserted a NIC in the telephony server that was set to the wrong bus speed. I had to send him home to change after the CIO threw him into the bay. The rule is that you need to know what you're doing — even if you are a Certified Network Engineer, or CNE, as they are commonly known.)

Second, even if traffic on the LAN slows things down, it will not be noticed by the callers who are waiting for service — unless, of course, it slows down that much. In general, the loss of time I'm talking about here is split seconds. Only one aspect does concern me, and that has to do with the telephonist console discussed in the following paragraphs.

This all may sound very complex. But what does such an assortment of protocols and software libraries achieve in functionality terms? How does the user become magically "empowered" with NTS? With reference to the discussion of third-party call control in the preceding chapter, the following may give you some ideas:

Screen or GUI-based call initiation. You can place outgoing calls by entering a telephone number in your application and by clicking a dial button. Alternatively, for all those numbers you don't remember, you can dial by name. The process is akin to having a telephonist or assistant place a call for you and then transfer the call to your telephone. When you lift the handset, you'll hear ringing.

This process may not seem so special if you have a perfectly usable telephone on your desk and no broken index fingers. But what if you have several calls scheduled at various times of the day? I sometimes get so engrossed in my work that I forget to make these calls. For this reason, I find this capability very useful. Also, when you have to make many calls and still must work in front of a monitor, the telephone set tends to detract from the flow of thoughts from the head to the typing fingers. A combination of headset and autodialer, a la NTS, can save you a great deal of time by cutting bother.

Screen or GUI-based Call Control. NTS provides a robust solution for achieving the third-party call control discussed in the preceding chapter, Via the NTS-compliant application on your screen, you can seize calls by pulling them off sequencers, ACD queues, and the PBX on-hold facility. You know about these calls because NTS also can provide you with this picture into the telephony world (I talk about this in more detail later in this chapter). You also can divert calls away from other users if necessary, which relates to the call-pickup feature that you can use from the telephone (but in this case, you don't have to remember if the code was *86 or #87).

You can forward calls, conference calls, and transfer calls without using your telephone. Setting up a conference between several people in the office or even a conference between two workgroups in separate locations can be fully automated. Speaker phones and headsets enable all callers to remain at their desks. At a given time of day, an NTS application canl hook up everyone. A application can auto-load at each workstation, showing who's in and who's out (relating to the callers that are connected). In meetings where everyone has to be physically present, call-conferencing gear can be used to provide the conference between several subsidiaries.

For example, in a conferencing demo I recently did with BMW (the German auto manufacturer), a conference had to be set up between several geographically dispersed locations. Setting up the conference itself kept the entire group waiting for 30 minutes. These conferences were repeated once a week, which translated into a waste of two hours for all executives. I'd bet, however, that BMW's shareholders wouldn't have a problem investing in technology that saves two hours a month for 45 of its highest paid executives (90 lost hours roughly translates into a loss of $4,500 or more, per month, of executive-level salary).

Telephonist services, call center management, and real-time call status information. The CTI link also achieves what I have always dreamed about in computer telephony application and CTI: Gaining a window into the status of all inbound and outbound calls. But having that window is not nearly enough. You need to be able to open this window, reach into the telephony world, and access the resources in several ways. Several key shifts exist in the telephone model thanks to NTS, and these shifts are described in the following paragraphs.

Telephonist consoles. Every telephonist console that I have worked with has the same limitations, no matter who makes the PBX. To start off, consoles are impossible to integrate with computer telephony systems. They are linked to the PBX via a proprietary data link (usually RS-232) and talk a proprietary language with the PBX, and no in-band control signal exists that all computer telephony systems speak and understand. Also, you have no way to connect consoles to a LAN.

Another problem stems from the fact that telephonists are no longer devoting all their time to taking and routing calls. The service domains of computer telephony — such as automated attendants, voice mail systems, and interactive voice-response systems — have, to a large extent, freed the telephonist from the answering and routing millstone. Now these workers have added time to handle other tasks, such as interviewing potential employees, doing word-processing, and performing data-processing tasks. To help handle these new duties, the telephonist's desk has a computer on it. It sits beside the PBX console, which the telephonist still needs for callers who dial 0 in the voice mail system or to perform some degree of call answering, routing, and transferring.

The combination of the PBX console and PC workstation takes up a great deal of space. Being required to work with a separate console also detracts from the human-computer interaction taking place with the PC. By moving the console to the GUI — that is, by integrating the console with the PC — you not only get eye-level information on the status of each call, but you also get control over the call from the computer telephony domain.

You may be able to better understand the computer telephony angle by considering what takes place between PBX and telephonist console from a real world example. It just so happens that the client in this case history (which occurred in September 1994) happened to be Novell — albeit Novell South Africa, which has offices in Cape Town and Johannesburg. The computer telephony system had been installed at Novell for several months and all was going well. Many clients, however, were still being processed by the telephonist. And Novell wanted it that way. When it came time to transfer a call to voice mail from the telephonist's console, however, the nightmare began.

At that time, the PBX provided for no in-band integration in the form of repeat or echo dialing. In order for the telephonist to transfer the calls into the correct mailbox for voice mail, the transfer had to be done *under consultation* (after first transferring the call to a tone-dial phone).

To refresh your memory from the preceding chapter's discussion of CTI, *under consultation* means that the telephonist first must put the caller on hold and then dial the voice-mail system; then when the system answers, he or she has to enter DTMF tones to drill down to the correct mailbox. As soon as the digits have been dialed, the telephonist has just microseconds to disconnect and affect the transfer of the call into the mailbox in order for the caller to catch the mailbox greeting. If the receptionist is not fast enough or get distracted, the caller only hears the last few words of the greeting played by the voice mail system.

This method of connecting the caller to voice mail is still widely used, even in the United States, which is at least three years ahead of the rest of the world in computer telephony integration (but losing ground every day). This method is possible from a touch-tone phone, but not from a console. Consoles only have the data connection to the PBX to affect (third-party) call control. Thus, the telephonist has no option but to revert back to message books and pink slips.

Because 70 percent of the calls to Novell were going to the telephonist, Novell had a problem with under-utilization of voice mail and the amount of time wasted in manual message-taking. Novell's management rightly questioned the investment with me (I was not the vendor). "There has to be a better way," said the head of Novell's South Africa operations. "There is," I said, "it's called NetWare Telephony Services, and it's made by . . . wait for it . . . Novell." The only problem was that the PBX industry had not delivered a NTS PBX at the time, which stuck Novell with the very problem it had begun to address.

With the console on the screen, the telephonist simply puts the caller on hold and transfers the call into the voice-mail system to the correct mailbox. The process is much faster than dialing repeatedly to the voice mail system. How does the voice mail system know which mailbox greeting it needs to play and where to store the message? NTS tells the computer telephony system who the call is for. The computer telephony system, if it is programmed to do so, can answer the call, bypass the default greeting, and play the mailbox greeting message. NTS makes this possible because it delivers real-time, call-status information.

Real-time, call-status information. The CTI link and NTS enables you, the telephonist or call-center manager, to view the status of every call in the system. This feature is great for the new model of software-based consoles. The call-status information displayed on consoles is rudimentary. The telephonist only gets flashing lights to indicate which extension is on hold and that a fresh call has arrived from the outside world or the computer telephony system. Although new models of consoles include large, liquid-crystal displays to convey as much information to the telephonist as possible, how do you beat a 17-inch, 256-color, high-resolution monitor and the graphics that go with it? Instead of just a flashing light, icons can change shape and colors or display different images to convey information about a call.

Will PBX companies scrap their physical consoles? I don't think so. You still may need to process calls if a LAN crashes or a monitor goes on the blink.

One aspect of the console remains that still concerns me, and after reading the preceding section, you should understand why I wanted to wait until now to discuss it. What if you use this new era, PC-based console and the network slows down long enough to cause a delay in answering the telephone? You don't want to ruin that alluring image and lose customers by allowing calls to run over the critical three-ring period just because someone decided to transfer 100MB of bitmaps over the network. You don't have to worry about this issue when using a console, but this problem is a concern when critical calls are being controlled over the network. You thus need to set aside the console/PBX domain from the rest of your applications and plan accordingly. Your answer may lie in some fancy network engineering, such as using a dedicated, LAN-based telephonist service.

The other vital link in the computer telephony chain is the provision of real-time status information to other computer telephony services. This status information can be used to provide information to the computer telephony system that has a real-time feed of call status information from the PBX. NTS can tell the voice mail system that the call ringing on its #6 port (extension 300) was diverted from extension 120. The voice mail system looks up extension 120 in its database and opens the appropriate mailbox as soon as it takes the call.

The provision of information can also be used to provide some sophisticated call accounting. NTS enables other applications as well, which I discuss in Chapter 7.

WINDOWS TELEPHONY SERVICES (TAPI, WOSA, AND WIN32)

When the Telephony Applications Programming Interface (TAPI) was first introduced in 1993 as a joint effort between Intel and Microsoft, it defined three levels of service:

✦ Basic Telephony

✦ Supplementary Telephony

✦ Extended Telephony

Basic Telephony is the lowest level of telephony service defined in the API. It provides a "guaranteed" set of functions that correspond to POTS . In other words, it only gives you direct (first-party) control of a telephone device to make and receive calls. As a result, Version 1.*x* of the API is very line- and phone-centric.

The *Supplementary Telephony* service provides (in-band) access to switch features, such as hold, transfer, conference, and so on. The *Extended Telephony* level provides numerous and well-defined API extension mechanisms that enable application developers to access service-provider-specific functions not directly defined by TAPI.

The primary reason for the various levels of service is that TAPI Version 1.0 primarily concerned itself with first-party call control (see Chapter 4 and the Lexicon). In other words, it only provided for direct control of a telephone device (and thus the call) if that device was installed on the data bus of the computer running a Windows client (3.1 and 95) or via a connector (such as a connection to the parallel port). This method is the converse of the logical connection, the keystone of NTS (described earlier).

As an API for defining first-party call control, TAPI has solicited a great deal of support for applications that automate the dialing process, especially software for smaller businesses. Microsoft was content (or so it appeared) to leave TAPI on Windows clients, satisfying its commitment to provide an API for first-party call control. This led the computer press to incorrectly report that third-party call control, or client/server telephony, did not work on the Windows platform. (As mentioned in other parts of this book, client/server telephony, especially on Windows platforms, had been achieved by many computer telephony companies even before Microsoft announced the provision of client/server facilities.)

The Windows 32-bit operating systems (especially Windows NT) are more than suitable platforms for client/server telephony, computer telephony integration, CTI, and third-party call control on the server, a la NTS style. Hence, TAPI Version 2.0 for Windows NT (and future versions of Windows 95) was born.

As of this writing (mid-1996), TAPI 2.0 is on the launch pad. After it is launched, it will provide third-party call control and client/server computer telephony for both Windows 95 and Windows NT. This service will serve the same objectives as NTS: providing a CTI connection between the telephony-enabled computer and the switch. (The computer telephony industry has dubbed Microsoft's operating system telephony services *Windows Telephony Services* (WTS), or simply *Windows Telephony.*)

Microsoft, however, is moving TAPI away from being a stand-alone API. In the first versions, TAPI was offered as a self-contained software development kit (SDK) that was mostly adopted by the computer telephony industry. Now it provides access to the telephony functions in the API as part of the Win32 API SDK.

What is the Win32 API?

Win32 API is the API that gives Microsoft engineers, independent software vendors, and programmers access to the *Win32 System Services*, which provides the core processing functions of the Windows 95 and Windows NT operating systems. System Services enables applications to access features such as hard-disk and printer services, network services, messaging, multi-tasking, file mapping, compression, security services and more. All the APIs are part of the Windows Open Services Architecture (WOSA), including the messaging API (MAPI).

The Win32 API also now includes all the necessary nuts and bolts to build the Internet and intranet "killer" applications that the world is waiting for with bated breath. Thus, it makes sense to lump everything into one whopper of a software development kit. Internet software will require access to telephony functions and vice versa. After all, in the age of cyberspace, if a person isn't on the phone, he or she is on the Web.

With WTS supported on both the client and the server sides, Windows can provide a rich telephony-services environment for 32-bit operating systems. TAPI 2.0 essentially will define services that enable Windows NT and Windows 95 to function as both telephony clients and telephony servers. For example, you will be able to run voice-processing cards, fax modems, and switch cards on the Windows server and, on the same machine, maintain a CTI link to a switch. This CTI link will provide the logical connection to devices on users' desktops (digital or analog telephones connected only to the switch).

Under Win32 system services, applications have access to the power of 32-bit OS features such as *symmetrical multiprocessing* (SMP, which I describe in a minute), preemptive multitasking, and multithreading. Support is also available (under Windows NT) for non-Intel processors, giving you a wide choice of hardware platforms on which to run computer telephony applications.

With the release of TAPI 2.0, you now can provide the kind of third-party call control power and functionality typically found in applications of call centers (or any busy office) as separate processes of the Win32 system architecture. You should understand, however, that call-center and third-party call control applications are not new to Windows operating systems — many of these applications have been running on Windows for some time. But these applications have only been *accessing* standard OS services. With switch makers now offering TAPI 2.0 drivers, call-control functionality can become part of the system services (rather than a feature built into the internals of an application).

This means that the switch, PBX, ACD, or other queuing device being used never needs to talk directly with the application running on the Windows client computer — it only needs to communicate with Win32 system services. Provided that the client or application (such as a Windows NT voice mail server) is TAPI 2.0 compliant, it will be able to request from the switch services such as checking to see whether a station (someone's telephone) is off-hook. CT applications only need to request the telephony services from the operating system, which acts as the mediator between the application software running on the PC and the devices providing the service (such as a PBX).

By fully integrating telephony services into the Win32 API, Microsoft has made Windows a true telephony/computer telephony operating system. CT applications now get the "full sniff" of what's cooking inside switch internals. Support is available for the following features:

✦ Monitoring station status

✦ ACD call queuing

✦ Routing

✦ Transferring and conferencing

✦ Outbound call processing and predictive dialing

✦ Agent monitoring and control (call data feeds)

✦ Call state and event timers and control

TAPI 2.0 also provides support for what Microsoft calls "quality of service parameters" — catering to new carrier technologies such as Asynchronous Transfer Mode (ATM).

Telephony services have also been extended for optimum integration with the other services in the Win32 API. TAPI is not concerned with providing access to the information exchanged via a call, the so-called media, or information streams (like the processing of a voice message); but telephony services can be processed in conjunction with other system services (such as the speech, audio, MCI, and fax services) to provide access to the information stream. This setup guarantees maximum interoperability with existing audio or fax applications, Internet telephony, distributed computing, intra-networking, and more.

The Win32 API also provides access to serial and parallel port services that control locally-attached devices (such as printers), network services (such as RPC), Winsock and Named Pipes, message transport service providers (MAPI), and more. In a nutshell, TAPI Version 2.0 serves up the full client/server computer telephony meal — appetizers, entrees, dessert, after-dinner mints, and all.

WINDOWS NT AND COMPUTER TELEPHONY

Though I believe that the Windows computer telephony services deal mostly with TAPI and the Win32 API, it also is very much about the Windows NT operating system. A discussion of Windows NT as the likely computer telephony operating system of choice thus completes my CTI overview.

The reliability of the operating system on which high-end computer telephony systems are deployed is paramount. Windows NT is that reliable operating system, especially for running high-end telephony applications, such as switching, IVR, and call-center solutions.

As mentioned earlier, computer telephony is becoming increasingly important at the desktop. In modern computer telephony, clients access critical telephony services via the GUI rather than the TUI (telephone user interface). By using Windows NT server on the back end, you get unmatched desktop integration because both the client and the server are part and parcel of the same operating system family. (The Win32 Systems Services is at the heart of both client and server. For mission critical call-control, this setup is essential.) With the PC emerging as the key communications client, seamless connectivity to the desktop PC is critical. (I need to reinforce here that my affection for the Windows 32-bit operating systems has to do with what lies "under the hood.")

Windows NT is a more than a suitable telephony server for Windows clients and, given its open networking architecture, can connect to a variety of heterogeneous clients. Support for Transmission Control Protocol/Internet Protocol (TCP/IP) — which is considered by many IT managers to be the essential ingredient in enterprise-wide connectivity and the intranet revolution — began with NT version 3.5. I explore this topic, and the new intranet paradigm further in Chapter 12.

TCP/IP provides access to TAPI 2.0 services on NT Servers. With NT comes significant remote procedure call (RPC) support, which is the capability for a client to summon processors and procedures that execute on the server. These features are essential for logically integrating computers and telephone systems over any network. The following list provides some of the key factors that make NT a good choice as a high-end computer telephony platform:

✦ Cruiser-class client/server and true symmetric-multiprocessing (SMP) architecture

✦ Scalability

✦ Preemptive multitasking and multithreading

✦ Redundancy and disaster recovery

✦ Great administration features, including the capability to remotely administer the system

✦ Big and growing array of "building blocks," such as voice-processing cards, databases (SQL servers), messaging systems (MAPI), and so on

SYMMETRIC-MULTIPROCESSING (SMP) ARCHITECTURE

Let's take an even closer look under the NT hood. Out of the box, Windows NT Server 3.51 can support up to four processors (CPUs). But Microsoft created this OS for high-end portability and customization. Theoretically, no ceiling exists on the power of Windows NT. With customization and the right hardware (if it is available), Windows NT could provide enough processing power to run a destroyer or, in keeping with the subject at hand, to handle the most demanding of central offices and call-center applications. To boost the power, you just need to add CPUs.

At the heart of every operating system is the *microkernel.* The microkernel consists of the minimum set of functions that have to reside in memory. Many computer telephony systems employ a similar kernel — not to replace the OS kernel, but to reside in memory and be ready to process callers at any time. NT merely executes another instance of its microkernel on any available processors. In a single CPU system, milliseconds pass while the telephony application waits for the processor to complete a cycle. In an SMP system, another processor comes to service.

Even with only one CPU — say, a high-end Pentium — NT will outperform its BIOSed interrupt-handling siblings. On other hardware platforms (this OS is truly portable) such as the DEC Alpha XT or IBM's Power PC, computer telephony applications will break the 30-port threshold in a single box, taking single-box deployment to the hundred port threshold and beyond. It is thus perfectly feasible to anticipate the advent of such systems in the near future.

PREEMPTIVE MULTITASKING AND MULTITHREADING

Computers waste a great deal of time. For enterprise-wide IT needs, they waste too much time. In DOS, when a request is made to read or write data to a hard disk, the CPU (which operates on to a nanosecond clock) goes to lunch while the hard disk (which operates on a millisecond clock) does its thing.

In NT, a component known as the Task Scheduler (or task switcher) makes sure that the CPU gets no such breaks. The CPU always has work to be done. Perhaps an appointment needs to be scheduled, or some high-priority calculation or memory scan must be done.

A number of applications may be running in NT. The voice mail administrator may be adding users, or a remote engineer may be performing some maintenance (connected via NT's built-in, remote-access service or via the LAN). The Task Scheduler keeps the CPU working on background and foreground processors, ensuring that foreground processes get higher priority. So, when a caller dials in and wants to listen to a ten-minute voice recording, the CPU can be engaged with other tasks while waiting for the drive to access the data. After the data becomes available, the processing resource can be switched to the Input/Output needs and the requesting processed will be serviced.

Computer telephony applications, whether voice mail or full-blown switching services, are I/O intensive. Disks are constantly on the move. Over the years, users have learned to squeeze as much juice as possible out of single-process computers. But the database and disk-thrashing activities in computer telephony applications are rocketing in accordance with user demands for service.

Every time a caller makes a request to be switched, leaves a voice message, or checks a bank balance, the machine experiences a substantial I/O strain. With enough RAM, it is possible to load all the necessary data (such as pointers to essential greetings or even the greetings themselves), but the application remains restricted to single-task processing. This brings me to the need for execution threads.

While the Task Scheduler is making sure that the CPU keeps busy, one caller waiting for a prompt or information will not notice any decrease in service. But sixteen callers accessing an IVR application running out of a single box are bound to notice that things are getting a little slow — the pauses between prompts taking longer. A multithreaded database application sitting under a computer telephony interface performs database I/O for several client processes simultaneously. Instead of waiting while a single thread completes a database read/write, another thread can be writing pointer records to voice messages stored in the message repository.

If you now take all the capabilities available to a single operating system described earlier and put the OS to work on a multiprocessor system, you end up with the horsepower and throughput for the highest of high-end computer telephony applications.

Both switching and human-computer dialog can be provided in a machine that is, essentially, a mainframe in PC clothing. Under SMP, database and I/O-intensive applications are catapulted to processing levels that far exceed anything possible with DOS, NetWare 3.x, and even several flavors of UNIX. (NetWare 4.1 has its similarities, including SMP; and of course, UNIX and OS/2 also are multitasking operating systems, but I won't delve into OS comparisons here.)

This point is where NT enters the realm of parallel processing. NT has the capability to clone as many copies of its microkernel as needed to match the number of processors in the system. The combined throughput from high-end processors is astonishing. A database application that reads and writes data through the IVR system's interface can delegate essential services to threads for an available processor to execute. Thus, a well-written NT application can merely apply for more horse-power as it needs it, regardless of the amount. This capability, built into the very "soul" of NT, is not available in any other OS.

REDUNDANCY AND FAULT TOLERANCE

Windows NT has other attributes that make it more than suitable for high-end, computer telephony applications. Not long ago, providing a client with redundant systems and sufficient disaster-recovery and fault-tolerant mechanisms was expensive and labor-intensive. Such items are absolutely essential in computer telephony systems, however. After all, you cannot afford to have the PC PBX go down and lose all the call-control records. The beauty of Windows NT, in this regard, is that it throws in the necessary software for these mechanisms as part of the deal.

The computer drives (hard-disks, floppy drives, tape drives and CD units) are the weakest components on the computer because they have moving parts. The NT file system (NTFS) redundancy is provided through transaction logging. All transactions or operations on a hard disk are logged to a special log file, which ensures that the hard disk structure (not a dead disk) can be recovered. NT also achieves its redundancy and fault tolerance through mirrored disk partitions, RAID5 support for disk arrays (the computer industry's latest specification for establishing redundant arrays of inexpensive disks), and disk duplexing.

The NTFS is a fully recoverable file system. With this system, cutting the power in the most intensive database or disk I/O results in no more than the loss of data that was being processed. The system restores to its previous state. To prevent the loss of data integrity, you merely need to make sure you have activated NT's built-in redundancy options.

Windows NT security is really a subject fit for an entire book, but I find it worth mentioning here because it touches on a subject getting lots of critical coverage lately: privacy and security. One monster that surfaces in client/server, desktop telephony applications like third-party call control and desktop messaging is *security*. Windows NT provides some very capable security features for your data's protection. NT's security system is so capable, in fact, that you could go war with NT and be confident that your information was protected.

Windows NT uses security built in accordance with the U.S. Federal Government's C2 and B security-level specifications — mechanisms put in place for the defense needs of the United States. What does that mean for computer telephony? Lots. Toll fraud and hacking is every IT manager's worst nightmare and also a very real threat. A PBX running in a PC and providing switching to a corporation is likely to become the target of every hacker on the planet. Part of the problem is that DOS has more backdoors for illegal entry than the TexMex border.

A DOS-based computer telephony system cannot adequately protect the sensitive messages of users from unauthorized access. Nor can administrators adequately screen certain users from messing with the mission-critical, call-control features that rely on information stored in databases.

In Windows NT, the files residing in a directory important only to the computer tele-phony server application are inaccessible by outsiders and unauthorized users. Secu-rity can be as tight as needed. Some applications require these files to be accessible only to cleared members of staff. To the rest of the enterprise and the outside, hacker-populated world, the files simply do not exist.

A WIDE CHOICE FOR USERS

TSAPI and TAPI were created for many reasons, and they are obviously self-serving to their creators and the supporters that have rallied around them. These standards may, in fact, determine who wins the network operating system wars. The ultimate achieve-ment, however, is that users have been empowered with reliable and supported stan-dards from powerful software companies. But in the end, the users win from this situation, because they can access any device that supports these standards from their system's software, as long as the software also conforms to the API.

Individuals in the computer telephony industry have been trying for years to achieve such standardization in computer-telephone integration. Their efforts have been re-warded with limited success and little support from hardware manufacturers (in this case, the PBX manufacturers).

Despite such setbacks, these individuals forged ahead with implementing computer telephony. After all, you don't really need either of the APIs to develop some fancy call-control or computer telephony system. Several computer telephony software developers managed to secure relationships with PBX companies that have resulted in computer-telephone integration via the RS-232 port (see Chapter 4). In other words, their systems can integrate with the PBX because the manufacturer has granted the CT developer access to the fundamental PBX control data. But don't expect wide adoption of these products because they support only a small selection of PBXs and thus offer little flexibility in the choice of PBX to deploy. On the other hand, NTS and WTS don't yet address all of your needs. And they probably never will.

But without the global or wide-ranging support of the major operating systems and the equipment manufacturers, TSAPI and TAPI would have had little chance of being widely adopted. Integration would have remained limited to the in-band (analog) and proprietary (digital) efforts of the old generation of CTI, as discussed in the previous chapter.

If you are an extensive user of NetWare, then you may be inclined to choose a prod-uct that supports NetWare Telephony Services (meaning it has been written to or conforms to the TSAPI). If you are a heavy user of Windows, especially Windows NT, then you're probably more partial to applications that support Windows Telephony Services (or that have been written for TAPI). Depending on the telephony equipment you use and your applications, you may even need to consider applications that sup-port both standards. For example, you may need a setup capable of running NTS applications on a Windows NT-dominant network or running WTS applications on a NetWare-dominant LAN.

In fact, you may need to run NTS and WTS side-by-side on the LAN or intranet. That could include such things as a voice-processing system running under Windows NT that works with a call-processing or call-center system running under NTS.

You, the user, now have the power to choose applications that suit your purpose: NTS, WTS, both, or neither. Your best option depends on several factors, but your choice will mainly hinge on the following: your applications and needs, your IT architecture and installed systems, and the telephony equipment already in place. I discuss all this and more in the chapters ahead. Until WTS for Windows NT (a.k.a. TAPI 2.00, or TAPI for Windows NT) officially ships, however, you will be limited to the first-party call control paradigm, unless you are working with a vendor or PBX manufacturer that has some fancy licensing deal with Microsoft.

I can only illustrate the dichotomy in user camps, and thus my point, by citing the example set by Microsoft. Although the company is partial to using its own software, it doesn't always have that option. The telephony environment in each subsidiary of the world's largest software company substantially differs from the next. In one office, they may have a switch that only supports the NTS-compliant applications; in another office, they may have a switch that only supports the WTS (TAPI)-compliant applications.

In 1994, a colleague and I installed a call-processing system in one of Microsoft's international offices. At first, it only ran on OS/2, but later we integrated it with a PBX from a vendor primarily supporting NetWare Telephony Services.

You can imagine the scene that this paradox caused. Senior engineers and management came down to the server room to see the debacle. One Windows NT technical support guru said, "I came to look out of curiosity, It's been so long since I've laid my eyes on OS/2, I can't remember what it looks like. And here it is, running our computer telephony system." Thank goodness we were able to use Microsoft's version of OS/2, which was put out to pasture long ago. Had we dared to suggest using IBM's OS/2, I may not have been around to write this book.

SUMMARY

This chapter gave an in-depth definition of CTI, including both first and second generation CTI. In addition, we talked about the concept of the Application Programming Interface and several specific APIs, including TAPI, TSAPI, and NTS.

I discuss the new models for computer telephony in the next chapter. But if you want to begin making some strategic decisions I suggest you read Part III and then come back to Part II. You also can refer to the Lexicon for general definitions on the important computer telephony standards.

In This Chapter

✦ Call processing, automated attendants, and voice processing

✦ Interactive telecommunications such as audiotext, fax-on-demand, and interactive voice response

✦ Messaging services such as voice mail, e-mail, and fax mail

"Either my answering machine tapes are running slow, or else I'm getting a lot of messages from Barry White."

CHAPTER

THE ELEMENTS OF COMPUTER TELEPHONY

This chapter serves as an introduction to the elements, or service domains, of computer telephony, the services about which you hear and read (see Figure 6-1). How do they work? What do you use them for? The answers are here.

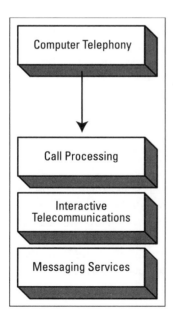

Figure 6-1: The service domains of computer telephony.

I introduce these services and the underlying basic concepts; in particular, I discuss call processing, automatic call distributors (ACD), fax-on-demand, interactive voice response, and so on. So, if you do not consider yourself a computer telephony "newbie," you can skim this chapter and move on. I deal with each service in more detail in Part II. Internet telephony (the process of establishing voice calls over TCP/IP networks) also is becoming extremely popular, and I discuss this new technology in Chapter 12.

Frequently, my clients manage to establish some of their needs but are not sure what CT services (or combinations of) are needed to address them or how to enable the IT people to take advantage of the technology. The following are just some of the tasks that these computer telephony systems perform:

✦ Process, route, distribute, and make calls (call processing)

✦ Interface with corporate databases, information bases and knowledge bases, and information retrieval systems (interactive telecommunications)

✦ Record and play voice messages; enable users to manage, forward, and reply to messages; send and receive faxes; and integrate with electronic mail systems (messaging services)

CALL PROCESSING

Call processing means using CT technology to do whatever it takes to successfully complete calls. *Inbound* or *inward call processing* is the processing of calls that come from the external environment of an enterprise; *outbound* or *outward call processing* is the processing of calls that originate from the enterprise and go to the external environment. A customer calling the help desk is processed inwardly, whereas the marketer or debt collector calling you at home uses outbound call processing. CT server systems should be capable of performing both inward and outward call processing (see Figure 6-2).

ANSWERING INBOUND CALLS

Computer telephony systems process inbound calls in several ways. The first way is to route or feed calls directly to a sophisticated automated call distributor (ACD). The caller does not need to know the number of an extension or how the routing of the call is handled. The caller simply dials a number and is connected to the first available operator, or the caller is put on hold or parked at a position on the PBX until a human can take the call. (How the CT system knows that a station is available is further discussed in Chapters 7 and 8.)

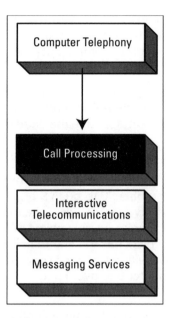

Figure 6-2: Call processing uses CT technology to successfully complete both inbound and outbound calls.

The CT system can be a dedicated ACD, or you can integrate ACD features with other telephony services, such as voice processing. ACD units typically are stand-alone devices or mostly digital, computerized PBX systems (also known as a CBX — computer branch exchange). But today, you can buy switching cards with built-in switching matrixes that you can insert into a workstation. These so-called "dumb switches" can be programmed to behave as PBX or ACD systems. The switching cards neatly coexist with other telephony components such as voice-processing cards, which means that you not only integrate the computer with the PBX, you bring it *into* the PBX. ACD is discussed further in Chapter 7.

Some applications for ACDs include help desks, order-processing centers, and customer-relations centers. In these environments, callers dial a number in the hope of getting a service; the callers do not really care about the person with whom they connect. Voice-processing features do not intercept these calls along the route unless the call must be diverted to alternative services, such as messaging and queuing.

VOICE PROCESSING

Computer telephony systems also can route inbound calls using voice prompts. With this method, the system operates like a human telephonist to route calls to the correct stations. Voice prompts, once the domain of stand-alone or bolt-on automated attendants, are now standard features integrated into the computer telephony software. With voice prompts, the system talks *digispeak* (analog recordings of phrases that have been digitized) to callers, asking them for the name of a person or an extension number (the station) to which they want to connect. The first phrase after the greeting is usually something like "If you know the extension number of the party with whom you wish to speak, enter it now or speak it."

This type of information processing is known as *voice processing* (as opposed to data or word processing). Callers are prompted to enter an extension number. After the caller enters the appropriate information, the tones are mapped to the extension number and the caller is transferred or re-routed.

Computer telephony systems do this by using DSP and sophisticated speech-recognition algorithms to listen to the caller's speech and act upon the commands. Most algorithms used today easily understand the numbers 0 through 9 and "yes" and "no." New advancements in speech recognition, however, will render tone or pulse recognition obsolete very soon. I provide several strategies on the subject of speech recognition in Part II. (If your computer telephony project has to cater to callers who are using rotary phones and you are about to go live with a system, I suggest that you stop reading this chapter now and go directly to Chapter 8 to avoid potential disaster and the mass suicide of the entire IT staff.)

Your computer telephony server should be smart enough to behave as both an automated attendant and as an ACD, either at the same time or in predetermined situations. For example, if technical support, order processing, and accounts are all dumped into the same call center with only one central telephone number, then one CT server can route calls to three ACD groups by first prompting callers to choose which service they want to connect to. Although the callers are voice-processed at first, the callers are concerned about using the service, not speaking with an individual.

If, however, a repeat caller wants to reach a person with whom a relationship has been established, the CT Server can tell the caller to enter the station number to bypass the ACD process and then park the caller at the entered extension. This situation often happens in technical support when the support person asks the caller to call back with additional information. Of course, how you use all this smart stuff is a matter of application and specifics. I get into that strategy stuff later.

If you already have a modern, open PBX, you should be able to integrate it sufficiently with the CT Server. If you are about to make a decision about buying a new PBX, I suggest that you read Chapter 7, which discusses PBX systems and how to choose one suited for CT applications or supported by CT products.

CALLING OR DIALING OUT

Outbound or outward call processing involves calling out to parties to connect them with services or to provide information. CT systems call out to deliver messages, notify people about events (the IT support engineer has gone bungee jumping with the LAN cable), or play information for the call recipients.

In the telemarketing business, sales and marketing people use this technology so aggressively that laws have been written specifically to curb certain practices. These laws vary from country to country and even state to state in the United States. You should get in touch with your local direct marketing association (DMA) for information. Then get an attorney to advise you on what you can and can't do if the laws are ambiguous.

All CT systems can seize a telephone line, establish a dial tone, and initiate a call. These tasks are all performed during the process of transferring callers. In the analog world, the CT system transfers a call in the same way that a human would. First, it flashes the switch-hook, which recalls the attention of the switch (you can manually press a recall button, which does the same thing but does it slicker). Then, the system dials another extension (which can be a remote extension) and connects the parties. I define this process in Chapter 5 as *first-party call processing*.

Call-processing systems also call out to parties on a proactive basis. This service is called *predictive dialing*. After the system dials a number and gets a live voice (it can detect an answering machine or another CT system), it connects the recipient with a live representative who just ended a call with an earlier party.

Predictive dialers get their information (who to call and when) from databases. A good example of databased information used in predictive dialing is, say, all accounts that are 60 days overdue or that need collection. Predictive dialers are often a little too enthusiastic, and when they can't find a free representative to talk to the customer, they terminate the call. Of course, you can intelligently manage the call threshold — increasing the outdialing as more representatives log in to the network.

INTERACTIVE TELECOMMUNICATIONS

As I mention in Chapter 1, computer telephony as a term has, in a sense, blurred the distinction between interactive and non-interactive telecommunications. Both are lumped under the rubric of computer telephony. I felt it better, for the purposes of understanding and distinguishing between these types, to return to the term *interactive telecommunications* when dealing with a real-time, interactive communication process that a caller has with a computer over the telephone (see Figure 6-3). Thus, this chapter deals with the interactive telecommunications as a division of computer telephony: interactive voice and fax response, fax-on-demand, and audiotext. The World Wide Web, discussed in Chapter 12, is another example of interactive telecommunications.

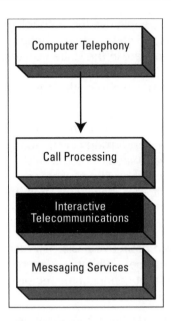

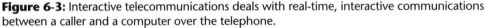

Figure 6-3: Interactive telecommunications deals with real-time, interactive communications between a caller and a computer over the telephone.

Messaging in the strict store-and-forward sense (S&F) is very much a non-interactive service in that, as you've seen, a caller sends a message to someone's mailbox and that's that. You could thus call all messaging non-interactive. You can send a message but do not receive a confirmation that the message has arrived at its original destination — only confirmation that it's been sent.

Interactive telecommunications, on the other hand, implies that a conversation of sorts is taking place between the two devices on either end of the communication; an interrogation of sorts is taking place, if you will. And when you, the caller, get a confirmation that the information you are seeking is at hand, you begin a transmission/ receiving process.

Computer telephony enables the telephone to act as an interface to data and information that resides in database tables and to information that resides in documents or multimedia files. I have placed this service in the interactive telecommunications section of the computer telephony schematic (refer to Figure 6-3).

Computer telephony also involves the processing, serving, and retrieval of information from your network. You can use your CT systems to provide electronic-based information to your callers and to receive information from callers. The features that perform these tasks are audiotext, fax-on-demand (FOD), fax-serving, and interactive voice response (IVR).

AUDIOTEXT

Audiotext (discussed in detail in Chapter 9) is essentially the playing of canned or pre-recorded sound files to the caller over the telephone. One of the most popular — and controversial — users of this technology is the "900" industry, known around the world as the *premium rate service*. With audiotext, digitized voice recordings are stored on the hard disk and played to callers on demand, or as part of customer service. In the 900 business, calls to the service are charged at a higher (premium) rate, earning the caller the privilege of listening to the sound bite. The audiotext file may contain health tips or a lurid sexual encounter.

Audiotext has a strong following, and a thriving audiotext industry now exists in the world. Recent well-known audiotext services in the 900 business include reports on the O.J. Simpson trial and Hugh Grant's sexual encounters. This great technology, however, has many applications: Talking Yellow Pages and talking classifieds are two prime examples.

Audiotext is also great for business. Retail chains waste a great deal of time repeating to callers directions to their locations. This task can be easily handled by a low-cost audiotext service running on a 486-class PC on the network. Audiotext does have several limitations, however; I discuss the pros and cons and strategies for using it in Chapter 9.

FAX-ON-DEMAND

Fax-on-demand (FOD) is a CT service that operates in a similar manner to audiotext. You can easily convert documents that reside on your LAN into fax format, so that you can transmit them to one of the millions of fax machines in the world. FOD is discussed in detail in Chapter 10. Examples of documents that you can convert include the following:

✦ Corporate literature

✦ Brochures

✦ Product information and technical sheets

✦ Order sheets

FOD essentially is a reactive service. People call in to get information from you. This service enables the caller to receive the fax right back on the same line (so that the server does not have to incur the cost of a new call), or it prompts the caller for an alternative fax number (usually restricted to a local or national area code) for later transmission or redirection to an alternative fax machine.

If you have fax capabilities on the server, you should also have fax-serving services. Fax serving is a proactive service similar to predictive dialing and outbound call processing; it enables you to fax documents to a group of people from the desktop. No more standing at the fax machine, faxing a notice to a customer base of several hundred — you can do it from your own PC. Businesses frequently use fax serving for marketing purposes. Junk faxing can be a nuisance to the receivers, but the weekly fax broadcast of a valuable newsletter often is handy.

IVR

Have you called your bank to check your bank balance lately? The CT service that greets you and performs this neat trick for you is called *interactive voice response* (IVR). IVR enables you to check your bank balance, confirm the last few transactions, and verify that certain checks have been processed.

IVR often is referred to as "giving a voice to data," and that's essentially what it does. Using the voice- and speech-processing services of computer telephony, your system can read data stored in database tables to callers over the telephone. Perhaps one of the best examples of this service is the U.S. Social Security Administration service (1-800-772-1213). This service provides callers with the location of their nearest Social Security office. All you need to do is enter your postal zip code.

IVR is probably the most complex of the computer telephony services to configure and operate because it requires interfacing the computer telephony systems to corporate databases that may be (and probably are) residing on a remote database server, whether the server is in the same room or half a world away. The CT system behaves as a client (or many clients) on the LAN. The database server treats the CT system no differently from human users extracting information from their computers.

IVR has many applications. A good idea for one would be to set up a system at the Olympics so that people can call in and check on records achieved in certain sporting events during the long history of the games. Here's another application that I was asked to help set up. South Africans love to run, as do the athletes of most nations. Every year, dozens of marathons are held in South Africa, and thousands of athletes from all over the world participate. This IVR system enables callers to check on race results by entering a year and a marathon ID code, and the name of the winner is then read to the caller.

You can go overboard with the way that you apply IVR. For example, the bank that handles my company's corporate account has gone nuts with its computer telephony system. Reaching a live person is now very difficult, and speaking to a person who works at the specific branch that holds the account is virtually impossible. The reason? The bank now publishes one telephone number that processes all calls via an IVR system that refuses to transfer you to the branch where you have your account. When you call to speak to a person about your bank account, you are routed to a system that asks you to try to gain the needed information via the CT system first before being transferred to a live representative. I'm convinced that my bank has retrenched everyone but the IT people.

MESSAGING SERVICES

The computer telephony industry has, in many respects, evolved out of the voice mail business. But the communications services (non-interactive) of CT still touch more people than any other service (see Figure 6-4).

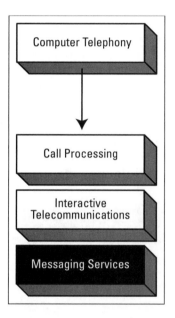

Figure 6-4: CT's messaging services — voice messaging, e-mail, and fax mail — handle the lion's share of contacts.

Many agree that the driving force behind voice-processing technology has been voice mail. Voice mail has been around for more than a decade. Even before CT services were extended to voice and call processing, people were leaving voice messages on computers.

Voice mail has evolved into more than just leaving a note that says something like "Hi, this is Jeff, get back to me at 555-1212." Voice mail has become a means by which two or more people can converse with only one party being present at a time. If used properly and wisely, *voice messaging* completely eliminates telephone tag (a human failing, not a machine one) between two parties who need to do nothing more than convey important information.

VOICE MESSAGING

Voice mail is accomplished by voice-processing components in telephony systems. Via the telephone interface, these components have the capability to capture speech and digitize it to a hard disk. The recipient then can retrieve the file from the CT system and play it back, forward it, reply to it, archive it, and so on. The capability to record voice in this fashion also led to the logging of conversations between live parties, an application that I often consult on and provide.

As I discuss in Chapter 3, many people hate voice mail because it failed them as a service and convenience. Improper use played an important part in bringing about this attitude, but the limitations of information technology have been the Achilles heel of voice mail until now. Voice mail is a drag to respond to because many users find it time-consuming to wade through a list of messages that you can only access serially. This method is so frustrating for some people that when the list of messages grows too big, it becomes impossible to deal with.

Computer telephony at the desktop changed all this. Now messages can be accessed at a graphical user interface and responded to based on information such as size, date, caller, and so on. You can also play messages over the computer speaker if you want (although this method is not a good idea, because not only does it disturb others in the office, but the content of the message may be sensitive) or via telephone handsets and head-sets. Computer telephony eliminates the "it's a pain to listen to all my voice mail" excuse.

Voice mail vs. voice messaging

I use the term voice mail when referring to the general concept of voice mail throughout the book. However, now that voice mail is being integrated as a message service with e-mail and fax-mail, many are referring to voice mail as *voice messaging*.

E-MAIL

You also can integrate voice messages into e-mail user interfaces where, along with fax, the user can access all message types in one convenient location. (The computer telephony model discussed in this book includes all the previously discussed communication types as part of the company's communication and messaging services.) Because e-mail is widely used on the LAN, it would be absurd to install a computer telephony system that forces the user to open separate applications at the desktop to listen to voice messages, read fax messages, and view e-mail. As more software becomes e-mail enabled and allows you to send a memo from within the working application, the e-mail interface is the logical place to provide access to voice messages.

Microsoft Exchange already pushes the integrated messaging desktop in Windows 95 with its capability to send and receive both e-mail and fax mail. New application software for computer telephony will soon enable you to receive voice mail in the Exchange interface, giving you an integrated and convenient gathering place from which to manage all three message types. Novell also offers an integrated messaging solution called GroupWise. In addition, companies such as Callware Technologies offer integration between their voice mail system and GroupWise. I have devoted an entire chapter to messaging, in particular the subject of integrated messaging (see Chapter 13).

FAX MAIL

Fax mail, the wayward member in the CT family, is another well-known CT communications service, although it is not used as widely as voice messaging and e-mail. Callers send fax mail to recipients in much the same way that they send a voice message. You call the party and, at the correct mailbox, the CT system prompts you to fax your message. Faxing is not a secure means of communication. Even if you use encryption, when you fax a message to a fax machine or fax server, you have to trust other eyes and hands with your fax. Sometimes faxes pile up at fax machines until a human can sort and distribute them. On the network, someone with a pulse has to look at the fax and reroute it into the e-mail system.

Many computer users have pondered the usefulness of fax mail for several years. The idea is a good one, but the rigid nature of the fax document makes it tough to work with after it arrives at its intended destination. You must have *optical character recognition* (OCR) to determine who at the enterprise fax number needs the fax — a computer cannot read it and determine which station on the LAN it should go to. So, to send a secure fax, the sender must first slip down menus in the voice processing system to arrive at a location that reads "Send here, this box is secure."

But unless they really want to send a fax that only the recipient will read, few users will want to endure the time and hassle of this process, especially if the call is long distance. DID (*direct inward dialing*) is an option, albeit an expensive one. I discuss this topic further in Chapter 7, but in the meantime you should appreciate that e-mail may be a better means of getting a secure document to someone. It beats fax mail hands down on price and ease of use. For security reasons, I predict that fax mail will disappear as a service as e-mail over the Internet matures.

I recently had to send fax mail to a client on the other side of the world. Because the mail was sensitive (it included invoices and financial information), we opted to use the fax mail facility on the CT system that I had helped him install. After several unsuccessful attempts that resulted in a horror story on my next telephone bill, we decided to use encrypted e-mail instead.

MOVING AHEAD

By implementing and using these services, you can greatly enhance the productivity of your enterprise and your workers — and enhance your customers' perceptions of your firm by being the anywhere, anytime enterprise.

To learn how CT can help out with a specific situation (yours, for example), we need to take a more in-depth look at the individual services — and that's exactly what Chapters 7 through 13 do.

SUMMARY

This chapter wraps up Part I. In Chapter 3, I discussed IT and where and how computer telephony fits into the information technology service domains. I also took some time to study telephony and the emerging standards for computer-telephone integration. This chapter introduced the new models of computer telephony and introduced the computer telephony services.

Having the general concepts in hand, let's now examine the CT services that you can use: Part II discusses these service domains in detail.

Part II

COMPUTER

TELEPHONY SERVICES

In This Chapter

✦ Enterprise-wide call management (EWCM)

✦ Switching and routing company calls intelligently

✦ Call paths

✦ Routing Option 1: Automatic number identification

✦ Routing Option 2: DNIS

✦ Routing Option 3: DID

✦ Routing Option 4: Centrex

✦ Routing Option 5: Voice response and voice processing

"I think we may be overworking
the phones. Our voice mail is
getting hoarse!"

CHAPTER 7

TELECOMMUNICATIONS: YOUR ELECTRONIC DRIVE-THROUGH

Y ou can communicate with your customers, clients, and associates in basically three ways: in the flesh, through the media and postal services, and through telecommunication. For the last several thousand years, the most common way in which people bought goods and services was to barter in person, physically shake hands on a deal, and exchange hard currency. Salespeople soon learned that they had to go out and "hit the pavement" in a proactive effort to sell goods — the most famous of which was the encyclopedia salesperson, a person selling knowledge, so to speak. It was in the twentieth century when the idea to buy goods through the mail really took off.

In the past 100 years, the physical communication method has slowly become outmoded in favor of deal making, relationship building, and purchasing without actually meeting the other party in person. Now as we rush headlong into the next millennium and cast our eyes on the Information Age, not only are we communicating person-to-person over the telephone, but we are doing most of the deal making, buying and selling, and relationship building in a virtual world.

The chief means by which this electronic contact currently takes place is via the telephone and the telecommunications network. To manage the surge in telephone traffic to and from the enterprise, all telephone traffic should be handled on an enterprise-wide basis, a function now referred to as *enterprise-wide call management,* or EWCM. (EWCM now has another source of voice calls to manage: people using the Internet or intranet. But rather than discuss this here, I have devoted Chapter 12 to the subject.) Placed under the authority of IT, enterprise-wide call management entails managing the following activities:

1. Call switching and routing (PBX systems)

2. Call distribution systems (ACD; outbound and inbound)

3. Queuing and sequencing

These EWCM activities all fall under the rubric of call processing. Figure 7-1 highlights call processing as a service domain of computer telephony.

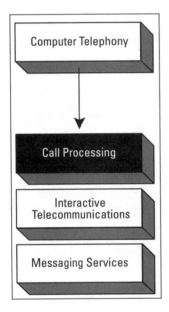

Figure 7-1: The call-processing organizational chart.

When I think of call processing, the first picture that comes to mind is the typical, American burger franchise with a drive-up lane. People on the go place orders at a signboard by speaking to the order processor via an intercom; then they drive to the window to pay for and collect their food.

The burger people employ technology like headsets and sophisticated wireless communications services so that they can keep moving all the time and sell more burgers. They can take your order while assembling someone else's dinner. Everything is coordinated and streamlined so that people don't bump into each other or get orders fouled up. When a bun arrives with dressings, a meat patty is ready to go on. When the burger hits the tray, the fries must arrive. The drive-up personnel try never to mistake onion rings for fries or switch cola for root beer. Intel's Andrew Grove referred to such business operations as the "breakfast factory." Industrialists call it "just-in-time" (JIT) manufacturing or delivery. The Japanese, as usual, perfected it.

But the burgers are not sold through the drive-through alone. If you do not need to be somewhere else at that time, you can walk in and sit down for your meal. The order processing in the sit-down side of the restaurant is supposed to be as efficient as the drive-through. If burger joints aren't managed properly and the lines get longer, customers go elsewhere.

This situation is how it is with the telephone and your enterprise. Many modern enterprises have, in effect, become electronic drive-through/sit-down joints for information.

Humans are rushing around so much these days that they do not have much time to "drive in" to (call) your enterprise and stick around for very long. As such, you don't want them sticking around too long or in the wrong lines either, because your electronic drive-through (call-processing system) is limited by telephone ports, attendants, and services. The callers who "drive up" and wait too long to get service will try someone else's drive-through.

Servicing your callers with your electronic drive-through is a rather tricky balancing act, because while you're trying to satisfy the people who've made it through to the station (drive-up window), you don't want to lose the ones on hold. And you have to assume that as soon as callers go on hold, they begin to think about abandoning the call.

Although the idea is to process the call to completion as soon as possible, you also have to keep the caller on the line as long as it takes to satisfy the customer. You walk this tight rope by deploying technology and strict call-handling procedures. Whether you can successfully accomplish this task depends on the availability and accessibility of the enterprise-wide information network: the data and knowledge bases on the LAN and telephone network, the available and enabling tools, and computer telephony tools that it uses.

I talk of a call center as being a room where many attendants do nothing else but process calls — such as a giant order-taking center or a help desk — but it's also clear that the entire enterprise has become one large call center. The term *call center* is thus better applied to a firm that processes calls for enterprises which do not have the capacity to process the number of calls they're receiving or the calls they need to make themselves. I thus refer to a corporate call center as an *informal* call center.

SWITCHING AND ROUTING COMPANY CALLS: YOUR PRIVATE TELEPHONE EXCHANGE

Not long after the invention (or more appropriately, the *invasion*) of the telephone (more than a century ago), the number of people making calls grew so large that a device was needed to connect, or switch, parties to their destinations. The invention of the so-called multiple switchboard — created by an American, Leroy B. Firman, in 1879 — can be attributed to the commercial success of the telephone, which soon became a critical service connecting mobs of people to each other in the U.S. By 1890, the number of people using the telephone in the U.S. was more than 250,000.

As the numbers of calls exploded, businesses realized that they were lacking some way to switch calls coming in on single and multiple lines to any of a number of telephones in the office. A device was created to handle just this task. Modeled on the principles of the multiple switch or telephone exchange, the device was known as the *private (automatic) branch exchange* (PBX). (European manufacturers added the "automatic" part for unassisted switching to form the acronym PABX.)

The early version of the PBX was nothing more than a device for connecting and switching callers, as illustrated by Figure 7-2. When a call arrived at the PBX, it was routed either directly to an extension or to a console manned by a human attendant. When the call arrived at the console, the attendant answered it, determined who the call was intended for, and then connected the parties. In turn, if the call was routed through an attendant, the attendant connected the call to the extension by first asking the PBX to "hold" it. Then the attendant would call the party and, if that person was available, would signal the PBX to connect the call to the extension.

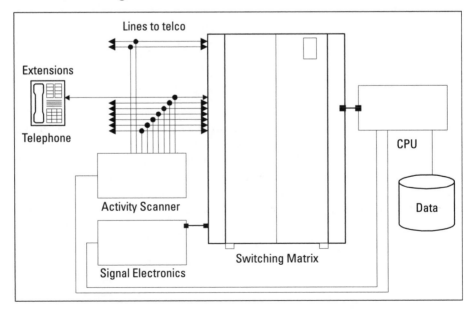

Figure 7-2: Schematic of a modern PBX.

In recent decades, the PBX has rapidly matured. In the early days of modern PBX technology (the mid-1970s and earlier), the PBX was basically an electromechanical device, just like every other machine at that time. Lines connected to other lines via mechanical crossbar switches and levers. These devices contained many moving parts and eventually proved to be unsuitable for the explosion in telephone usage.

Operating these devices with any form of automation was impossible, so it became necessary to replace the moving parts with microcircuitry that a computer could control (any computer, however primitive.) This technological advance was a major step forward in telecommunications.

The modern-day PBX has a central-processing unit that, using stored program control, can process calls; scan all extensions for activity; control the switching logic and the thousands of possible call paths; service user requests for specific functions, like signaling to place a call or to transfer a caller; and more — all at a much faster pace than the previous generations of switching devices. With the number of options now available to users and the new flexibility and speed available for handling calls, the PBX spurred a productivity increase in the enterprise and enabled the enterprise to better manage its communication activity.

Although the office telephone system is generally referred to as the office switch or PBX, several types of switching devices are available to the business. These variations include the following:

✦ Key systems

✦ Hybrid key/PBX systems

✦ True PBX systems

✦ Automatic call distributors (ACDs)

In addition, analog-transmission PBX systems and full digital switches that can transmit both voice and data are available. But how does each flavor of switch empower businesses to route callers and service people who need to use the telephone?

KEY SYSTEMS

A *key system* is an ideal device for a small business that needs more than one telephone line but does not employ enough people to warrant switching callers to extensions. The principle behind a key system's operating process is that all telephone sets have direct access to the telephone lines. A button on the telephone set represents a particular line, and by depressing that button, the caller gets a dial tone and can make or answer a call. This setup is often referred to as a *square plan* (see "The mysterious square" sidebar).

The mysterious square

The reason why this setup is called a "square" plan seems to be somewhat of a mystery. I have asked many switch manufacturers where the term "square" comes from, and no one knows, not even the "techies" who work in the labs at AT&T.

I do know that using the term can unexpectedly get you into trouble, though. I remember once talking to a computer telephony engineer in Melbourn, the land of OZ, to whom I said, "You've set the PBX up rather square, haven't you?" He replied, "Is that an insult, mate, or a South African term?" It's neither, but every PBX technician in North America will know what you mean when you refer to a "square plan."

The key system distributes calls to the stations over lines that make up part of a hunting group, and all stations have direct access to these lines. If, for example, line 1 has been seized by someone making a call, the telephone exchange is alerted of this fact with the "in-use" or "busy" signal; now anyone dialing the central number of the enterprise shunts to the next line in the hunting group (see Chapter 4). This shunting process carries on until all lines are busy and the caller receives a busy signal.

Although the business has three numbers, they are all part of the next available hunting group, so the callers only need to know one number to call rather than three. Workers have buttons for the hunting group's three lines on their phone sets and can press these buttons to get direct access to the lines. Figure 7-3 shows the telephone for a square-key system.

The key system, also known as a *direct inward system access* (DISA) system outside the U.S., can be programmed so that calls first ring at only one station — typically the station where the telephonist sits. However, a person at any other station also can seize or answer the lines from that station as well.

With this system, typically the telephonist answers the ringing line and then puts the call on hold. The telephonist then announces the call to the party for whom it is intended over an intercom system or similar setup.

Unfortunately, many key systems — especially the European models — do not provide intercom features, so the poor telephonist has to shout across the office passages and through reception room walls: "Edwin, call for you on line 1. It's the bank manager again." This not only is frustrating for the small business; it can be irritating and rather disruptive for its employees as well.

Without intercom facilities or the capability to transfer a caller, the telecommunications system begins to break down: People may end up shouting at each other in the office, making embarrassing statements like "Bindle can't take your call, she's in the Ladies" that the whole office staff hears, or they may seize a busy line by mistake, interrupting each other's calls even though each telephone has line-in-use indicators.

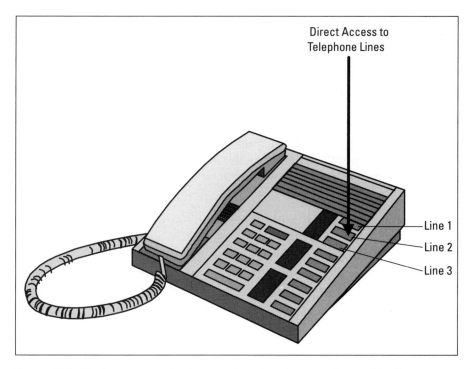

Direct Access to
Telephone Lines

Line 1
Line 2
Line 3

Figure 7-3: The key system telephone set has three buttons that enable direct access to hunting group lines.

To help counter that last problem, some key systems have a "private" button to protect a conversation. The party in the office can release the button if he or she wants to invite another member of the enterprise into the conversation.

Computer-telephone integration with key systems is not really a sound solution or even an option, especially in Europe. The reason lies in how these systems are used: Users access the systems via manual key pressing, a mechanical process of handling calls and communicating with the switching functions, rather than by sending electronic signals or data communication to a CPU for service requests, a central principle on which computer telephony is based.

To use computer telephony features and services to your best advantage, you will need to upgrade to a PBX. For example, if you have a plain, old, mechanical key system, you only can get a very limited voice-mail system by using crude add-ons and contraptions. You may be able to get your key system wired so that it can pass a call through to an answering machine after hours, but that's about as far as it will take you.

Although thousands of key systems are still in use today, production of new key systems has slowed considerably and many countries are phasing out key systems entirely. This scenario is especially prevalent for equipment manufactured in Europe and other countries outside the U.S.. In South Africa, for example, all push-button key system manufacturing has come to an end. The service available for this equipment is on a tiny scale, so the owners of these systems trash anything that needs more extensive fixing.

Like most countries, the trend is to build "business telephone systems" — that is, small, cheap, hybrid PBX systems. As the more capable PBX systems rapidly render key systems obsolete, your biggest headache will stem from how to dispose of the junk.

PBX AND ACD SYSTEMS

The volume of inbound calls that enterprises experience began to rocket upward in the '70s, not only because more people were buying goods over the telephone, but also because customers were demanding more after-sales service and satisfaction. Customers were no longer willing to just mail a letter to the service department and wait weeks for a reply. Instead, they picked up the handset and dialed a service number.

Compounding the call traffic problem was the business' need to make more outbound calls. With all the calls flying in, a potential caller had little chance of seizing a line without interrupting a conversation. As more and more people began to make similar calls, companies found the PBX to be the central technology for handling the increase in call traffic with computer telephony.

The PBX's capability to satisfy any number of requests — without the users having to worry about "invading" other calls — led to its increase in popularity. The user simply picks up the handset and dials the request for dial tone (usually digit 9 or 8 in North America and usually 0 in other parts of the world). If all lines are busy (blocked), the PBX (not the telephone company) indicates this fact to the user with a reorder tone (which sounds like a busy signal on steroids), which means "try again later, all company lines are in use."

If your workers frequently come across this situation with your enterprise's PBX, it may be time to order more lines or it may be an indicator of other problems in the enterprise-wide distribution and use of the telephone system (such as excessive on-hold use, which is discussed in Chapter 14).

The capabilities just described make up the first steps in any computer-telephone integration. In other words, if you can perform these functions, then you are at the first rung in the CTI ladder. As Chapter 5 explains, computer telephony systems may have to do these tasks and more.

As the PBX's popularity grew, a new need began to arise — how to optimally manage a PBX so that the PBX and telephony needs of the enterprise were met. PBX manufacturers responded by adding more features to the PBX's software to enable users to handle calls in a myriad of different ways, such as conferencing, parking, camping a caller at an extension (which means that as soon as the extension is free, the call goes through) and by providing data on call traffic (SMDR and SMDI; see Chapter 5). By doing this, PBX manufacturers enabled the enterprise to handle more callers.

As businesses grew, their telephony requirements also changed. Enterprises employed people to manage telecommunications needs and focus on the PBX, as well as attendants to process calls. But, as illustrated in Chapter 1, the enterprise began to run out of human capacity to handle calls, finally reaching the point where employing more humans to process calls began to have negative impact on operations and thus on the business.

Ironically, the enterprise now found itself in a situation similar to that in which AT&T found itself in 1919, when it reached the endpoint of a human's ability to process calls. Without the introduction of dial phones in this year, attendants (who were essentially connecting people to people by joining two wires) would have gone on strike and the telephone industry might have collapsed. Without the ability to employ a computer to process calls, the enterprise would have lost a lot of business.

Manufacturers provided an interim solution to the call-handling problem by introducing more sophisticated features on the PBX itself, controlled by embedded software. Although this Band-Aid worked for a time, it wasn't a particularly efficient solution because the PBX did not have the CPU capacity to intelligently route calls, nor was the existing technology flexible enough to cater to the ever burgeoning needs of the enterprise. Third-party intelligence and technology were needed.

The third-party technology came in the forms of artificial intelligence, object-oriented software engineering, microprocessor- and digital-signal-based operating systems, neural networking, and heuristics. This stuff is what many good computer telephony software gurus use to make sophisticated applications, such as call processing and voice response, work the way they do.

These engineering fields never fell into the expertise of telephony and PBX specialists. Many PBX companies simply ignored these new frontiers in technology, or were simply too busy making money to worry about them. That's a pity because they soon will fry as a result of their shortsightedness. If you own stock in one of these PBX companies, bail out now.

Enterprises suddenly had a new, vitally important need to process calls as quickly as possible, service people sufficiently, and get them off the line, enabling others to get through to the organization (especially new customers). Users needed to park callers at extensions, hold callers for service, route calls to different departments, be able to conduct conference calls, and more.

Enterprises also discovered a need to get information about the switch operations. Without data on the inbound and outbound traffic, the people in charge of telecommunications had a hard time estimating how best to improve the service to provide maximum efficiency. Having information about the workload that operators were under was also critical, so that their managers could monitor stress levels and better coordinate staffing shifts.

Companies needed a system that could intelligently distribute calls to the correct resources in the enterprise. The device used for this purpose is known as the *automatic call distributor* (ACD). The ACD works on the same principles and technology as the PBX, but it can work with larger volumes of callers and distributes calls according to data supplied by the caller or a database. The callers or databases provide this data via *in-band signaling,* digital data that provides information about extension status (on-hook/off-hook), interactive input from the caller, or external information, such as agents logging in to and out of the work group. Another key feature of the ACD system is that it can provide statistical information on call flows.

Up until now, I differentiated between the PBX and ACD by comparing the central features of the systems. PBX systems are designed to provide a central (star topology) processing and switching of calls, as well as ad hoc or on-demand services. The ACD was designed chiefly to distribute and route inbound and outbound calls to agents.

Today, the software and technology driving PBX systems and ACD units are practically the same. Many PBX manufacturers are shipping PBX systems with advanced ACD capabilities. Add to this setup good reporting capabilities, and the difference between the PBX and the ACD begins to blur. It won't be long (probably before the end of this decade) until the PBX and the ACD become the same device — fully computerized, open, and interoperable with the other systems on the enterprise information network.

The switching components will likely operate in microprocessor- and DSP-based systems and draw all their processing instructions from applications running on operating systems such as the likes of Windows NT or UNIX. By the end of the century, the modern switch will likely be a switching card and telephone interface card sitting in a PC. You will have as much as 64MB of "flat" memory available for application software. In contrast, many of today's switches, costing on the order of $100,000, have little more processing power and memory (640K) than a 1985 IBM personal computer or a latter-day smart calculator.

HYBRID PBX SYSTEMS

Some of the more modern key systems in the U.S. have the technology to behave like a PBX or have some limited PBX functions. These systems are called key/PBX hybrid systems. In key/PBX hybrid systems, users can use plain old telephones and can access lines through a central service that selects the line used.

This means that although the system has a square setup, when switched to PBX mode, you can attach a plain old telephone to it, dial an access digit, and get a dial tone; also, you can simply lift the handset to answer the call when your phone rings (choosing between speaker or handset) without first having to seize the line (important for CTI).

One trend that has emerged in the current decade is to manufacture fully featured PBX systems that can behave as key systems if a business wants them to behave that way. The equipment lets you set up your office systems as either a square plan or a PBX plan. The AT&T Merlin is one such system.

As stated earlier, the square plan — or rather, the key or DISA plan system — is not ideal for computer-telephone integration, especially for automated answering and telephony services. The reason is that the system (usually) cannot directly route multiple calls to the voice-processing ports on the computer telephony server, and the server may be unable to signal the telephone system's CPU for service. If setting up the system with a square plan prevents the CT system from being able to use a plain old telephone port, you may have to change the entire system to a PBX plan.

But I am not sure why even a small business would want to set up "square" anymore (a practice still popular in the U.S.). The PBX plan makes so much more sense, especially considering that CTI is now as important and accessible to the small business as it is to the large enterprise. I can vouch for the fact that in many parts of the world, small businesses are opting for PBX systems, even when they need only two extensions. (And the reason is that they want computer telephony.)

CALL PATHS AND ROUTING

Formulating policies on how your firm takes and handles calls is no longer enough. Now, through enterprise-wide call management, your central focus should be on how you *wisely* distribute calls on an enterprise-wide basis (on a global scale), without needing additional human effort to route the calls. To better understand the difference, you can divide your call traffic into the following two simple categories. From there, you can derive further definitions.

GROUP A: RANDOM CALL TRAFFIC

Random call traffic is miscellaneous calls made by or received by anyone in your enterprise as part of their normal course of business. Calls are received at the enterprise's main number (a hunt group into the PBX) and are processed by humans. These random calls involve individuals who need a specific service, product, or information.

Usually, these calls only can be handled at an individual level. Although companies typically employ several people to handle such calls, here the enterprise does not need to manage the path of the calls by routing them to services according to the caller's needs, although the enterprise may want to filter or group them. "We take them as they come," one IT specialist said to me. But when I pointed out that at least 20 percent of the calls requiring technical support could be rerouted directly to the computer center of the business and showed him how much of an impact this setup would have on the workload of the general staff, he changed his mind.

People receiving miscellaneous call traffic may not receive any calls during a certain day, or they may receive hundreds of calls. Each call may be for a different purpose and from people with different intentions. The callers could be new customers, family members, or a number of clients with different needs.

By following the policy of enterprise-wide call management (EWCM), companies use computer telephony to ensure that calls can be routed to the correct people without human intervention. Computerized telephonists and automated attendant systems enable the caller to select the correct extension number (if they have called before and know the path they want to take or with whom they want to speak). By striving to minimize the number of random calls that end up at the incorrect station this way, you eliminate the need to have humans route calls — as well as problems like telephonist burnout and the hour-glass syndrome.

Random callers who do not know with whom they need to speak can be filtered into predetermined groups, if so desired by the business — or when the business realizes how useful this practice can be, by having callers select single options from a voice-processing menu. I deal with these services in the next chapter. Workers who receive random calls do not wait for calls to arrive or work in a call processing (state-of-mind) mode, although it often seems that way. (This is the function of the service and knowledge workers in Group B.)

You also can use computer telephony to move calls along a customer "path" in the enterprise. Each enterprise has different needs, and often the call needs to be processed according to a specific plan that a manager has prepared.

GROUP B: HOMOGENOUS CALL TRAFFIC

This second type of call traffic emerges when call volume increases enough to classify the number of callers as belonging to a specific group, even when a great deal of callers do not know with whom they want to speak but have the same (or similar reason) for making the call. This group also applies when you start a service that will result in people calling the enterprise specifically for that service, such as with sales/marketing efforts and help desk/technical support services.

Having this type of call-traffic control requires IT and the EWCM strategy to consolidate and group several knowledge workers, whose focus will be to interface with callers. In other words, the worker's primary focus will be dealing with callers, and it may be the only task they perform in the course of their normal workday.

With these types of calls, it is especially important to employ ACD equipment, computer telephony, information bases, and technology for the enterprise information network and intranet (see Chapter 12) so that you not only distribute the calls to the groups who can best handle them, but can *intelligently* distribute the call (work) load within that group.

This capability is the chief difference between an ACD system and a PBX. An ACD system can use information to decide how best to distribute the calls so that no single agent in a group is overloaded. The PBX, on the other hand, was designed to enable people to decide how to best switch or transfer a call, and to provide centralized access to dial tone and PBX services for both internal and external random telecommunications.

The ACD determines to which stations calls should be routed. It "knows" how many calls a station has received and which station the next call should go to. It determines this according to top-down, bottom-up, sequential, or random processing algorithms. The database also records every call transaction so that the ACD knows (for example) that station A has received 20 calls, station B has received 19 calls, and station C — which was logged out for the telephonist's lunch or smoke break — received 12 calls. When station C logs back on, the next call goes there, relieving the other stations.

To achieve EWCM objectives, a new trend is emerging that hasn't quite matured; it involves linking computer telephony and the EIN into the ACD scenario. Here, calls are handled by the ACD according to (1) external information supplied by logarithmic and time-management parameters and (2) skill, knowledge, and experience levels. To illustrate the latter: A smart, informed ACD can query a database to determine who in the station pool is more able to handle the next call, if all callers have taken 100 calls. It's not simply a matter of sending the call to just anyone — after all, what if one of the agents worked late the previous day and is due to sign off in five minutes? The ACD would be putting the caller at a disadvantage by routing the call to this agent.

The ACD determines which stations are available to take calls by the busy condition data provided by line-activity scanners and by other sources that tell the ACD whether the station is logged out or logged in. The information sources provide this data internally to the ACD (via a data or digital connection) Alternatively, the ACD can get the information from a database where an external line/extension activity scanner writes the off-hook/on-hook status information of every extension.

The best ACD equipment employs robust operating systems, powerfully structured query databases, and telephony equipment designed to keep it abreast of line and extension conditions. This ACD equipment distributes inbound calls or those that resulted from proactive dialing routines.

Can you use a PBX as an ACD? The answer is yes — if your needs are not critical or if the PBX has the features discussed earlier. Although most PBXs can distribute calls to station pools, you need to add computer telephony services (such as a voice-response unit or voice-processing system) and engage CTI to simulate critical ACD services.

Call distribution can be easily handled by a CT system that can distribute calls randomly or in a sequential fashion. This option may be a good one for a small, growing business because ACD systems are very expensive.

What about having the PBX route calls according to a least recently used (LRU) or most recently used algorithm? To use a PBX and CT system for simple grouping and distribution of calls into departments, you need to make sure that the information the CT system and PBX gets is reliable. The CT system and the PBX (or both) need to gather real-time, station-status information from the enterprise information network. Can a CT system do this task by gathering and analyzing the information received from the stations? Yes — it can perform this task in two ways:

1. It can monitor the lines for call progress information.

2. It can scan the extensions for activity by measuring the changes in the loop current.

Option 1 is, however, too iffy and slow for critical call distribution; Option 2 isn't that much better because it requires messing around with electronics and devices, and that can cause problems.

All CT services use DSP capability to decide how to route calls and transfer callers, but such inband monitoring is not sufficient for critical ACD services. Some integrators find inband signaling weak across the board of CT features and services. And inband signaling is not ideal for critical or loaded call processing. It keeps callers on hold longer (blocking levels rise) because it first has to call the station or extension and do call-progress analysis before the call is routed elsewhere.

This brings me to the subject of computer-telephone integration. By understanding CTI, you will be able to better understand the broader concepts of computer telephony. (You may want to return to Chapter 5 at this point.) Remember that the fastest means by which a computer telephony system can get real-time station status information is via a digital CTI link. This is now possible in an open, interoperable fashion thanks to the advent of NetWare Telephony Services and Windows Telephony Services (the TSAPI and TAPI standards).

To add to our basic definitions and understanding, let's discuss four automated routing options available to (many) enterprises that want to muscle up on computer telephony. They include, in no particular order, the following:

✦ Automatic number identification

✦ Dialed number information services

✦ Direct inward dialing

✦ Voice processing

ROUTING OPTION 1: AUTOMATIC NUMBER IDENTIFICATION

Automatic number identification (ANI) is made (widely) possible by the capability to convert digital information that originates at the telephone company (telco) into analog information that can be transmitted to a device at the end of a POTS line. This information is the telephone number of the person or party who has subscribed to that line — in other words, the party responsible for paying the telephone bills. Thanks to this nifty feature made possible by the smart integration of digital and analog telecommunications technology, the telephone companies found a way to make more money (it costs between $7.00 and $10.00 in most regions of the U.S.). It invented a service called Caller ID (CID), or Calling Line ID (CLID or CLI) as it is known mostly in Europe. These are services provided by telephone companies around the world that enable the called party to identify the telephone number being used to make the call.

Caller ID is the marketing name that many telephone companies use to identify the service in the U.S. This name suggests that the service may also include the name of the subscriber whose line is being used to make the call. ANI is the technology and is not universally available (as a service), and some territories restrict or limit its scope of use and implementation.

This is how it works: Basically, the local or long-distance telephone company uses equipment attached to (or part of) a central office switch to transmit all or part of a telephone number of the person making the call to the called party. The number can be sent just before the call, during the first three rings, or just after the three rings. (Usually, the phone company transmits the number during the first few rings — most often just after the first ring.) The party receiving the call can wait for the number to flash up and then decide what to do with the call. Of course, this has raised all sorts of rights and privacy issues. But we are not going to debate that because we want to use ANI for computer telephony strategy, not to invade privacy or violate rights.

ANI digits are usually transmitted over the same voice channel as the call; that is, as inband signals or touch tones. Telcos also are able to transmit them digitally on ISDN and data lines.

Before looking further into the use of ANI for routing calls, I want to clarify something. Telephone companies and the media have attributed special, omniscient, paranormal features to ANI that do not exist. I've read countless articles and received many calls from telephone companies suggesting that Caller ID service tells the recipient exactly who is on the line. That statement is not true; caller ID cannot do this. How on earth does the telephone department know who is doing the dialing on the other end? The telco only knows which line has been seized to make the call, and it transmits that information.

Many businesses have thus installed Caller ID with the hope that every call can be intelligently routed, managed, and processed according to the information transmitted. Sorry — in order to use this information to route calls, you have to create an association in your information systems that governs how to handle repeat calls from the subscriber's number. In other words, you can route calls based on ANI only because your information tells you that you can assume, with a level of confidence, that the party on the line is a certain individual who has called before or who always calls from this number. Caller ID technology, however, can be made to work for you for consumer-to-business transactions when the calls originate in the home. When individuals call a party from home, the Caller ID information can be matched against a database with some level of security. The information originates in the home and identifies the subscriber's name. But when a call is made from a business, how do you know who is calling? All you get is the business name and telephone number. Thus, only certain applications will benefit from the integration of ANI and computer telephony. Here are two examples that may highlight the difference.

I have a number of small businesses exploring computer telephony strategy. Two make great case studies for ANI. One is a family-run Thai take-out kitchen; the other is (was) a sex/lonely hearts line I consulted for a few years back (they had quite a call center).

My Thai client was concerned about missing calls when things become hectic during lunch hour. Calls would come in and be abandoned before he had a chance to reach the telephone within three rings. To try to solve the problem, he installed Caller ID with the hope that if the caller abandoned, he would be able to call right back and hold on to the business. That's where I came into the picture to provide an alternative.

My Thai client (Rodney) told me that the service did not really work for him. In fact, on some days it did not work at all. On a given day, almost every call for a delivery came from a business. All my client could do was call back the number and hope for the best. When he got a computer telephony system on the line, he would just abandon and write off the business. When he got a live person on the line, it took so long for the receptionist or telephonist to find out who ordered the take out that other calls were being lost.

Scrap the Caller ID idea, I told him. What Rodney needed was a mini ACD that could route calls to the whole family, fitted out with headsets. If Rodney (the order taker) was too busy to take the order, his wife (the chef) could hand the shrimp to the assistant chef and take the call.

My sex/lonely hearts line client was a bit different. The problem was that the 900 number industry had blocked my client from the pay-per-call billing benefits it needed to set up direct-billing relationships with its callers. The solution was easy — arrange for a customer to always call from a certain number. This use of ANI works because the call can be associated, with confidence, to database information related to that number. Now my client can link the database information into billing systems, which automatically debit credit cards or a credit account (called *bill back*) and route calls. For example, clients could be routed to an "agent" of first choice based on the ANI/Caller ID information. If you have the application, ANI can be rather useful.

How does it work on the computer telephony end? The enterprise's computer telephony systems trap and use the digits to route callers who have had previous contact or experience with the enterprise. A voice-processing system can answer the call; if it "hears" the digits, it can, using a mask, compare the numbers to information residing in the database to determine how best to route the call.

Let's say that Mr. E. Smith on 011-750-9870 calls the enterprise. The voice-processing system's DTMF (dual-tone multifrequency) detection technology can trap the digits, mask out 9870, match them to Mr. E. Smith, record 9870 to the database, and route the call to the agent best positioned to assist Mr. Smith.

If the ANI digits arrive digitally, the enterprise will have to place external technology in front of the voice-response unit (perhaps even in front of the PBX) to pick up the digits and do one of two things: either convert them to DTMF for inband signaling to the voice-processing boards or pass them, through a RS-232 data link, to the enterprise information network (EIN) and into database tables that the voice-processing system can access.

But the enterprise needs to use this identifying information for more than just routing. If a call can be identified and looked up in a database, it would also make sense to send a message across the LAN to the agent about to receive the call, indicating that the call is "en route" and that E. Smith is the caller. The agent then determines how best to handle the call. He or she also can use the information to pull up recent records related to E. Smith.

Utility companies that typically get several thousand calls an hour are ideal candidates for ANI. Many customers call from home between the hours of 7 p.m. and 8 p.m. Here, the company can have its system trap ANI digits and use them to associate the number with the account holder (they may still have to verify the caller), pull up records, and then route the call and the records to an agent best suited to handle the call (I talk about this later in the chapter). If the database shows that E. Smith is about to have his water cut off due to a late payment, the call can be routed directly to the agents who know how to deal with callers strapped for cash and get people to pay their bills.

As I said earlier, ANI will not work for every call, but if you do the math you'll see that you can easily save thousands of hours a year in call-processing time. That translates not into soft dollars, but hard cash saved from an actual reduction in expenses. If ANI does not work for your situation you may have to route your calls or group and filter them using Option 5, discussed later.

Here's an interesting example of modern computer telephony at work. On our feature phone at home, my wife and I have a redial button and several others that have preprogrammed numbers. The manufacturer, Sony, had thoughtfully recorded 911 as one of the preprogrammed numbers.

One day, my wife accidentally hit this number and connected with emergency services. After apologizing profusely, my wife was given a lesson in 911 computer telephony. The agent said that because the services were not busy right then, she could just check the records for accuracy, and so proceeded to confirm our address. She explained that as soon as the 911 call came in, our home address and other details popped up on the screen. I later told my wife that the time it takes to provide these details, especially under stress, could mean the difference between life and death.

It is sad that this technology is not available for such domestic use throughout the world. As for the so-called psychic lines — well, they have a connection to a higher authority and, on the advice of the spirits, they use Caller ID extensively. While moderating several discussion groups at the Computer Telephony Expo in March 1996, one Caller ID consultant demonstrated the use of this technology on psychic lines. When you call your psychic hotline, your Caller ID information digs up every known fact about your life from a global database. Then, thanks to computer telephony, your call and your "life history" are routed to the next available psychic. When the psychic takes your call, the computer telephony system (and Windows 95) goes into trance state and tells the psychic everything he or she needs to know about you. Your entire conversation is noted, and the database is updated for the next time you call. And that's one of the main reasons why these services insist that you call from your home telephone for your reading.

ROUTING OPTION 2: DNIS

DNIS stands for *dialed number identification service,* which uses the same technology as ANI to provide information that helps the system automatically route, group, and filter callers. The main difference is that DNIS information is the number being dialed rather than the number of the person making the call. Toll-free and premium-rate services, also known as 800- and 900-number services in the U.S., use this service.

Large enterprise call centers and commercial call-center operations use DNIS for marketing/sales campaigns and to enhance customer satisfaction. The DNIS information can be collected, for example, to route all callers that dialed 800-987-8765 to an ACD group. When creating a telemarketing "campaign," the call centers set up parameters that will route the calls according to the number the advertiser publishes in the media.

The call center then can give its customers a toll-free number to use via the advertising and marketing campaign. All calls dialed by potential customers can be routed to agents who have been trained to handle the calls to the toll-free number.

Like ANI, the DNIS information should be fed to the EIN so that records and collateral information can be "popped" onto the agent's screen at the same time or just before the call reaches the agent's telephone. If the toll-free number is an order line, the DNIS information can be programmed to "pop" order-entry screens for different products and campaigns according to the 800 number called.

DNIS information also can be effectively used by the voice-processing system to play various information to callers before the call is routed. For example, a call to 800-987-6543 can be answered with the knowledge that the caller wants information on vacations in the Caribbean, whereas a call to 800-987-6542 can be answered with the latest information on the umpteenth hurricane that has formed in the Caribbean.

Note that the call center or enterprise does not always need a different line for every toll-free or premium-rate number dialed (I say not always because the services vary around the world). Telcos provide a service that will transfer DNIS information to any of the lines used by the subscriber.

Call centers are using computer telephony and DNIS to process more calls for more customers faster. The agents work hard to take as many different callers as they can at the station. They can be processing a call for a small utility or service company on the one hand, when suddenly an order screen "pops" onto the monitor. The agent can then put the one caller on hold (if the campaign provides for that action) to take the next caller.

ROUTING OPTION 3: DID

Direct inward dialing (DID), also known as *direct dialing inward* (DDI), is another means of routing calls automatically. This service is almost universally available; I have found it being used in many countries that I have consulted in, Africa and the Middle East included. PBX systems, both analog and digital, that are DID-capable (as many are) can route a call to an extension based on the number that the subscriber dials, bypassing a live attendant or telephonist in the process.

The DID service varies around the world, but it basically works as follows: The enterprise subscribes to a group of numbers that share a common exchange grouping. For example, the enterprise may be able to acquire the use of exchange number 437, typically catering to x number of concurrent conversations for which the enterprise determines it needs capacity.

The enterprise's main number could thus be 437-0000, and any numbers above 0000 will represent extensions connected to the DID-capable PBX owned by the enterprise. The number of extensions can be 30 or 3,000. The number of lines configured for DID depends on the resources of the telco and other central-office-related factors.

A simple explanation follows: When a caller dials a DID number, the telco signals the enterprise's PBX that a call has arrived by seizing a line. The PBX returns a signal to advise the telco to send the remaining four digits. Let's say the telco sends the number 2100. The telco "pipes" the number dialed (that is, the number 2100) to the PBX in similar fashion to the way DNIS and ANI transmit information.

After the PBX receives the digits, it performs attending functions to facilitate the call. First, it tests for the availability of the extension; if the extension is busy, it sends a busy signal back to the telco or diverts the call elsewhere according to stored data. If the extension is not busy, the PBX sets up a ringing connection to the extension (switched) and sends a ring-back connection to the caller. If data provides for ringing timeout, the PBX will transfer the call to another extension if no one picks up at the first one. The next extension could be a live attendant, a telephonist, a coworker, or the voice-messaging system. The next extension is known as the *coverage extension*.

If the called extension goes off hook to indicate an answer, the PBX drops the ringing connections and sets up a connection between the DID line and the called extension. If either of the parties hang up, this action sends an on-hook signal to the PBX and the telco, and the connection is torn down.

DID has a notorious history. The central principle behind DID is to route calls directly to extensions, thereby avoiding the attendant or telephonist. This principle is the PBX and telephony company solution to the bottleneck or hour-glass syndrome.

PBX companies forget something when they recommend DID as an hour-glass syndrome solver. As I have said repeatedly, calls interrupt important work; most of the time, the reason for the call is less important than the work interrupted. Thus, DID users will often call-forward, or divert, the extension to a coverage extension, usually the telephonist. If this case applies, several things now happen.

The enterprise, thinking that DID will relieve the telephonists, installs more regular lines on its main number (437-0000). But because almost 80 percent of DID lines will be diverted to the telephonists, the hour-glass syndrome not only returns, but with a vengeance.

In many of the sites where I consulted, the DID situation was a nightmare. Let's sit in the caller's chair: You call Barney on extension 2100. But Barney is busy or out of the office, so the call is diverted to an overloaded telephonist. This person answers the phone: "XYZ Corp., how may I direct your call?"

You've already heard this greeting once, so it peeves you a little. But you remain calm and say, "I'm trying to reach Barney Smith." Before you can say anything more, the tired telephonist transfers your call back to extension 2100 that you just dialed directly. You wait the three or less rings (not knowing if this is correct), and call forwarding transfers you back to the telephonist. Now you may view this situation as déjà vu on steroids. Didn't you just do all this? The telephonists are not impressed by your gripe because thousands of callers do this to them all day long.

Meanwhile, you find the enterprise repulsive and start thinking about abandoning the call.

The golden rule to follow with DID is that computer telephony should be employed as a "safety net" under DID. All calls should be forwarded to the computer telephony system for intelligent routing or messaging services. If the PBX can notify the voice-messaging system, via inband or digital signals, of which extension or user needs service, or signal the voice-processing system to offer the caller a menu, or both, then the DID system will live on. If not, the PBX must come out, lest it destroy the entire business and every bit of customer satisfaction effort it has garnered for you.

If you can't take such drastic measures, you need to make sure that users do not forward their phones to the telephonists rather than forward to their office colleagues or assistants when the users plan to be out of the office. The chance of this rule being obeyed to the letter is as slim as trying to grow hair on your tongue. Fortunately, we have entered the new wave of computer telephony described in the next part and Chapter 11. If your PBX manufacturer has joined this elite club (NetWare Telephony Services and Windows Telephony), you're in luck.

ROUTING OPTION 4: CENTREX

Although it's more of a service rather than a routing option, *Centrex* or *central exchange* (its more common name) is essentially a DID-type service with one important difference. The PBX is not on your premises — it resides at the central office; in fact, it *is* the central office.

Centrex does not require the user to have any PBX or switch on site. In fact, the only customer on-premise equipment may be the telephone sets and a voice-messaging system. All switching done by the telephone company and all individual lines in your office are connected to the central office as if it were one giant PBX.

The central office enables Centrex customers to use the central exchange like an on-premise PBX. You can put callers on hold, transfer them to other telephones in your office or off-site, conference callers, and much more. You also can get a separate data line for immediate call accounting.

Many users feel that to engage in the full range of features and benefits that the new wave of computer telephony is bringing, the enterprise needs its own private branch exchange or ACD. This theory may be true, depending on the applications and needs. However, the new wave of computer telephony, especially call control from the desktop PC, will be accessible from Centrex services as well.

Centrex, like DID, can do serious damage if calls are not routed intelligently or caught with an on-premise, voice-processing and messaging system. It is all too easy to call-forward a phone to a coverage extension that's not prepared or able to process the additional load.

ROUTING OPTION 5: VOICE RESPONSE AND VOICE PROCESSING

I have devoted the whole of Chapter 8 to this subject, so I won't go into it much here, save to say that calls can be automatically routed and processed with the aid of voice-processing technology. I also call these systems *voice response units* or *VRUs*, although I prefer to talk about voice processing.

You need voice processing because the options listed earlier are, at best, incomplete automatic call-routing and filtering solutions; at worst, they are dangerous. I use the word *incomplete* for two reasons: First, you have to acknowledge that you will not always get ANI, and second, you cannot always expect the ANI information to be true or pertinent for a particular call. In these cases, you depend on the caller input to a voice-processing system, which detects touch tones or voice input, to assist the call-routing process.

So, it's safe to say that the methods provided earlier are not really as intelligent as they at first appear to be, nor can intelligent routing be easily accomplished.

What if you want to route the call or provide services based on information that has nothing to do with telephone numbers? This information could be a serial number of a product; an order or purchase number; customer number; passwords; ticket, docket, or file numbers; area code; ZIP or postal code; social security number, identity number, or passport number; driver's license number; confirmation number; and much, much more. Only a voice-processing system can provide this service, which is why it deserves a chapter on its own.

Coupled with intelligent call routing (as described in the following section), the capability of a voice-processing unit to intelligently route a call makes for an alluring proposition.

INTELLIGENT CALL ROUTING

Most ACD and smart PBX systems today have the capability to use data to best route a call according to the skills of the agent. This method often is referred to as *skills-based routing*. Although the ACD can go a long way to routing a call to the correct agent, its capability to intelligently route calls is limited by that which you feed to it. You thus need to capture and maintain as much information as you can about each of your callers and store this information in databases on the enterprise information network, where it can be used by all, human and machine alike.

The end result of maintaining such data is that your switching system can route callers to agents or representatives in the enterprise who have the necessary skills and experience to best handle the call. The alternative is to put callers on hold while the first agent the caller connects to tries to find someone better equipped for the call, or else the agent is forced to stumble through the call, which helps no one.

The following list corresponds to the information you want to get to better handle a call:

✦ For ANI, note the people that regularly call from a particular number if there is more than one. If more than one family member calls your company, you will find it more difficult to match enterprise records with ANI. If this happens, you will need to route the caller to voice processing.

✦ For DNIS, trap and database the numbers called to map the behavior of the party.

✦ Information obtained from the voice-processing system

✦ Sociologic information (what does the person do for a living, hobbies, sports, spending habits, responsibilities, and more)

✦ Demographic information

✦ Geographic information

I am not suggesting that you build a database that rivals the FBI's or the one used by the large, credit-reporting agencies in the U.S.; the idea is to use the information in the database to transfer a caller to someone who is best able (via skills and experience) to process the caller to satisfaction.

My software company, for example, is a member of several developer programs sponsored by Microsoft, not the least of which is the computer telephony developers program. Every time we call Microsoft, the technical support engineers almost have nervous breakdowns over some of the questions we ask. The result is that although we do have valid questions — some seemingly very simple ones — we always end up being transferred to several engineers who have to do some serious thinking.

Whenever we call, we enter an identifying code into the voice-processing system. Such information should be used to transfer or route our call to the most intelligent engineer in the company.

Using the technology I described, the EIN, the voice-processing systems, and computer telephony systems described in the next chapters add up to saved time, more productive time, satisfied customers, and calm and collected workers.

SUMMARY

Very few business in the world exist without telecommunications. The fact that so much business is done on the telephone warrants the enterprise putting telephony and computer telephony systems under direct IT control, such as with the other service domains of IT (database servers, application servers, and so on). I am often astonished at how little attention telephony gets in many enterprises. I often find that even in a big company employing two or three dozen IT people, no person has been delegated the responsibility of telephony, nor is it considered a strategic advantage.

It's time to change this way of thinking. You need to formulate an enterprise-wide call-management plan. Start now. Chapters 15 and 16 can give you some (strategic) guidance.

In This Chapter

✦ The computerized telephonist: what it is and what it does

✦ Justifying the need

✦ Determining your needs

✦ Scripting the call flow

✦ The pilot project

"Please press 1 to transfer your call.
If you're calling from a rotary phone, please
make a beepy noise that sounds like you just
pressed 1 on a touch-tone phone."

CHAPTER 8

VOICE PROCESSING AND COMPUTER TELEPHONIST SERVICES

How long does it take to lose a customer? Pick the correct answer below and win the computer telephony merit award!

A. Between three and six seconds

B. Between 30 and 60 seconds

C. Between three and six minutes

D. All of the above

If you read the opening chapter to this book, then you know the answer. If not, go back and read it. (Just kidding — sort of.) What do you think the correct answer is?

If you picked A, pat yourself on the back — you're right! Did you know that people form an opinion about your business as soon as you answer the telephone (computer or human)? What you say and how you say it when you answer the phone forms an imprint on the caller's brain that you cannot easily remove. Whomever or whatever answers the telephone is representing the enterprise.

HUMAN-COMPUTER DIALOG

Before I launch into this chapter, I want to talk about a concept mentioned in several previous chapters: *human-computer dialog*. It's important to note, from the engineering or technical perspective, that, in this book, human-computer dialog refers to a dialog over the telephone and a one-on-one dialog that happens with the computer in front of you, in a way that humans are accustomed to and feel comfortable with (that is, voice).

But human-computer dialog also implies data input, word processing, mathematical calculations, graphical design, and more. Although I use the term mostly to discuss human-computer dialog over the telephone, I also use it here to discuss the dialog between humans and computers on the World Wide Web (see Chapter 12). Remember, too, that the underlying principle of computer telephony is humans communicating with humans. The computer is merely a representative, or a stand-in, if you will.

However you decide to configure and set up the interactive computer telephony systems discussed in the following chapters, first doing as much research as possible on the audience and how they will use the system is important. This point is where you have to focus on human-computer dialog. The extent to which this dialog will be possible depends on a number of factors (discussed later in this book). In the chapters that follow, I provide several suggestions for optimizing the way this dialog works. Some strategies may be valid for your situation, others not; it all depends on your application.

For example, although I hate rotary detection and wouldn't recommend using it (unpleasant past experiences have soured me against this technology), that doesn't mean that computer telephony is no good for you if your city's or country's PSTN (public switched telephone network) is 100 percent pulse-dial driven. Your audience may be able to tolerate a level of interaction that's not as feasible, say, in the U.S. Unless a critical need to do otherwise exists, people do not like to be inconvenienced. Nor do they particularly like having to learn new things when they otherwise wouldn't have to. How many people, for example, learn sign language unless they have a deaf child or relative (sad though it may be)?

For this reason, you need to keep your audience in mind as much as possible while you're establishing needs, designing the system, and acquiring and deploying the technology. I'll expand on that thought in a later chapter, but for now I suggest that you interview focus groups composed of the potential internal and external users of the system before going live (switching on the system) or starting the buying process. This researching process can provide you with valuable insight on the type of human-computer dialog that suits your situation best — and help you avoid making a costly mistake.

To quote James Martin, the most well-known writer of books on information systems and the person who popularized the concept of information engineering: "To bring the power of computers and the information in their data banks to the maximum number of people, careful attention must be made to the man-machine interface. People must be the prime focus of computer systems design. The computer is there to *serve them, to obtain information for them, to help them do their jobs. The ease with which people communicate with the computer will determine the extent to which they use it. . . .*"

THE COMPUTER TELEPHONIST: WHAT IT IS, WHAT IT DOES

A computer that answers the phone and routes callers is commonly known as an *automated attendant*. I'm not sure where the terms *auto-attendant* and *automated attendant* came from or who coined them (I've asked a dozen people). No matter what the origin or the source, an automated attendant originally referred to a 1,000-pound gorilla machine that shared its "closet" with the PBX. These old dinosaurs had three functions: to route calls, lose clients, and collect dust.

Why do I cite the last two unflattering functions, you ask? Because for many users, the terms auto-attendant and voice mail system are synonymous with a technology that was unfriendly and repulsive, but, paradoxically, a necessary technology.

In the new frontier of computer telephony, this technology has "come out of the closet," so to speak. It's time to shed that evil label that once attached itself to the call-processing technologies. Figure 8-1 highlights the call-processing service domain of computer telephony.

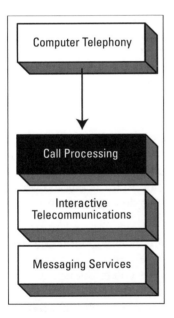

Figure 8-1: The call processing service domain of computer telephony: computer telephonist services.

To help this process along, I like to think of a *computerized telephonist* as being the computer that answers the telephone or makes calls for your enterprise and is thus the first representative of your organization that your clients encounter. The term *telephonist* has a more international ring (wow, what a pun) to it than the alternative —

seldom have I heard my clients in Europe or Africa use the attendant term. (Actually, they usually call it "the machine that answers the phone" or "that thing that answers the phone — and then cuts you off." Of course, that last description only fits for machines that are not set up properly.)

This substitute term comes in handy in my role as a consultant; whenever I use the terms automated attendant or voice mail, my clients either pity me or trash me. But they do take interest when I introduce the term computer telephonist. Also, the term computer telephonist fits the new frontier of computer telephony better — the technology being used is called computer telephony; hence, a machine that supports it is a computer telephonist. I hereby relegate this term to technology dictionaries and lexicons of the IT world.

In the old frontier of IT, the automated attendant usually was a "bolt-on" computer attached to the PBX, that is, a legacy system bolted on to (or wired to) another legacy system (see Chapter 3 to learn more about bolt-ons). Following the advent of the digital signal processing (DSP) card, these services were incorporated into PCs and coupled with software that also provides voice mail facilities.

A few of these old systems that do little more than auto-attend still are manufactured today, and too many of them remain in use. In today's new frontier of integrated computer telephony technology, the computer (or automated) telephonist service is an integral part of the whole telecommunications picture — because no state-of-the-art product provides the automated routing of calls as a stand-alone, single feature. Rather, automated call routing is just one of the service features provided, along with audiotext, fax-on-demand, voice mail, IVR, and more.

The bottom line of what a computer telephonist does is this: The computer gets callers directly to live agents or extensions of their choice without the aid of a human telephonist. The defining difference between this service and an automatic call distribution (ACD) system or DID is that the computer telephonist is a voice-processing service (using the DSP card) that prompts the caller to determine switching information by entering an extension number (see Chapter 5).

The ACD system, on the other hand, does not require callers to input information for switching; rather, that information is predetermined and preprogrammed. As explained in the preceding chapter, an ACD connects the call to the agent when the caller does not know with whom he or she needs to speak. Callers do not encounter any stops between the two destinations other than when they end up on hold in a call queue.

In the random call scenario, an intervening party has to determine routing information. For me, providing the caller with the ability to choose which extension or station he or she wants to connect to tops the list of critical computer telephony services because it eliminates the need to involve a human telephonist. This feature can be a boon for both the caller and the enterprise if you use your machine wisely.

Because of its capabilities, computer telephonists are the most widely used of the computer telephony services. Many callers incorrectly assume that the system is voice mail when the system answers — it's not. Voice mail is merely the additional service callers are routed to after the computer telephonist answers the phone. Don't get confused by the term *service* though, because the messaging side of it can be a software module in one whopping computer telephony program. With the new computer telephony models however, users are opting for a separate messaging system that integrates with another vendor's computer telephonist.

Many enterprises install computer telephonist systems to answer and process calls without really looking at the overall needs of the enterprise, and frequently the motivation driving the installation of computer telephony is the need to cut back on staff. Because of this fact, this service is rarely used wisely. In turn, poor management of the computer telephonist system is one of the chief reasons why callers to these corporations often say things like "Oh, voice mail answered and I simply put the phone down."

Ideally, an enterprise should find out as much as it can about a computer telephonist system to determine whether it is appropriate for their work environment and to learn how to implement and use it so that customers don't come back with choice words about the new system. So, let me step right up to the plate and tell you a little about what a computer telephonist can do for you.

WHAT THE SERVICE PROVIDES

With a computer telephonist, you get a wide variety of capabilities, as the following list shows:

1. The computer telephonist can answer the telephone and greet you ("Good morning! Thank you for calling . . .").

2. It can prompt you for a particular service ("For customer relations, press 1; for sales . . .").

3. It can prompt you for an extension or station number ("If you know the extension, enter it now").

4. It can capture ANI (automatic number identification) or DNIS (dialed number identification service) information and make this data available for other services.

5. It can transfer the caller to another computer telephony service or move the caller to the next realm of computer telephony options within the same program (such as audiotext or voice mail).

The computer telephonist is reactive in that the software processes inbound calls — it reacts to the calls. Of course, the system you use may do outbound services and place calls (such as delivering mail), but these features are merely the product of another service running on the same system (or within the same software) as a separate process.

JUSTIFYING THE NEED

Now you know what a computer telephonist can do for you, but do you need it? Let's take a look.

If you have callers who call regularly and know the extension or station number they want to end up at, the routing service should be automatically handled by the computer. If your enterprise is in this position, you can immediately justify implementing a computer telephonist service. This service, perhaps more than all the others, can pay for itself within a matter of months.

Callers learn the extension numbers by calling the party regularly or from reading the information off enterprise stationery, such as business cards, letterheads, envelopes, and so on. Why employ a human to switch calls to the correct extension if the callers can get to the correct destination themselves? In today's business jungle, employing humans for this sole purpose is a waste of resources.

But wait — what about the benefits that you get in the customer's perception of the enterprise when he or she gets through to a human rather than a machine? Nearly all the enterprises for which I have been a computer telephony consultant or system installer have confronted me with the outdated maxim that "having a computer answer the telephone is bad for our image."

Well, they would have been correct a decade or two ago, if computer telephony had been possible then. In the days of typewriters and telex machines, a company typically employed a handful of people as switchboard operators whose sole purpose was to answer the telephone and connect the callers to extensions. (These people certainly left an impression on many of us — you still see the stereotypical switchboard operator in many cartoons, complete with horn-rimmed glasses and a supply of emery boards.)

Today, however, a successful business may need to employ 30 to 40 people just to project that sterling personal-service image and handle the barrage of calls coming into it. Clearly, this option is absurd.

What's more absurd is that some of these successful enterprises still try to employ only a handful of people to route these calls and service callers, which puts these poor humans into situations where it's impossible for them to answer the calls calmly. The critical time-slice of three rings — after which callers start to consider abandoning the call and the enterprise risks losing a customer — approaches rapidly when the operators have to look up extensions, take down messages, and do other things they would not have to do if a computer telephony system were installed. Because of the explosion in growth of message traffic over the years, often a company's telecommunications cannot be handled by a router that eats, breathes, and has a pulse.

So, instead of garnering a polished professional image, the reverse happens without computer telephony. Customers abandon their calls to the company and either retry (which compounds the problem if the result is the same) or call elsewhere. Research has shown that in the Information Age of the 1990s, callers are more likely to lose respect for an enterprise because their calls are not answered quickly rather than because a computer represented the enterprise in the first six seconds. I also found this to be true when I did a study (a requirements analysis) for a major chain of hospitals I consulted for in 1993.

There *are* situations where you would not want to replace a human being with a computer telephonist service, but the reasons have nothing to do with image. So, if you publish numbers that attract a great deal of call traffic, the need for computer telephony is justifiable because you will lose clients if the human telephonist cannot answer calls fast enough or process them soon after putting callers on hold.

Consider the following call scenarios associated with inbound traffic on a particular number. In the following scenarios, Group 1 and 2 know with whom they wish to speak or the extension they need.

+ **Group 1: Established human-to-service callers.** You have callers that have called the enterprise before and are likely to call it again. They do not necessarily need to talk to a human; they may just need to access your enterprise information network. A bank is a good example of an enterprise that callers will likely call using the same number several times a month. These callers are a group of regular human-to-service callers.

+ **Group 2: Established human-to-human callers.** You have callers that have formed business relationships with the enterprise. Strategic partners, OEMs (original equipment manufacturers) and VARs (value-added resellers) are good examples. This group consists of regular, human-to-human callers who know who they want and how to reach them.

+ **Group 3: Infrequent human-to-service and human-to-human callers.** You have multiple departments and all fit in with the preceding scenarios. Callers establish contacts in the company and know with whom they wish to speak and which extensions they want to dial. It's unlikely that callers to this line will call only once. At the minimum, they may call again after long intervals.

+ **Group 4: Frequent human-to-workgroup callers.** In the preceding scenarios, you have a variety of callers at this number that need to be filtered to several departments or workgroups; for example, to sales, technical support, or business relations.

+ **Group 5: First-time, human-to-human callers.** You have callers who have never called the enterprise. These callers are calling for the first time and are unfamiliar with the enterprise. The impression they get from the way you handle their first call will be a lasting and influencing one. I once termed these telephone users "virgin callers," a phrase that raised some eyebrows.

✦ **Group 6: First-time, human-to-workgroup callers.** You have callers that have never called the enterprise, but they need to be filtered to one or more of several departments.

In these situations, if call volume is large enough that you have to put a caller on hold while the human telephonist performs another job-related task, then you can justify the need for computer telephonist services.

How do you know if this is the case? You just have to do a bit of research. Sit down at the PBX console (as I have done many times) and wait for the first call. When you take the call, remember that you have to convey an alluring image of your company to the caller within the first few seconds after the first ring. While talking to the caller does another line on the PBX console light up? Do you start to speed up the call you're presently on to catch the next call within three rings? Do you watch the fourth ring and then tell the caller you are in the middle of servicing to "hold a moment"? Then, when you take the second call, do you see another light blink on?

If this is the case, ask yourself this question — What image of my company am I conveying now? How many fading inbound call lights (abandoned calls) will it take to convince you that you need another solution: the intervention of a computer?

People will drop the line and try elsewhere if you take too long to grab the call; believe me, that's no lie invented by the industry to sell more computer telephony products. You've likely been in the same position when calling a company; if no one answers within a certain amount of time, you become restless.

In 1993, I consulted for two competing software resellers, both vying for each other's business. Both companies carried Microsoft, Novell, and Lotus products, so when one firm lost a call, often the business went to the competitor. In this situation, I was able to compare the telephony services at both companies (with their knowledge) and get an idea of how computer telephony affected their sales.

One company was further along the road of CT deployment and implementation than the other. When a customer called the first company and the product he or she needed was not carried by it, the company representative would refer the caller to my other client. Often, however, the caller's response was along the lines of "I tried calling them already, but they took too long to answer so I thought I would check to see if you also carry the item." As you can see, price is not always the determining factor for customers. Companies that I have interviewed regarding this same subject have made these statements:

> Call volume is high, and without the computerized routing of calls, we would need to employ several humans to perform the function, doing little else. Thus the installation of an eight-port (eight lines serviced) system costing, say, $35,000 is saving us the cost of salaries and facilities for six to eight people — an expense of more than $100,000. The system paid for itself in under eight months.

> Besides the savings, we service a large number of callers who repeatedly call our offices and know exactly with whom they wish to speak or what service they need. They consider it a waste of time to have to talk to a human in this situation.

WHEN VOICE PROCESSING IS NOT JUSTIFIED OR RECOMMENDED

There are situations where the commission of a computer telephonist is not appropriate. In fact, in some cases I'd advise against any form of voice processing to process calls. The following scenarios give some examples of situations in which you probably would be better off using a different approach.

Do not use voice processing when callers need to talk to a human as a matter of extreme urgency. In these situations, the callers usually are under considerable stress, and any form of voice processing will aggravate an already tense situation. It may also leave your facility open to damages and liability. Imagine calling a system that prompts callers this way: "If you wish to report a shooting, press 1. If you wish to report a stabbing, press 2." If a situation arises in which all operators are busy, the only possible computerized call intervention you should consider is to have the computer take a message and keep the caller on hold.

No computer has the capability of a practiced paramedic to establish the nature of an emergency and make critical decisions when a life hangs in the balance. Yet I have come across situations where an emergency facility was closed and a message told the caller, "This facility is not a 24-hour operation, please call (somebody else)." Here, the calls should have been diverted to the 24-hour facility; asking an emergency patient to waste time with a voice message is absurd. The local switch or central office exchange should be able to provide this after-hours service. If these devices are not sophisticated enough to handle the task (but they should be), the enterprise switch and CT system can do the job. One emergency service that I know of set free lines to an off-hook state so that callers would get busy signals. The telephony people at this site felt it was better for the callers to try to get help elsewhere rather than stay on hold. Clearly, this decision was a bad one — what was needed was a wide-area routing service.

Do not use voice-processing or computer telephonist services in sales situations. When callers dial toll-free numbers, particularly in response to commercials that prompt impulse actions on the caller's part, using a computer to route the calls is tantamount to burning your banknotes. In these cases, you need to take the calls through an ACD, with no computerized filtering, and keep overflow callers on hold no more than two to three minutes (keeping them abreast of their call status during that time).

After that time period elapses, the impulse actions are replaced by aggravation and the caller drops the line, unlikely to ever return (see Chapter 14). The optimum scenario is to have another call center on standby during commercials, to which the first call center can reroute calls to handle the load. This situation requires some strategic planning, but it applies to all call-center operations, from the large commercial situations to enterprise-owned facilities.

Do not use computer telephonist services when catering primarily to elderly callers. Some older folks, although intrigued with what computers can do, don't appreciate the gains made by new technology and resent being forced to change their ways. (Although I have heard rumors claiming that over a million grannies surf the Internet regularly). A good example is the ATM (automatic teller machine). Many older folks still prefer to stand in line (although all the ATMs are free) to do their banking, even if that means waiting all morning. (Also, you may run into problems when some users can't hear the prompts, although this problem definitely is not limited to the elderly. You can install a feature that enables callers to increase the volume, but voice files tend to become distorted very quickly. And don't forget that you're introducing another step by doing so.)

DETERMINING YOUR NEEDS

Now that you have justified the need to provide computerized telephonist services, you must determine your needs before you invest in a product or hardware. The first question you should ask is this: How many ports do I need? Because this is one of the most important decisions you will make and one that requires some research regarding *all* your computer telephony services (even your PBX), I have devoted Chapter 17 to the subject.

SCRIPTING THE CALL FLOW

When you are employing computer telephony to answer and process your organization's calls, you have one objective: Take the calls and get the callers transferred to the services they need as efficiently and quickly as possible. Do not do anything that will put successful call completion at risk. Figure 8-2 represents a simple flow-diagram to achieve this result in as short a time as possible.

I call the process of designing the opening prompts and service that perform these functions *scripting the call flow*. Call flow also can be referred to as the *call path*, or the path that the caller will take to reach the correct destination as soon as possible. To achieve this, you need to design a quality call-flow script. The following criteria are important considerations for scripting the call flow:

Choosing the right software	Dialing the extension now
Choosing the salutation	Filtering callers
Employing the notion of time and season	Using multiple levels
	Offering clear choices
Applying character, image, and identity	Using multiple languages
Avoiding fooling the caller	Dealing with the inactive caller
Throwing out the gumph	Using a company directory
Pressing 0 for assistance	Sticking to a formula that works

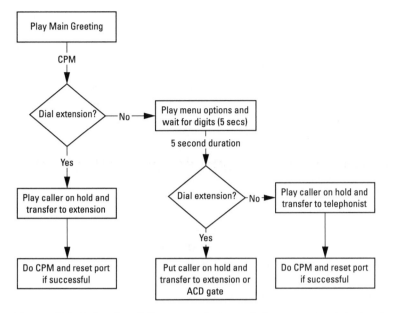

Figure 8-2: A simple call flow or path through the computer telephonist service.

This discussion of the call-flow script applies to the majority of enterprises that have or want to put computer telephony on their general or main numbers. Of course, you may have special or particular needs, so the script should be flexible enough to cater to your objectives. You'll want to invest in a system that lets you design and set up exactly what you need according to commonsense practices. Here are some thoughts about choosing the right software.

CHOOSING THE RIGHT SOFTWARE

Many older automated attendants were difficult to optimize because you could not change the call-flow script very easily. This problem also is true of some newer, PC-based platforms that have been poorly designed. So, when you're choosing a product, keep in mind the following considerations:

Do invest in a system that you can easily manage and that lets you update (re-record) the salutation with ease. Do *not* invest in a product where the recording and changing of the salutation is a major exercise (such as bringing the entire computer telephony system down). You may discover a need to change the opening phrases at any time, and you won't like performing this task if its fun factor is akin to that of having dental work done.

Do invest in a system that can play multiple phrases one after the other, so that you have maximum flexibility when designing the call-flow script. You'll want to be able to swap phrases around or insert and remove phrases in the script without having to re-record the entire script from beginning to end.

Do invest in a system that can play multiple phrases one after the other, so that you have maximum flexibility when designing the call-flow script. You'll want to be able to swap phrases around or insert and remove phrases in the script without having to re-record the entire script from beginning to end.

Do make sure that — if you have the preceding feature — you also can insert (and have the system play) the phrases based on time and date. This important capability enables the system to swap phrases based on the time of day and time of year. We will talk a little more about this later in this chapter.

Do make sure that you invest in a system which can detect both single digits and strings of digits at any time in the script. This capability allows you to prompt the caller for a single digit (press 1 for . . .) or a string (enter the extension now . . .) at any time in the call-flow script.

This basic necessity enables you to set up a system according to your special needs and circumstances. You should be able to design and deploy a script that caters to extension routing and filtering simultaneously or one service at a time. In many cases, you will want to filter the callers and do nothing else, using the system in front of the ACD as a low-cost ACD for small shops.

CHOOSING THE SALUTATION

Getting back to the subject of image, you want to use the clearest and friendliest voice possible to greet the caller. Unpleasant voices, poor scripts, and poor call processing dole out pictures of a repulsive enterprise, repulsive products, and repulsive staff to the caller in the few brief moments that he or she encounters the salutation.

You may recall that I said it can take as little as six seconds for a caller to form an indelible impression about your company, either positive or negative. Often, I think it takes less time; three seconds is more likely. As a comparison, the salutation is typically delivered within the first three to four seconds of the call — something to consider when you're deciding what to say and how to say it.

When I attended a sales seminar in New York City in 1984, the advertising sales manager of *Omni* magazine, Charlie Mandel, advised us to view every customer as representing several other customers and repeat business, not just as a single sale. He told us to look at the forehead of the client and imagine a million dollars inscribed there. This inscription represented the repeat sales and good word-of-mouth that would emanate from the happy buyer.

Well, I still look at foreheads and imagine a million bucks. You should look at your callers in the same light. They represent repeat sales, and their good and kind words about you will bring you more customers. Let's call this Charlie's forehead law. Violate the six-second-rule, and Charlie's forehead law has the opposite effect. You lose repeat business, and you lose new customers.

Karl Slatner, my partner, says that you know your customers are saying good things about you when you no longer need to cold-call. The best example of this credo is Intuit. This company sold 1.5 million copies of its Quicken personal finance software in 1994, more than any other retail software company.

How was this achieved? Scot Cook, Quicken's creator, says this: "Word of mouth. When customer satisfaction creates demand, salespeople don't have to convince potential buyers the product is good."

Keeping that in mind, make sure that your customers hear your salutation within six seconds and that the greeting they hear is as pleasant and inviting as you can make it. (Alternatively, don't make it so sickly sweet that it sounds insincere or makes them nauseous.)

For more on recording strategies, refer to Chapter 9.

EMPLOYING THE NOTION OF TIME AND SEASON

It takes just under a second to say "good morning," or "good evening," in a salutation and, although some of my peers may disagree with this practice, adding this little nicety pays off with other benefits. This greeting is a no-brainer feature in computer telephony software. If you can't add this greeting in your current system, then it's time to get a new system. The time/season phrase is merely a phrase or two inserted in front of the filtering or menu part of the script that plays according to the time of day or year.

This time indicator provides the callers with an immediate picture of the time of day at the facility they are calling, which can be appealing to the caller. It also promotes the image of the anywhere, anytime enterprise. This little reminder tells long-distance callers from other time zones that you are working harder to accommodate them when the system answers with good evening, but it also gives a subtle hint that the caller should not expect to get live assistance from a full complement of employees. (In highly productive countries, such as Taiwan, you'll get a human answering the phone at any time of day or night, seven days a week.)

Providing a notion of time on toll-free calls also is a good idea. These days, long-distance calls are a fact of business, and toll-free numbers do not provide information about where the enterprise is located because the area code is generic (such as 800, which is the toll-free code for North America, and 0800, which is the toll-free code for all of southern Africa). Of course, you may want to tell the caller that it's "after hours," but you should still enable the caller to get some business done by routing the call to voice messaging or to a member of staff on night duty.

The seasonal phrase also can be alluring if used wisely and kept short. Many companies use the following phrase during November and December: "Good morning and happy holidays!"

If you really want to make an effort, you can record some holiday season background music in the greeting. One firm did this, and the firm's callers said it gave them the impression that everyone was in a good mood, so business must be good. A live telephonist cannot answer the telephone and have the CEO standing behind singing " 'Tis the season to be jolly, tra la la la la . . . ," but the CT systems can play this prerecorded song.

The other school of thought says not to use time in the salutation but simply to say "Hello." Citibank uses this practice. (I call the Citibank system a great deal to do a quick check-up of my account balances). But I find the single "Hello" unsettling. Many others would agree that this practice tends to encourage you to wait for the next word to make sure that you are not talking to a human before you launch into giving your account number.

If you do not want to convey time but instead the notion that you are open all day and night and all year round, then the hello greeting may be appropriate. If you transfer callers between several locations spread across several time zones, then time of day may not be necessary. (You may think you're calling California, but the British accent on the line gives away the actual situation. When I suspect that my call has been switched to a remote location, I always ask the representative where he or she is located. I often am amazed at where my call ends up; often it's in Ireland because Ireland offers good incentives as a place to set up a call center.)

APPLYING CHARACTER, IMAGE, AND IDENTITY

You need to be aware of the character, image, and identity you're portraying to the caller (and this applies to mailbox greetings; see Chapter 13). In this area, you'll need to apply a bit of logic and common sense here rather than take any specific advice from me, except for the following consideration:

Putting all political correctness debates aside, if you feel that using the voice of a particular sex or race in a salutation is more appropriate for what you're trying to achieve, then do it. But whatever you decide to do, do it wisely and do some research first. What image are you portraying if you answer the call at a women's services enterprise, say a baby-care clinic or gynecology center, in a male voice? You have to evaluate your own situation because every situation is different.

One veteran of the voice recording and prompt business is Richard Snider, the president of Marketing Messages in Newton, Massachusetts. Richard has been consulting for the IVR and audiotext industry for more than ten years and hesitated to lay down any rules, except to say that one generally accepted theory is that "for a comforting, welcome, or helpful image, use a female voice; for authority, use a male voice." But he adds that this rule is not a hard and fast one and that "one huge financial services company who thought a male voice would sound more authoritative when relating financial information later changed its mind."

AVOIDING FOOLING THE CALLER

Some systems try to sound as human-like as possible, but there's really no need to follow this practice. It won't take the caller long to figure out that the voice belongs to a computer, so go straight from the salutation to the menu options. Programming the salutation to say "How may I help you?" is redundant and wastes time and may leave some callers feeling patronized and angry.

THROWING OUT THE GUMPH

At this stage, it's vitally important that you offer service options and allow callers to make their selections with haste. I prefer not to use any gumph (promotional hype) and risk violating the six-second rule. If you must have gumph at some time during the call — and often you must — leave it to the on-hold facility or the enterprise information service.

By taking out the gumph, you will process calls faster and save time for the caller. It's a hassle for the callers to be required to listen to promotional hype about the service or the enterprise repeatedly and for eternity (every time they call). Besides, the callers that know your system will just drill past that $10,000 promotional recording that the consultant convinced Kenny Rogers to do.

So why not leave the gumph in there then? Although callers can cut through any greeting or message and drill down to the service that they need, new callers, and sometimes even the regular ones, don't always know this fact. Even the customers who have been advised of this technique in your letters and introductory promotions (we'll get to this later) may forget how to do it, particularly if they call so many other systems that they can't remember what can be done where and when in the script. Instead, they wait for the gumph to finish, which can be annoying.

Also, not knowing about the capability to cut through these messages (which, by the way, is an essential feature of every CT system) may not even be the customer's problem. During the past five years, I have seen many people wait for the initial prompts to finish before they start drilling down to the services they need even though they know that they can bypass these prompts. Why? Because so many systems failed when the customers tried to bypass them before that the callers are too petrified to do something that will foul up their calls.

For example, many repulsive systems respond with "Invalid entry" or shunt a customer into something akin to Dante's Hell. The caller often is told to hit any key to stop the prompt but hears something such as "If you've completed the action, press pound" when he or she follows the instructions. Then the caller hits pound and again hears "Invalid entry" or "That extension does not exist." What is the caller supposed to do next?

Here's another reason to avoid using gumph in your initial salutation: Ask yourself whether the human telephonist answers the telephone and reads three minutes of promotional hype before saying "How may I direct your call?" NO. So, why should you make the computer do this?

Although quality of voice is important, the part of the script that prompts action requires critical attention. This part of the computer telephonist service can quickly destroy any good impression that the salutation may have created. Depending on what happens after the salutation, you could lose clients or gain new business.

Your next phrase should immediately indicate to the caller that he or she is dealing with a computer telephonist service by saying something like "You may enter an extension at any time during this call" (if appropriate to do so).

Thus far, the greeting that I've talked about goes as follows: "Good Morning! Thank you for calling ABC Corp."

Pressing 0 for assistance

This line, which usually follows the salutation, may be the most trite expression in computer telephony. Why do I regard it as trite? Because everywhere in the world, 0 is the universal digit that callers press on a computer telephony system when they want to go directly to a live receptionist or assistant. In the past, systems have been so difficult to use and navigate that many callers learned to hit the 0 key as soon as the system answered. This practice was derived from dialing 0 for Operator, a facility provided by every telephone company in North America.

The problem here is not the phrase — including it in the script will not affect the call flow and only adds a second to the script. The problem here is in the switching. If the caller presses 0 and gets nothing, you're likely to lose the call. See the section on switching later in this chapter.

Dialing the extension now

As soon as the system finishes the salutation, it should prompt the callers who know the extensions that they want to reach to "dial the extension now." Only repeat callers with experience navigating your system will know that they can dial the extension at any time during the script. For first time and infrequent callers, you need a prompt that notifies callers — if this is what you want them to do — that they can dial the extension number if they have it. Otherwise, the callers simply have to listen to the entire script.

Remember that, in computer telephony in general and voice processing in particular, callers will listen to your instructions and do exactly what you tell them. I have never found an exception to this rule — as long as the instructions were within reason, of course. If you instruct the callers to key in a number that they have or know, they do it. If you instruct the callers to speak the number, they do it. If you instruct the callers to "speak louder, the computer can't hear you," they start talking louder. If you instruct the callers to make beeping sounds, many will do just that (remember Randy's cartoon on the opening page of this chapter).

It's best if you keep the prompt to enter the extension number as simple as possible: "If you know the extension number of the person with whom you wish to speak, enter it now."

Filtering callers

After you've scripted in the salutation and first routing prompts, go directly to the filtering options, and keep the list short. Don't keep it *too* short: A menu of one option is uncommon, so if you have one of these single option menus, you should have a good reason for it (touch-tone callers, press 1; rotary callers, hang up and go elsewhere).

Listing two options is okay, but three is a good number. Providing four options also is okay; five options, however, is pushing your luck; and providing more options borders on making your call-processing scenario repulsive and too complex for callers to use. Few companies have more than five departments that have strong calling groups.

The following example shows a pretty good menu:

> For sales, press 1.
>
> For product support, press 2.
>
> To check on the status of your order, press 3.
>
> To repeat the options, press 4.

Because callers cannot see the menu, they must rely on hearing and memory to navigate your system. You must remember this fact and plan your system accordingly. Have your people try out the menus and see if they can remember all the prompts on the first call.

I've seen dozens of situations where callers get to the fourth option and decide that an earlier option actually was the best choice for what they need to do. By that time, however, the probability that the caller remembers what the first option was is only around 25 percent. The probability of the caller remembering the first option by the time he or she reaches the fifth option drops to 10 percent. Add to that probability a situation in which you have tense callers or callers under pressure of time and place, and your caller stands virtually no chance of remembering the first option on the list.

Most callers can remember three options without too much difficulty. If you do offer more than three menu choices and do not offer an option to replay the menu, you risk losing the caller at this point. Using the last option to repeat the menu is the alternative to losing the caller or having them take a chance on picking the correct menu option and becoming more frustrated. If you're filtering callers, remember that you are asking them to do some work that is supposed to make life easier for them and your staff (both must benefit). So, be considerate and offer as much help as possible — consider all the things that can go wrong, and take action to correct the problems you encounter while testing your system.

USING MULTIPLE LEVELS

If you have several departments or facilities in your enterprise and you want to filter callers into more groups (let's say nine groups, for example), take your callers down one more layer and limit each layer to three options. When you try to take callers down further levels, you're no longer performing a service, and callers are unlikely to stay tuned.

Again, you should give callers the option of replaying the menu. At this level, however, you also need to offer the caller another option: going back to the previous menu. Thus, you will be offering the caller five menu options, as follows:

> For support on product X, press 1.
>
> For support on product Y, press 2.
>
> For support on product Z, press 3.
>
> To repeat this menu, press 4.
>
> To go back to the previous menu, press 5.

Using a whole series of cascading menus is a bad idea in my view. I don't even like using a second level of menus unless it's absolutely necessary. Yet I have called companies that have installed a system with dozens of levels.

OFFERING CLEAR CHOICES

Make sure that your callers can determine which services they gain access to when they select a particular option. Your system violates the six-second rule if callers press a digit and find that it doesn't provide the service they expected it to. Different financial services can sound the same if you're not careful when you name options. When scripting your call flow, make your menu choices as clear as spring water and use different nouns to describe different services. For example, the following menu is confusing:

> For customer relations, press 1.
>
> For customer support, press 2.
>
> For customer satisfaction, press 3.

A better menu would be this one:

> For customer relations, press 1.
>
> For product support, press 2.
>
> For sales, press 3.

Notice that these menu items consist of two parts: the "for" phrase (for sales) and the "press" phrase (press 1). I've tried transposing these two parts so that the menu item reads "Press 1 for sales." It's workable, but I have found the first structure to be the best of the two, especially in long sentences. The following example is rather stressful for the caller:

> Press 1 if you have your forms but do not know how to fill in the red section.
>
> Press 2 if you do not have your forms and need to be transferred to the fax-on-demand delivery system.

By the time you've figured out which choice corresponds with your needs, you've forgotten which number to press. Word order is important for clarity, so list the service first and then tell the caller what number to press.

Here's another dilemma to consider regarding your menus: What should come first — the menu options or the self-routing service?

That depends on the nature of the enterprise or facility servicing the caller. If most of your callers have established relationships with particular employees, consider placing the self-routing prompt before the menu options. Conversely, if most of your callers need a service rather than an individual, it pays to place the self-routing prompt after the menu.

In both scenarios, one important rule applies: The caller must be able to dial an extension number in the middle of a menu. Your CT software should be sophisticated enough to quickly determine whether a caller is selecting a menu option or entering an extension. If the caller presses a single digit and pauses, the software should be able to read the corresponding menu option and handle the call accordingly. Likewise, a quick succession of key presses should prompt the software to buffer and read the digits, retrieve the extension or station number from the database, and transfer the call.

You may be wondering, does your organization need these services? In many cases, there's no real need to filter callers; the menus are there more to impress callers than to serve some other purpose. A small company whose employees all perform the same tasks is a good example.

However, if *your* small company has a good reason for using menus to filter callers, then do it. Using a menu does have benefits. Firstly, a menu can give callers the impression that your enterprise is bigger than it really is — your callers may think you are a sprawling concern in a fancy building, when in reality your work force consists of five software gurus cooped up in an attic.

Secondly, if you wear several hats on the job, menus can provide inbound notification (on your screen or on the telephone) of calls that can put you in the right frame of mind to handle the calls more effectively. For example, suppose that your system displays the message "Inbound call for customer complaints" when your phone rings. Now you can answer the phone as follows: "Hi, thank you for calling the people who care! How may I serve you on this beautiful day?"

USING MULTIPLE LANGUAGES

Some companies reside in multilingual societies; if this situation describes your company, you should determine the dominant language and greet your callers in this language first. For most situations, using multiple languages is not necessary. But if you have many callers that speak a different language, you may want to provide a second language as a menu option.

Filtering calls based on language is a disconcerting service that should be used very carefully. Although you may be tempted to provide more language options with your system, your rule of thumb should be to provide the same languages you did before installing the CT system. If you previously answered the telephone in English and the company employees only speak English, it's not smart to provide the caller with 170 language options ("For Zulu, press 95; for Swahili, press 97 . . ."). Your callers will expect you to answer in that language when the call transfers to your extension.

For example, I had a client in South Africa who wanted to provide five languages in his system. (He said that this was the politically correct thing to do now that Apartheid was over.) I pointed out that the telephonist who answered the phone before the installation of the CT system only spoke two languages and was really only fluent in English. If the caller selects Zulu and eventually gets an English-speaking representative, what good does that option do? I also knew that although most South Africans can speak as many as ten languages, they all speak English.

Don't waste a caller's valuable time by forcing him or her to listen to a list of several languages. Two languages is generally the maximum number of options that you should provide in a multilingual society. In this situation, have your system answer in the main language of your company's location and then offer a second language only if you get several callers who speak that language.

For example, the language of choice in the U.S. is English; however, several companies in Miami have predominantly Hispanic clienteles, so they greet callers in Spanish and then offer the option to switch to English. (Some Miami-based companies later dropped the Spanish option at the request of their English-speaking customers who felt patronized.)

DEALING WITH THE INACTIVE CALLER

If a caller doesn't respond to the provided choices in a call-processing situation, your system should be able to drop the call to a live telephonist. DSP cards listen for a predetermined period of silence or inactivity at a certain point in the script and then assume that the caller cannot make a selection. Don't invest in a system that cannot perform this standard feature; even the less productive systems can act on a "time-out" period at the end of the script.

Many callers expect to be transferred to a live representative if they do nothing, so it's not wise to route a caller to another automated location after a period of inactivity. Therefore, when building menus, it's okay to offer just two menu choices and then have a third — albeit unmentioned — option that transfers the caller to a live telephonist.

If you offer the option to repeat the menu and nothing happens, it's particularly important to connect the caller directly to a person. Do not repeat the menu; more than likely the caller has a pulse or rotary dial telephone or is disabled and requires live assistance. Repeating the prompts only serves to annoy the caller in this situation.

You should keep in mind that not all your callers will be calling from modern telephones. For example, my cousins Ellen and Jake Azrael have more telephones per square foot than anyone I know, and Jake seems to have a fetish for the old, rotary-dial models.

Although pulse dialing is now the exception rather than the rule in the U.S., the same cannot be said for other modern-day cities such as London, Tel Aviv, Johannesburg, and Lisbon. In these parts of the world, pulse dialing is still very common.

As a result, some U.S. companies still receive a high percentage of callers from pulse-dial phones. These callers have to be moved through the prompts as quickly as possible because rotary callers can't use the menus and must wait for the time-out to land at the live telephonist. To speed this process, some companies filter callers by prompting touch-tone callers to press 1. ("If you are calling on a touch-tone phone, press 1; all other callers please hold and a live attendant will be with you shortly.") After this prompt, the system can process calls with only touch-tone callers in mind.

The only problem with this prompt is that it tempts dishonest touch-tone callers *not* to press 1. Also, prompting callers to press 1 if they are calling from touch-tone phones is, in many cases, an exercise in redundancy. You may find that 99.9 to 100 percent of your callers are using touch-tone anyway. Also, if a caller doesn't have a touch-tone phone and intends to call frequently, he or she will probably get one after having to wait through the menu several times.

You do have another alternative available — you can use a system that has pulse detection. I don't recommend using this detection method in the modern CT era, however, simply because it does not work consistently. Trying to have a pulse "conversation" with a computer telephony system can be a nightmare for many callers; few people want to endure the torture. For IT it's often a nightmare. In high-volume situations, you will discover just how valuable each port is (see Chapter 17), and rotary interaction chews up ports fast and leads to call blocking. Even using pulse-to-tone converters does not solve the time factor; besides, it's expensive and sends the cost of a computer telephony system soaring. I have found myself in many situations where knowledgeable workers using pulse dial telephones (because their local PBX interprets the pulses as requests for service) actually disconnect themselves from the remote computer telephony system because their PBX mistook the dialing as a request for service. This was true for users in the U.K. and South Africa.

USING A COMPANY DIRECTORY

Two methods exist that you can use to assist callers in self-routing when they do not know the number of the extension they want to reach: a company directory or dial-by-name service. Modern CT systems give you the capability to do both.

A company directory is easy to set up. You simply record a list of names and extension numbers and enable the callers to enter the number when they hear it. But it presents some problems.

First off, it's not that easy to maintain, particularly if your company is fairly dynamic. The person maintaining the system has to re-record parts of the list every time a staff member leaves or moves to a different extension number. If your company experiences a large turnover of staff, you'll need to re-record the directory voice file from scratch or else it begins to sound like a riot, with the dozens of different voices. This task becomes more difficult if you have a large staff because you'll have to break down the files alphabetically.

Secondly, few people use the directory when you make it available, which makes creating and maintaining it a waste of time and tedious effort. The directories that I implemented in my earlier systems were hardly used, so I dropped the practice.

If you do decide to use this service, make sure that the software you buy can build this list automatically for you. Also, a short list of departments and services makes a better choice for a directory than an alphabetical listing of the staff.

The second option, the dial-by-name service, is easier to set up and maintain. The CT system database contains a list of all the users and their respective extension numbers. With a dial-by-name service, you get the correct extension number by simply entering the first few letters of the last name of the person you want to reach.

You run into problems when you have more than one employee with the same last name. When this happens, the system has to take up more of the caller's valuable time by prompting something such as "For Bob Smith, press 1; for Bill Smith, press 2." Again, your callers are more likely to make a bee-line for live assistance than endure such torture.

STICKING TO A FORMULA THAT WORKS

Once your callers become familiar with a system that works, do not change it. If you must change a system, make the changes subtly and stretch out the implementation over a long period of time. Otherwise, you will have to re-educate callers with costly promotional material because the change will impact the caller's ability to obtain the correct service as quickly as possible.

Remember that the callers who frequently interact with your enterprise will have a map of how your CT system works imprinted on their brains. If some lunatic with a burst of energy changes the whole system overnight, these callers end up doing the equivalent of groping around in the dark. This can turn your alluring enterprise into a repulsive gorilla of a company overnight.

For example, Rhetorex, Inc., one of the leading manufacturers of voice-processing boards, has used the same call-flow script since I first called the company in 1991, even though the system has been upgraded and new versions of the software added to it several times. When I called the company for some material for this book — the first time I had called in many months — nothing had changed. I knew where to find the directory, and the extension numbers I needed were the same. Like always, the system invited me in.

Rhetorex follows a tactic used by many CIOs and IT people, something I call the KISS principle: Keep It Simple, Stupid. If your customers cannot easily complete their calls, they will go away and you'll earn the reputation of being a repulsive enterprise.

I once read the following passages regarding computer telephony systems in an old issue of *Teleconnect* magazine, the paragon of telecommunications industry periodicals:

Choose any extension. They all say "The extension cannot be dialed at this time." It then gives you choices. Your best bet is 9 and then to hang up. If you dial 0 for the operator you are told "You can't leave a message, the system has no space left." You can't get through to anyone. It's impossible to speak to a live person. At least it was the day we called.

If you hit 0 to default to an operator, you are immediately cut off.

So, word does get around about poor computer telephony systems.

Here's an example of what *not* to do: One credit-card processing software company publishes a number that they require you to call to set up the package. This CT system prompts you to "Press 3 for validation." Know what happens next? This does: "Please hang up and dial 1-800 . . . ." When you dial the new 800 number, you get another system that goes through the same choices; when you press 3 here, you get another toll-free number to call — the third in the list. The only thing that did work was the "Press 0" option. To make matters worse, I later determined from the human telephonist that all three numbers were listed in the same building, in the same office, to the same CT machine. Enough said.

THE PILOT PROJECT

The most important exercise that you must go through when implementing a computer telephonist service for the first time — or even when changing a product or service — is the *pilot project*. The pilot project is essentially the phased implementation of a service and is a critical part of deploying computer telephony. A pilot project phase is especially important when callers will be directly affected by voice processing and computerized intervention in the call-completion process. (The pilot project described here is valid for all computer telephony services.)

The pilot project consists of several stages:

1. Testing the switching process

2. Service curves and reliability factors

3. Educating the staff

4. Educating the callers

5. Phased implementation

These stages are discussed in detail in sections that follow.

TESTING THE SWITCHING PROCESS

Your computer telephony system must send calls to the proper extensions or ACD services as soon as the callers make their choices. The minute you set up the system and enter all the names, extensions, and station numbers into the database, it's time to do a little switch testing.

No system should go live (process actual calls) without extensive testing. The test phase should begin as soon as the desirable script and voice prompts are in place. Your test phase should also take place over several days, if not weeks, to make sure that it's working the way you intend it. Otherwise, you risk losing callers.

The only testing that you can really do at your enterprise is to make sure that your system (in terms of script and so forth) works the way that it should. You cannot do any service curve or stress-level testing at the enterprise site because you need call volume for this, and your callers should not be your proverbial guinea pigs. (See the following section on service curves and reliability factors.)

Go through every extension number or service set up in the system, and make sure that you get the correct results. Too often, the IT people or consultants fail to check this and assume that the PBX will handle the calls. Do not assume that the list of extension numbers on the PBX was entered correctly or that your system will switch your callers to the intended party. Otherwise, your callers may end up at extensions that are incorrect, out of service, or simply unavailable, in which case they are met with silence or extension unavailable notification.

The most important services to test are the 0 key and what I call the "fall-through-to-live assistant" feature. These services provide the safety net for callers who cannot — whether willingly or unwilling — go anywhere but to the operator. For that reason, these two services need to work reliably and consistently.

Make sure that the people who receive these calls know what's required of them; they are the CT system's safety net, so to speak. If the call gets through to these workers' stations, it's inexcusable for a call to go unanswered. Calls can be easily "snatched" by dialing a call pick-up code (often you need to dial the extension that is ringing "off-the-hook"). Granted, telephonists, receptionists, and attendants are human, too; they need smoke breaks, refreshment breaks, and visits to the rest rooms from time to time. But if a call cannot be answered at one extension, the system should divert it to another station monitored by a living, breathing person. Someone should always be there, so insist that they do not all take breaks at the same time. Always — I repeat, *always* — back up the system with a live attendant during normal office hours. If you truly want to be the anywhere, anytime enterprise, then you need to back up the system with people 24 hours a day.

For example, the CIO and CEO of one of my first clients, Comprehensive Property Services, asked me to go over the live assistant part of the project with them. When I asked the CIO who would answer calls when the telephonist or other attending staff were busy with other calls or away from their desks, the CEO jumped in and said

"Me." That's how important the callers are to this organization. At another client, Workgroup Systems (one of Microsoft's leading resellers), the CEO designated the entire company for taking calls that fall out of the call-flow script.

The bottom line is this: The caller should never be told that the receptionist is unavailable or asked to "Please leave a message."

SERVICE CURVES AND RELIABILITY FACTORS

Few manufacturers of computer telephony systems publish sufficient service curve statistics and reliability information for their products. I have yet to come across the equivalent of the MTBF (mean time between failure) for the software and hardware in computer telephony systems.

However, if you want to process a large volume of callers, you need to make sure that the system is as reliable at processing 30 callers simultaneously as it is at processing 4 or 8. You have a slight catch-22 situation here because you won't know how the system shapes up until it either works or doesn't work. You definitely don't want to wait until you have 30 customers in the system to find out this information, especially if you're the consultant or IT guy or gal who will be responsible if the system *doesn't* work.

On most systems, pushing 30 ports in one PC is risky business. A great deal of debate is going on about the reliability of new-era computer telephony systems. In this regard, the old legacy systems were closed and proprietary, but at least they were reliable.

The most reliable system that I have encountered to date is Applied Voice Technology's CallXpress (I do not have shares in this company, nor am I selling this product) which runs on the old Microsoft version of OS/2 (Version 1.3). Even with CallXpress, I am hesitant to have more than 20 or 24 ports processing on one PC. This fact is not based so much on the service curve as on reliability. PCs break down, networks crash, and you don't want to risk losing 30 callers because of a system failure. I strongly recommend cascading PCs together and drawing up a redundancy and reliability plan (see Chapter 17 for more details).

EDUCATING THE STAFF

When I say educate the staff, I don't mean sending around a circular that says "Hi from your lovable IT manager. This is just a short note to tell you we are installing a computer telephony system in the office tonight and you're all expected to like it and know how to use it by noon tomorrow. Please pick up a user manual on the desk outside my office."

If you do this, you're walking the plank. Any consultant that proposes such a scheme *should* be fed to the sharks.

I also don't mean that you should worry about getting them on board now (selling the system to the users). It's a bit too late for that at the pilot project stage (see Chapter 16 for more details). The pilot project is something that members of the enterprise have been expecting for some time. The staff members who you select to involve in the pilot project should be fully briefed on what the system does and how it does it. Now is also the time to get your live safety net assistants into the act, explaining to them how the system works and what happens to callers when they press 0.

After you inform and train the pilot project team, it's time to begin the phased implementation. Do you go live at this stage? *NO.* Not before you educate the external environment — that is, your callers.

EDUCATING THE CALLERS

Educating your callers is necessary. Few companies do this — they just expect their callers to gleefully accept the new system that suddenly appeared at the other end of the line. Your callers — especially your most trusted and valuable clients — need to be prepared for the change and, in some cases, properly trained to use the system.

One way to do this is to send out a letter announcing the new system and the pilot project. In the letter, describe the phase-in strategy that you're using to implement the system. Tell your customers when the system will go live, how many lines will initially be serviced, and, most importantly, why you are implementing the system. Make sure that they understand the system is also for their benefit and that if anything does not please them, they must report this to you. Provide a mail box, physical address — even a secure meeting place in the park — where customers can give you honest and accurate feedback. You especially want to know about cases when they hit 0 . . . and got zero.

Also include a diagram in your letter that shows the call-flow script and the call path a caller will take to reach a particular station or service. Show the processing of the call, from the time the system goes off-hook to the switching process. Emphasize the "press 0" safety-switch option with several live representatives waiting at the end of the line.

In short, provide all options that the caller needs to know about. You should instruct your regular clients to keep this diagram close at hand because it provides a visual representation of the layout of your system. This layout will help callers *see* and navigate the call path.

If you have long-established clients or clients with large accounts, I recommend going out to their offices so that you can personally demonstrate how to navigate the new system. It would be nice if you could do this customer service bit for all your clients, but that's probably not possible.

When I first installed a CT system at the Johannesburg offices of Microsoft, I went to their important resellers and demonstrated the system to them. When they eventually encountered the new voice on the line, they knew exactly what was required, making the transition to this system somewhat painless (some pain is always involved — you just have to minimize it).

Printing up some informational cards for the benefit of your customers is a good idea. Many consultants do this only for the enterprise — they forget that the callers are also users. If you decide to do this task, make sure that the card provides sufficient information that is neither overpowering nor too complex to fathom. If your staff members shove these cards in their top desk drawers because they cannot understand them, what do you think your callers will do?

PHASED IMPLEMENTATION

Phased implementation, in a nutshell, is a strategy for implementing a new service or fundamental change while cushioning the shock to the existing systems and users.

In computer telephony, you have four distinct implementation areas:

+ Internal system implementation

+ Live system implementation as an overflow service behind the telephonist

+ Live system implementation parallel with telephonists

+ Live system implementation in front of telephonists

Internal system implementation. In this phase, the system is fully operational but is only used internally. Callers do not encounter the system; only a selected team of IT and general staff are allowed to "play" with the system as much as possible. For this to work, your staff must make a commitment to use the system to make interoffice and intradepartmental calls. This way, you give the employees involved in the pilot project a chance to make suggestions for implementing the system in other areas.

This phase encourages staff members to provide valuable information to the IT department because their lives are also on the line. The sales manager will be the first person to make sure that the system works, so there better not be any gremlins hiding in the system that could send important customers packing. The technical support people also will give the system the once-over. The customer service manager (as well as the CIO and the CEO) makes sure that technical support and service people are involved in the pilot project.

Live system implementation as an overflow service behind the telephonists. In this phase, you enable callers to get their feet wet by switching over a small number of lines to the computer telephony system. To do this, you simply reduce the load of calls handled by the current system and then flow the additional calls to the new computer telephony system. This phase enables you to watch two important activities: the caller's behavior when interacting with the new service and the behavior of the IT and IS systems affected by or integrated with the new system.

At this stage, you'll be carefully monitoring the paths of the calls moving through the system, the performance of the PBX, and so on. This phase is important because you'll see how your system reacts to a real call-processing load. Anything can go wrong at this stage: The PBX can suddenly bomb out; the whole lot can go dead on you; and so on. You want to be around if this happens and make sure that you get things back up ASAP. Here, at least, you will not inconvenience many people if the services crash.

The LAN people also will be watching closely as callers begin to populate the ports of the CT system. With LAN integration, you can't predict how existing systems will behave. While installing CallXpress3 at Microsoft, fellow consultant Gil Caplan and I were able to convince Microsoft to integrate one of its old operating systems (OS/2 Version 1.3) with a whopping NT network running several hundred NT and early Windows 95 clients. (Any later version of OS/2 was refused because they were true-blue IBM versions introduced in 1992 after the famous OS/2 split.)

Microsoft's systems are impressive, to say the least. At this particular site, the remote access server (RAS) was crowded with callers accessing the networks, hard-disk arrays, and a CD-ROM array containing about 30,000 MB of information and software. That's when the incredible happened. As we switched on the telephony server, the RAS collapsed. (You can imagine what happened then — you would have thought the third world war had started.)

After everyone calmed down, Gil — perhaps one of the most experienced network specialists in the world — said, "I doubt the CT system caused the crash — it was just a coincidence that the RAS crashed at the same time we switched on the CT server." He was right. As I said earlier, anything can happen, so you want to be there for any event . . . to either allay fears or die like a hero.

Live system implementation parallel with telephonists. This phase is merely the process of increasing the system's inbound-call load. You can increase the load to the CT system by simply asking the human telephonists to answer less calls flowing to the PBX consoles. The CT system "feels" the calls in synch with telephonists and takes the callers who are not answered within the first three rings.

The nice aspect of this phase is that during dips in inbound-call traffic, the telephonists can leave the processing of calls to the CT system. The consoles can be completely abandoned during lunch, smoke, or coffee/tea breaks. You also can use this phase when you want to monitor the telephonists handling the calls in which callers have pressed the 0 (zero) option.

Live system implementation in front of telephonists. This is your final phase before complete roll-out of the system. Here, you give the CT system free access to all calls in front of the PBX consoles while putting the telephonists on standby. If any problems exist, you can simply switch off the system and have the human telephonists take the calls.

After the pilot project is complete, you can reprogram the PBX to pass all calls to the CT system's ports. Now you have your own CT baby.

SUMMARY

There are many reasons to install a computer telephonist service. In many cases, this decision is not so much a matter of justifying the need for computer telephony as determining the type of need. This critical service has now become as essential an item as the LAN. Many enterprises feel that the computer telephonist service (that is, the automated attendant) is the cost of doing business. In other words, they would not be in business without it.

In This Chapter

"Welcome to the Fantasy Hotline!
This call is $3.99 a minute.
But since this is a fantasy,
let's *pretend* the call is free
and we can talk for hours
without paying a cent!"

CHAPTER 9

AUDIOTEXT

One of the most popular and widely used computer telephony services is audiotext. Like voice mail, audiotext has been around for as long as humans have been able to digitize sound files and store them on a computer's hard disk. You could argue that audiotext's history stretches beyond the age of digitized media — in the early days of the premium rate business, people connected huge, reel-to-reel tape systems to telephone lines, although it was a costly and cumbersome means to play sound bites over the telephone.

Today, audiotext is a solid member of the computer telephony service domains, as the organizational chart in Figure 9-1 illustrates.

Audiotext or audiotex?

Many computer telephony gurus prefer to lose the *t* at the end of *audiotext* to form the term *audiotex*. It's believed that the *t* took a chop because audiotext suppliers wanted to draw out the connection with the term *videotex*, a service that really only took off in France.

The two terms are used interchangeably; however, I prefer to use the term *audiotext* so that I don't have to explain to South Africans, Australians, and the people of other remnants of the British Empire that the idea was not invented by a cowboy.

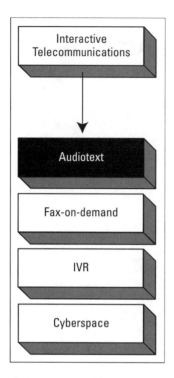

Figure 9-1: Audiotext is the interactive telecommunications service domain of computer telephony.

This chapter takes a closer look at audiotext and the elements of the voice (or sound) file, the medium behind audiotext services. Because the voice message consists of the same elements and format, the information provided here also applies to the discussion on voice messaging in the chapters that follow.

WHAT IS AUDIOTEXT?

Audiotext is the playing of pre-recorded sound files over the telephone to callers. No more, no less. Audiotext relies on the voice-processing functions of computer telephony hardware to play sound files.

Like voice-mail files, digital-signal-processing cards with built-in voice-processing technology play audiotext files to the caller over the telephone. (Although DSP is not the only technology that you can use to digitize sound, it's the most powerful technology around for this purpose.)

The complex technology involved in processing sound and content is completely transparent to your caller. As a result, callers use audiotext in much the same way that seeing people use their sight — they do not think about how they see, they just see. Callers do not have to enable anything on the telephone for audiotext. They just make a file selection and listen to its contents. That's some of the strategy stuff (like using audiotext services to provide callers with directions) that comes up later in this chapter; for now, however, let's talk about the makeup of a sound file or a voice file (basically these files are the same thing; they just have different content).

WHAT IS DIGITIZED SOUND?

A digitized sound file is an analog sound recording converted to a digital representation and stored on a magnetic medium, such as a hard disk. Figure 9-2 illustrates the different formats.

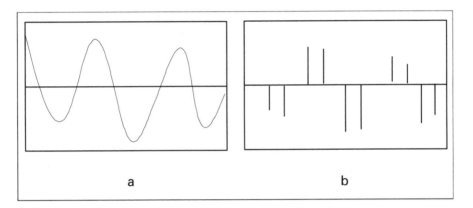

Figure 9-2: The analog wave form of a snippet of speech is illustrated by A; B illustrates the same snippet of speech in its digital form.

Analog recordings can be stored on magnetic tape, but this medium stores the recordings serially and only can play them back on a single device, such as a tape player. This arrangement severely limits using audiotext services on multiple lines. First off, the device has to rewind the tape to the beginning of the message as soon as the caller is done listening to the file on the telephone. This restriction takes away valuable time that the system could use to answer another call.

In this format, you also must deal with the many moving and degradable parts of the playing device: capstans, motors, rubber bands, and so on. Tape players cannot withstand the demands placed on the equipment by large numbers of callers — at least, not for very long. The risk of foul-up is extremely high, especially when the machine is under duress.

If you digitize a sound file, however, many callers can randomly access it by connecting to the computer via the voice-processing cards. These callers listen to sound files stored on a single hard disk. Your computer does not need to rewind a digitized sound file stored in this format, and the sound file can be started, stopped, fast-forwarded, and replayed at a rate several thousand times faster than the rate you get from a tape-playing machine.

The voice-processing hardware then copies the digitized files into memory in real time, so many people can listen to the same sound file although they may be at different points in the content. This capability means that you do not need to make another copy of the file in order to service a large number of users simultaneously. Of course, the original file can be cloned in real time for as many callers that need to access it.

Your only limitations will be in the computing power and distribution of computer resources over several computers and the bandwidth that the LAN provides. Thus, if your audiotext application calls for several hundred files, you can meet this requirement with one decent hard disk (500MB or more) instead of several hundred tape players.

Sound files are identical in makeup in that they are a collection of 1s and 0s (binary data that's treated differently by various devices). The voice message files that you leave in a person's mailbox have this same make-up as well.

The old days of tape-played sound files are almost over. I say almost because many modern-day situations still use the technology, including domestic answering machines. Tape-played sound files are not limited in terms of the reproduction quality of the digitized sound, but rather in the way that they manage (juggle) large numbers of files and the available editing software.

Figure 9-3 depicts one such editing program, a popular shareware editing suite called Cool Edit. It was written by David Johnston, and if you want me to send you a demonstration copy, drop me a note at `js@wizzkids.com`.

My last days in daily news reporting provide a good example of the problems that tape-played sound files pose. I was working for an independent radio station in Johannesburg as the night news editor. At the time, South Africans were still living in the dark age of apartheid. My job was to interview people over the telephone and record the conversations on a huge, reel-to-reel system. After the interview, I edited the sound bites by cutting and splicing the tape, editing conversation bits into a usable clip, and then copying these slices to a tape cartridge, or cart. (I learned a great deal from watching the "Iron Force" in action in *Mission: Impossible* reruns — how to cut out unwanted words, sighs, and heavy breathing.)

This format, however, provided a wide margin for error; if you consider the pressure of working for a radio station's newsroom — airing news every 30 minutes — you can probably imagine the foul-ups that happen. The day that the station's newscaster mixed up my sound bite from an interview of an ultra-right-wing party leader with a story about a 50-year-old elephant suffering from diarrhea at the Johannesburg zoo was the day I first had thoughts about changing my career to information technology. (The station manager agreed.)

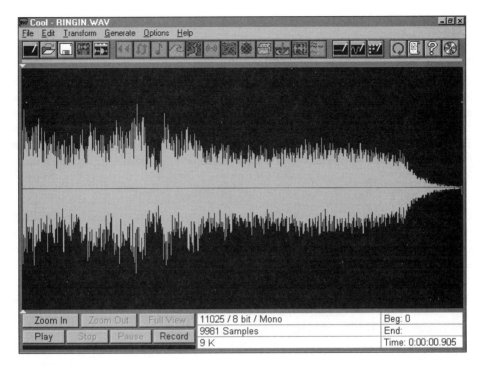

Figure 9-3: Software for the editing and managing of digitized audio is plentiful and mature, such as this shareware product called Cool Edit.

I had simply mixed up the labels on the tapes. I knew that there had to be a better way of recording, storing, editing, and playing recorded sound than the method my station was using. For example, every time that you played a tape cart, you had to rewind it. This task wasted valuable time, especially when you only had a few minutes to go before news time. Many newscasters, embarrassed by foul-ups similar to the one described earlier, try to make sure that they have the right carts in the right order before news time, but they don't always have the time to do a double check.

One solution would have been to use a graphical user interface to work with the files. If all the files were accessible from a GUI, playing each file would have been a simple matter of a double click.

APPLICATIONS FOR AUDIOTEXT

Computer telephony and its audiotext service enable users to play files of information to several concurrent callers while working with just one file. It also enables the user to copy files to distributed computer telephony servers. Are there uses for this service? There sure are.

The most obvious use deals with electronic publishing: the premium rate services or pay-per-call industry. These systems, which you can call up to glean information such as "The loosest slots in Nevada," "100 golf courses O.J. has played on," and "How to make $1,000 a day doing nothing," are audiotext systems.

This industry has been so aggressive that many countries have legislated it heavily to control abuse, fraud, and the proliferation of pornography. With everyone connecting to the Internet, lawmakers started rethinking some of these laws. In many countries, audiotext abuse led to the demise of all public audiotext services; the situation became so bad that the governments decided to close down the lines permanently. That's a shame because audiotext can be a wonderful public service when used correctly. One reason why the responsible electronics publishers floundered was that they were unable to bill their callers when the telephone companies quit including premium-rate billing with regular telephone service billing.

South Africa is a good example of a place with an audiotext premium-rate industry disaster. The one and only telephone company in South Africa (Telkom), once wholly government-owned, did not have decent billing technology in place, which tempted some vendors of audiotext technology to take advantage of their customers. One audiotext business owner set up a computer telephony system for Telkom that automatically called his own audiotext lines, running up fantastic bills that Telkom, in turn, had to pay him. This little scam went on for quite a while before Telkom realized what was happening. The government shut down the young premium-rate industry because of an incredible amount of similar fraud that would have ruined Telkom if it had continued.

Lots of audiotext success stories exist, however. An outstanding audiotext service can be found in the U.S. Yellow Pages. This service is known as Consumer Tips. Under each service category, the directory lists a telephone number that you can call for general information. Say that you want to rent a car. The automobile category includes a Consumer Tips entry exclusively devoted to this service. You dial the number and enter a number code related to the information you are looking for. The menu sounds something like this:

> Enter 1647 for information on where to rent.
>
> Enter 1648 for reasons to rent.
>
> Enter 1649 for insurance of rental automobiles.
>
> Enter 1650 in the event of an accident.

These services are usually sponsored by the vendors and service providers who advertise in the Yellow Pages. The computer telephony system can transfer you to a sponsoring vendor in the middle of the voice file.

AUDIOTEXT AND INFORMATION EXCHANGE

I concentrate on the realm of enterprise information and information exchange next. You can use audiotext to save time and resources. Some people must repeat snippets of information to callers several times a day — the number of times is astonishing. This information may range from the most basic information to important instructions or directions.

SALUTATIONS

If your people work in sales rooms, they probably say something like "Good morning, thank you for calling . . ." several hundred times a day. If your company takes 1,000 calls a day and it takes two seconds to greet each caller, 33 minutes of your workers' time is being devoted each day to this task. An audiotext system could greet callers for you and free up your workers to concentrate on other tasks.

Does that add up to savings and money? Sure — after all, time is money. I wouldn't mind saving ten minutes of stress on my voice box per day. I can use that time to finish a few sentences (and maybe wrap up another sale). Say good-bye to another caller. Swallow some lunch. As you can tell, the benefits all add up.

Telephony services, which are built into Windows 95 (thanks to Microsoft's TAPI), provide a great answering service by using a dialer and audiotext. The dialer mentioned in Chapter 5 can answer the telephone for you, using a device like Comdial's PATI, and play any audiotext file you choose to greet the caller. In my quest to preview the TAPI-compliant Visual Voice (a computer telephony, visual software development platform from Stylus Innovation), this capability was the first feature I wanted to use. Again, if this nifty feature grabs your imagination, I will send you a shareware copy of the software. You just need a TAPI-compliant dialer or modem.

DIRECTIONS

Providing directions daily can be a killer on the enterprise. The process is simple, but employees still spend as much as five minutes on the phone, several times a day, providing people with directions. For this reason, I always insist that my consulting clients record an audiotext file that provides directions to its location.

An audiotext file works well for this situation. If a caller phones to get directions, the telephonist puts the caller on hold and transfers the call to the audiotext service on the CT server. The audiotext system provides the desired information; then the caller can prompt it to replay the information (if they still have a problem) or divert to a fax-on-demand service to get a map.

I introduced the audiotext directions service to one of my clients, a real-estate services company that offered training courses on processing mortgages. The telephonists were receiving hundreds of calls from clients who needed directions to get to their classes. This caused a problem because by tending to these calls, the telephonists were putting other callers on hold, abandoning people in the reception area, and experiencing a steep decline in productivity. One telephonist complained that she couldn't get any work done and needed a temp to help out during busy days.

My solution was to record several audiotext files that provided directions to the firm from different routes. The enterprise inserted a menu option in the CT main menu that said "For directions to our facility, press 4." The next menu provided options based on route: "If you're coming on the M1 South, press 1. If you're coming on the N3 East, press 2," and so on. The audiotext system read the instructions to the caller slowly and clearly, and the caller could repeat the directions if he or she didn't get all the information the first time.

After it was installed, this service cut down 75 percent of the telephonist's calls. Some callers opted to leave a message after the audiotext service and have a map faxed back to them. The service also referred people to product literature containing a map and directions. At least five percent of the callers abandoned their calls after realizing they already had a map in their materials.

Some companies that invest millions in computer telephony overlook this small option when building their menus, but providing it makes a company that much more attractive to customers. An audiotext service running after hours makes the enterprise accessible 24 hours a day. People who have early morning appointments will not find someone there to call for directions, but they will appreciate having the audiotext service as a substitute. I've said it before and I'll say it again — with a computer telephony system, your company becomes the anywhere, anytime enterprise.

REPETITIVE PRODUCT OR SERVICE INFORMATION

Greetings and directions aren't the only examples of information that is given out repeatedly. Lots of other informative stuff exists that your staff spends valuable time repeating to volumes of callers. Like the preceding examples, audiotext can (and should) provide this information, too.

PRODUCT OR SERVICE DESCRIPTIONS

An audiotext file that provides information on a business or investment opportunity is a good example of an audiotext system that can help an enterprise reduce the amount of time its employees have to spend on the phone.

I advised a Florida business broker to invest in a four-line CT system to handle the hundreds of calls it received daily regarding businesses for sale. Most callers were inquiring about the 10–20 businesses advertised in the classifieds. My suggestion was to record a description of each business and place a corresponding CT menu number in the classified ad. When callers called the service, they entered the listed number and listened to a description of the business for sale. (The broker didn't have to use sterling recordings; employees with nice voices did the trick.) After listening to the description, callers could repeat the information; if they were interested in the opportunity, they could press 0 to reach a broker in a small, automatic-call-distributor (ACD) group.

The broker saved hours of time that his employees would have spent filtering the callers, and the representatives saved their voices (before the audiotext system arrived, each had to repeat a four-minute description of a business as many as 20 times a day). Also, the system weeded out callers who were only mildly interested in the businesses, enabling the brokers to treat the callers who selected the 0 key as possible buyers. If your firm has a similar setup, an audiotext system can provide these benefits for your company, too.

CONFIGURATION AND ENABLING INSTRUCTIONS

Seagate Electronics provides another good example of how to use audiotext wisely. The company manufactures computer hardware and is one of the leading (if not the leading) hard disk suppliers. Its product line ranges from older 20MB models to models that can hold over 1GB of information.

To give you a little background on the product, every hard disk has settings that the user must enter into the motherboard CMOS (a memory chip where hardware information resides). When you install a new hard disk in a computer, this information has to be entered correctly; otherwise, the computer cannot communicate with the hard disk. The information contains the number or sectors, landing zones (where the heads rest during power-down or idle time), and cylinders.

Because it's human nature to lose things, thousands of novices and systems integrators call Seagate every year to get this information after losing the installation guides. Seagate installed an audiotext system to manage the related call load for information. Thus, when you call the Seagate audiotext system, it prompts you to enter your hard disk's model number. The model number activates a corresponding audiotext file that describes the proper setup and installation for the product.

I suspect that Seagate will keep this information on audiotext even after it becomes accessible from the Internet. After all, you can hardly access a Web page with your PC when the information you seek is needed to get your computer up and running in the first place.

IMPLEMENTING AUDIOTEXT

Audiotext is not a difficult service to implement. When you invest in a CT system, it should provide you with the basic features for using audiotext. You should make sure that your system includes the following options:

✦ **The capability to configure any number of audiotext files.** If the system is set up to detect five digits, then you can feasibly publish 99,999 audiotext files. Every good CT system has a numbering scheme for every service or a flow scheme that points the caller to the file and then plays it. For example, you assign a number to a file ready for caller access; when the caller enters the number, the audiotext file plays immediately. This number can be directly assigned to the file or be a pointer to the file.

✦ **VCR or cassette-tape player type controls.** As Figure 9-4 shows, the CT system must give the caller the option to fast forward, rewind, (usually in five-second increments), stop, pause, and resume (usually the second press of the pause key) the audiotext message while the file is being played. You are essentially turning the telephone keypad into VCR-like controls. Your CT system should enable you to set up these audiotext controls so that you can map them to any number on the telephone keypad (and allow you to disable the control in certain cases).

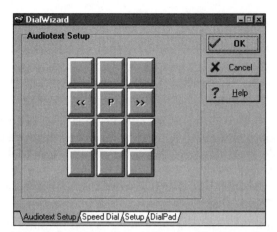

Figure 9-4: The caller can listen to files as well as rewind, fast-forward, and pause them from the keypad.

Consider this example: "To talk to a live representative now, press 1." You could place this option in the middle of the audiotext file as the Yellow Pages Consumer Tips example (described earlier) lets you do. The caller is able to reach the sponsoring companies from the audiotext service without dialing another phone number. "This Consumer Tip information is sponsored by AA Car Rental; to talk to a representative now, press 1."

✦ **The capability to integrate audiotext service with other telephony services.** You can integrate audiotext services with messaging, IVR, fax, and call-processing services of the CT system. That is, while the audiotext message plays, the caller should be able to transfer to a live representative or (ACD) gate, request a fax, request additional data, or communicate information.

✦ **High-quality sound recording and playback.** Your CT system should include tools (editing suites) and hardware to make high-quality audiotext files. If possible, invest in a CT system (or platform) that enables you to digitize recordings in the Microsoft WAV file format in addition to the proprietary format (every system has its own format) of the voice-processing platform. The reason for using WAV is that, as noted earlier, many superb WAV editors are on the market.

✦ **The capability to transfer callers to audiotext services from the main system.** Extensive audiotext services should not be offered as options on the general public reception lines because it makes the menu long and cumbersome (see Chapter 8). But you can include the service as a main menu option. If you need to include audiotext services on the general public lines, offering one audiotext file — such as directions to the office — or a menu option that diverts the caller into audiotext services is available. For example:

- For sales, press 1.

- For marketing, press 2.

- For information on our products and services, press 3.

The third option diverts the callers to audiotext services where they can enter published numbers or select a file from a short list of options.

In early 1995, I consulted again for Telkom, the public telephone service provider in South Africa. Telkom's IT department in Pretoria has a large field staff (several hundred employees), and it runs a very busy help desk for employees having problems with office equipment, computers, or the network.

When a circuit goes down, the field technicians call in to find out when services will be restored, repairs made, and generally whatever information they can. They may even convey information that can assist in correcting the problem.

We decided to install audiotext services so that the help desk could post information regarding the nature of certain problems and when it expected to have the problems fixed. The service reduced traffic to the help desk's live attendants by as much as 95 percent.

The system's design enabled a help-desk attendant or a technician out in the field to call a voice-message facility and leave a message concerning the problem. The facility enabled the person leaving the message to update it from time to time and to record it from a remote location.

AUDIOTEXT TIPS

Like any good service, a few variables exist that you can control to optimize your system for audiotext. The following sections provide a few tips that you should follow to get the most from audiotext.

LENGTH

Audiotext files should not be longer than four minutes at best. If your file plays longer than that, the listener begins to tire and will abandon the call before reaching the end of the file. Breaking up large amounts of material into several files and cascading them together, almost like chapters in a book, is a good idea. O.J. Simpson's audiotext service (if he had decided to run one, which I think he did) covering the so-called trial of the century might have gone like this:

Thank you for calling 1-900-THEJUICE. This call is costing you $1.75 a minute.

If you do not agree with the verdict, press 1.

If you do agree with the verdict, press 2.

If you think you know who the guilty party is, press 3.

For information about licensing the name O.J. and The Juice, press 4.

To listen to the options again, press the star.

This modular approach would be far better than providing one long text file.

QUALITY

The best quality recordings are only as good as the telephone circuit's frequency range (between 480 Hz and 3,850 Hz) in terms of the speech and fidelity performance that the sound board or voice-processing component provides. This fact leads many people to ask: "Why do you need to record prompts or files in a studio then?"

The reasons are simple: Firstly, recording studios and other soundproof booths, such as those found at radio stations, block out audio material that you cannot hear but that exists in a "quiet room." If you examined the analog wave form of the recording on a scope or waveform editor, you would be astonished to see the number of extraneous sounds that crept into the recording.

Secondly, recording studios are controlled environments and the equipment used creates the truest recording of the voice and any associated sounds that you want to use. With high-quality professional analog recordings, you now can work in a comfortable environment to transfer the recording to the digital representation for your audiotext project.

Thirdly, with the assistance of a professional recording artist and sound engineer, you gain access to expensive technology such as high-quality microphones and headphones. Also, by using a professional voice artist, you benefit from his or her experience in vocal technique and dialogue.

It is not a good idea, especially in a multi-ethnic society like the U.S., to use an accent that is linked to any region of the nation. For example, southern accents are not wise choices for general audiotext publishing, unless your audiotext service is offering the equivalent of "100 ways to make gumbo or jambalaya." Professional voice artists can change their accents easily enough to render speech that is "American" in accent and representative of the nation, not a particular culture or creed.

While doing audiotext recordings for a client offering a service in the U.K. and South Africa, I was specifically asked to provide an American voice artist. The client felt that because the products and services being offered were made in America, an American accent would help promote the "made in America" quality being reinforced in the documentation.

I could not find an American voice artist in the time given. I then noticed in the "catalog of voices" that several artists described their abilities as "can do American (Brooklyn, Deep South, and so on), British (Cockney, and so on), French, Italian, Greek . . ."

and so on. We thus found an American voice artist for our client, and I learned a great deal about the voice artist profession.

Voice artists also know how to breathe while reading the scripts and how to place less or more emphasis on words, phrases, and certain letters that cause problems once digitized, such as the "S" sound.

One quick word of advice regarding voice artists: Make sure that he or she is healthy when recording your scripts. In one case, I used an artist who failed to tell me that she had caught a cold. Nobody noticed a problem until we finished the final recording and handed the tape to the sound engineer for digitizing. He came back later saying that the recordings were unusable and that, from the quality of the digitized recordings, it was quite evident that the voice artist was having trouble breathing.

On another occasion, we used a voice artist who — for some reason — salivated excessively. Our sound engineer had to spend a whole day cutting out clicks, pops, and clucking sounds that were clearly visible in the visual voice editor.

It also pays to get started with the voice artist first thing in the morning so that the artist's voice is fresh.

RULES FOR USING AUDIOTEXT

Many applications exist where you should consider using audiotext, and also many situations where using it is inappropriate. You also need to consider a number of facts when using audiotext to convey information:

✦ **Length.** Use audiotext over the printed word (whether screen-based, such as e-mail, or published in paper-form) when the file length makes for comfortable listening. If you use audiotext for anything longer than four minutes, you run the risk of the caller abandoning the call. Files that contain too much information are not a good idea for audiotext; other mediums, such as printed documents (tsk, tsk) or a document on the World Wide Web (yea!) would be a better choice.

✦ **Updating the contents.** Audiotext files can be more costly and time-consuming to maintain and update (especially if you're running a professional service). If the file content changes frequently or the material is likely to become dated soon, it may be better to stick to documents. You can bend this rule for some situations (such as the Telkom example discussed earlier) where small, informative files of information have to be updated several times a day. In this case, the message and not the information is the important factor.

✦ **Access.** Audiotext makes perfect sense in situations where the telephone is the only interface to the information. The Yellow Pages Consumer Tips idea or the audiotext services of many newspapers are ideal candidates in that the reader is scanning a "hard" medium and all that the reader must do to get to the promoted information is pick up the phone and dial a few numbers.

✦ **Catering to impulsive action.** Clearly, you won't succeed in getting anyone to log on to their Internet host, launch a Web Browser, and surf over to the home page on the Web just to read a snippet of casual information. Nor will your readers send away for a snippet of information that they want on the spur of the moment. For catering to quick impulse actions, audiotext is a great service. In fact, this area is where all aspects of CT shine.

✦ **Conveying information.** Be careful not to overburden the caller by requiring him or her to write down tons of information. If you have a great deal of information that you want callers to write down, such as addresses, telephone numbers, or access codes, it may be better to convey it via fax-on-demand or the World Wide Web.

Nothing is more frustrating for a caller than missing vital information because he or she couldn't find a pen or failed to hear a word accurately. Nobody likes to backtrack, especially on the telephone. Callers who miss information in an audiotext service are more likely to abandon the call than to try to figure out how to loop back to it, particularly if this process is not readily apparent. Also, do not assume that all callers will be able to write down the information (they may be handicapped or not have writing material handy).

Instead, publish information that callers find easy to memorize. A description of your enterprise (perhaps a few words from your founding statement) may be fun in audiotext; a description of the telephony interface on a voice processing card would be horrid to listen to, though. An audiotext service that provides directions to your facility (like in a previous example) works great for people who know the city and its transport network. But, for example, I have never been to Timbuktu — thus, an audiotext file explaining how to get from the airport to the destination site would be pretty useless to me. Rather, I'd just have the cab driver call "control" and have an officer convey directions over the two-way radio.

TECHNICAL STRATEGIES IN ESTABLISHING AN AUDIOTEXT SERVICE

Like all good marketing or media campaigns, an audiotext campaign or service needs to be thought out and tested before you go live with it. Here are some considerations to take care of before you go live:

✦ **Transfer to agent.** If you allow callers to transfer out of the audiotext file to a live representative, make sure that the transfer actually works when they press that digit. It's frustrating when you press 1 to talk to an agent and end up in the telecosmos.

✦ **File-play controls.** Designate the keys 4, 5, and 6 as file-play controls. In other words, 4 makes a good "rewind five seconds" key, 5 makes a good "pause/ resume" key, and 6 makes a great "fast-forward five seconds" key. Why?

First of all, the digits are in the center of the telephone keypad, which many people prefer to press (yes, I have research supporting this fact) and all the digits are in one line. Second, keys 1 and 2 are reserved mostly for branching away from a point in the CT application, such as "Press 1 for yes, press 2 for no." If you use 3 as a file-play control key, you run the risk of the caller accidentally hitting the 2 key instead of the 3 key on the first line. Third, if you look down at the numeric keypad on your keyboard, you will notice that keys 4, 5, and 6 are in the middle while the other lines are transposed. Key 4 has a left arrow signifying "go back," and key 6 has a right arrow signifying "go forward." These marks are almost universal.

✦ **Replay the file.** If you want to enable callers to replay the file, make sure that only one key-press gets them back to the beginning of the *same* file. For example, if you say something like "To listen to the information again, press 9" and then take the caller back to an earlier option (hopefully not a menu), you run the risk of call abandonment. This is a no-no if your audiotext service is promoting a product that you want callers to buy when they transfer to the agent.

SUMMARY

Audiotext can become a very useful and powerful service for your enterprise, provided, as with other service domains, that you use it wisely. Audiotext also plays an important role as a supplementary service to the other computer telephony service domains, which I deal with in the next chapters. You also need to couple audiotext services with the computer telephonist or automated attendant services described in the preceding chapter.

So, where do you need to go from here?

✦ If you need to set up an audiotext service as soon as possible and plan to integrate fax services into the setup, you should read the next chapter (Chapter 10) and then move on to Chapters 15, 16, and 17.

✦ If you do not need fax, go directly to the chapters in Part III.

IN THIS CHAPTER

✦ A brief history of fax

✦ Why fax became the critical service for business

✦ Fax-on-demand and strategies for its implementation

Mrs. Branderbundt frequently whines in a high, squeaky tone and is often mistaken for an incoming fax transmission.

FAX-ON-DEMAND

One of the most popular computer telephony services is fax-on-demand (often referred to as fax-back, or FOD). FOD is closely related to audiotext in that the caller needs only to enter a code to receive the information; no database link exists as with IVR (which I discuss in the next chapter). Like audiotext, FOD is a great way to get information from the LAN to the caller without requiring your knowledge workers to waste time assisting in the delivery process.

At this point in the book, I also discuss fax from a historical perspective, comparing fax as both an interactive and non-interactive telecommunications service in the next three chapters.

I will not deal with fax communications per se and therefore will not provide any general descriptions of how the technology works, such as compression, handshaking, and so on. Dozens of books have already done that. The purpose of this chapter is to discuss uses for fax technology for information exchange, as interactive telecommunications. Chapter 13 discusses fax as a non-interactive communications or message service — that is, as fax mail or f-mail.

A BRIEF HISTORY OF FAX

Facsimile, which has become popularly known as *fax,* has been around for more than a century. The idea of transmitting an image over telegraphic transmission lines was patented in 1853, long before Alexander Bell made his famous telephone call in 1876. The technology, however, has only recently (within the past two decades) become cheap enough to be a worthwhile, critical service for businesses. There are two important reasons why fax took off the way it did over the past 20 years: the drop in the cost of the equipment and the drop in the cost of transmission, both attributable to the wide adoption of a standard (see Chapter 5).

Which is better — the WWW or FOD?

Although I devote Chapter 12 to discussing the World Wide Web, I want you to know that as of this writing (May 1996), the Web really is not critical enough as a service to replace FOD. I've received several questions asking for help on whether to use the Web or FOD as the CT service. The following answer to that question should be valid for several years yet.

The Web certainly is going to go far. By the end of the decade, I believe it will become the preferred choice for retrieving information. My company, Nortech Software, Inc., has a site on the Web. And I definitely prefer accessing and downloading information from the Web rather than using a FOD system to retrieve the info. Despite its snail pace, surfing the Web still is a better method than FOD for retrieving information if the company you want information from has a Web site. I would even say that the death of FOD as a critical service is only a few years away, thanks to the Web.

Keep in mind, however, that currently only seven percent of North Americans have access to the Web, even just to enjoy the graphical and colorful world seen through browsers. In other parts of the world, the Web has considerably less penetration. In some countries, Web penetration is almost zero. And in some regions, using the Internet costs a great deal more than using the fax. Fax machines, on the other hand, can be accessed by millions of people from nearly anywhere in the world.

Does the number of existing fax machines mean that you should not consider a Web site yet? No. I feel that you should do both. If you have a need for a FOD service, then set one up. At the same time, you can put up a few Web pages for less than $50 per month — so why not do it? I recommend, however, that you build your document management system around the HTML standard (see Chapter 12 for more on this) so that you can serve both FOD users and Web users from a single source of information and content. Many FOD systems can now read HTML, so the document that emerges from the fax machine looks identical (except for color and resolution of course) to the page you see on the Web with a Web browser. The big advantage of storing HTML files rather than PCX or bitmap files is size. HTML files are just text and take up very little space in a document management system. Fax-formatted files, on the other hand, are huge, so you need oodles of hard-disk space just to store a few hundred pages without graphics! Besides, if you go the HTML route, you'll be building a great Web information base for the future. Your FOD system and Web server will be accessing the same documents.

Fax transmission times dropped rapidly between 1976 and 1978 with the advent of the CCITT Group 2 standard, which was universally adopted. The average transmission speeds went from six minutes a page (the Group 1 specification) to three minutes a page. Despite the faster transmission speed, however, the quality of the resulting fax was still very poor.

Fax was used mostly by select organizations such as government offices, law enforcement agencies, news agencies, publishers, and banks. Fax service became more widely available, but it was still unaffordable for many businesses. Only organizations like Interpol, the KGB, and the CIA had budgets for copious use of facsimile communications. They would often transmit photographs of spies and contacts around the world. The material was needed for identification of suspects or agency members.

Then, in 1980, the Group 3 standard was published. Group 3 is a digital standard that made the machines even faster. Transmission speeds improved from the average three minutes a page to between 20 and 30 seconds a page (depending on the resolution) by 1982. During this same year, the cost of transmitting a page had dropped from about $4.00 to $1.00.

The new fax machines were also cheaper to manufacture, and by 1983, the U.S. had more than 350,000 machines in use, up from the 69,000 installed base in 1976. (For small businesses, though, fax was still more expensive than telex service, which most telephone companies around the world provided.) The first directory of fax users was published in that same year. Japan was considered the leader in fax machine manufacturing. Leading the field of Japanese exporters of fax machines to the U.S. was the Tokyo Shibaura Electric Co., better known as Toshiba.

As the Group 3 standard matured and the cost of the communications service became affordable, fax, in turn, became an essential communications process for transmitting a facsimile of a document from point A to point B. Today, more than 25 million fax machines are installed throughout the world. In the United States alone, more than 100 million faxes are transmitted between businesses every day.

How is it possible to use fax technology as an interactive service to exchange information over the telephone network? Let's look at the technology a little closer.

As Figure 10-1 illustrates, the fax machine consists of the following technological components:

✦ A printer for printing out the assembled data (usually a thermal printer)

✦ A modem for the sending and receiving digitized information and communications between the fax machines

✦ A scanner that passes over the surface of the document about to be transmitted

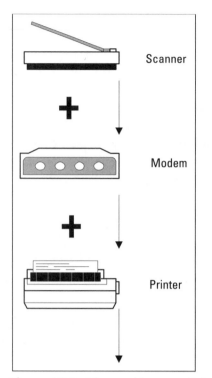

Figure 10-1: A fax machine essentially consists of (a) a printer, (b) a modem, and (c) a scanner. You can attach all three components to the workstation or server as peripheral devices, but you only need the modem and software for communications.

If you take out the modem, mount it on a card, and plug it into a computer, you've basically done away with two of the nonessential (for computer-based faxing, any-way) components needed for communication: the scanner and the printer.

What this means is that to send a fax, you no longer need to print out the document, walk over to the fax machine, and stand behind a long line of people waiting for ser-vice (so you also don't have to try to sneak your fax to the top of a pile of outgoing documents anymore). You can simply send the document, via the LAN, to a fax server consisting of several fax modems and have the server do the work for you. If the transmission is successful, the server notifies you that the remote machine said "document received." You can be sure that your transmission has indeed been re-ceived, but you still can't be sure that the person for whom it was intended is staring at it (this service is non-interactive, which I explain in more detail in Chapter 13).

Conversely, if you receive a fax via the computer-based fax modem, you thus have the opportunity to view this information on the screen or send it to the print server (discussed further in Chapter 13). If you need to send a hard copy of the document to the remote fax and have junked your fax machine, as I have, you will need to use a stand-alone scanner to digitize the information and transmit it to a computer on the LAN.

After a document has been scanned into the computer or prepared from the software, it's still not ready for faxing. A conversion process has to take place first. You need to convert the file to a format that the fax modem can transmit. Typically, the format you need to convert to is PCX, the most common format for faxing. Many modems and software now perform the conversions for you on the fly. You simply print the document to a fax driver, and off it goes.

That said, if you now want to junk the fax machine and stick the modem onto a card that plugs into a PC (like I did), you're going to need some hardware — namely, the modem card. You can turn to U.S. manufacturers such as Intel, GammaLink, and Brooktrout to get the card. Because the PC is attached to your LAN, it logically follows that a caller can "request" the fax from the computer telephony system interface, which in turn "processes" the document so that it gets transmitted back to the person requesting it (via the same telephone line or to an alternate fax number). This capability is known as *fax-on-demand* — or, as mentioned earlier, just "fax-back." Why is this service useful, you ask? Read on.

FAX-ON-DEMAND

In early 1990, I got involved in a project to create and publish an information base of all the adventure-prone destinations and facilities that one can find in southern Africa. The project was ambitious: We had to work with several wildlife, conservation, adventure, and outdoor-life groups to gather and place all the related information into a huge database management system (DBMS). I was responsible for designing, creating, and maintaining the DBMS. The information would then be processed and printed as tourist guides for the international travel industry and tourists. The countries involved extended as far north as Zambia and Kenya.

But the guides never made it to print. One of the problems was that the information in the database was changing and expanding so fast that, as soon as one guide was ready for the press, the material in it was either outdated or inadequate. By press time, the facilities would contact us with new information. At one point, the book was suspended so that a government or two could lose or take power. The map of South Africa, at that time, was changing monthly.

I began to ponder how best to put the information into a giant bulletin board system, where it could be updated and managed every day and where people all over the world, especially travel agents, could access the information as soon as the authorities and facilities released it. I began to do some research, which entailed faxing a number of BBS software developers around the world.

It was then, during the faxing, that I thought about the possibility of providing an interactive telecommunications (computer telephony) service that would allow callers to interrogate (or at the least, simply request) any of several thousand documents that we had in the information base. They could receive the information on their fax machines during the same telephone call, anywhere in the world, at any time. In essence, the millions of fax machines in the world would be transformed into remote printers.

This idea was not a new one. Back in the early 1980s, Peter Drucker, author of *New Realities,* suggested the following: "Within 22 to 25 years, it can be predicted with high confidence, the bulk of what we call newspapers and magazines today will be transmitted through electronics and through the printing plant of a telephone or television set."

Now that same idea is happening with fax and the World Wide Web. Despite the advent of the on-line commercial services (such as America Online and CompuServe) and the Internet, a massive installed base of fax machines still exists.

Even if e-mail does become more popular that fax, which is predicted, you cannot escape the fact that more than 25 million fax machines are in use throughout the world. (And that number will soon be 30 million.) With fax resolution improving and approaching 300 dots-per-inch (DPI) — the same resolution as the majority of installed laser printers — these devices have become that personal "printing plant" about which Drucker spoke more than a decade ago.

With that idea in mind, we proposed a fax-on-demand service for distributing the adventure guides. Without many commercial products available for that service in 1990–1991, we had to develop one from scratch that met the existing telephony approval standards in South Africa. Although this product now exists as a commercially available system (which I no longer have any financial interest in), I learned a great deal about FOD and computer-based fax (CBF) from designing and developing it.

Just sending a fax from point A to point B is an example of a non-interactive telecommunications process when you compare it to FOD. The sender simply sends the document without really being sure that the other party has received the document; you only know that the remote fax machine *says* it was received. It's a simple telephone process: The calling fax machine initiates a handshaking process with the receiving fax machine and requests an "all clear" signal to transmit the document. The only communication that takes place is a message saying "received okay," or "we fluffed up along the way, Babe; try again." Apart from this transaction, little else takes place.

In contrast, a FOD system is interactive and works this way: Through the TUI *(telephone user interface),* callers navigate the remote computer telephony system and request certain files that they know about from previous information. The caller may find out about the documents residing in the information base from information that you publish in a brochure, a television commercial, or in other print media. Regardless of where the information comes from, either the caller has to know about it, or the system needs to offer the caller a list of documents and their corresponding numbers during the interaction process (see Figure 10-2). You should, as a rule, provide a regularly updated contents page. (See the section later in this chapter in which I talk about rules for using FOD wisely.)

You may be wondering, "Can this model of interactive telecommunications and information exchange be put to good use in my situation?" It sure can.

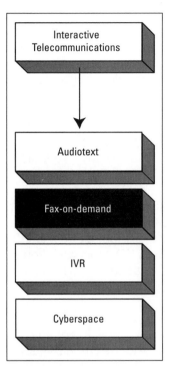

Figure 10-2: Fax-on-demand is an interactive telecommunications service domain of computer telephony.

IDEAL USES FOR FAX-ON-DEMAND

During 1993 or 1994, a media story reported that an IBM employee received a prize of $100,000 dollars for suggesting a FOD system. The corporation was able to show incredible savings by using such a system. How and where do you save by using FOD? Maybe the following list will help:

+ **Cost of paper, printing and binding.** Corporations go to incredible lengths and expense to prepare and publish brochures, white papers, and spec sheets for the sales and marketing functions. By cutting out this manufacturing process and allowing a customer to directly request such documents via FOD, a corporation can save a bundle.

+ **Cost of shipping, handling, and postage.** The buck does not stop with printing. It costs big money to have people package, insert, and collate material. It also costs big time and money to have people stuff the information sheets into envelopes. These envelopes still have to be addressed, which takes time — a great deal of it. Licking stamps and the backs of envelopes is not particularly pleasant, either. If you do this enough times, your lips start to stick together. If that's not enough to convince you, the final dent in the bank account that comes when you have to schlep off to the post office and pay a wad for postage will.

✦ **Getting the information to your prospect.** This time-related expense is a big cost even though it's not a direct, hard-dollar cost. When customers want information, they want it today. Taking a week — or even a month, if you're sending information around the world — to deliver the information may cost you the sale. If your competitor can get information to users before you do, chances are that a decision will be made to buy the other guy's stuff before you even have a chance to lick the stamp.

✦ **Maintaining the *customer satisfaction index* (CSI).** The CSI is a very important factor. By installing and offering information to customers and clients around the world, you are, in essence, providing them with a direct interface to the information on your LAN they need. By using FOD this way, you become that alluring anywhere, anytime enterprise about which I have spoken so often. Use FOD *wisely* and your customers will love you.

I strongly emphasize the word *wisely* here because it's the key word used in this list. Many FOD systems are installed without much thought and upkeep. When you follow that practice, what once was alluring and accessible becomes repulsive and repelling. Before dealing with the "rules" of wise use, let's take a more in-depth look at how a FOD system works.

The voice- and call-processing components of a computer telephony system, just as with the IVR and IFR systems described in the next chapter, enable the caller to navigate the system and probe it for information. In case the caller is not armed with a FOD version of a contents page that provides a list of items available for reception, the menus will — or should — provide this reference as the first option. The caller usually hears the following prompt:

> "Key in the code number of the document that you want to receive . . .
> or, to receive a list of available documents, enter 999."

The computer telephony system accesses the document as would any client PC on the network. This document can then be queued for transmission while the caller selects additional documents. The queue information should contain pointers to the file or directory where the file has been copied for transmission. To help you to better understand what happens next, I have provided an amusing tale of the first fax-on-demand system that my company created back in 1991.

When we first suggested the fax-on-demand option for the South African adventure guide, we aroused the interests of not only the conservation authorities, but also an investment bank that was getting sick of printing out forms for its customers and then faxing them from the various fax machines scattered around its multilevel building. The bank had considered using computer-based fax as a solution, but besides providing the advantage of the higher quality of faxes, all the server did was cut out the fax machine ritual.

In other words, the staff still needed to spend time interacting with callers, searching for documents (which meant interrupting work), and sending the material to the fax device. Each call took approximately five minutes to process. If you have to deal with 20 to 40 callers a day, you still lose a great deal of time. By using FOD, however, customers could download information at their expense (time and telephone calls) and anytime of the day, night, or weekend.

With that in mind, we proposed that the bank use a FOD system. The only problem was that, at the time, no product really existed for this service. It was still *vaporware*— a form of software that exists only in the software developer's mind. (About 90 percent of all software written and talked about today is vaporware. Windows 95, to many users who do not live at One Microsoft Way, was vaporware for many years.) We explained this concept to the bank, and the management team immediately fell in love with the idea. We agreed to show them a working prototype within a month.

Because users can call a fax modem (or any modern fax machine) and request it to send a document instead of receive one (a process known as *polling*), the voice-processing interface to the FOD features was needed to enable the caller to poll the computer and have it transmit documents *back* to the caller's fax machine. Once the computer had selected the document (according to the document ID number entered by the caller), it could simply hand over the remaining program execution to the fax board and cut the voice-processing card out of the process.

In this case, a T-piece or Y-connection connected both the fax card and the voice-processing card to the single telephone line, as illustrated in Figure 10-3. Today, computer telephony components have become more sophisticated. Several digital bus standards have emerged that connect the various computer telephony components via a ribbon-based bus (see the entries for MVIP and SCSA in the Lexicon).

As sometimes happens, the software took longer to develop than expected, even though it was a simple, single-line state machine (see the Lexicon). An hour before the presentation, during which the bank planned to have customers call the system for the first FOD demo, the fax side of the effort was still not working.

Using guru logic, we brought the fax machine into the picture. When the bank's team called to prepare for the demo (which included the CEO), we advised them that only one document was prepared for transmission. So, they called in from their fax machine, and we listened in on an audio coupler as they navigated the system and entered the number for the document. As the prompt requested them to press start on their fax machine, we pressed start on our fax machine and transmitted the document. The demo was a success. This setup essentially illustrates how FOD works.

Nowadays, fax-on-demand software and turnkey systems have matured. They are feature-rich and enable you to control just how much you transmit and where you transmit to. Today's FOD systems, for example, enable you to choose between one-call and two-call processes. The one-call option means that the caller can receive the document on the same telephone call. The two-call option means the caller can enter an alternate number to receive the document.

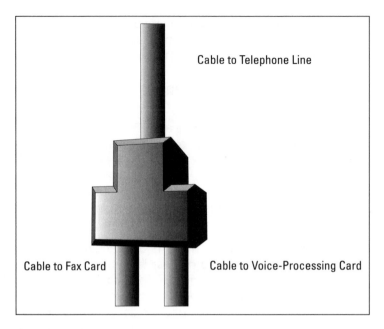

Cable to Telephone Line

Cable to Fax Card

Cable to Voice-Processing Card

Figure 10-3: A T-piece or Y-connection connects the voice-processing card and the fax card to a single telephone line.

The two-call option is used a great deal with systems that get a lot of caller traffic. The option enables the caller to get off the telephone and allow another caller to access the service. Meanwhile, the fax queues up to transmit the requested information to another port or to route it to a fax server (not true, interactive fax-on-demand, but delayed transmission nevertheless).

A major difference between the two-call and one-call processes is cost. When the caller receives the faxes on the same telephone line, he or she bears the cost. But the enterprise bears the cost of transmitting the fax in the two-call process because the system initiates the call to the customer's fax machine. This option can be rather expensive if a caller from, say, Moscow calls a system in Provost, Utah. An important feature of the FOD system, therefore, is that it can enable the administrator to limit the area codes to which it can transmit.

Computer telephony systems, FOD in particular, also enable you to charge for the information that you provide. The system can prompt callers for credit card information before it retrieves a document, or you can make the FOD system accessible via a premium rate or pay-per-call service. FOD works the same way that audiotext does.

WISE RULES TO FOLLOW WITH FOD

The key to making your FOD system — and any other computer telephony service, for that matter — work effectively is using it *wisely*. The following rules give you a few ideas that you should mull over when using FOD.

KEEP THE NUMBER OF PAGES IN EACH DOCUMENT TO A MINIMUM

I have found that five pages is about as much as the caller wants to receive for each document. If the customer requests three documents, he or she will have to download 15 pages of information. Fax paper is expensive, and few people want to blow this money on a lengthy download.

Fax paper not only costs a whack, it's also difficult to manage. Some expensive machines cut and collate the fax pages for you, but if you've ever had to chop up a long ribbon of fax paper manually, you know how miserable this process can be. More than likely, the caller will want to photocopy the fax pages before they turn gray and fade away. Photocopying 5 to 15 curly fax sheets is not my idea of using the enterprise's time productively.

In addition, if the caller only has one telephone line, a long download will tie up the line and likely have the caller abandoning the call halfway through the transmission. Many corporations are infamous for overloading their FOD systems. In fact, I now refuse to access several such systems, turning instead to the WWW to see if their home pages (if the firms have them) provide the documents.

Keep the number of documents to no more than three, four at the most, so that the caller can download them during one call. This rule is especially important if you are at a busy site. Despite the marvels that the Group 3 standard introduced, faxing still takes a great deal of time. Twenty pages of fax can keep the line tied up for between 15 and 20 minutes; not a good idea if your company is in demand. Add that to the five to ten minutes the caller took to call and navigate the computer telephony system and you can see how that time adds up. You also have to remember that many callers will probably be calling you long distance, and every minute counts.

KEEP THE HEAVY AND HIGHLY DETAILED GRAPHICS TO A MINIMUM

Too many graphics slows down the transmission and places a heavy load on the receiving machine's thermal printer components. The ideal document should contain mostly text or a mix of text and light-line drawings. Many companies simply scan in a color brochure without much regard for the consequences it will have for the user.

KEEP THE DOCUMENTS FRESH AND UP TO DATE

Nothing is worse than spending time on a system to find a document that you need and then, when you download it, discovering it's a year out-of-date. Make sure that your documents are updated regularly.

ALWAYS PROVIDE A CONTENTS PAGE

Every FOD system should include this bit of customer service. When you do, make sure that you tell callers how to access it as soon as they connect to the system — in the greeting, if possible.

Also, keep the contents page as current as possible. Every time you make a change to the system, update the contents page. You also can include instructions on how best to use the system. This could either be a separate document or part of the contents page. Remember to be brief and to the point.

LIMIT THE MARKETING MATERIAL PROVIDED IN YOUR DOCUMENTS

Many FOD users like to include some corporate information in their documents. You don't have to attach public relations or corporate ID and advertising gumph to every page or document in the system. Almost all FOD software enables you attach this information to the end of the document stream.

A word of advice: Make sure that the system does not attach the PR gumph to the end of *every* document. This slick trick really upsets the users who have to put up with it. The best place to include this information, I think, is in the contents page. Then callers only get the gumph when they retrieve the contents page and not at the end of every transmission.

You also can attach an order form to the end of every document stream; however, I think attaching the order form *ID code* to every document is a better idea than repeatedly faxing the form itself to the caller. Let the caller retrieve the order form when he or she is ready to get it. If the caller discovers that the three documents selected will require several fax rolls because of these order forms, you may lose a potential customer.

OTHER CONSIDERATIONS FOR USING FOD

As mentioned earlier, long documents are not suited to FOD. The longer the document, the more expensive and time-consuming it is to retrieve it. You could argue that faxing long documents takes you into the realm of publishing rather than information exchange. Long white papers and product overview documents are more suited to other forms of electronic publishing, such as the World Wide Web discussed in Chapter 12.

A great way to use FOD is when you need to provide blank forms that people can fill in. These forms may include tax returns, application forms, request forms, and so on. You also may agree that FOD is great for providing users with an on-the-fly, electronic front door to your information base. If all someone needs is a one-page document or a blank form that he or she can fill in, then FOD is the way to go. Leave longer documents to the World Wide Web and on-line bulletin board systems.

One of the biggest users of fax-on-demand is the New York City-based PR Newswire. The "newswire" gathers information about companies (their operations, products and services, and shares) from 20-plus offices around the world. Newswire then makes this information available to the media and its subscribers via an FOD system. Subscribers — who typically include reporters, private investors, money managers, and brokers — can call the system daily to receive information on the stocks of a particular company or other pertinent data via the fax.

As you can tell, FOD and fax have a wide potential for improving the way your enterprise interacts with customers, users, and other corporations. What you need to do is determine how it can best serve you.

SUMMARY

This chapter provided a brief history of facsimile technology and discussed the fax-on-demand service domain of computer telephony. I discuss the technology further in Chapter 12 by comparing it to the World Wide Web. If you need to provide an interactive telecommunications service, a front end to your enterprise information base, or have many long documents that you want to make available, I recommend turning to Chapter 12, which discusses cyberspace and WWW publishing as an alternative.

IN THIS CHAPTER

✦ What are IVR and IFR?

✦ The telephone interface to data

✦ Justifying the need

✦ Human factors to consider

✦ Implementing and deploying IVR

"Thank you for calling the Psychic Hotline!
If you'd like to know what the future has in store for you,
leave your name and address after the beep and we will
mail you a copy of next week's TV Guide magazine."

11

IVR

*I*nteractive voice response (IVR) is the computer telephony service that enables the telephone to act as a data retrieval and submission interface. This service falls in the interactive telecommunication and information exchange section of the computer telephony schematic (see Figure 11-1).

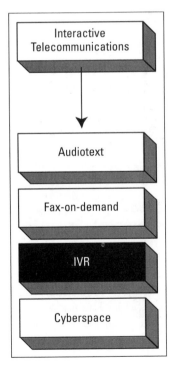

Figure 11-1: The IVR service domain of computer telephony.

Although many in the CT industry use the terms IVR, voice processing, and audiotext interchangeably (as subsets of each other), I prefer to focus on how IVR uniquely gives you telephone access to a real-time data service. IVR is the data-centric service of computer telephony: It provides the capability to "speak" data from the database management system over the telephone network. IVR also is a more expensive service than audiotext due to the interfacing that you need to do with the database.

You may also have heard of the term *IFR*, which is the acronym for *interactive fax response*. IFR systems refer to the coupling of IVR systems to fax-on-demand capability. In other words, IVR systems "talk" data to you, but with FOD capability, they can fax you this information as well. The essential service is IVR, however.

WHAT IS IVR?

One of the most important tasks for which we use computers is to record, manage, and deliver data. Every enterprise owns data. Therefore, every enterprise has a need for database management software that can input, sort, manage, and retrieve its data. Just managing a list of ten telephone numbers or birthdays can be called database management.

If you have a lot of friends (like many celebrities or heads of state have), you may need a database management system (DBMS) to manage this data; if you plan to invite all those wayward relatives for Thanksgiving, you need a DBMS; if your Jewish New Year mailing list is like mine, you need a DBMS.

DATA RETRIEVAL AND DOCUMENT RETRIEVAL

Understanding the difference between document retrieval and data retrieval is important when discussing IT and, in particular, computer telephony. Consider the following:

✦ **Data retrieval** is the retrieval of specific information based on a direct query. The retrieved information answers a specific query such as "When is my niece's birthday?" or "How much money do I have in this bank account?"

   Document retrieval, on the other hand, is the retrieval of a document or set of documents about a subject. The inquirers access the information base to retrieve documents that *may* have the information they seek. IVR is a data-centric service; fax-on-demand is mostly a document-centric service.

✦ **Data retrieval** is deterministic in nature. In other words, a necessary relationship exists between the request and the answer. The question "How much money do I have in the bank?" is met with the answer "–$1,500." The answer may not be the one that the inquirer wants to receive, but correct or not, it's the one stored in the database.

Document **retrieval**, however, is non-deterministic in nature. The inquirer retrieves documents in search of something, hoping to find a satisfactory answer or information within the requested document.

THE CLIENT/SERVER MODEL AND IVR

An *intranet* makes data available to users via computer screens. In the old IT frontier, users entered search and retrieve commands on dumb terminals to get data. Today, the client/server model of data retrieval is the norm (and fast becoming the standard) in many enterprises. Users request data from their computers via interfaces that send requests to the server.

Getting information from the World Wide Web is one of the best examples of this model. Logging on to one of the search engines, such as Yahoo! or Alta Vista, is a data-serving process. The flow of information travels by direct queries and direct responses across the network. For example, after the server receives a query for a bank account balance, it performs the necessary procedures and routines to retrieve the appropriate data; then it sends the information back to the client. (For a more in-depth discussion of intranets and telephony, see Chapter 12.)

The most common type of client/server database management system (DBMS) is known as the *full C/S*. A full C/S means that the data can reside on several servers on the LAN or on geographically dispersed servers. These servers perform all the necessary DBMS processing, and users access the data from the DBMS on the servers.

The two advantages of client/server technology — which have in recent years provided the impetus for IVR — are multiple clients (or front ends) and interoperability.

INTEROPERABILITY

Using client/server architecture enables the client user interfaces to run on any platform. The workstations can be IBM PC and compatibles, Macintoshes, UNIX boxes, or any combination of these devices. You can even extend the life of the older computers by using this format because client software does not do any of the processor- and memory-intensive work on the DBMS. The server side does it.

This fact is important because the computers on which IVR applications run may be platform independent (of the DBMS). I discuss why it needs this independence in the next section.

MULTIPLE CLIENTS

For modern enterprises, making data available to internal and external environments is a necessary function. Their users want to know about debits, credits, and balances; they want to know about shipping times, dispatch dates, and the exact locations of letters and parcels that they send; they want to know data related to their personal lives, such as how many sick days they have left or how much medical insurance they have; they want to know how much time they have left to pay traffic fines; they want to find out about the availability of products, costs, and versions; and more. The C/S model empowers the enterprise to serve up such data and enables specialists to manage it while keeping unauthorized hands off the DBMS.

An important reason why enterprises have made the switch to client/server DBMS can be directly attributed to the fact that multiple clients need access to the DBMS from multiple platforms. This issue encompasses more than interoperability; it means that servers take requests not only from a common front end, but also must handle several requests from many different front ends or clients. Without this model, the Internet would not have become the critical service it is today. That it can even provide telephony services is testament to the model's success.

IT specialists want a data-serving environment that does not care about the myriad of different clients and platforms requesting the server for information. As long as the server DBMS understands and interprets the requests, it can process the query and send the data back to the client.

The C/S architecture (it can be argued) is a more sensible platform for protecting and keeping data secure. Different clients request and work with data in the internal and external environments of the enterprise.

The clients that work with data in the internal environment are

✦ Personal computers running Windows (3.*x*, 95, and NT clients)

✦ Macintoshes

✦ Workstations (Power PCs, NEXT, and SPARCS)

✦ Mainframe and minicomputer dumb terminals

In the external environment, the following clients deal with data:

✦ EDI terminals

✦ Remote-access clients (these clients typically are the same as clients in the internal environment, but their main source for accessing data is via the Web clients or the intranet and remote-access services)

✦ IVR (using the TUI or telephone user interface)

✦ Internet and the World Wide Web (using a browser)

With this model in place, the enterprise can choose and install the client/server architecture that best suits it. Perhaps UNIX works better for you, or maybe you've standardized on Windows NT and SQL Server. Or, is an OS/2 environment more in line with your current systems? No matter what you have, you do not want to alter or replace server software just to suit a particular client running on a particular platform. One of those clients may be the IVR system; the one you decide to use may be galaxies apart from the operating systems and database software at the server end.

WHY IVR?

With so much data in the enterprise's DBMS, the staff and systems are under considerable strain to relay database requests from the external environment (customers, clients, and partners contacting you on the phone) to the DBMS and back. People call in and take up your staff's time in search of data that they need to keep their lives and businesses running smoothly. The number of times a bank gets calls for nothing more than a bank balance forced this industry to invent ways in which the callers do the work themselves. Hence the advent of IVR, another critical computer telephony service that caters to the hectic traffic of data. (The alternative was to employ thousands of people to sit at computer screens and look up the information, 24 hours a day, 7 days a week.)

The IVR system is nothing more than a client of the DBMS that runs on the database server. The DBMS does not care what the user interface looks like; after the request is made, it sends the data to the client. The client then must translate the data into a form that humans can easily recognize. In the case of IVR, the data is converted from digital information into audible information rather than being presented on the screen.

Think of an IVR system as a super-efficient data processor that can help a number of people with their data needs over the telephone — whether that number is 1 person or 200. Enabling a computer to take requests from the caller and query the DBMS makes perfect sense because many enterprises can rapidly establish the cost justification of IVR systems.

THE TELEPHONE INTERFACE TO DATA

The telephone interface to data is simply an alternative screen interface for requesting and receiving data. However, understanding the differences between the two interfaces is important when considering and implementing IVR. Although these differences should be apparent, I am constantly amazed when intelligent people forget or ignore them when designing IVR applications. In the following sections, I emphasize these differences and hopefully awaken some people to their waning customer satisfaction index.

SCREEN-BASED USER INTERFACE

The screen-based user interface has undergone a fundamental paradigm shift in recent years. Since the advent of the Microsoft Windows and Apple Macintosh graphical user interfaces (GUIs), client software has been empowered to take advantage of graphical, icon-laden interfaces, making it easier for users to access and understand data drawn from the LAN or intranet. The process of querying, retrieving, and managing data now centers around events: clicking buttons, selecting choices from menus with a mouse pointer, dragging and dropping objects to different parts of the screen, and so on.

Thanks to object-oriented design and modularity in software engineering, users can perform complex routines on a DBMS with a simple mouse click. The commands and messages that the client sends to the server to complete certain tasks are embedded in the software and screened from the users. You can predetermine the complexity (to the user) of performing tasks from the client end as needed.

For example, you can enable the user to create a direct SQL query on the DBMS, such as this one for house prices: "*Select* all records that equal = $100,000, *where* the city is West Palm Beach." Or, for novice users, you can specify a similar query to run as the result of an event, such as a mouse click on a button. (Here the button can be represented by an icon of a house with a dollar sign on it, communicating the event that occurs when you click it.) The button pops up a list of cities in southern Florida for the user to choose from. After the user double-clicks on a selection, the query runs, and the retrieved data appears in a scroll-down list on the user's screen for easy perusal.

In the old IT age of dumb terminals and character-based interfaces, users were forced to make selections from sedate, fixed menus or to directly enter commands into an edit field. A fixed list of options limited the user's choices; the user pressed Enter to make a selection, which then activated the query. Sometimes another step required users to type cryptic commands in a field that popped up over the menu. These systems were bland, difficult to use, and very limited in the way data was presented.

Even with these old interfaces, users were able to *see* the query results and manipulate them — albeit in a limited way — to best suit their methods of interpreting and understanding the data. I remember my first dBASE program. When I needed to build a way to present lists or several records on-screen, I made sure that the user could at least scroll through the data. Alternative data presentations were more complex for the user to work with, however. The source code pages for building alternative presentation formats would run in the thousands of lines. (Today, I need only write 15 lines of source code with a product such as Borland's Delphi — Object Pascal — to achieve the same results and better serve the user's senses.) Even here, at least the data remained on the screen for as long as the user needed it to remain there.

TELEPHONE USER INTERFACE

The *telephone user interface* (TUI), however, puts the person requesting the data at an even greater disadvantage: You not only are unable to see the data (which the brain can interpret quicker than sound), but the data is fluid and temporary. In other words, you only hear it for a moment, and then you have to reaccess it. Imagine what it would be like if, in the previous example, the scroll-down list of house prices popped onto the screen and then vanished after a second or two. As the interface builder, I would have been fed to the sharks!

All computer telephony services have this disadvantage by their very nature. However, this disadvantage is an important consideration when planning IVR systems because of the additional actions that users perform while interacting with the system. The users have to listen hard to catch the temporary string of data. If they do hear the string, they have to write it down, understand it, interpret it, and react to it — simultaneously.

Although the object of IVR systems is to self-empower the user and reduce the load on your firm's internal resources (and get the call completed as soon as possible), the TUI (the telephone keypad and the spoken menu) sets the caller back 20 or more years in terms of accessing data and interpreting it easily. Even a good IVR script walks a fine line between customer satisfaction and disservice.

Keeping this limitation in mind and *remembering* the differences between the interfaces, you then should sit down and consider your needs for IVR.

JUSTIFYING THE NEED

Despite its limitations, many callers use the IVR system because it saves time and bother and because many enterprises do not offer an alternative. IVR systems also offer more privacy. Many people do not want to talk to humans about private or trivial information. Take the banking scenario from earlier: Many callers prefer to have a computer to tell them what their bank balance is because (a) they are paranoid about another human knowing this data, and (b) they can access the data far more quickly over the IVR system (if all they need is a bank balance).

If you receive many callers who request repetitive information from databases, you can justify installing an IVR system. Discussions in the earlier chapters that centered around justifying the need for other computer telephony services apply to IVR as well.

HUMAN FACTORS TO CONSIDER

Many firms install IVR systems without considering the limitations of the telephone user interface. Although you can employ IVR as a means of making life easier for employees and saving money, the gains should not come at the expense of your customers. If the IVR system is too difficult and cumbersome to use, the customer will abandon the call to seek alternative sources of information and relief.

DO NOT OVERLOAD THE CALLER WITH INFORMATION

If you force your users to access an IVR system for *all* database queries and complex data rather than employing more people to better serve the customer, your customer satisfaction index begins to dive and your company's alluring image begins to take on a repulsive form.

To avoid this problem, limit the IVR to providing only the most frequently accessed data. Do research. Use customer satisfaction surveys and the reports of your computer telephony system to determine which data is requested most frequently.

For example, in banking and other financial institutions, the account balance is the most frequently used data. In fact, this request is so frequent that you do not have to make it a menu option at all. Instead, have your system read the account balance or other frequently accessed information to the callers as soon as they enter the account number and password/security code. Consider the following script that plays as soon as the user has entered his or her password:

The available balance is $1,300.95.

For the last ten transactions, press 1.

To verify a specific check, press 2.

For the last ten deposits, press 3.

To transfer funds, press 4.

To replay the menu, press pound.

This menu offers several benefits, such as the following:

✦ The menu is brief and to the point. The idea is to get the data to the caller as quickly as possible. If all the caller needs is the balance, the caller can write it down and then repeat the menu to verify it by pressing the pound sign.

✦ The user can quickly select the desired options and nothing more; these options represent the most frequently asked questions that tellers and other bank staff receive. More complex questions, such as the amount of money in a float/hold, the reason behind an unusual debit charge or unexpected withdrawal, and so on, require the user to press 0 to talk to a representative. Such data is difficult to fathom or evaluate over the telephone and would require the user to perform several actions to repeat the data.

✦ The brevity of the menu gives the user time to write down the data and still listen to the menu options going by. By the time the menu has been read, the user can replay it by selecting the pound sign or work from memory and previous experience. The thought process underway here is this: "I have heard the balance now; the first thing I want to do is go over the recent activity." This particular menu enables the caller, after selecting the first option, to access all data on file simply by selecting 1 after every ten items. The caller can exit the first option and return to the preceding menu simply by choosing pound.

✦ The caller can make a choice by selecting from a list of options rather than being forced to use the often hazardous Yes/No menu in an IVR situation (see Chapter 8). I say *hazardous* because a telephone can kill when an irate customer flings it across a busy open-plan office. Banks that use this style of menu are trying to make the IVR menu the same as the automatic teller machine (ATM). However, you can't see the ATM screen over the plain old telephone. While concentrating hard on the data or options flying by, you don't need the additional burden of making sure that you hit the 1 or 2 key at the right moment in the prompt of six or eight options.

This menu achieves the objective of an IVR system. It enables the caller to quickly access important — yet superficial — data that the caller needs primarily to make sure that he or she has sufficient funds in the bank or has met certain obligations.

Besides their balance, most callers want to know whether a certain check has cleared yet. Anything more complex requires the individual to use all of his or her senses when accessing and interpreting the data. Thus, when you force your customers to access checking, credit cards, borrowing and loan information, securities, interest rates, and more, you're essentially repelling them by asking them to do too much work. Nobody wants to sit on the telephone longer than they would have to otherwise, straining to make sense of all the data whizzing by their ears.

BLOCK THE CALLERS FROM THE ZERO OPTION AT YOUR RISK

Never, *never* prevent callers from accessing live assistance in a customer service and satisfaction scenario. Although the IVR system is in place to take the majority of trivial calls away from employees, the caller may need to further query certain data at any time. Remember that I said data retrieval is deterministic. The answer that the caller gets is the only answer (take it or leave it) because that's the one in the database at the time. Any further investigation, such as why the data is what it is, requires the assistance of a live representative.

IMPLEMENTING AND DEPLOYING IVR

Hardware, voice-processing components, and operating system requirements are no different for IVR than they are for other computer telephony services. Most of the scripting and general computer telephony routines handled by IVR systems — such as answering calls, presenting menus, switching to live attendants, putting callers on hold, taking messages, and more — are the same. Two components of IVR software, however, are more pertinent to the data-centric service of IVR than the other CT services. They are

✦ The interface to the enterprise DBMS

✦ The capability to convert text to speech (known as text-to-speech, or TTS)

IVR applications revolve around the enterprise DBMS. Whatever product you invest in, its strengths should center on providing the telephone-based interface to the data, giving that data a voice, so to speak. Although it is possible to invest in a voice-processing product, ACD, fax-on-demand system, or audiotext system that does not require additional source code, script language, or interface work by a specialist, this is not usually the case with IVR.

Granted, some systems offer various flavors of terminal emulation so that your IVR client behaves the same way that the dumb terminals do in the internal environment. But, if your enterprise has downsized (or rightsized) and standardized around client/server architecture, you need to consider an IVR system that provides you with the tools for tailoring and managing it to fit the ever-evolving enterprise DBMS, the needs of the internal user base, and the needs of the caller base.

You need tools and flexibility on two levels: the menus and the database. (The database level includes processing database requests, updating the database with new information, and reading data to the caller.) You can best achieve this functionality by using an applications generator, known throughout the software world as the *app gen*.

What Is an App Gen?

Applications generators (app gens) come from the world of *computer-aided software engineering* (CASE), which assists engineers in conceptualizing and planning applications, and *rapid application development* (RAD). RAD consists of tools, such as compilers, libraries, and off-the-shelf software components, that help bring software to market more quickly. An app gen is a software suite that combines CASE and RAD to create applications as rapidly as possible with minimal code writing. We use app gens for IVR applications because this service needs to be created and deployed rapidly in the enterprise and tailored to your database management processes. You cannot simply go out and buy a database application, hope that it will suit your needs, and that's that.

Why do you need RAD, and therefore an app gen or software development interface, in IVR? Every enterprise has unique and proprietary data. Each entity manages and controls that data in a way that best suits its business needs, culture, habits, and practices. Each DBMS also is managed and updated according to the needs of individuals in the organization.

For example, suppose that Tom from marketing goes to the database guru and asks for the capability to extract information, which he can then present in a way that communicates how certain advertising programs affect sales. Mary Beth from sales, on the other hand, may ask the guru to add a feature that enables her to quickly see the average time it takes for each of her sales representatives to close a deal. Neither of the two workers can simply go out and pick up a software package at the mall and expect it to provide them with the information they need automatically.

Acquiring and installing an IVR system is very different than the procedures for installing other CT services. Voice-messaging and call-processing products remain the same in that you can generally install and maintain them without ever needing to access the internal workings of the product. You can buy a turnkey product for these services and reliably use it — once users know how to use it, you seldom need to worry about it (assuming that it does what you want it to do). The developer provides new features, updates, enhancements, and bug fixes for you.

You can't say the same about IVR though, because the enterprise is constantly evolving and improving the DBMS. If you make any changes to the server functions, you'll have to update and change the client software that accesses the data for the client/server architecture to work properly; this includes updating the IVR system.

Newer client/server architectures do not always require you to make changes in the client end at the same time you make changes in the server end. Eventually, however, the client software may require updates to enable certain processes to run on the server, depending on how the two distribute the processing load. You do not want an IVR system that dictates how you manage and configure the database server because you have other clients to consider, especially the local, LAN-based clients. For that reason, you may need to update the DBMS functions just to move data from one table to another in the DBMS.

Does this mean that you need to invest more time and money in training and delegating IVR system maintenance than with the other CT services? Yes, if you plan to do a great deal of work in-house and want to support the constantly evolving needs of your enterprise. You'll need to invest in a robust development package and then delegate responsibility for it to an individual or team in your enterprise. Another option would be to employ an IVR specialist to handle the system for you.

THE IVR SPECIALIST

Going the IVR specialist or consultant route has two advantages: experience and experience. By that I mean experience in creating and deploying the IVR application and experience in using the right product.

By employing a professional who has set up many IVR applications, you not only draw on the consultant's experience with database access, you also draw on the individual's experience in dealing with different switches and the often puzzling world of telephony. Hundreds of different PBX systems are in use today, and each one is different from the next. Even PBX systems manufactured by the same company may be different: The first one's reorder tone may be different than the reorder tone on another, or the string that you dial to light a message lamp on the telephone may be different from the string that performs the same task on another system.

With so many divergent issues to consider, rolling your own IVR system may not be a good idea, unless you have some critical need to do otherwise. If you do purchase your own product, you still need the assistance of an experienced computer telephony systems integrator to steer the way for you. (IVR is so specialized that many manufacturers of IVR systems refuse to allow integrators and computer telephony consultants to sell and install IVR without first doing a course on the subject and getting certified. Applied Voice Technology (AVT) is one company that requires its VARs to do an IVR course before they can offer and sell the IVR module to CallXpress3, probably the most popular system in use today.)

The second issue deals with the specialist's experience in the products and the app gens on the market. More than likely, the IVR consultant will have worked with several different products and be in a better position to advise you on which platform is better for you. The consultant can get the IVR application up and running more quickly and with less debugging and testing than you. If the consultant has a great deal of experience, he or she can implement your system without having to do the equivalent of re-inventing the wheel; the specialist will have a proven set of canned routines and procedures that were used to test other clients' systems. All you have to do is purchase the hardware and a run-time executable license from the consultant.

The consultant route may also be cheaper for you in the short term because you will not have to buy an entire development platform and all the add-ons, tools, and utilities that the consultant needs to develop new IVR systems every week for different clients.

Of course, the downside to using the consultant is inherent. If the consulting firm goes out of business, or if the consultant dies or decides to take a year-long trek through the Amazon in search of the golden piranha, your enterprise needs to survive this loss. (This fact applies for all applications/services that you develop.)

If you go with a consultant, make sure that the individual (or firm) you choose uses a popular package that another specialist can take over later and that you get adequate documentation on it. The documentation should describe not only the source code or script language, but the design, objectives, and philosophy that the consultant used to get the app up and running.

Finally, keep in mind that consultants come in all shapes and shades. What is more important, however, is that you grab a guru who knows the database business like the back of his or her hand. Databases are extremely complex products. Every system performs file- and record-locking according to its particular design or architecture. A system's setup also affects how it handles volume. For example, if you plan to inject a million records into a fluid database, then forget about using the Xbase family for speed, integrity and reliability — especially in multi-user, concurrent-access situations. Xbase tables tend to become a bit brittle when the number of records exceeds 10,000.

Or, if you plan to have Internet users access the database simultaneously, some SQL databases will perform the job better than others. Still others may provide a level of security that is unacceptable to your situation. As a result, your guru — when armed with adequate information — needs to know enough about the DBMS business to act in your best interests. I have found that pulling in several gurus — each a specialist in his or her field — is often better than going with the proverbial "Jack of all trades" consultant. This fact is especially true now that the Internet visitors have arrived with their Web browsers. You want a solution that caters to both the telephony and Internet worlds from a single DBMS.

TEXT-TO-SPEECH

Text-to-speech is an essential component of the IVR application. Text-to-speech (TTS) is the voice of data. Your application uses TTS to read data to your callers from its screen. You could use concatenated phrases with some applications, but the problem is that data changes all the time. For example, one caller may update a field with data; then a second or two later, another client changes this information. TTS simply "reads" whatever the database server sends back to the IVR system. TTS technology is discussed in Chapter 4 and the Lexicon.

SUMMARY

IVR has become a critical service in the Information Age. Quick access to data is a valuable enterprise-empowering tool. Many computer telephony industry insiders believe that IVR usage will increase by 50 percent each year and will become as popular a service as voice messaging.

You must remember that the interface and human-computer dialog is very limiting. For working remotely with more complex data and information, your clients may be better off accessing their information via screen-based interfaces. I discuss this setup in the forthcoming chapters dealing with intranets and cyberspace.

IN THIS CHAPTER

- ✦ Computer telephony and cyberspace

- ✦ The Internet

- ✦ The World Wide Web

- ✦ The World Wide Web versus IVR and fax-on-demand

- ✦ Intranets

- ✦ Internet/Intranet Telephony

"The Wizard says if we want more information on his services, we should visit his Web page on the Internet."

CHAPTER 12

COMPUTER TELEPHONY AND THE CYBERSPACE PHENOMENON

The preceding chapters look at all the interactive services of computer telephony and how you apply them as tools of customer satisfaction and productivity. As a computer telephony user, you have to evaluate new and emerging technologies as they arrive and empower yourself with this knowledge.

The headlines tell the story: "Net War Looms in Hong Kong," "Cyberspace Juggernaut Unstoppable," "Millions of Gophers on the Loose," "A Hundred Million People by 2000." Are we about to be invaded from another galaxy? No — these headlines are talking about the incredible phenomenon known as cyberspace (or the *information superhighway*, Washington's pet name for it).

You could argue that the cyberspace frontier has been here for more than two decades because the Internet has been around for a while. But the tumbling costs of personal computing and the spiraling speeds and capabilities of hardware and software have just recently made the Internet and the world of on-line communications available to everyone.

No other aspect of information technology has flourished this quickly. More than a million computers have been connected to the Internet over the past ten years, and some experts estimate that more than 1,000 new users connect each day. The Internet is international in scope — more than 50,000 networks in around 160 countries connect to the Internet. And as LANs around the world standardize on TCP/IP (Transmission Control Protocol/Internet Protocol), the number of networks on the Net will swell to the millions. Thus, the Internet provides a great example of the power of open systems and global standardization in telecommunications.

As a consultant, this means I also have to align myself with consultants who specialize in other IT fields so that I can bring more than just information to my clients. If I did not do this — recommending the same solutions year in and year out instead — I would not be in business for much longer. One subject that turned my consulting life upside down (but I'm especially enamored of it anyway) is the Internet and its hypertext service, the World Wide Web.

COMPUTER TELEPHONY AND CYBERSPACE

Let's go to the IT road map (Figure 12-1). Both CT and Internet services share common objectives in the customer service area: exchanging information and communicating. In the future, I believe that Internet services will gradually replace (for many organizations) a significant number of audiotext, IVR, and fax applications. In many cases the Internet services will completely supplant them as customer satisfaction and information exchange tools. This transition could be wide-spread and possibly come before the end of the century, although telephone access to quick information will still be needed.

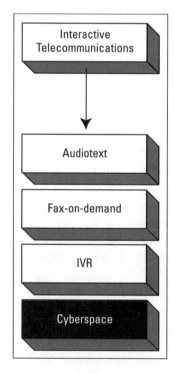

Figure 12-1: Cyberspace and the IT service domains.

When it does happen, this transition will take place in the same fashion that the fax machine replaced telex and teletext in the mid-1980s. Undoubtedly, today's Internet has already reached critical mass (more than 100 million users may be on it by the year 2000); over the next decade, this technology can expect to see mass participation by business.

Is it fair to devote so much time to the Internet in a book about computer telephony? *Yes.* Strategy-wise, I have to discuss it. As a business owner or IT manager (or both), you have to lay the two technologies and communications models side-by-side. Right now, investing in the Internet is the most important strategic decision you can make (if you haven't already) when evaluating your computer telephony needs and your overall IT needs.

You may be wondering, will cyberspace replace computer telephony or voice communications in the business arena? No. Voice services (call-processing, voice-processing, and voice-messaging services) will always be there to assist and facilitate the chief means by which you communicate with your customers (at least, until humans evolve into telepaths and no longer need our voice boxes to communicate with each other). Voice communications will always be the first line of service in the CSI (customer satisfaction index) picture. This scenario will change as users opt for more online dialogue (via electronic mail and the World Wide Web, for example) with your enterprise. In the coming years, the information exchange (information and data retrieval) services of computer telephony will be the ones challenged by the Internet.

E-mail is another popular Internet service now competing with computer telephony messaging services, most directly with fax mail and voice mail, as a way to empower users and customers alike. E-mail can provide several advantages as a messaging service, which we'll discuss in the next chapter, but it also has its drawbacks. For now, just know that e-mail is an alternative you need to consider as the Internet and its services grow in popularity, and that it can be used in combination with CT messaging services to increase productivity (the next chapter discusses this subject in more detail.)

The following list provides some guidelines and rationale for using Internet services over computer telephony services (when you can):

✦ **Send or invite e-mail before you make that call or send a fax if the recipient has an e-mail address.** E-mail eliminates telephone tag and the hassles of fax, and also gets you a faster response. If your business associates have e-mail, use it for negotiating or corresponding with them. You'll take less calls, deal with less voice mail and fax-mail, and be able to respond more easily and quickly as a result.

I recently began talking to a large software company about how they can enter the computer telephony industry. During our first voice contact, the firm's representatives told me that future discussion would be via e-mail. We exchanged a great deal of e-mail without really knowing where either party was when the message was sent. On one occasion, I got a reply from the floor of an expo, which impressed me. When I got e-mail from an executive jet traveling at 35,000 feet, I started shaking with excitement. I also like the idea that I have an electronic record of every conversation (as do they).

✦ **Send or invite e-mail before faxes or fax-mail.** E-mail eliminates the need to engage in extensive fax transmission of preliminary negotiation and discussions. It is easier and less expensive to send someone e-mail and prompt them for a response than to repeatedly send faxes. Corresponding initially via e-mail enables you to measure the penetration of your message and the value of your correspondence before incurring expenses with voice and fax communication.

✦ **Send information from the enterprise information network via e-mail.** Using e-mail eliminates the need for extensive fax transmissions of corporate literature, documents, price lists, and so on. Besides freeing up the time it took to scan or convert the items, the information contained in the literature will be clearer and easier to read. For example, I asked Qualcom, Inc. (via the telephone) to send me literature on their Internet e-mail package, Eudora. They simply e-mailed me a trial version of the software. The person receiving the information via e-mail also finds it easier to zero in on a specific item (or lack of one) in the documentation and request immediate clarification or further information, such as cost and availability of an item.

✦ **Attach documents and files to your e-mail in their native formats.** This practice eliminates the need to fax documents to parties, who cannot easily edit, review, change, or otherwise work comfortably with the documents once they receive them. A good example is the transmission of a spreadsheet, report, or graphic that needs to be reviewed. If you faxed these documents, the receiver can only annotate or scribble over them manually. E-mail copies of the documents, sent as binary attachments, are identical to the original copy. If the receiver has the same software used to create the application, he or she can work directly on the file. You don't have to go through any time-consuming conversions (which degrade the format and layout in any event). On-line document conferencing further enhances this concept.

✦ **Make the resources of your enterprise information network accessible via the Web.** By using this format, you reduce the load on the fax-on-demand system and make it easier to manage. Users can access the information for the cost of a local call from anywhere on earth (or above it) and avoid the heady long-distance charges you'd get by faxing to people on the other side of the planet.

The Web interface for resources you place on it is much more user-friendly than the interface for fax-on-demand or IVR. Rather than endure tedious and time-consuming menus via the TUI (telephone user interface), your users will find it easier to surf over to your Web site and find the information there. You can place information on the Web as an HTML (Hypertext Markup Language) document or in a portable document format (the best known being the Adobe Acrobat Portable Document Format, or PDF). These files are easier to create, edit, and manage than files that have to be converted into fax form. As a result, many of the faxes I have retrieved over the past few years were too outdated to make me appreciate what the enterprise was offering (see Chapter 10 for managing fax-on-demand systems).

THE INTERNET

Until recently, few people outside of governments, educational institutions, and the military knew about the Internet. Part of the reason may be that it was so hard to use (without a GUI) that few people cared to consider what a marvelous communications tool it was. Or perhaps we still had to get over fax fever and voice mail sickness. As recently as one year ago, some software engineers still shied away from the Net jungle, preferring to blow budgets on modem-to-modem file transfers instead. And, don't forget, the Internet community barred business from the Internet until 1991. That's when the Commercial Internet Exchange (CIX) was formed, a body that serves the interests of commercial Internet service providers (ISPs).

So what's so good about cyberspace? Graphical user interfaces on operating systems like the Apple Mac and Microsoft Windows (the user interface is everything) and fast modems open a window to the Internet right from our homes and offices. The Internet user is like Alice falling into Wonderland. *Dial, connect, experience.* Dial some numbers and suddenly you can *surf* around the world from computer to computer, fish around in mountains (or gopher holes) of information, send people e-mail, advertise to millions for the cost of a classified ad in print, make new friends, check out the competition, and — well — make new enemies.

Although cyberspace potential is great, few people really know how to use it. For example, most users don't know how to place a document or image on it, and little is really known about the demographics, users and its uses, and the geography of cyberspace. Part of the problem is that the Internet is growing faster than it can be quantified; the most accurate statement to date is that the Internet population is growing at the rate of ten percent per month. The Net is like the universe — constantly expanding in all directions.

As a small business owner or an IT specialist, you need to be in cyberspace, and you need to be there now. The reason is not that it's a "window of opportunity" that some say is going to close soon. The Internet is not some on-line business park selling prime space fast (although *domain names* may soon be as valuable as an address at the Empire State Building). You need to be connected because it's good business, because your competition may already be there, and because your customers are out there — in cyberspace — waiting for you. Don't forget that you want to represent the anywhere, anytime, alluring enterprise; and that includes cyberspace.

THE WORLD WIDE WEB

The World Wide Web, or just plain Web, is the hypertext/hypermedia service of the Internet. Many books deal with the Web in detail and almost every computer book publisher has this subject already covered (including IDG Books Worldwide, Inc.). Thus, I have nothing new to offer on the basic composition of the Web and refer you to these good books (you have several hundred to choose from).

But in terms of discussing computer telephony, you should understand that the Web is undergoing a rapid transformation from a hypertext service to a full-blown hyper-media service that offers simultaneous access to text, data, audio, images, and voice. This capability involves computer telephony, so we discuss the Web in this book from that respect.

THE WORLD WIDE WEB VERSUS IVR/IFR AND FAX-ON-DEMAND

As other chapters already discussed, both interactive voice response (IVR) and fax-on-demand (FOD) offer limited and often restrictive interfaces to the information re-siding in the enterprise information network. For this reason, you need to use these services carefully. Several factors must be considered when designing and imple-menting these systems, as follows:

✦ Cost

✦ Convenience

✦ Users

I am not suggesting that you drop the IVR or FOD service and just go Web, Web, Web or Net, Net, Net (although some firms are doing this for some good reasons, as ex-plained later). All services have their place in the computer telephony picture, and you should use one service over another if that's what the users want. Again, talk to your customers, do customer satisfaction interviews, undertake needs syntheses, and find out what your users want. Find out what works best to make your enterprise alluring while enabling your firm to be the anywhere, anytime enterprise.

Many enterprises throw everything at their customers and users over the telephone or fax machine. They stick thousands of documents on the FOD service (most of which go out-of-date and stay that way) and provide access to tons of data on the IVR side. If you ask the users what they think of these systems, however, you get answers simi-lar to the following ones, which I culled from users of an IVR system installed on a medical insurance line and an FOD system installed at a software reseller:

> We don't know how long the faxes are when we access them. After finally making the selection, we end up with 10 or 20 pages coming in over the fax machine, which wastes paper and keeps out other callers.

Some faxes are poor scans of the original glossy brochures that contain high quality photographs. When the faxes comes through, we get nothing but a black blob we can't identify.

The IVR system has too many menus and too many options. We spend a lot of time on the telephone going from level to level, writing down the information furiously and often incorrectly.

Often we miss the information and have to loop around and go through the menus again to get the information repeated, so we don't save that much time.

If we hit the wrong button or are distracted, then it can take as much as another five minutes to get back to the point where we were.

Many times the system just shuts down and that's the end of it. We then have to go out to the ATM anyway.

Why give the users such hardships when the detailed information they seek could be accessed visually from the World Wide Web? Many banks opt for this solution. Is security an issue? I don't think so — nothing could be less secure than the four or five password tones you key in over the telephone to access all your information. You don't need to be a member of the *Mission: Impossible* team to record a user's tones from a wire tap. One software engineer I know, who spent four years developing voice-response systems, could imitate the tones with his voice.

IVR was a critical service before the advent of the Web (I once called it the killer app that kills — developers and users alike). It gave users and customers access to data and information they were seeking without having to bother the firm's workers. But the extent to which users can access, update, or change information is limited by an interface that caters only to the sense of sound, and over a medium (the telephone) that itself is very limiting. The Web, on the other hand, opens the window to the enterprise information system. You can control exactly what you want the user to see and how you want the person to work with and manipulate the data.

But, to add a feather to IVR's cap, nothing beats the ability to pick up the telephone, dial a number, enter a password, and glean critical data (like a bank balance). Logging onto the Internet, however, can take ten minutes; and then you have to launch the browser (and the server might be busy). In short, if you're going to log onto the Internet you should plan to spend some time there.

By the time this book is published, the WWW will have become a true multi-media medium. Enterprises will be putting live audio-visual data on their Web sites and creating snazzy 3D presentations that jump to life when you access the page. I say *live* because the Web interface is a direct port to the enterprise's database management system from the remote monitor which can be anywhere in the world and accessed at the cost of local telephone tariffs. Web users will be able to work with their data as if they were sitting in the same office as the server machine that contains the database. IVR and FOD systems, on the other hand, are hardly as user-friendly. To a large extent they can be repulsive, while the Web can be very alluring.

As the Internet and the World Wide Web become more secure and popular, it may make sense for you to offer a simpler telephone (IVR) interface to your organization's data than you currently offer and to scale down the complexity and size of the FOD. You'll save money in addition to providing added customer convenience, because a good, robust IVR system can cost an enterprise more than $100,000 in software alone. Then you have to factor in upkeep and hardware. Alternatively, an enterprise can install a Web server for under $10,000.

As the popular southern Florida radio station *Y100* now promotes: "Hear us, see us on the World Wide Web."

INTRANETS

What may be more significant for business right now than the Internet is a new model of business networking known as *intranetworking*, or intranets. How did the IT industry suddenly inherit this new child being cloned, adopted, or seriously considered by almost every IT manager on the planet? Let's go back to the critical emergence of the Internet for the answers.

The global love-affair with the Internet has led to capitalists feverishly investing billions of dollars into any technology company creating or adapting a product for use on the Internet. I have not been able to put my finger on the real reason why Wall Street and other stock trading posts have placed such high value on anything for the Internet. I won't go into the subject (lest this book turns majorly philosophical on you), but I'm sure that many of the reasons you can come up with still do not warrant such "valuable" attention.

Many experts view the feeding-frenzy of Internet investment with a jaundiced eye. Does it not seem incredible that companies with very little technological prowess, no patents, no new genius, and no new algorithms or breakthrough can go public and be given market capitalization in amounts as high as a billion dollars? All of this money is pouring into the Internet while other companies, some developing critical medical and biotechnological wizardry, go unnoticed. Their time will come, however, because their products will be even more attractive when the Internet becomes as much a part of life as I-95 is to motoring America. Bubbles will burst — that much I am sure about.

The upside of all this money going into the Internet is that many companies are developing Internet products, hoping to see riches come from the massive size of the Internet audience. Every software or computer company in the world would be nuts to ignore what is happening on the Internet. All of these companies are creating some component of their software to work on the Internet and, in many respects, are coming up with new Internet products. Just to remain competitive, these companies need to label anything and everything they produce as Internet-ready.

Perhaps the most famous example to date is a programming language known as Java. Created some years ago by Sun Microsystems, Inc., the original motivation for this new language was to easily program intelligence into consumer electronics. Sun and its partners needed new technology to make it easier to program toasters, cellular phones, washing machines, cars, and so on. But then the Internet train stopped at their platform, and now Java has 100,000 developers around the world furiously creating Java software for the Internet. The computer telephony industry is on the same train, too, as you will see later. As a result of this investment fever, companies are now creating more products for the Internet than for any other sector of the technology industry (more patents are pending for Internet products than for any other products).

As discussed earlier, the Internet is not new. The critical component of the Internet is its set of network protocols known as TCP/IP, which stands for Transmission Control Protocol/Internet Protocol. TCP/IP has been used in business networking on LANs and legacy networks for many years. Digital Equipment Corporation's (DEC) DECNET is a good example of an Ethernet LAN that has been running TCP/IP services for a while. NetWare also had TCP/IP before any of my clients or I considered connecting to the Internet.

The TCP/IP set of protocols was intially developed by the U.S. Department of Defense to link different kinds of computers across an ocean of disparate networks. After it was adopted by business, TCP/IP became the most popular protocol to be deployed across Ethernet and X.25 networks. Although it has become the de facto suite of networking protocols, the successor to TCP/IP — which will be based on the Open Systems Interconnection (OSI) architecture, a child of the International Standards Organization (ISO) — is already being tested.

Back in 1992, my company needed to build TCP/IP support into a computer telephony product to get the product to interoperate with mainframe computers running on DECNET via TCP/IP. To enable Windows applications to talk down to TCP/IP networks (from the application and presentation layer to the network layer), software needed to be hooked up to the Winsock network API. Considering the vast number of computers running Microsoft Windows, had I (like many software entrepreneurs now kicking themselves) devoted more energy to TCP/IP and Winsock development, I would be a multi-millionaire.

If the Internet were a train, TCP/IP would be its tracks. TCP is the "New Master of the Domain" as *LAN Magazine* proclaimed in its October 1995 issue. As a result, corporations that have adopted TCP/IP as their chief LAN protocol (and many did years ago) have suddenly found a host of new products and development tools to install on their LANs that can make their people more productive. LAN managers and IT staff have, for example, found it far easier to set up a corporate Web site and give their users Web browsers than to maintain the old bulletin board systems that were so popular but hard to use in the late '80s and early '90s.

Also, BBS required dedicated connections from client to server over the PSTN, which is the chief reason why it did not become a pervasive technology, and why the BBS from as late as 1995 will be dead and buried by 1997. Even voice-mail distribution lists cannot compete with the capability to publish information on a Web server.

What's more, much of the client Internet software is free, and the server software is very affordable. As a result, IT managers are bringing Internet technology into the business like bees bringing pollen into the hives. It's cheap, it's abundant, and it works. This is what intranetworking is all about. Intranets are nothing more than LANs running TCP/IP to support Internet technology such as Web servers, Web browsers and other Internet client applications such as FTP applets and data-rendering technology. That said, managing a TCP/IP network is not as easy a task as slicing cheese. But the task is getting easier every day, especially because the likes of Microsoft are sinking so much money (billions) and programming effort (thousands of geeks) into Internet development.

Office automation and groupware are being rapidly adapted to support intranetworking and the TCP/IP protocols. A whole new generation of software is emerging that has the Internet flowing through its heart and soul. I call this phenomenon the "paradigms smashed" phenomenon, which caused the leading technology companies to rethink their strategic objectives. Software must to be built on groupware principals and be communicative in nature, because the Internet enables even the loneliest computer user (such as my marine biologist friend who lives in the most isolated regions of the North Pole) to connect to others and share resources.

Computer telephony is communications software, but without the Internet (and by default, Intranet connectivity and support), computer telephony software is outmoded, outdated, and less effective. This point is where the new paradigms of Internet and intranet telephony come into being. I'd even go as far as to say that, by 1997, any software company whose product cannot connect to the Internet and reliably talk to the new emerging Internet protocols will be dead meat.

INTERNET TELEPHONY

Internet telephony is a new territory that deals with cutting-edge technology, most of which is still in the trial-and-error stage. Using the definitions provided in Chapter 1, the Internet telephony being discussed here consists of voice communications that are facilitated, enhanced, or carried by the Internet. Internet telephony uses the Internet as the carrier rather than the public switched telephone network (PSTN), although the boundaries of PSTN and the Internet are blurring more every day.

In fact, many people no longer are surprised that you can have a telephone (voice) conversation over the Internet. You could say that the PSTN and the Internet are part of the same network "cloud," because many telephone companies and long-distance providers now offer Internet access over the same wires that provide voice communications. The difference between PSTN and the Internet really boils down to a matter of protocols and the sending and receiving equipment at the origination, interconnection, and termination points of the network, the technical details of which are beyond the scope of this book.

By the turn of the century, the international telephone network and all the interconnecting networks, both private and public, will be part and parcel of one huge, information superhighway. Even today, setting up a conference call among callers using telephones and those using computers is not too difficult. You can even conference in a Web site and listen to a Web-borne hypertext document. Hence, you have the advent of Internet telephones.

The *Internet telephone* is a simple hardware/software device made up of existing PC technology. The "netphone" hardware has existed in the LAN world for many years, and adapting it to deliver voice along primarily data-centric networks (digital networks) was not shuttle science. LAN engineers have long pondered such a concept; in fact, LAN manufacturer Artisoft, Inc., actually invented a voice-enabled LAN card some years back (although it was not widely adopted). Many IT managers considered using ISDN/PBX technology just to be able to use the PBX as a gateway for data. ISDN access for many companies is provided by the telephone company, and an intranet (a LAN running TCP/IP and Internet technology) enables a company to connect to the Internet through the ISDN PBX (although this option is very expensive if you really just want an ISDN connection to the Internet).

Internet telephone software, as illustrated by NetSpeak Corporation's WebPhone in Figure 12-2, manages a digital voice conversation and controls the required hardware for converting data to analog form so that humans can hear the information and reply by voice. To imitate the standard telephone, Internet telephone software needs to access sound cards, PC speakers, and PC microphones. The sending and receiving of the data is done no differently by the modem or network interface card at the hardware and network levels of the Internet.

Figure 12-2: Whereas other Internet telephones sport traditional Windows user interfaces, NetSpeak's WebPhone has been modeled after cellular phones and emphasizes the critical business application of the product.

What made the idea of Internet telephones so hot is that the Internet is practically a free resource, especially in North America. To the Internet, voice data traveling along its network is no different than other data. But the Internet is not owned by anyone (although that topic is a sizzler for debate), and over the years, a "freebie" culture has developed that persists today. That culture has made charging for anything on the Internet difficult.

But the free Internet is already a thing of the past. Though access in the U.S. is close to free, other parts of the world do not have the same benefit. In some countries, Internet access is even more expensive than long-distance calling. Why would you go to the pain of setting up a telephone call on a computer via the Internet when the telephone is cheaper and carries the promise of more than a century of service and sound quality?

For example, I wanted to set up an Internet connection with my mother and sister who live in South Africa because my telephone bill was high. But the effort of getting them a decent PC, a decent modem, and an Internet connection proved to be too expensive. I would have needed a year of free Internet telephone calls to pay for the investment. Not much logic in that. Business-wise, I may not find it useful to talk via the Internet to a business associate only a city away — but that feature could be useful if I were based in New York City and my learned friend were based in San Diego.

Something else to consider is that serious moves are afoot in Washington, D.C. and at state-legislature levels to impose taxes on the Internet. In addition, a number of traditional telephone-industry (long-distance of course) members have lobbied the FCC to either ban Internet telephones or impose taxes and trade tariffs on them. With a fair amount of cynicism, I have to admit that any tax or tariff placed on the Internet may make using Internet telephones a nonsensical idea for "chatting" with family members over long distances.

If you plan on investing in Internet telephone technology, be sure to consider items that may not have an obvious price tag on your needs-synthesis clipboard. These include the following:

◆ The cost of the peripheral equipment, such as speakers, headsets, microphones, soundboards, and other multimedia equipment

◆ The cost of Internet access, which is very high in many parts of the world

◆ The time it takes to set up a call, considering that your party needs to be online at the same time

◆ The time it takes to "tune" the Internet phone to get the best voice quality

Keep in mind that Internet telephones need hardware. Hardware may be affordable to many in the U.S., where consumers benefit from the huge economy of scale, but elsewhere their price tags may outweigh the benefits gained. Computing is expensive: In the European Economic Union, just stick a CD player into a PC and see what happens to the price. The import tariffs triple because the computer is no longer taxed as a computer but rather as a consumer electronics item.

Also, it will not be long before some countries reclassify a computer with Internet telephony software and an internal sound-card as a telephone. That means such a device will fall under PTT (Post, Telephone and Telegraph) administration, and so a user may have to take out a license just to own the computer.

The non-U.S. import duties on Internet telephone software also may go through the roof. Software is taxed by as much as 500 percent in some countries, so an Internet telephone may be taxed as software once and then again as a telephone. An example: A voice-mail system that costs under $5,000 in the U.S. can cost a foreign corporation as much as $100,000.

INTRANET TELEPHONY

Although I have mixed feelings about using Internet telephony as a tool to circumvent long-distance charges, I think it's a cooker as far as using it with intranets.

Take a group (or several groups) of people in an office, for example. Now give them a high-bandwidth Ethernet LAN or WAN (or an interconnection of corporate LANs, WANs, and Web servers). Have TCP/IP drive the whole show and put Internet telephones on every PC, and you have the making of a marvelous new concept in inter/intraoffice multimedia telecommunications. Figure 12-3 illustrates the interconnection of data and telephone networks on the Internet and intranet.

As Figure 12-3 illustrates, the center of the corporate intranet is the Web server (a), which provides users in the internal and external environment of the corporation with a "doorway" to the EIN. The Web pages stored there typically can support sales, customer satisfaction, technical support, and so on. Internet phone technology can be easily accessed from the Web page. A company installing intranet telephony would need to install an Internet/intranet telephone PBX as well. This device is a network-based version of the standard PBX, which extends the traditional CTI and telephony features (such as ACD and call processing) to the intranet telephone system.

A gateway to the PSTN or telephone exchange (c) is essential for connecting Internet telephone callers with standard telephones via the PSTN (f). Employees and users on an intranet now have easy access to Web services, intranet telephony services, and standard computer telephony systems from their workstations (d).

An intranet-telephony control center (e) is a system that manages the intranet PBX system. From such a control center (a component of NetSpeak's Business WebPhone System), IT and call-center technicians can manage inbound and outbound Internet telephony traffic. By using their WebPhones and Web browsers for secure transactions, shoppers can benefit from the availability of simultaneous voice, image, and data communication for making credit-card payment through banking networks such as VisaNet (g). With Internet telephony, traditional computer telephony (switching and voice processing) and Internet/intranet-PSTN gateways (h, i, and j), cyberspace is a happy place where everyone can communicate with each other.

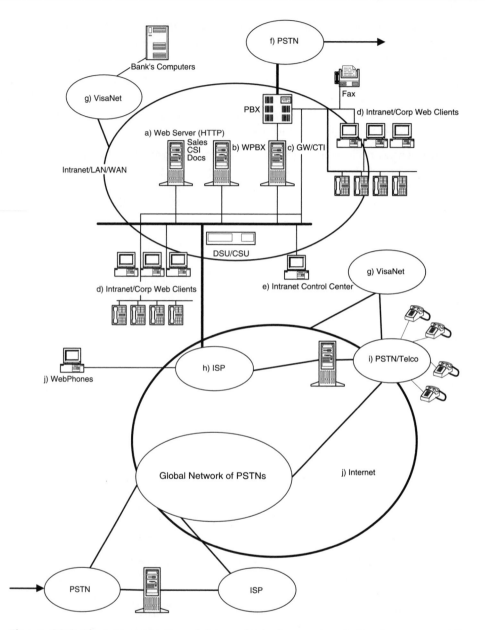

Figure 12-3: The interconnection of data and telephone networks in cyberspace and the relationship between the Internet and corporate or private intranet.

For some time now, through Electronic Data Interchange technology (EDI), many enterprises have exchanged data with their clients and suppliers over wide-area networks. IT has invested heavily in e-mail to help relieve the load on office telephone systems and PBXs. Now, with intranet technology deployed over LANs, companies can talk with their clients over the same network.

Using an intranet as an alternative method of interoffice communication is a good idea because it helps keep people off the "physical" telephone. In some large corporations, the staff spends as much time on the telephone with other members of the company as they do with customers and clients. And if staff members are talking on the phone between groups and departments and even leaving voice mail for each another, someone else trying to call in (the customer) may end up being dumped into voice messaging and may abandon the call. The result? The caller may have to call back, a sale may be lost, or the caller may have to be put on hold, forcing telephonists and administrators to waste time monitoring telephone traffic.

In short, you get an unnecessary waste of time and money. Communicating via a system that provides a unified, integrated multimedia messaging capability (including voice, fax, e-mail, video, and file transfer functions) is much more efficient. I will admit, however, that nothing beats the ease of dialing a person, even to ask a question as simple as "Do you have a paper clip?" The ease with which a telephone enables you to communicate to someone is simply irreplaceable.

At the time of this writing, the only Internet/intranet telephone company I would invest in, if it was public, is NetSpeak Corporation in Boca Raton, Florida. NetSpeak is the only Internet telephony software maker concentrating on the intranet or business corner of the Internet market, although their WebPhone can be used to chat to your heart's content. I spent a great deal of time with their cofounder, Chief Technical Officer Shane D. Mattaway, pondering the application of Internet telephony on corporate intranets.

NetSpeak's technology is based on point-to-point communication on a TCP/IP network (IP address-to-IP address). Most other Internet telephones rely on the Internet Relay Chat (IRC) service, which is essentially bandwidth reserved for Internet chat "lines." This means you have to log on to an IRC chat server to use the device, and making such a connection to another person not only takes more time, but will never be a suitable replacement for a real-time telephone conversation. Also, server-based architectures place severe limitations on the development of switched networks that function efficiently for organizations with widely dispersed sites.

Another problem with relying on the Internet Relay Chat service is that the Internet also is frightfully unsecure. You may think you're having a one-to-one conversation, but there's no telling how many ears are listening in the dark. Hiding from a determined *cyberspy* on the Internet is very difficult, as the movie *The Net* demonstrated.

Point-to-point Internet telephony is more akin to regular telephony because you simply look for an IP address or a friendly name and then "dial" that number. Over the Internet, the person (or rather, the machine) you are calling may not be online at the time, but on an intranet, the computers are permanently connected and always online (if the techies are doing their jobs).

With an intranet, every computer in the company has an address and is connected to the LAN; in turn, the LANs are connected to each other and to other LANs at remote offices of the corporation. Thus, whether you are a company that only maintains one small LAN spread over several offices, or the likes of IBM, which has a corporate net-work about as large as the Internet, intranet telephones may be boon for your business.

The quality of the voice is acceptable over the WAN and no different than talking on the telephone, when all parties are connected to the same LAN. Over the Internet, a conversation is mostly akin to having a Citizens Band (CB) chat, with a single-duplex phone, and a cellular phone conversation with a full-duplex phone. On the intranet, the phones, like the LAN, and the corporate telephone network are always up and running; thus, you can talk to someone on the other side of the company simply by clicking a button. Connecting this way with someone working on the other side of the world for the same company can save a firm huge volumes of time and money.

The benefit of keeping people off phones for interoffice communication is not the only marvel I can single out for intranet telephony. Shane Mattaway showed me how a voice call made over an intranet can be routed to a PSTN or PBX gateway so that the caller can connect to any standard telephone. At the time of this writing, NetSpeak's gateway product is the only one of its kind ready for commercial exploitation by business.

The following information was provided by Shane and is based on information found in NetSpeak's media kit. This information describes the hottest of the hot Internet/intranet telephony technology, created by NetSpeak Corporation:

WEBPHONE INTRANET SERVER AND PBX

This product provides you with the following features and more:

✦ Selectable directory-assistance publishing scope and access

✦ The capability to initiate telephone calls to other users by selecting e-mail addresses or aliases

✦ Directory assistance (similar to dialing 555-1212 in the U.S.)

✦ Configurable isolation from other WebPhone users

✦ Follow-me services (more a feature of the Internet's IP addressing scheme)

✦ Secure transmission using RSA public-key encryption technology

✦ Remote system administration

WEBPHONE AUTOMATIC CALL DISTRIBUTOR

This is a software application that runs on servers to provide an organization with a TCP/IP-based LAN or WAN call-center for its Web-driven business. Features include the following:

+ Real-time call routing

+ Queuing

+ Messaging-on-hold

+ Connection to voice mail

It also includes many of the goodies you'd find in traditional call centers, such as call-center management software for statistics analysis and reporting.

WEBPHONE PSTN GATEWAY

This gateway is a hardware and software product that enables WebPhone users to place calls to conventional telephones on the PSTN (Public Switched Telephone Network). It makes the connection to the telephone subscriber through any switch, PBX, or ACD unit. It can exist in the central office of the telephone company or be connected to the office PBX.

The gateway also enables both parties on conventional telephones to use the Internet or intranet to connect two or more gateways. This means that all parties can use their standard telephones to converse over the TCP/IP network.

An outstanding aspect of the gateway is the added RSA security feature for secure conversations. And you can connect any fax machine to the gateway (via the PBX or direct) meaning the age of long-distance fax calls may be over for many adopters.

As of June 1996, the WebPhone business system is still in Beta.

USING INTRANET TELEPHONY WISELY

Using the intranet/Internet-PSTN gateway means that you can make a voice call over the Internet and intranet to any standard telephone in the world, as long as a gateway has been installed in the local vicinity of the recipient. My family in South Africa, for example, doesn't need a PC and an Internet connection if a gateway is supported in Johannesburg.

This setup changes everything and is rather scary for the long-distance industry. A company that connects its offices over a wide-area network can, with little bother, connect an intranet-PBX gateway in its remote office. With hardware as simple as telephony interface cards and voice-processing cards, the intranet caller can establish dial-tone at the remote site via the PBX and call someone in the remote city as if he or she was calling from that city.

Take a company like IBM, which owns the world's largest channel for computer technology in the world. It has such a huge global network in place that intranet telephony could wipe out millions in long-distance charges. The airlines companies, too, are good examples of companies that own global enterprise information networks.

Intranet telephony, which is supported by business, comes loaded with features. You get everything that comes with your usual feature phones and then some. For starters, you can conference up to 250 people on an intranet phone PBX; you also can receive and make up to four calls at the same time, so someone can call you on Line 2 while you are talking on Line 1. Intranet telephones also support the Internet version of Caller ID because you know the IP or e-mail address of the person calling. And you can do a lot of things in a business environment if you know who is calling. You certainly can better prepare yourself to handle the call, and if you're away from your PC, you can set up a different voice message greeting for every caller.

In the new and exploding Web business, Internet/intranet telephony may prove to be a real winner. A whole new paradigm is emerging: the concept of switching Internet voice calls to standard telephones and PCs right from the Web pages. Thus, if the customer sees something he or she likes and needs further assistance, the customer simply needs to click on a button on the page. You (as the vendor) then can have two things happen: You can enable the customer to connect with a representative and have a live voice conversation right from the Web page, or you can have the representative call the customer back at his or her regular telephone number. This feature is great for Web business because it means callers can connect with sales people without having to make a regular — and often long-distance — call.

The Internet and computer telephony industries have met and formed a love affair. The result of this union is Internet/intranet telephony. This new paradigm will flourish and go a long way in the world of intranets.

Although this technology has great potential, we have to be careful not to make the same mistakes with Internet or intranet telephony that our PBX and telephony cousins have made over the years. As mentioned in earlier chapters, PBX companies have made the same mistake for decades: producing equipment that few people can use. Many PBX extension sets provide such a ridiculous amount of feature buttons that are hardly ever needed or used that, as a result, few people in an office know how to set up a conference or how to program a button that automatically calls the voice-messaging system.

The last thing, then, that you want to do is throw Internet telephones at users and have them face yet another struggle with dozens of cryptic buttons and features that detract from, rather enhance or facilitate, making a call. The computer telephony industry exerts a great deal of effort to reduce the complexity of making calls and using PBX systems. Making a call from a computer should be as simple as saying "Computer, call Karl and conference in Erik, Wayne, Lars, and Bryan, and then record the conversation for posterity."

The following list describes several features that you'll want to make sure your Internet telephone includes:

✦ **Point-to-point calling.** This feature should have been called person-to-person calling because it more accurately describes a Net phone feature that operates similar to the way standard voice telephony works. In other words, you attempt to connect to the other party by "dialing" his or her e-mail address, an IP address (if it is fixed rather than dynamically assigned for every Internet login), or an alias (to the IP or e-mail address). (Don't let the point-to-point part confuse you — this isn't the same as the PPP connection protocol.)

Some phones have you connect to other parties by logging on to an IRC facility, which is insecure and unstable. When lots of people log on to the IRC server, call conditions worsen, and you could lose your connection. The IRC option does not permit many of the features that resemble "old era" computer telephony, such as voice messaging and music, while on hold.

✦ **Full-duplex communication.**

✦ **Caller ID and the capability to screen or bar callers.** This feature is important for preventing uninvited guests from gate-crashing your conversation or eavesdropping by breaking in another line.

✦ **Multiple-line support.** For concurrent conversations and the capability to conference in other callers

✦ **Call holding.**

✦ **Voice mail services.** The phones vendor should deploy several servers around the world that enable you to leave voice mail for users who are not logged on to the Internet or who may be otherwise unavailable.

✦ **Party-specific voice mail.**

✦ **Complete access to sound-card electronics.** Naturally, the better the sound card, the better the quality of voice conversation. Access to the sound card enables you to best configure your telephone (although the phone software should be doing this for you) and permit user-definable sound effects, such as ringing and music (or MIDI) on hold.

✦ **Conversation encryption.** The conversation is scrambled and can only be deciphered by the receiving telephone. This means that anyone tapping into the middle of the connection will only hear garbage. The Internet is chock-full of eavesdroppers, and you should always assume that your telephone conversations will never be private. This feature is one of the most important.

SUMMARY

The Internet (and its hypertext service called the World Wide Web) is evolving into a critical service that business can use as a premium customer satisfaction tool and to gain competitive advantage. More importantly, the Internet is turning the world of telephony on its head, and you should watch this technology closely. If this chapter convinced you that the Web is more appropriate for your needs, I direct you to Part III because you will be needing some expertise. If you plan to do further reading on this subject, IDG Books Worldwide, Inc., has some excellent titles. One of my favorites is by fellow cyberpal Dave Taylor, called *Creating Cool Web Pages with HTML.*

In This Chapter

"Thank you for calling. Please leave a message. In case I forget to check my messages, please send your message as an audio file to my e-mail, then send me a fax to remind me to check my e-mail, then call back to remind me to check my fax."

CHAPTER 13

ELECTRONIC MESSAGING AND THE PRODIGIOUS MAILBOX

O ne of the most exciting pay-offs of the new frontier in information technology is that you are no longer a slave to the limitations of the information systems you employ in your enterprise. You can choose exactly how and when you want to communicate to customers and co-workers alike. You can communicate in real-time by picking up the telephone and dialing a number, or you can send someone a message by fax, e-mail, or voice mail.

You now also have the ability to choose how you want others to communicate with you. You can choose the medium that will bear the message to and from the parties with whom you're conversing. Indeed, many people I talk to now refuse to get back to me over the telephone or via fax. I, too, try to avoid having someone send me a fax, preferring instead to "talk" via the Internet, using e-mail.

Now, that's real business power. It's kind of scary even, and many factors play a part in it. It makes me wonder: When we meet our maker, are we going to first lay down the rules for communication?

This chapter thus deals with the world of (non-interactive) electronic messaging, or *electronic mail* (see Figure 13-1). The three message formats that this chapter reviews are v-mail (voice mail), f-mail (fax mail), and e-mail (electronic mail). All three types employ the so-called architecture of *store-and-forward* mail, or S&F mail, as many choose to refer to it.

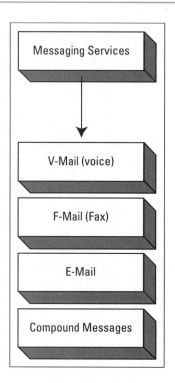

Figure 13-1: The messaging service domain of computer telephony.

The principle under which S&F mail operates is simple: A message is sent to a virtual mailbox in a virtual post office that resides somewhere in the world. The physical machine may be located in an office belonging to your enterprise or it may be a host computer on the vast Internet. To retrieve the mail, the recipient (that's you, the human) logs in to the mailbox from a computer screen or telephone. The mail is then transferred from the post office to you.

New advances in technology have enabled users to employ means that automate the retrieving process. You can send out software agents to return with news and information. With v-mail, you can actually log in to the message storehouse directly and receive a copy of the message over the telephone. Nowadays, you can have agents keep track of your mail, in all its forms, and report to you whenever they turn up a memo or note meant for your attention.

The message type that conforms the most to true S&F is e-mail, and you can find it in its purest form on a LAN-based, workgroup post office. The post office enables you to peek into your mailbox, and if you do have mail, transfer the message and any attachments to your screen.

The post offices also are proactive in nature. Wanting to keep clutter and unretrieved mail from piling up, the post office can beep you on the screen or call you wherever you may be. You can also send or forward a message onwards to another computer somewhere else in the world, for someone else to listen to or read.

Understanding that all these message types are a form of non-interactive communications that work on S&F principles is important in preparing the way for the merging and "morphing" of the messages into a single compound message that will contain sound, text, graphics, and video elements.

VOICE MAIL: THE OMNIPRESENT MESSAGE

Several years ago, I took a call from the telephone manager of the University of South Africa in Pretoria. Better known as UNISA, this university is the largest correspondence institution in the world.

"We're having problems with our answering machines," he said. "How can you help?"

"We don't fix or sell answering machines," I replied.

"No, let me explain, I'm about to buy the thousandth machine. And this one, like all the others, is not going to last. I've been told we need something called a voice-mail machine."

I thought this poor soul was joking. When I arrived at his office, he showed me to a storeroom where I saw a mountain of broken answering machines piled high, one on top of the other. He was right — they did indeed need voice mail.

Hundreds of lecturers worked at the university, and like all university or college lecturers, these teachers of higher learning are hardly ever in their offices. When they're lecturing, no one can reach them. They communicate with other lecturers, with staff, and mostly with students. Without voice mail, they did not have many options for communicating with these people, other than through fax and three-dimensional mail. And there was no way on earth that the university could afford to give every member of staff a human personal assistant.

Voice mail was the only sensible option. Although it has a notorious reputation among some users, it nevertheless provides a critical service.

More than 200 million people in the world use voice mail. This technology has been around since the early 1980s. Since then, voice mail has become the fastest way to leave a message for someone, thanks to the wonder of the telephone's lift-dial-ring-speak service. But voice mail is no longer just a convenient means of leaving a message: It has become a replacement for conversation when the other party cannot be present.

Paul Finnigan, one of voice processing's founding fathers, believes that voice mail is fast becoming a primary method of communication. "The shift is from telephone answering to call messaging, with the ultimate aim being integration with the PC workstation," he says.

Voice mail is not only undergoing a transformation, it's taking on a whole new form and purpose in the new IT frontier, including cyberspace and on-line communications. It's being transformed from a medium confined to the telephone interface to one that can be accessed and managed from a computer screen anywhere in the world.

Let's review and assess the benefits of voice mail and the strategies for wisely using this ubiquitous message format within the contexts of the emerging and future technologies, from both the pay-off and trade-off points of view.

VOICE MAIL: THE TECHNOLOGY PAY-OFF

Do you remember the game we played as kids in school to demonstrate and learn communication skills? Teacher would give one kid in the class a message, and that child would relay the information to the next child by whispering it in his or her ear. Each child, in turn, would then relay the message until the last person in class was given the message. At the end of the exercise, the first child and the last child would stand in front of the class and compare messages. The final message was never close to the original (kind of like what happens in the adult game of politics).

This problem is the same type of thing that happens to messages taken down on pink slips or scraps of paper and relayed to people in the enterprise. It's a wonder that some companies still use this outmoded communications method in the digital age in which we live and work. But go to any stationery store and you'll still find pink message pads, as well as people snatching them up.

What are the voice mail pay-offs over paper-based messages in particular and as an enabling technology in general? I guess you can apply the following discussion to all electronic message types. Here is a list of them, not necessarily in any order. (Most of these pay-offs can be backed up by research from the likes of the Voice Mail Educational Committee (VMEC), but they are based on my own experience setting up and training more than a thousand voice mail users.)

PAY-OFF 1: THE FULL MESSAGE IS RECORDED

Every word that the person leaves is recorded. In the dictation scenario, it is very difficult, if not impossible, for a human to take down every word verbatim, even while typing the information into the e-mail system.

Microsoft's people often used this tactic when callers reached its human telephonists on its main number. I should know — I looked over the shoulders of the people I trained and watched the fun and games commence. This experience helped me figure out how to integrate computer telephony in the reception area. The e-mail interface was easier for the users to access, although the message they left often was less accurate than one left on v-mail. (No matter how furiously the telephonists typed into the MS-Mail mailboxes, the messages were never complete and the recipients invariably had to return the calls.)

I've installed several systems for sales applications where clients can call account executives and leave orders and requests in the voice mailbox, including order numbers, part numbers, and instructions. In these cases, the voice-mail systems filled a critical need.

Motor Vehicle Insurance Services, Inc. (MVIS), is a good example. Thousands of callers left full descriptions of motor vehicle accidents and thefts, dates and times of the incidents, locations, details, policy numbers, and more. The real test came in transcribing the voice mail messages, but any message was always available for replay and confirmation.

PAY-OFF 2: ACCURACY IN THE MESSAGE

The voice message is 100 percent accurate (as a record) in content as opposed to the paper-based message. This pay-off concept is a little different from Pay-off 1. Although the full message can be painfully dictated and recorded, you have no guarantee that it's accurate. The message may say Mrs. Shapiro called, but that message could be from my wife, my mother, or the spouse of a well-known attorney. With the paper-based method, the caller also may have a later dispute with the assistant who took the message, should a conflict arise (see the next pay-off).

While training the telephonist at Novell's Johannesburg office, I encouraged this person to tell callers who could not reach a technical support person to leave messages in voice mail, explaining in detail the particular problem they were having with a LAN installation. This strategy worked and had an ancillary pay-off. The mailbox owners were forced to learn how to access their mail when they realized that Novell's customer service index was at stake.

These pay-offs really take on new meaning when you consider the problems that arise from delivering incomplete messages to busy executives who are on the road, away from their offices, out of town for a while, or in some way unable to return to their desks to retrieve messages (see Pay-off 8). Messages that are written down and then relayed to sales executives when they call in are even further eroded.

Who needs data encryption? Just pass the data through the message-taking and relaying process, and no chain of supercomputers or mob of KGB agents will be able to decipher the final translation.

To make matters worse, the harried people who receive these incomplete, unintelligible messages usually find that the only free times they have to call the office and check messages is while sitting in rush-hour traffic or thundering down I-95 at 75 m.p.h. It's very difficult and often uncomfortable to access messages from a client's premises.

I remember one time I was riding with a client's IT executive around Johannesburg, a city as busy with traffic as New York City, L.A., or Tel Aviv. The IT guy had just installed a trial CT system but had been too busy to take time out so that I could train him to use the system.

His assistant called on the cellular phone with information that a network had gone down. She began to relay the message, saying that such and such error messages had appeared on the screen, implying disaster and telling them how to recover from it. I listened to this exchange of words with amusement at first: "What do you mean you can't read the words . . . who gave you this message . . . where's he now . . . what IRQ?" and so on.

Then my heart almost jumped through my ribcage. I noticed that my client had taken the pen out of his pocket and started writing down details on a notepad. One hand was holding the pad, the other hand was writing, and his head was cocked to the left, holding the phone between his ear and shoulder. *No hand was holding the wheel, and now he was viewing the road at a 90-degree angle.* Naturally, I began to panic.

I forced him to pull over and told him that *now* was as good a time as any to start using his new voice-messaging system.

"Call your assistant back," I ordered him. "Have her get the LAN people to read the message into your mailbox, and we'll call back in ten minutes to get the message and suggest the solution. The server's not going anywhere in a hurry." Done.

Fifteen minutes later, we pulled over again and called the mailbox. This particular experience marked the first time I had ever shown someone how to get his voice messages from a car on the highway. He listened to the message, and I told him to press the selection to reply to the message. With the exact information in the mailbox, read directly from the server's monitor, he was able to point the LAN support staff to the solution. "What a fantastic experience," he said. "Give us a quote to install the system in all our locations."

Other examples come from the hospitality industry, which I group hospitals and clinics into. I've consulted for these industries in both computer telephony and workgroup computing, and many of my experiences have not been pleasant. Installing voice-messaging systems in hotels is one of the most complicated exercises an integrator will encounter. Hospitals are even more scary. The integrators have to deal with very different norms from the ones found in the typical enterprise, where people work reasonable hours and stay at their desks. In hotels and hospitals, you first have to deal with staffs that move around a great deal; then you have to deal with the users — patients and patrons — who will only be using the voice-messaging facility for a short while, and maybe never again.

When I called on an international corporation, a large chain of hotels and casinos in southern Africa, Europe, and the Caribbean, I was confronted with such a spaghetti mix of interrelated and interconnected information systems that I wanted to escape at the first opportunity. They wanted a voice-message system that could deliver messages to a gambler in the process of throwing craps: "You have no money left in the bank — to arrange for a line of credit, press 1 . . . ."

But all jokes aside, the hotel, the hospital, and the casino have the same basic needs.

Guests and patients move into a room and frequently leave a day or two later. Any messages they receive are written down and popped into "pigeon" holes from which the patients or guests can collect them on their way out for the day. Staff members are far too busy to take down anything other than "*X* called; call back."

Some hospitality enterprises have thus sought to improve or add value to their client's stay by adding voice-messaging services. But the problems presented by the way the organizations operate are enormous, and few have thought out the processes or done their logistics homework. How busy executives can be expected to check into hotel rooms, change the greetings on their mailboxes, and then figure out how to access the messages while away for the day is beyond me.

Hospitals also have another major problem. The busy ones I have called on receive tens of thousand of calls a day. They employ scads of telephonists to manage the chaos. Out of all the thousands of calls they *do* get, I have found that almost a third are repeat calls that could not be completed on the first attempt. Take the following two scenarios that occur at hospitals:

The caller reaches the telephonist and asks to speak to Mr. X, who was admitted last night. The telephonist, faced with the flashing lines of dozens of callers, looks up Mr. X's ward and room from another screen and then transfers the caller. If the patient is asleep, unable to answer, in surgery, or (gulp) dead, the call will do a U-turn and come flying back to the telephonist. As a result, the telephonist has to reprocess the caller.

Just to get rid of the call, more than likely the telephonist will send it back to the room, where it may do another U-turn. When this happens, you can imagine the collateral damage that occurs at the telephonist's room. The biggest headache the hospital has then is dealing with callers, many of whom have emergencies, who cannot get through because calls are circling endlessly around the hospital and tying up the lines and sending blocking levels to new records.

At one hospital, telephonists in their sixties sat in front of three screens from a DOS system, a UNIX system, and a legacy mainframe system. (Who says that older folks can't learn computers?) The PBX console often was on their laps as they struggled with the keyboards, looking up rooms and extensions. They entered and manipulated data and information from all three screens.

Our job was to provide a needs synthesis and clean up the mess, then add computer telephony solutions, replace the PBX, and integrate everything to work as one. "Where do we start?" the IT executive at this clinic asked. I replied in dry humor as we surveyed the scene, "All over again — what you have here cannot be fixed."

"You can say that again" quipped Mrs. Rosen, a telephonist who had been working the switch for about 30 years. "I've come to the conclusion that I won't be checking out of here."

At one maternity hospital, the biggest problem I observed was callers leaving congratulatory messages for newborn mothers with the telephonists. We considered having callers leave messages in a mailbox account that the mother opened when she booked the facility. She could then access the messages after the birth and even from home for a week or two before the mailbox "evaporated." Like flowers, such a service could generate funds for the clinic and help pay off the CT system.

I don't want to delve too deeply into the problems of integration in the preceding scenarios; they were complicated and arduous and better left to a book devoted to system integration and interconnection. However, what's important to learn from these examples is that people away from their offices, who have to get clear and accurate messages, will certainly benefit from having a voice-messaging service.

You no longer need justification to invest. Workers in similar situations need a service that they can respond to in their own time, for complete and accurate messages. In this respect, these workers can satisfy clients and customers, even from a remote location. Without this service, they might as well check out for a while and deal with the mail when they get back to the office.

PAY-OFF 3: PROOF OF CONTENT

This pay-off is something that Microsoft, more than any other client, found the most important when it came to technical support and dealing with corporate clients, typically the Fortune 500 companies that order "a few thousand of this, a few thousand of that" at the push of a button.

Some callers would call management and complain that "your technical support person messed up. I never said that." The Microsoft people had an answer: "Oh, but you did, Sir; we have a copy of the voice message that you left."

The "permanence" of the voice-mail message has other twists, which I get into in the "Pay-off 6: Privacy" and "Trade-off 5: Voice messages are not private" sections later in this chapter.

PAY-OFF 4: IDENTIFYING CALLERS FROM THEIR VOICES

Because a voice message provides you with the tone and inflection of the voice leaving it, you can usually tell whether that person is angry, sad, happy, or "high" and, of course, often deduce the person's gender, nationality, race, and religion.

With this information, you can prepare (mentally and with information resources) for the return call. I often get voice mail from Mother; she's my severest critic but an unfailing supporter. Depending on the tone of voice in the message, I either call back right away, take an hour to prepare myself, take a Valium, or leave town for a week. The written message cannot convey this element.

PAY-OFF 5: THE VOICE MESSAGE *IS* A COMMUNICATION

Whereas some people just leave a note that says "call me," many who use voice-messaging systems to their fullest potential launch into full conversation as if you were listening at the same time. You are listening, in a sense, but you won't hear the message until you access the voice file (basically, voice-messaging is a form of S&F conversation). Thus, voice mail has become a means by which two or more people can hold a conversation with only one person present in the dialog.

Research indicates that more than 50 percent of the reason why people make a call is to convey information, not to engage in conversation. Voice mail is a great way to do just that because it offers a one-way, asynchronous, noninteractive telecommunication.

In the message dictation scenario, having a human take down a lengthy communication is almost impossible. The person taking the message will invariably say something like "Why don't I just tell her to call you?" Conversation always drags out and wastes productive time. Live, two-way conversation encourages chit-chat, whereas voice mail gets to the point.

PAY-OFF 6: PRIVACY

Voice mail is more private than a message on paper that tends to get circulated or can be left for prying eyes to see. Computers don't spread rumors, but people do. It's easier for people to gain access to private information on paper-based or relayed messages and then start rumors.

I once employed a software engineer who did not like his work. I discovered that he was leaving his job because the receptionist could not transfer the call to his voice mail and I saw the written message from a placement office on her desk. I called him into my office and said, "I had no problem with your desire to seek work you enjoy. What use is an unproductive software guru who is devoid of vision and inspiration?"

The situation would have been better had he come to me with his reasons for wanting to leave, rather than skulking around the office like a KGB mole and making his colleagues wonder why a placement agency had left a message for him. Later, I called the agency and told them off for (a) calling my office and "head hunting" without my knowledge, and (b) conveying such a private message to a loyal staff member of the company. A revengeful or uncouth employer might have fired the employee before he had a chance to resign.

On the other hand, employers often want to know this information; I talk about the question of voice-mail privacy and the law later in this chapter.

PAY-OFF 7: RETENTION

Although it is possible to lose paper-based messages or have a person forget to give you the message, voice mail cannot be lost — at least 99.99 percent of the time, anyway.

Many voice-mail specialists will tell you that voice messages are almost never lost — deleted unintentionally, yes; but lost? Never. After users learn how to use their mailboxes, they will not lose their messages. Computers don't scheme to delete a message for no good reason. *Software logic* and *control* does that, at least for now.

If the user deletes the message, the IT executive or system administrator can recover it. Almost all systems that I know can recover a deleted message or fish it out of a recycle bin. I even had a guy from Microsoft once ask me to recover a message from Bill Gates that he wanted to preserve for posterity. "Who knows? I suddenly thought my grandchildren might be able to auction off the voice file for millions in the next 50 years."

PAY-OFF 8: TELEPHONE TAG

By leaving a detailed, clear message for the person you want to reach, you eliminate the need to have them get back to you for further information. Leaving short notes on paper, usually no more than three or four words, results in telephone tag because the people may not be available when you call back. The waste of time and money on phone calls is enormous.

About 75 percent of telephone calls cannot be successfully completed on the first attempt because of one of the following:

✦ People are on the phone (usually checking messages).

✦ They are in the office but cannot be interrupted.

✦ They are away on leave and cannot be reached.

✦ They are in meetings.

✦ They are away from the office on business.

PAY-OFF 9: INTERRUPTION OF WORK

At least *two-thirds* of the reasons for which people call are less important than the work they interrupt for the called party (this statistic is the most famous statistic a sales executive will quote when trying to sell a voice-mail system).

By setting a "do-not-interrupt" indicator to on, the recipient of a voice message can choose when to take the message and act on its content. Voice-mail vendors and system integrators need to be aware of the interruption factors in work settings. A very powerful and persistent computer telephony system can bring a company to its knees (see "Trade-off 4: CT is intrusive" later in this chapter).

The greatest attribute of the telephone is its immediacy and the ease with which you can "reach out and touch" someone. If you need to call someone, you simply lift the handset, wait for the dial tone, and dial. For this gift, you can thank Alexander Graham Bell. But the immediacy and the ease with which you can use the phone has its trade-off. When you're in the middle of something important and don't want to be disturbed, the telephone can be a very obnoxious technology, as Thomas Watson discovered on the receiving end of probably the most famous phrase in the history of technology and science: *"Watson, come here."*

People who call don't know that you're busy, and some expect you to take the call even if it's interrupting very serious work. When the age of video phones arrives, you will not be able to fob off a call with something like "Call me back, I'm bathing the baby," when in fact you're doing something more adventurous.

In this respect, humans tend to be slaves to the telephone. Voice mail empowers you to answer the phone at any time of day or night and enables the people calling to dispense their business. When your work is complete and you're finally in the frame of mind to get back to these people, you can go through the messages as often as you want and formulate the replies before you make the return call. Voice mail is thus an immensely powerful tool because you can use it to screen out those callers you determine to be undesirable, such as debt collectors, telemarketers, and persistent admirers for whom you do not share a similar affection.

PAY-OFF 10: STORE, FORWARD, AND ARCHIVE

Voice messages can be forwarded to an associate, and you can even reply to the sender while listening to the message. You also can annotate and append information to the voice message. If you want, you can archive and store important messages for later use. I have several voice messages that I have kept for many years, some for sentimental reasons. Voice messages also are kept because they have legal ramifications and implications.

Two professions that find the store-and-forward capability an important feature of voice mail are law and journalism. Attorneys, after they understand the technology and the features, use voice mail extensively. These people spend a great deal of time dictating briefs and correspondence into cassette tape recorders and dictaphones, so sending a long voice message is a trivial matter for them (a legal paragraph can run to more than 100 words). I once asked a skeptical voice-mail trainee of the Rubber Pencils law firm, who was planning to leave long messages for the "learned" associates in the U.K., if she was experienced in closing arguments. When she replied that she was *prima facie* — not a dunce — I told her to imagine that the voice mailbox was the judge or jury and use it to practice.

The same concept applies to journalists, especially the broadcasters who spend a great deal of time in front of microphones or cameras, talking to millions of people as if they were talking one-on-one. These professionals can use voice mail to practice their techniques.

Voice-mail systems also can be networked. In 1994, I helped a computer reseller with offices in three southern U.S. states formulate a message interchange and networking service. The company installed ISDN between all three offices and networked everything that was telephony-related over T1 lines. Rather than go into the complexities of networking voice-mail systems, I refer you to AMIS (Audio Messaging Interchange Specification) in the Lexicon.

PAY-OFF 11: CUSTOMER SERVICE, CONVENIENCE, AND SATISFACTION

Voice mail enables your customers to communicate with you any time of day and night, and, as long you respond to your messages promptly and wisely, you will notice the pay-off when people say "Thank you for acting so fast." If your customers know how to use your voice-mail system and how to navigate mailboxes, you will see the pay-off in terms of personal productivity.

Despite what many vociferous people say, research has shown that nearly 60 percent of callers prefer to talk to voice mail if you are not available, rather than to a live executive assistant or telephonist. Nowadays, leaving a message with a human has become a painful process, and when faced with the option of going on hold or abandoning and calling back, 78 percent of callers would rather leave voice mail.

PAY-OFF 12: PROMPT NOTICE

Voice-mail systems are designed to make sure that you "get the message." These systems can call out to any part of the world, send messages to e-mail, rattle the pager, fire up message lamps on phone sets, sing songs to you on your PC, and prompt the PBX to alert you of messages every time you lift the receiver and have not cleared the messages.

Many personal assistants or telephonists vouch that they too know how to reach you, but the telephonists and executive assistants I have trained admit they will not go to the same lengths that voice mail does to get you your messages. Will your executive assistants call you at three in the morning to remind you to take a shower and write another report? Will they stay up until midnight and make a long-distance call to you three time zones away? Will they attempt to alert you via all the listed technologies every 30 minutes? Some years ago, the only "person" who remembered my birthday was my voice mail; everyone else was too busy.

Besides, these workers have other work to do, and voice mail can end up being their ultimate productivity and empowerment tool.

WHY VOICE MAIL INDEED? THE TECHNOLOGY TRADE-OFFS

Despite its obvious pay-offs, voice mail has drawn harsh criticism from many quarters, including voice mail users themselves — even from me. Tim Andrews wrote this about the technology in his April 1995 column in *PC Week:*

We fervently believe that new technology is inherently good. We are ever ready to impose radical technologies upon our culture with no fear of the consequences.

That's got to stop. Technology is never neutral. It is binding. And every time we blindly embrace The Next Big Thing, we bind ourselves a little bit more. The smartest IT executives must anticipate how a technology's best attributes can turn out to be its worst.

That's exactly what happened with voice mail. Simply put, that little red light on the corner of the phone has become the ugliest sight in the office. Voice mail actually is anti-empowering . . . .

Although I don't agree that voice mail is anti-empowering, this technology has its problems, as do all technologies. However, voice mail touches everyone. It pops up in the middle of the most widely used communication and technology process that mankind uses every day — the telephone.

The irony is that voice mail is a technology that humans cannot live with and, yet, one that humans cannot live without. If we put more thought into using it wisely and making it a more attractive, empowering, integrated technology to use, voice mail may become less infamous. We may even fall in love with it on the same scale that people now love its sibling, e-mail. But to do this, let's discuss and understand the trade-offs, many of which are perceived drawbacks rather than actual ones.

TRADE-OFF 1: PEOPLE ARE UNREACHABLE, THANKS TO VOICE MAIL

This fallacy is more a notion on the caller's part and not *really* a trade-off. Humans can be selfish and narrow-minded when it comes to trying to reach someone. Just because the caller has an urgent need to speak to someone, he or she expects that person to drop everything and take the calls, even if that person is in the middle of a life and death situation, as my company found out when consulting for hospitals.

Doctors complained that callers hounded them while they were doing rounds or even while they were in surgery. This fact was a prime motivator to installing voice mail in a medical facility. My company, however, had to ensure that the systems could reliably offer alternative call paths and solutions if the phone call was critical or urgent in nature. The most important question we had to consider was this: What if you have to be reached as a matter of life and death?

On the flip side, when humans want to talk to someone and repeatedly get sent to voice mail, they blame the technology for the hassle. People are unreachable because they want to be or need to be, don't care about your call, are too lazy to pick up the phone, or have lost the passion for life. The tool these people now use to remain out of reach is computer telephony and voice messaging. Many reasonable circumstances exist for not being available to take a call. After all, humans have to eat, drink, and sleep, as well as visit the rest rooms several times a day. If people want to remain out of reach, let them — as long as it's not *your* staff or customer satisfaction and sales going to the dogs as a result.

Bad experiences with voice mail lead many to assume that when they confront voice messaging at the enterprise, it's time to head south. My most vivid example of how quick people are to accuse you of "hiding behind" voice mail occurred with my former associate, Dr. Michael Edwards. In 1993, in the middle of discussions with several *very important* clients, Michael left the following voice mail message on his mailbox: "You have reached the voice-mail box of Michael Edwards. I will be taking a long trip. In the event that I take longer than I expect, please leave a detailed message because the system will try to find me. If I don't get back to you, please contact Jeffrey Shapiro on extension 300."

Michael did take longer than expected. He admitted himself into a clinic to check on a pain in his abdomen. He died a week later of stomach cancer. For several weeks after that, I took his voice mail messages from several important clients who were concerned that he had not returned their calls; some felt that for a voice-mail evangelist, he was not setting a very high standard.

You *can* hide behind voice mail systems, and many people do. But if they decide to take this route, you need to realize that the problem stems mostly from the individuals — their discipline (or lack of it), their lack of purpose and common vision, and their lack of education and skills. Poor software and poor integration of the system into the enterprise information network also can be a contributing factor.

However, if you want to assign a portion of the blame to the technology itself, you should have voice mail as the last item on the list of culprits. Voice mail, in my opinion anyway, will certainly be the most important link in business communications after the telephone for many decades.

I blame the technology's limitations for the reputation that voice mail has of being an evasive tool (I discuss this later). Reporters complain that voice mail prevents them from reaching people for quotes and comments on developing stories. Because these journalists (and other information and knowledge workers) are working against tight deadlines, the voice-mail systems are obstructive and get in the way because these callers expect that at the end of the lift-dial-ring sequence, they should be able to reach a human. But what if the reporters did get the person on the line? Is the comment "No comment" any good? I have never seen a report in which a journalist wrote the following: "We tried repeatedly to get hold of Simpson, but his voice mail says 'I am either on the phone or away from my desk.'"

Voice mail is not the reason why people can't be reached. Before voice mail arrived, people were just as elusive. When it comes to customer satisfaction, sales, and service, however, you dare not hide behind voice mail.

TRADE-OFF 2: THE TECHNOLOGY IS ENSLAVING

This point has a great deal of merit when you are dealing with a voice mail or computer telephony system with a poor design and a weak architecture. By weak architecture, I mean a lack of a visual interface from which the users can *see* their voice messages from the PC monitor. This setup is the flaw in the voice mail paradigm — the inability to manage and work with the messages visually.

The chief reason why some people hate using voice mail so much is that the access to messages is limited to a sequential process. Retrieving and responding to messages also is a process adversely influenced by the limitations of the telephony user interface, or the TUI, as it is known in CT circles. In many respects, voice-mail *is* enslaving; just like the character-based dumb terminals I talk about in Part I.

Here again, not having adequate function in the technology or failing to use your guru smarts sufficiently are the reasons for the trade-off — and not really the fault of the technology itself. If a young guru named Marc Andreeson can use his guru smarts to build a browser that opens a window to the Internet, effectively bringing it to critical mass and "reinventing" the World Wide Web, then computer telephony gurus can do the same with the mail explosion.

In my own software company, my gurus have achieved incredible things that were generally felt to be impossible to do in the time available and with the technology at hand. Granted, you have programmers and you have gurus. The world is full of programmers, but not enough super gurus are available to go around. There also are not enough creative managers to channel super gurus in the right directions — and the lack of vision has stymied the critical growth of voice mail.

Of course, the engineers, designers, and dreamers are not entirely to blame. Operating systems, software stability, APIs, and applications have been the limiting factors. My company, however, developed software that accesses and manages voice mail from a visual interface with MS-DOS way back in 1992. The system has been restricted from wide acceptance, however, for several reasons that I discuss later in this chapter.

Consider the environment in which most humans now find themselves at work, be it at the home office, the remote office, or in rooms or offices with several hundred other people. Work lives now center around the computer screen, a keyboard, and a "rodent" that points and activates software events. Many users are more or less attached to the computer and its appendages while working. When the telephone rings, users have to stop what they are doing on screen and divert attention to the telephone — something that many are loathe to do.

But this discussion is not about how to integrate the telephone with the computer — that subject comes up later. It's more about how humans use the computer and the telephone. Since Alexander Bell's eventful day in 1876, the telephone's main function has been little else other than as a tool to enable people to speak to people and listen to their replies in real time. In this respect, humans really use only two physiological processes or senses on the phone: speech and hearing.

Since the beginning, the telephone user interface has hardly changed. Humans once *dialed* numbers on a *rotary dial* (you still have to in some parts of the world). Now you dial, key, enter, push, punch, and speak numbers, and — I almost forgot — click them on a "soft" dial pad. Other than the keypad and the transmission type (analog and digital), nothing much has changed in the way that you make a call. Nor should it; nor *can* it. Humans still use only hearing and speaking senses to communicate with other humans in a conference in an easy-going, relaxed state, at least until videophones become widely used and the bandwidth of all telephone networks increases. This telephone works so well because it emulates the way humans communicate with others in the flesh.

But as the telephone's popularity grew, so did the problem of not being able to reach people as easily and as readily as before. People can take down messages for you, mostly hand-written. But humans frequently cannot take down detailed messages accurately. This process is no substitute for being part of the conversation. Recipients of messages often find that they have to call people back to find out why the caller called in the first place, only to find the other party away. The process then repeats itself in reverse.

In the U.S., this problem is called *telephone tag*. I guess baseball had some influence in the description of the problem, but because no source of mine could confirm this, I will. As a Little League shortstop, I remember well trying to "tag" a runner between second and third. I've heard other cultures call this aggravating problem ping-pong.

Suddenly, in the late 1970s, an inventor named Gordon Matthews threw down the gauntlet on all the paper-born messages piling up on his desk. He invented a digital device called the *voice message exchange* (VMX) to record messages like an analog answering machine but with the (digital) capability to access, manipulate, and manage them. Because the messages were accessed over the phone, they had to be stored in a virtual mailbox that no one could see, controlled and manipulated from an invisible menu, and be able to have additional information attached to them, such as date and time. You cannot see these things; you can only hear the information.

Gordon Matthews made a fortune on his idea, as did others, such as the switching giant, Octel, which finally absorbed VMX. As Octel's chairman said in a 1994 interview with the *Wall Street Journal,* people cannot write down messages reliably; that's "why my children eat so well."

Make no mistake — the TUI has worked well for voice mail and will continue to do so. For people who travel and spend a great deal of time away from their desks, the ability to walk up to the nearest available telephone and contact the office or desktop is too important to ignore, no matter how small or how large the enterprise for which the people work.

Using a touch-tone phone, the user can manage the messages by responding to a spoken menu with key presses. You can replay the message, reply to it, discard it, save it, skip to the next message, and so on. Even if you do get too many messages to manage from your location, in a mental "scan mode," you can still be kept abreast of important events and make a mental or physical note of urgent issues and people you have to get back to within a certain time frame. Many clients of mine begged for a feature that would enable them to listen to messages in "scan mode," by joining all the messages together in one long message. They can press keys on the dial pad to rewind and fast forward as needed by using this feature. The TUI can work this way, but this setup presents a problem, as you'll see in a moment.

Inventors, product enhancers, and value adders essentially give users a form of intelligent digital messaging to replace the ineffective stand-ins. That's great — as long as you do not receive very many messages. The reason: Voice mail comes to you sequentially, so you have to manage the mail sequentially, using first in/first out or last in/first out sequencing. Although the system stores the messages digitally, you can only access them serially. Trying to sort them or jump around is too cumbersome and complex without being able to visually manipulate them. Thus, this format puts you at a disadvantage.

Why wasn't this problem a big deal 15 years ago? Because voice mail took users from one extreme to the other. First, people used it as a stand-in. People who were "unprepared to talk to a machine" took their business elsewhere or refused to leave a message. I've talked to many callers who felt this way over the years — they just felt that making them leave a message was no way to treat a customer. As a result, when these callers heard the computer step in, callers would just abandon the call. (Many callers left snide remarks such as "bloody machine," or "I've been a customer for 20 years and don't expect this kind of service from you.")

Of course, several other factors helped influence the callers' attitudes. These factors included a mistrust of the technology, cultural resistance to accepting the technology (the Japanese still balk at voice mail), and the fact that many callers were unaware that users had introduced a new voice mail system because the users never bothered to tell them or prepare them for it.

For example, in the U.S., many people may agree that voice mail now is as much a part of the American cultural fabric as baseball, Halloween, and hot dogs. In parts of Europe, Asia, and Africa, however, voice mail remains an alien concept. In many cities outside North America, this alienation factor results from customers' expectations of service and personal attention.

On the other hand, I've watched many people who have used the telephone perhaps once or twice in their life start responding to voice mail rather easily. Voice mail provides a great means of leaving a message for those who can't read. These people have the patience and the time to listen to messages, and their listening skills are good. They respond to the spoken messages more easily and feel comfortable "talking" to the voice on the other end of the line.

Today, people view voice mail as a necessary service. Although most people prefer that you talk to them if you can, the idea of people leaving messages is no longer as abhorrent in the U.S. This idea is catching on fast everywhere else, too. Even in Ireland, voice mail penetration is expected to reach 100 percent before the U.S. or Canada. People who used to mistrust the technology now prefer to talk to the machine.

Research has shown that over 60 percent of callers in North America would prefer to leave a message with the machine rather than with a human. If the alternative is to go on hold for hours (see Chapter 14), the percentage of callers who would prefer to deal with the machine increases to 80 or 90 percent. But now, a new problem arises that is the opposite of the problem faced at the start of the CT industry in the late 1970s. Now there's *too* much mail to process through the telephone interface alone.

The PC's screen-based user interface enables you to manipulate and access information visually. Although the brain is a marvelous tool, you have to remember that it functions like an analog device (naturally, a great deal of debate exists about this topic). Unlike a digital computer, humans cannot listen to a message with one ear, scan a second with one eye, and then manage a third message with the other eye.

But on screen, you can manage information in a much more "spatial" environment, composed of signs, symbols, icons, and metaphors. By being able to use your sight, not only can you scan messages faster, but trained and experienced users can process information faster via pattern matching and glancing. Put voice mail management onto this visual plane, and you empower the users to manage their voice mail more intrinsically. Basically, you provide the sense of being "within" the mailbox.

ATMs in the South African bush country

A few years ago, I was traveling to a place called Sodwana Bay in South Africa, a marvelous scuba diving resort on the Indian Ocean not far from the South African/Mozambique border. The setting is as rural as rural Africa gets. Not so long ago, to make a telephone call in Sodwana, you had to crank a handle rapidly to raise the operator who makes the call for you. (I believe a more modern exchange is in place there today.) While driving along a long, dusty trail to the ocean, my friend and I stumbled across a small village; standing in the middle of nowhere was an ATM (automatic teller machine). A line of tribal members stood waiting to access their savings and deposit money.

Despite the hyena teeth marks on its case, the machine was in good condition. I noticed that most of the people using the machine could not read but were easily responding to voice prompts in English and Zulu. The screen-based user interface also made copious use of icons, and written instructions were kept to a minimum. Many people used the machine to deposit their daily revenues from so-called "bush stores." One gentleman typically deposited several thousand Rand a day from sales of nothing more than soap and paraffin.

When I got back to the office, I called the bank that had installed the machine, and they told me the ATM had been an experiment that turned out very different from what it had expected. The machine had become so popular that the bank was planning to install more machines in other remote locations. The clever use of voice instructions and icons made it simple to use. Once the user had an idea of what the symbols meant, the rest was easy. Users also had voice prompts to follow.

I've discovered that nothing is worse than using an ATM in a foreign language. While working in Israel, I learned that most of the machines displayed Hebrew text. Without symbols and voice instructions, getting a cash advance in that country was akin to extracting teeth. I managed to master the Israeli ATMs by first matching the patterns of the advanced Hebrew instructions with the results they represented. Later, as my Hebrew improved, I was able to read and understand the meanings of the words, rather than use pattern matching.

I found myself asking the following questions: "What about voice mail? How can voice mail stand in for all the millions of disadvantaged people in the world who don't have access to the telephone, either because they are poor or because there aren't enough telephones to go around?" In the U.S., the people-to-telephone ratio is approximately two to one; that is, two people to one telephone. In Africa and Asia, this ratio rockets to around 20 or 50 people to one telephone. In China, this inequality is exactly what voice mail is catering to. If you only have one telephone among 50 families it becomes very difficult to get through to someone. Many Chinese citizens who use the telephone have never had a live conversation.

The number of voice-mail messages that you can comfortably access (and further manage) from the TUI, compared to the number of messages that you can comfortably access from the screen-based interface, is considerably less. After the message list builds past five messages, the user's ability and desire to access and do something with the message wanes. Of course, the amount of decrease varies from person to person. But once a message file gets past ten messages, the ability that most humans have to manage the messages from the TUI diminishes substantially.

The ability to deal with mail (all mail) depends on the character, experience, and daily regimen of the person receiving the mail. Some people can handle 10 or 20 messages simultaneously, whereas others can only handle five. Busy telephonists will likely only handle three before they have to take a call. Once the voice mail box fills up, the busy telephonist will not be able to find the time (nor the mental strength, especially at the end of a busy day) to process the voice mail. As a result, the mail piles up until it's almost impossible for anyone to manage.

As soon as mail becomes two to three days old, it makes little sense to listen to the messages. In any event, it's more than likely that the callers already have called back or have called elsewhere, especially if they really needed to talk to someone at the enterprise,. The resulting call from customers and clients usually goes like this: "I don't trust your voice mail because my call was not returned."

I call this problem "the capacity to deal with voice mail." By capacity, I mean the following:

✦ **Time.** The available time and date devoted to accessing voice mail

✦ **Location.** The place and position of the person accessing voice mail

✦ **State of mind.** The patience, mood, temper, worry, and more of the person receiving the call. Busy IT executives are never in a state of mind that's conducive to the enslaving process of accessing and processing huge volumes of voice mail over the telephone. You can't really expect them to, but few people understand this.

✦ **Experience.** How often has the person accessed voice mail in the past? Not only does the person's knowledge of the voice-mail system (which is gained through proper training) contribute to the amount of usage, but if you use the system often enough, you will soon be able to "see" the menus with your mind's eye. At one time, I used voice mail so extensively that I often dreamed about it.

A person's capacity to access voice mail often depends on how these factors combine. A busy executive at Chicago's O'Hare airport on a late Friday evening, a day after Thanksgiving, in the middle of blizzard, will probably be unlikely respond to messages until several days later . . . if ever.

The reason for the low threshold again stems from the sequential and sightless process of accessing and managing voice mail messages. I have seldom come across an exception to this problem after almost four years of training people to work with their voice mail. The only exceptions occurred when the poor employees stayed late at the office, fearing for the future of their jobs, to wade through the messages and with dedicated sales people.

This situation held true for many enterprises I worked with across the U.S., EEC, and southern Africa. I periodically accessed various mailboxes at my clients to check on the contents and activity of the mailboxes. At first, this action was a safety check to make sure that the PBX was properly integrated, that the system was up and running, and that callers were accepting the service. Later, this exercise became one in which I pondered the ability of users to retrieve their voice mail — whether working with the worst or the best of products. As a result, I began advising my students to set aside 10 to 30 minutes a day to go through voice mail and messages. Few could fit in that time slice.

The busier and more in demand the person is, the more his or her voice mail would pile up. Perhaps one of the busiest executives I worked with was Brad Bews, a senior IT executive for Microsoft. Brad is hardly ever at his desk, so his voice mailbox explodes. "My mail has to be strictly sorted, filtered, and prioritized," he once told me. "Otherwise, I would be responding to the least important messages first, and the most important ones six weeks later." Often, I would bump into him in the server room just after he had beamed over from another part of the office complex. "Hi Brad! I left you voice mail . . . ." But Brad would just reply, "Yeah, you and 3,000 others." Then he would be gone again.

One day, I just had to get a message to Brad at all costs, so I entered "Free Bottle of Bacardi Gold" in the subject field. Brad replied within an hour and responded to my message. At the end of his message, he added: ". . . now about that "Free Bottle of Bacardi Gold."

The limiting effect of voice mail's sound-only, sequential access is not the only hurdle you encounter with CT software. Managing and working with the message (using it) after you hear it also presents a problem — one that only dedicated individuals can overcome. Few busy executives seem to have this attribute. I have trained all sorts of people to use and manage their mailboxes, from CEOs to cooks in a large enterprise canteen, to users who receive only a few messages a month. The situation is always the same: Very few users have the "capacity" to manage and manipulate voice mail after they hear it.

At the very best, I have managed to get only about 20 percent of a staff to use advanced voice mail capabilities shortly after training. That figure drops to between five and ten percent several weeks after training. Six months later, almost nobody uses the advanced features of their mailboxes, and very few users have changed their greetings. And I have never had the benefit of working with an enterprise where 100 percent of users used their voice mail.

Here are some of the most basic of the "advanced" features and options that voice mail provides (and few take advantage of):

✦ **Reply.** If the message leaver has called from an extension or station within the enterprise or if the voice mail system can capture the number he or she called from, you can reply to a voice mail message by entering one digit ("To reply to the message, press 1").

✦ **Forward.** The user can forward the message to the mailbox of another user in the enterprise. This process is similar to the Reply function.

✦ **Append/annotate.** The user can add to a message received and then forward it.

✦ **Date and time information.** You can obtain this information by entering a single digit option or by choosing the option from an advanced submenu. Some voice mail systems automatically attach this information to the end of the message.

✦ **Archiving.** The user can prevent the message from being automatically deleted by the CT system's purge capability.

✦ **Changing a password.** The user can change the password to his or her mailbox as often as needed. This precaution is a good one to follow because mailbox espionage is not uncommon.

✦ **Changing a reception message.** The reception message is the greeting that you provide for people who end up at your mailbox. You should use this message to tell people why you can't take the call.

Another common problem that arises is that few companies recall the consultant to train new staff members, who had not yet been hired at the time of the last course, how to use the system. When the enterprise experiences high turnover or reorganizes, the enterprise often cannot retrain these new members itself because it did not designate an IT person (or any member of staff for that matter) to champion the system and make sure that people know how to use it. (That strategy was one of the first items of which I made special note in Chapter 1.)

After all, you can't expect a new member of staff to just arrive at the enterprise and start using the voice mail system as if the person had invented it (unless, of course, he or she did). The result is that the amount of usage that the enterprise gets out of the voice mail system drops over the years, until few people who know how to really use the product remain in the enterprise. This problem would be less important if the voice mail system was accessible via the PC GUI, not a service that "lives and dies" by the phone. Almost every knowledge or service worker knows how to get around, even as a novice, in Windows. According to Microsoft, more than 100 million people know how to point and click. How many know how to switch off a message lamp when no two telephone systems are alike?

So, how do you make sure that people use these features and that they remember them? *User manuals.* The first little booklet I wrote for training purposes was too long and too complex. The sight of dozens of cascading menu options looks horrendous. I then opted for much simpler booklets with very pared-down information. This solution worked better, but I still had a problem. The booklets get misplaced, get buried under office work, and eventually fade from the enterprise altogether. My final attempt was to make Windows help files containing the how-to information, which worked much better.

What then, is the key to improving the way people use voice mail and increasing the number of people using it? For many years, I believed that the answer lied with the PC. The perfect interface to voice messaging is the graphical user interface. And the application that will empower you thus is e-mail. Why?

First, let's talk a little about the GUI. Earlier I touched on the changes that arrived with the new frontier in IT. Voice mail is about to go through the same transformation: from an enslaving technology to a truly empowering technology that you will love to use and, for the anti-workers, one that you will not be able to leave behind.

The graphical user interface has brought with it standards to interface design and concept. Before the advent of the GUI, every software application was different. Few people could go from one application to another and start working with it. Even starting the application was a mystery. What cryptic command did you have to type at the prompt? And then, once you had the app up and running, where did you go from there? Even the paragon of word processors, WordPerfect, had to migrate the DOS version to a product that had a similar look and feel to its Windows sibling. The Windows version was a late starter for WordPerfect Corp. that no doubt cost it market share.

Today, first-time users can simply click on icons and work with several applications at the same time. Access to on-line, hypertext help is a standard feature. Many people can start applications and begin working with the most basic features without any significant training. I recently helped a staff of several hundred people upgrade to Windows for Workgroups and migrated them to the latest version of a popular office suite. All it took was a video tape in a meeting room that users could review now and then.

Today's software lends itself to on-the-job training. Users learn the software as they go, although the advanced features may require some training. With e-mail, however, after you know the ropes of sending and replying, what more do you need to know? Few users find it hard to migrate from one e-mail product to another.

This is how it has to be with voice mail. Without visual access, we'll all eventually stick to e-mail and use the telephone only for personal communication. This idea may sound great, but the transition from voice mail to voice messaging at the desktop has started. This next statement may be a bitter pill for many vendors and developers to swallow, but I say that if you cannot take your voice mail system and integrate it with the enterprise-wide e-mail service, your product will be cast out as a relic. I know. I've had to junk voice-mail systems in favor of a product that had to have desktop access at the behest of my clients.

But building an application that enables users to access and manage voice messages from a GUI does not do enough. As humans go through the Information Age, they are waging a war of messages with associates, customers, clients, and friends. Humans send and receive electronic messages via e-mail, v-mail, f-mail, telex (yes telex), video, and alphanumeric pagers and other wireless message broadcast technologies. Humans not only receive more messages, but they use many more messaging types as well. Thus, you cannot expect the users (who will certainly be losers) to sit back and calmly process their messages through six or seven applications — you should be able to use one application for every message type.

The only sensible interface is an e-mail application that offers true, electronic-mail interchange. Any popular package will do, as long as it provides an open and accessible architecture that humbly migrates voice mail to the world of desktop messaging. The three main message-interchange candidates with which voice mail systems should integrate are Novell Messagewise, Lotus Notes, and Microsoft Exchange.

Why e-mail? If you have not realized this fact already, e-mail has already seized the desktop and captured the favor of users. Here are some thoughts to consider:

✦ People love using e-mail. Unlike voice mail manufacturers, e-mail vendors do not need to wander around Comdex wearing "I love e-mail" badges. Why do people love using e-mail? For starters, you can read and reply to your mail a great deal faster. Humans read about six times faster than they can listen, and that's without scanning or speed-reading.

✦ Because e-mail is easy to reply to on the fly, people can process and respond to thousands of e-mail messages. People have a hard time processing more than ten voice messages at a time, so the messages go unanswered. Voice mail is harder to reply to on the fly.

✦ You can easily send e-mail replies to any e-mail address in existence. Voice mail cannot be replied to (OTF or otherwise) to anyone outside your organization, unless you have a voice-message routing facility between two identical voice-mail systems.

✦ E-mail is easy to forward and share with others, and you can attach, append, and annotate messages with ease using many multimedia message types. Conversely, voice mail is a drag to share with others and sometimes impossible to share with people outside the enterprise, unless you conference them with your voice mailbox.

✦ E-mail is easier to manage than voice mail, and most e-mail products work the same way.

✦ E-mail's usage rate is growing fast, and it will soon become the chief, preferred means by which people want to communicate. People now have the power to choose their communication method. If they want you to "talk" e-mail and you want to call instead, tough. You'd better get used to the idea of people dictating the method of communication that you use. So, voice mail has to jump on the gravy train now — or be left in the old IT frontier. As an example, I receive many messages from people that read: "Don't call; e-mail me."

In the new frontier of IT, the ability and ease with which people can manage e-mail can be extended to voice mail and fax mail. Newer, cheaper, and more powerful software development tools, coupled with newer, cheaper, and more powerful computers (servers and clients) have made the new messaging paradigm a reality: integrated message services and universal mailboxes.

A shakeout has to happen now: The computer telephony software industry probably has more companies vying for market share than any other segment of the software development world. Vendors are offering hundreds of products. The industry magazines review the products they know about in the U.S. and Europe, but hundreds of other products exist that these publications have not even heard about.

In contrast, no more than 12 leading e-mail packages exist. Four or five of them have the lion's share of the market.

Despite this fact, voice mail is, at present, the most important and widely used medium for business to business communication after real-time conversation on the telephone. That may sound paradoxical, enigmatic, even false, if you give respectable editorializing in the *Wall Street Journal* and other main street press any credence. Although I suspect trillions of bytes of voice mail messages get deleted without ever being accessed, the majority of knowledge and service workers say they use the service more extensively than any messaging technology. It has been voted the chief productivity booster by many.

Without giving way to cynicism, I have to say that hundreds of millions of people use voice mail because (a) hundreds of millions of people use the telephone and (b) the omnipresent voice mailbox resides at the end of almost every telephone number. It's also darn easy to leave a message.

How different is using voice mail from actually having the conversation? Very little. Any further steps that need to be taken, like re-recording the message or appending to it, are up to the caller. Receiving and acting on the message is another story, so the challenge now presented is how to provide users with a service that couples the ease of e-mail access with the ubiquitous capabilities of the voice message.

CT software developers who recognized the hurdles and limited nature of the telephone user interface are preparing to bring users the new frontier in voice messaging in 1996 and 1997. Here's a sneak preview of two models that bring voice messaging to the desktop: the integrated mailbox and the universal mailbox.

The two paradigms discussed here are very different at the conceptual level. But one outstanding objective is common to both models: empowering the user to manage voice messages from the screen-based user interface, just as the user does when receiving and responding to e-mail. If you plan to upgrade or purchase a new system, you'll want to consider these two models. First, let's look at how difficult it is to manage messages with these systems.

Managing messages is a complex and difficult process. Messages have to be stored in secure locations on your enterprise information network. But just storing and retrieving the messages is not where the job of messaging software ends. Messaging software on the server uses sophisticated binary information, usually stored in database tables, to maintain information about every message, new or old. The messaging software needs to know whether the message can be deleted; whether it has to be archived; whether it has to be copied, moved, or forwarded; whether it has to be mothballed; and when to activate and send it. The messaging software also needs to know whether the message has relationships with other messages (especially with different types of messages) such as a voice-annotated fax, the length of the message, the date and time the message arrived, who sent it, who to reply to (the original sender or forwarder), and so on.

Presenting the contents of a mailbox in a graphical list box that incorporates all the features of the TUI is not a difficult task to do (see Figure 13-2). The messaging "engine" is the same for the TUI and the GUI. The differences between the two include the capability to select any message in the list, or several. Just by clicking on the message, the user sends a command back to the server that basically says "Call me on extension XXX, and play me the message I just selected," or "Play the messages on the PC speaker."

The client software directly touches the server with instructions on how to handle and play the message; that is, rewind, forward, repeat, and so on. This process can usually be achieved by sending data to the sever via a direct network connection, such as a named pipe or a TCP/IP datagram. Such a function requires complex software engineering but is doable nonetheless. Software developers have been doing similar tasks for several years now.

The pay-off for creating this solution is that the software creator only has to deal with messages created by the proprietary voice- and fax-mail application. Using the intrinsic knowledge of the message storehouse for both these message types and the message database, the engineers can wire up the desktop with little effort. I don't call this device an integrated mailbox. It's simply a GUI to the TUI with some nifty client/server features added which further empower the user to manage mail. This system goes far but not far enough.

When presenting such solutions to my clients, I have found that they used the interface for voice mail often — at first. At the same time, however, e-mail arrived on the desktop scene and rapidly dominated communications from the screen. My clients then called me back to say they wanted me to integrate the voice and fax messages into their e-mail application's user interface.

The reason was clear. The fallout from the GUI explosion is the avalanche of software and applets that now populates users' desktops. In the old IT frontier, most of power users dealt with no more than four or five applications. Some developers tried integrating all the applications (word processing, databases, and spreadsheets) into one application. Ashton Tate's Framework was a good example. But these applications did not fly under the old operating systems because they were islands of technology that could not communicate with other applications and soft-ware. Today, the opposite situation holds true: Thousands of software developers are fighting to get their individual icons onto your screen. At last count, my Windows 95 desktop provided access to more than 200 applications.

The *last* thing that a user wants is to have to open and work in two or more messaging centers. Therefore, all message types should be accessible from one application's user interface.

THE INTEGRATED MAILBOX

Time to go back to the thinking tank. The creative and daring side of you says: "Let's give them e-mail in the same interface; after all, we have the message store- house, and we're already doing voice and fax." The business and commonsense side should say: "Hold it — who says the users want to give up their Lotus Notes, their CC-mail, or their MS-Mail?" You'll have to abandon the dream and traipse voice and fax messages to the e-mail interface in the hope that an open API will enable you to mix messages with e-mail. And if you think your solution is on the Internet . . . it's not.

What you're talking about is the *integrated mailbox*. A big difference exists between this application and the separate, yet graphical, voice-mailbox-like screen-based interface. The integrated mailbox, depicted in Figure 13-2, can provide access to all message types from one application, which saves the user from having to manage three separate applets. The integrated mailbox, however, still is not an optimum solution because you have to maintain separate message storehouses for separate types of messages. It unifies the message information, but the message storehouses remain separate. Under the hood, the interface merely points to messages stored and referenced in three separate databases or message warehouses. The user interface is easy to create from the client software point of view. You merely extract the information in the list boxes from the different message databases located on the servers of each message type.

To the message's recipient, the fact that these messages are stored separately is not really important. The messages behave differently anyway. You can't read your voice mail, and playing your e-mail only makes sense when you can't be in front of the PC's monitor. The real concern of using the integrated mailbox involves the IT department and the computer telephony people. The question you have to answer is this: Who manages and controls what service? Until now, e-mail was the domain and responsibility of the IT people, whereas voice and fax mail was the domain and responsibility of the computer telephony consultants. This separation of specialties will likely remain for many years, although eventually the scenario will change.

Although e-mail travels from the mail server, across the LAN, to the e-mail client interface, voice mail travels to the user via the telephone network — and the PBX sits in the middle of the route. Both technologies are of very different worlds as far as information technology is concerned. Most CIOs and IT executives are more comfortable

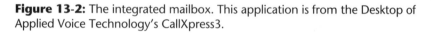

Figure 13-2: The integrated mailbox. This application is from the Desktop of Applied Voice Technology's CallXpress3.

leaving telephony to the telephony people, whereas the telephony people feel as at home with the enterprise's computer and IT needs as humans do to flying with the birds.

By having three or more separate servers for the different message types, you, the IT executives, must maintain and manage more equipment and software. If you already have a substantial investment in these servers, then the integrated approach will at least provide the notion of a unified message box while keeping the storehouses separate but connected (that is, if the vendor can provide this setup). If you do not have substantial investment in a modern computer telephony product, or if your voice mail system harks back to the days of the legacy/bolt-on era, then your next big decision will be making the move to a universal solution, no matter how big or complex your enterprise. This decision is one you'll have to make in the next two or three years. Let's talk about that now.

THE POWER OF ONE: THE UNIVERSAL MAILBOX

The single most important factor that sets the universal mailbox apart is that the server holds and maintains a single message storehouse for all message types. How the messages traverse the enterprise information network (LAN and telephone) will be determined by the vendors of these message or mail servers. The vendors include Microsoft (Microsoft Exchange), IBM (Lotus Notes), and Novell (GroupWise). The e-mail vendors place their e-mail into these storehouses as do the voice and fax vendors with their messages. (See Figure 13-3.)

A major advantage of this approach is the ease of managing a compound message, such as an e-mail file that has a voice message attached to it, or vice versa. The next few years will see the arrival of the compound message. The user will be able to access both message types and the various components of the compound message from either the TUI or the GUI.

It probably goes without saying that Applied Voice Technology (AVT), although not the first vendor to enable users to access voice messages from the GUI, was the first one to provide users with an integrated mailbox from which they can easily access and manage voice and fax messages.

TRADE-OFF 3: CT MAKES THE ENTERPRISE REPULSIVE

This fact applies when you're dealing with callers who've worked with other enterprises' systems that were confusing, complicated, poorly designed, and difficult to navigate. Callers who have experienced "voice mail jail" are left with a bitter taste for the technology, and removing it requires a great deal of effort. The result is that a community of voice mail haters now exists, so the industry needs good PR and educational committees to ensure that the new breed of integrators, the LAN value-added resellers touting Novell Telephony and Windows Telephony, do not further sour customers on this technology.

This trade-off also holds true from the user's perspective in the internal environment of the enterprise. If users find it difficult to access the computer telephony system and navigate their mailboxes, they will not respond to messages. The result is that customers will find the enterprise repulsive as well because no one gets back to them. There *are* some companies that you simply cannot reach and that simply do not return voice mail. You have to wonder how these companies are able to stay in business because they can't be making that much money offering that kind of customer service.

The upside to this trade-off is the emerging trends in personal computer software and client/server technology. The manufacturers of DSP voice-processing cards for PCs stepped onto the right path years ago by building components that can survive not only the terrible versions of software that software developers first supplied for the component, but also software from other manufacturers. In other words, a past investment into a voice-processing card, like the Rhetorex RDSP series and the Dialogic D41/D that came out in 1992, is a pay-off strategy that will start to reap rewards now with the new and future software hitting the market.

In this regard, the DSP voice-processing card/telephony component may go down in history as the most innovative PC add-in ever invented. The fact that few other devices can boast such survival rates and such hardiness is a tribute to the computer telephony industry. To understand what the software in the new frontier of computer telephony can do for you, read on.

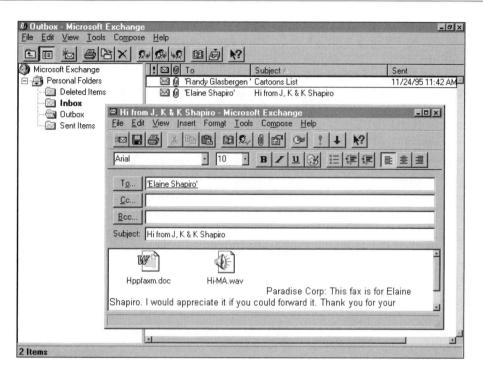

Figure 13-3: The universal mailbox provided by Microsoft Exchange.

TRADE-OFF 4: CT IS INTRUSIVE

Whether or not CT is intrusive depends a great deal on (a) the attitude and work regimen of the user and (b) the product being used and the way it is set up. Users who feel that CT is intrusive are probably attached (not in the romantic sense) to voice mail systems that enslave them. Fighting with a blinking message lamp on the telephone or having to endure the annoying stutter and stammer of the "you have messages" dial tone every time you lift the telephone can be frustrating.

These CT systems offer users no means of managing *how much* the system can intrude in their lives and work regimen — it's an all-or-none situation. The intrusion factor leads many people to either vanish behind voice mail or — to avoid being accused of "hiding behind it" — to switch it off. In both scenarios, the users have chosen, for various reasons, to be out of reach.

Let's talk about message notification. A fancy catch word in the industry is *cascading notification*. This process means that the CT system will try all means of delivering a message to you if you provide such information in the message-storing database. In other words, if you carry a pager on your hip, it can alert you via that device; if you carry a cell phone, it can call you on the cellular phone; if you have e-mail, it can alert you via e-mail; if your phone has a message lamp, the system can turn it on.

The CT system also can instruct the PBX to notify you of messages when you pick up your handset to make a call. The PBX can be programmed to change the cadence of the dial tone, play a digitized message, or play a sound file. I have even worked with some systems that make an intercom call, just to say "You have new mail," and then wait for a password to continue or reset. The term *cascade* alludes to the system's capability to try alternatives or *next* options to alert the user or deliver a message. Cascading notification is good idea, but make sure that it is user definable (that is, each user can define to what extent they need to be interrupted).

A CIO or IT executive typically is responsible for making sure that users get the mail by all possible means. I heard of one setup that routed users directly to the CT system every time they lifted the handset to make a call. The intentions may have been good, but I would take an ax to such a product. It's too intrusive. If a CEO demanded this setup from me, I'd explain that in order for the firm's workers to be productive, the users need to define how they want to be alerted when messages arrive. It's important to deploy software that users can easily manage from the desktop themselves, graphically at best or via the TUI at worst.

Here's an example: I have worked with several people who get tons of voice messages every day. Many prefer not to be notified of messages by their systems at all. They have set times or patterns in their behavior that determine when accessing and responding to voice messages will be most convenient.

A computer telephony system that lets calls ring endlessly at extensions, alters dial tones (causing havoc with modems trying to signal for service), crashes the PBX by consistent hammering at the message lamps, and generally hunts down people to make sure that they get their messages also will be considered too intrusive. You can bring users to their voice messages or vice versa, but you cannot make the user utilize the system. The user still has to act on the message and respond to it; you don't have much control over that part of the deal. But if you enable your people to decide for themselves how they want to be interrupted for messages, the intrusion factor will disappear, as will the desire of your users to escape from the system.

How do you make sure that people are checking their mail? One option does exist, but I really don't think you want to do this regularly. The problem here deals with the users, and its solution does not lie in computer telephony (see Chapters 15, 16, and 17).

But if you have to keep informed from time to time, or when certain factors or incidents (like complaining clients) motivate you to do it, the answer is to have the vendor provide utilities to read the message database. With these utilities, you will be able to see who is not accessing and responding to voice messages and how long he or she has been avoiding the service. Then you can take action on an individual basis, instead of forcing proactive, cascading-message notification on every member of the enterprise.

TRADE-OFF 5: VOICE MESSAGES ARE NOT PRIVATE

This trade-off has to do with the employee's right, or assumed right, to privacy and protection from prying eyes, as well as from espionage or an attack on the enterprise in general.

The right to privacy is a tricky one, and employees and users should be aware that even if they have these rights, as they do in many parts of the world, their rights and privacy may be infringed on or ignored. Many companies routinely monitor v-mail, e-mail, and fax mail. In some cases, the enterprise insists that the employee understand that he or she is to use the voice-messaging facility for business use only and that management will monitor the messaging services to ensure proper use. Advising your employees to keep sensitive, personal information out of the enterprise's voice message facility is a good idea, for their own good.

A voice mailbox is not 100 percent safe — not from management, however justified it feels in listening to messages; not from disgruntled employees or peers; and not from hackers, internal or external. Users need to be aware that their passwords are accessible to systems administrators and that the possibility exists that someone could "hack" into the message storehouse and listen to the messages in user directories. Someone may be able to externally access the voice message and wreak havoc with it. Even if the user is obeying the business-use-only rules, their messages may be valuable to someone else in the enterprise. Sales people are especially prone to attack, and several sales executives have expressed concern to me about the safety of the messages their clients leave.

Two widely publicized cases come to mind regarding the right to message privacy. In the first case, which hit the press in early 1995, management at a McDonald's facility learned of an affair that an employee was having and promptly dismissed the person. Management was alerted to the affair by another employee who had managed to infiltrate the offending employee's mailbox.

In another case, a New York woman left a sexually explicit message on the system at a law office. This message has since been circulated to thousands of users like a worn-out cartoon. The debate raging around this event is not one about privacy but whether or not the story is true. Many men believe it is a genuine account of a sexual encounter, whereas many women say it's just voice mail pornography. I have not personally heard the message, but I hear that it's a remarkable recording.

A bigger problem for the enterprise, however, is protection from outside attack. So-called hackers find the thousands of voice mail and computer telephony systems in use easy targets. Many hack them just for the challenge, whereas others have more sinister and lucrative reasons. These reasons include the following:

+ **Industrial espionage.** Hackers break into mailboxes to listen for information they can use or sell for competitive advantage. Legal firms, stock brokers, financial advisers, accounting firms, and many others receive and process extremely sensitive information. People even leave credit card numbers, passwords, PIN numbers, access codes, and more in mailboxes.

✦ **Toll fraud.** This activity could cost you millions and even force the enterprise into bankruptcy. By enabling remote users to access your outgoing trunks to make long-distance calls, you're providing a very tempting service for someone to hack into. After the perpetrator has opened a gateway and gained dial tone from your system, he or she can resell this service for shiploads of money. In the meantime, you end up paying through the nose for someone else's long-distance calls.

✦ **The uninvited guest.** The third, yet not the least, problem is the so-called uninvited guest who probes your system to find unused mailboxes, which he or she then rents out or uses for transacting illegal business, such as coordinating drug deals. Some hackers are smart enough to hack the administration software and set up their own mailboxes. Basically, they set up a voice messaging service within a voice-messaging service.

ROCK SOLID: STRATEGIES FOR SECURE MESSAGE SERVICES

Protecting the computer telephony system (and mail servers) from attack should be part of the general security plan that governs the entire LAN. Why some products allow extensive system management over the phone, such as fully functional mailbox setup, I can't figure out. I shut off these features or disable them from the management suite. Unfortunately, that strategy still doesn't provide 100 percent protection. The CT system can also be reached through the LAN, through dial-up and serial (RS-232) ports used for remote management, and through any remote access server (RAS) that you may have provided for the benefit of users and customers.

The CT system thus needs to be "tucked" neatly away behind the network's firewalls. Many such products have emerged in tandem with the increase in popularity of the Internet and World Wide Web. As different message types merge into one message storehouse, an attack via voice "windows" could be an attack that hits both e-mail and f-mail as well.

The information and the security strategies that follow are based on material provided to me by the Voice Messaging Education Committee (VMEC), the industry-sponsored organization that is the leading spokesbody and advocate for the wise use of voice mail. I also have added my own experience as a computer telephony consultant, as well as the experience of other IT executive and systems integrators:

✦ Regularly communicate enterprise policy on matters of security and what you consider to be acceptable use of messaging services and the network to employees.

✦ Make sure that the security issue is covered in training classes and that user material includes such information. A good place to put this information is in the help file of the enterprise's on-line telephone directory. Update your users as often as necessary via the LAN's e-mail service.

✦ Advise telephonists to be alert, prudent, and security-conscious all the time. It's a good idea to keep these people updated with training and information. I was once put on hold by a telephonist who mistakenly provided me with a dial tone on one of the company trunks. I realized that I had an opportunity to gain access to the firm's sensitive service by merely asking for the service. Problems also arise when a member of the enterprise stands in for the telephonist. This action is like dropping your shield. A caller may request a service, and the stand-in may oblige without much forethought.

✦ Carefully and astutely manage and control the outbound activities of the CT system. These services, especially those that are part of the message notification process, are the weak links in the armor of the security system that protects your data.

✦ Establish password protection and changing routines. Also consider having users regularly change their passwords but not so regularly that they run out of passwords.

✦ Keep track of members who leave, temporarily or permanently. When a disgruntled member is booted out of the enterprise, he or she can call into a previously used mailbox and leave a damaging message that gets broadcast all over the place. In one of my cases, a dismissed user felt a need to vent his anger and opinion about the chairman by leaving a message in the mailbox that distributed messages to a number of senior executives. The disgruntled person knew the password and, after leaving the company, was able to leave a message for all to hear. The information in this case was not damaging, but it was embarrassing. In another case, a mailbox user who was routinely forwarded sales leads left to work for a competitor. Not only did he call in and routinely collect information after leaving, but the system *called him* to update him several times a day. These events went unnoticed for nearly six months by his previous employer.

The final word on privacy and security is to keep a watch on the systems by regularly checking SMDR and call-accounting information for unusual activity. Spotting problems is fairly easy. If you notice regular calls from a single extension or mailbox at certain times of the day, drawn out over a long time period, little bells should start ringing.

GETTING THE MOST OUT OF VOICE MESSAGING

The following strategies are drawn from several years and thousands of hours of training users to get the most out of messaging. Remember that by using the system wisely, you can go beyond just having the callers leave a voice message and can engage in a full conversation. Proper use and management of your system will help callers feel more secure and comfortable leaving you voice messages.

Getting back to callers or acting on their needs promptly also improves customer satisfaction and makes your enterprise and you that much more alluring, accessible, and available — key ingredients to your success. You also can get a great deal more out of voice messaging if you learn how to leave a voice message properly.

THE MAILBOX GREETING

You should change mailbox greetings regularly. Recording a new message at the start of every workweek is a good idea. You should also let your callers know where you will be for the week — if you plan to be out of the office, say so, but keep it short. Callers will keep calling back until they get through to another person. If they later hear "Oh, he hasn't been at his desk all week," then when you finally connect with the callers, they will not be too impressed with you.

Make sure that you personalize the greeting; nothing is worse for your callers than leaving a message in a mailbox with a generic greeting or one where they cannot rest assured that they have the right mailbox.

Leave detailed greetings that don't leave the callers wondering whether you really exist. Choose your words carefully so as not to make the greeting too long for callers. One of the worst mailbox greetings is the generic "I am either on the phone or away from my desk . . . ." If you don't want to say much in the greeting, use something like "Sorry I could not take your call . . . ."

It is a good idea to provide the caller with as much information as possible (without being too graphic) to help him or her decide whether to leave a message or call back in five minutes. A detailed greeting prompts the caller to leave a detailed message. The "on the phone *or* . . ." message prompts many callers to leave an excuse for a message — something like "Call me back when you've made up your mind . . . ." Of course, the caller does not know that in reality you're a thousand miles away in the Caribbean hunting down UFOs (or giant cockroaches).

Again, I blame the inflexible and hard-to-use voice mail system for making the task of updating your greeting repulsive. Asking many users to keep greetings up-to-date is like giving a 15-year-old who wants to learn to drive an eight-gear, double-clutch, 18-wheeler. I know it's not easy to record a good greeting message; it's not easy to keep changing the message every hour either. That's why some people have greetings that are often weeks or months out-of-date.

One exception to this problem occurs in the computer industry, where greetings are often posted a bit *too* early. Around the festive season (late November to mid-January), many IT people and hardware and software vendors seem to get caught up in a distortion in the time-space continuum. They leave voice mail greetings such as "I will be attending Comdex Fall from November 23 to 27 and will be returning on . . . ." What is happening here: The voice-mail greeting has gone unchanged for two months and sometimes longer. Comdex has come and gone, and it sounds like the greeting is now months too early.

The good news is that the shifts in CTI, which I discuss in Chapter 5, will bring forth new products that will enable you to change a message by clicking on an icon. A microphone attached to the PC, likely via universal serial bus, will allow you to say your piece and go. You'll even be able to record your greeting remotely and e-mail it to the system . . . . I've already said too much. Many telephone headsets will likely double as microphones so you won't need to touch the telephone.

The opposite extreme is the mailbox greeting that sounds like a diary or consists of the abridged version of your autobiography. It's also not a good idea to say "but I will be calling in to check my messages." Yeah, right. How many times have you been lied to like this? The caller will tell you that "If you listened to your messages, you would have gotten back to me or provided me with service. Besides, your mailbox greeting said you would be out until the 16th, and now it's the end of the month. Who are ya kidding?" Your callers expect you to check your messages. You should not have to entice them to leave a message.

As far as greeting content goes, you need to consider the type of caller that will be leaving messages in the mailbox. If you get all types of callers, try leaving a greeting that caters to all. You may be wondering: Who are *you* to dictate to me what message I leave? Well, consider that CSI can go downhill fast if callers abandon because they run out of patience, two minutes into your greeting.

It's also become redundant to tell the caller to "leave the message after the beep," unless your system plays several beeps (like Morse code) or is confusing to the caller. Callers know that the time to start speaking is after the beep, just as they know that you have to turn the key to start the car.

The new wave in CT technology will enable you to select a different mailbox greeting for different times and circumstances. These greeting can be changed easily via the GUI. If, however, you have to leave a generic message, simply say, "Sorry I could not take your call . . . ."

CALL-SCREENING POLICY

Call screening is a very popular service that all CT systems have. But, if I had my way, I would ban it from the CT standards. I still don't understand why some people screen calls when better ways to route and filter callers are available without running the risk of offending people and damaging the CSI.

The problem with screening calls is that the caller always knows when you are doing it. The CT system says "Please say who is calling." Then it leaves the callers hanging. Look at the situation as if you were the caller: If the person you called decides he or she wants to talk to you, the called party can take the call; if not, you get dumped into the mailbox. How unflattering. How demoralizing.

Unfortunately, most CT systems available today are too dumb to work in such a way that they don't screen the caller when the called party really can't take the call. The callers get dumped into voice mail because you were out of the office; but the callers get the impression that they ended up in voice mail because they were screened. Ask yourself whether this is what you want the caller to think when the caller wants to know where to send the check you're waiting for or when the caller wants to place an order.

My colleagues and I pondered this problem during software development, and many wanted to include the feature "because the competition did." But after several clients of mine banned their staffs from using the screening function, I realized that this practice had survived from the days when humans screened calls for busy executives and could change their screening tactics from call to call, but the CT system does not provide that same flexibility.

Today, the solution lies in using CT screening tactics that do not inconvenience or upset the caller. As discussed in the other chapters, especially Chapter 7, it helps to anticipate the calls and prepare for them accordingly. If you want to work without being interrupted but have to take some important calls, try having those callers dial a different extension number that calls first before diverting to the mailbox. All other callers can go directly to a mailbox or, better still, to a human who can take the calls *and can service the callers* without risking the callers leaving voice mail. Again, it depends on the situation. A nifty feature that has arrived in the new era of computer telephony, a la NetWare Telephony Services, goes like this:

Technical assistant to caller: "I'll tell you what we are going to do. Since John is the only person who can help you on this problem, I am going to conference you into his voice mail so that together we can explain the problem, okay? Then when we're done, I will send him an urgent e-mail and make sure that he gets back to you. I also have made a note here which will have the system call me back to check if this problem was resolved."

MAKE SURE THAT THE CALLER CAN GET ADDITIONAL SERVICE

Always provide callers with a way out of a mailbox. I don't care where you want them to go afterwards, as long as they can reach a *live* person if they have to. The *only* exception to this rule is when the caller knows the system is a messaging service or audiotext system. Such examples are the voice mail systems used to process classified ads and dating services.

If the caller needs to reach a live person, they must be able to. If they press 0 (zero) at any time in your mailbox, they must go to a telephonist, operator, attendant, expert, uncle, Batman, anyone you choose — as long as it's not another mailbox. The industry calls such a situation "voice mail jail"; I call it bad business.

You should also, as part of the message or as a system prompt, advise and enable the callers to "go elsewhere" after they leave a message or even before they leave a message. Callers should be aware that they can re-record the message or forward it elsewhere if they so choose. If you want to advise callers that alternatives to leaving a message are available, that's fine; just keep in mind what I said earlier about message brevity.

The worst message I ever heard is the one by a professor at MIT. This guy listed every possible telephone, fax, and e-mail option where he could be reached and a dozen other ways to get service in his greeting. The e-mail addresses went on for five minutes. I finally hit 0 and told the telephonist that "I never want to be sent to his voice mail again. Just give me his main e-mail address and let me talk to him in cyberspace."

LEAVING MESSAGES: HOW TO HAVE A TELEPHONE CONVERSATION WITH A COMPUTER

If everyone knew how to have a conversation with a computer or how to leave voice messages that people can act on without having to call back, no one would have to endure boring mailbox greetings that remind you of these services every time you get voice mail.

Almost everyone using the telephone finds him- or herself on both the sending and receiving side of voice mail at one time or another. It's likely, then, that you know how unnecessarily time-consuming it is to call someone back just to find out why they called in the first place. Unless you want to talk person-to-person or unless what you have to say will not work as a message, leave the recipient with enough information to act on. When I call people, I try to leave a message that will make sure that when they get back to me, whichever way they choose, they will have the information or answers I need. Often, I just get e-mail confirming an arrangement.

Go beyond the surface of the message: Leave part numbers, invoice numbers, and whatever instructions are necessary to accomplish the request. In fact, close your eyes and try to imagine that the person is on the other end of the line listening to you. I find this strategy works well. I call it *staying in conversation mode,* as opposed to going into message mode. If you stay in conversation mode when you reach a mailbox, you be able to leave a detailed message.

Many callers know what they want to say, but as soon as they hear voice mail, they lose the power of speech. Others sound like they're choking on a burger. Staying in conversation mode will help you avoid this problem.

BEYOND JUST MESSAGING: OTHER USES FOR VOICE MESSAGING

The capability of the CT software to record voice goes further in application than voice mail does. Many clients need to cascade or join several voice message boxes together or set up voice forms. Many applications exist for this task. I designed one for a chain of hospitals that could no longer keep up with the volume of callers that needed to pre-register before coming in for surgery. The system is a combination of mailboxes that allows the caller to leave details such as name and address, medical insurance information, referring doctors, prescribed medication, and so on.

Or how about this one: An associate of mine designed a system that allowed morticians to describe autopsy work while having both hands free. You may ask "why use voice mail?" The company that needed the service provided an autopsy service that linked hundreds of morticians working in a number of cities. So interested parties, such as officers investigating violent crimes, could listen to the descriptions of cause of death over the telephone (think about how much time that saved). It was probably one of the most macabre computer telephony systems ever commissioned. Talk about "bleeding edge" technology.

But you have to remember that deciphering and transcribing is a tiresome and tedious process. You may have to rewind a voice mailbox several times to take down all the details. Don't use a system that only enable access to voice mail via the TUI. An integrated or universal mailbox application will enables you to click on VCR-like controls on the screen. In the end, it may not be worth the effort you have to expend to set up this application, and you should explore the more interactive technologies available, as discussed in the preceding chapters.

F-Mail

Great things can be said about fax, and it has enjoyed wide application. But I don't think fax mail is one of the brightest ideas around. Before getting into that idea further, a statement that might get me shot, let's recap the discussion about fax from Chapter 12.

Right now, more than 25 million faxes (some say 30 million) are in service around the world. Fax machines are getting smaller and cheaper by the day. You now can get a fax machine, scanner, printer, and photocopier all in one device for around $300.

Fax machines also are found in jetliners, trucks, automobiles, trains, and ships. For the past decade, the fax machine has been one of the chief means by which enterprises have corresponded with each other. The chief reason for the popularity of fax communication (as a non-interactive technology) has been that it's easy to use. You stick in a letter, dial a telephone number, and press Start. The fax device on the other end receives the transmission and prints out a facsimile of the original or it saves it on a hard disk.

Faxing is used by people who have a need to communicate the contents of a document as rapidly as possible. Fax has become ubiquitous throughout the world as the chief form of business communication. But as you venture deeper into the Information Age, you will find that fax mail, as a premium message format and medium, does not readily suit the global business village that has emerged.

What is fax mail? With the advent of the fax card in a PC, it became obvious just how much better it is to fax from the desktop. You can write a letter, prepare a document, and fax it to someone without getting up from your desk. While the document is faxing, you can start another letter or get down to other work on the PC. You don't have to wait for the job to finish, as you do when you stand next to a fax machine to catch the scanned pages so that no one else sees what you're sending.

But the message format betrays the usefulness of the technology because, unless you are faxing to a fax machine, which inconveniences the receiver, the effort required to route the fax into a mailbox so that it pops up on your addressee's screen is Herculean. To address this paradoxical fact of f-mail (and v-mail to a lesser extent), I took a shot at writing some poetry:

> If we can sit at our screens,
> and click "send" on the fly,
> what's wrong in the spec,
> that it's hard to receive and reply?

Fax mail is much harder to receive and reply to than it is to send. It can take an instant to send a message; it takes a great deal more effort for the recipient to receive the message and reply. With e-mail, which is discussed next, receiving and replying to messages are easier.

Consider the following points:

The problem with fax mail is that it's inherently difficult to route faxes to the recipient. Unfortunately, the Group 3 standard provides no guidelines for a header or address information to facilitate the routing of fax mail after it has been received by the fax gateway of the enterprise information network.

With the arrival of fax cards, which at first could only send faxes, some began to use the new electronic-messaging service without fully considering how the message would be routed to the user, who would be one of many in the remote enterprise.

Several ways of routing fax mail to an individual's desktop are available, but they all have drawbacks.

The first and probably most widely used method, but not the best one, is human filtering. The enterprise that receives fax mail from a wide audience has to employ a person to sit at a screen and determine for whom the fax is intended. If this is not apparent from the cover page or log information, then the attendant has to go into the body of the message for this information.

Two problems with this method are that (1) it's time consuming and (2) any confidentiality in the letter is at risk. Few enterprises want to employ people just to filter and route faxes. It defeats the objectives of employing technology in the first place.

The next most widely used routing option, for large organizations, is direct inward dialing (DID). Without going into the technology of DID here, this option is probably the best available for routing inbound faxes to the desktop. This method involves the central office and the DID-capable PBX or DID add-on hardware and software. No human intervention is necessary with this method.

For many, the DID option is expensive or unavailable. Although DID service is easy to access in the U.S., many countries do not provide readily available and affordable DID service. A DID-capable PBX and equipment, added to the cost of the CT system, is out of the financial reach of many of my clients who wanted to explore fax mail.

Voice processing is the third option and probably one of the most difficult to implement. When computer telephony consultants or sales people refer to fax mail, they are most likely referring to the process of reaching someone's voice mailbox and being presented with the opportunity to send a fax at the same time.

This kills the whole idea of fax as an easy-to-use technology and turns it into one that requires dedication and indulgence on the part of the caller. You are unlikely to have many callers who will agree to go through the process of sending fax mail to the desktop via the voice-processing and voice-mail facility of the enterprise, especially if calling long distance. The other problem is that the sender may be faxing from the desktop, in which case it's impossible for him or her to navigate the CT system on the other end. If this happens, the CT system should default to receiving the message in a single corporate fax mailbox, which goes back to using the first routing option — a human attendant.

The last, least-used, and hardly reliable method of routing is optical character recognition (OCR). The idea, or madness, behind this facility was to include a mailbox number at the top of the letter. OCR scans the digits and then converts the bitmap (a mapping of digital information) into text. Once in text form, the number can be matched against a database of mailboxes and routed accordingly. Many people believe that OCR will one day be accurate enough to recognize the information on the cover page of the fax and use the information for routing. I don't think so. OCR is great for scanning manuscripts, but not for routing faxes. Even if it works 100 percent one day, and it might, the bigger problem of having an inflexible format arrive at the desktop computer still lies ahead.

Even with the advent of newer standards and technologies, such as X.400, better options are available. Instead of discussing these options here and comparing them to fax mail, I have left this to the discussion of e-mail that follows.

Before going into detail about e-mail, it is worthwhile to note that now — and more so in the future— the mail you receive should be in a format that will enable you to easily annotate it, reply to it, edit it, manipulate it, and database it for whatever reasons. The current format of fax makes this impossible. Fax mail thus has two major drawbacks that you need to consider:

1. It is not cheap or easy to route fax mail to the desktop.

2. After it's at the desktop, fax mail is almost impossible to work with.

Despite these limitations, many enterprises have invested substantially in fax mail because few options were available. It made no sense to buy a fax machine for everyone in the enterprise. The challenge now is not to keep investing in overcoming the problems you have with fax mail, but to try and adopt the other models and technologies.

The solution will take a change of heart throughout industry and will not occur overnight without bold planning and courage. If you're stuck in fax mail, it's time to look at e-mail.

E-MAIL: THE CRITICAL SERVICE

Electronic mail is old hat. This service has been around since the turn of the century and the days of the telegraph. E-mail is the posting of messages electronically — it includes telex, teletext, facsimile, store-and-forward electronic mail (or *just e-mail*), and electronic document and information interchange (exchange). You could argue that voice messaging is also a form of e-mail.

An e-mail communication is composed of two parts: the header and the content. The header contains the routing information and the recipient's address. The content contains the body of the message and any file attachments. E-mail software reads the message headers that arrive in mailboxes to decide where to route the message and how to notify the recipient.

The whole idea of e-mail is that someone sends a message to a host computer where you (the subscriber) have a mailbox or a post office account. The mailbox stores the message and waits to hear from you. After you connect to the host computer, you can read the message while connected or you can download it (which forwards it to your local computer; your computer is known as the mail-transfer agent). Voice mail works on identical principles. Software agents now go out onto the Net and probe your various mailboxes for your mail; then they download them and transfer them directly to your desktop.

The origins of store-and-forward electronic mail can be traced to the predecessor of the Internet: the *ARPAnet,* or the Advanced Research Projects Agency (the ARPA) network. The purpose of ARPAnet was to connect universities and other learning centers, especially institutes funded by the ARPA. Imagine how lonely it must have been for those scientists to sit in an isolated office in the basement of some huge campus, not being able to discuss, debate, and "shoot the breeze" with fellow "profs." As a result, the scientists began sending messages to each other on the ARPAnet. This easy message interchange led to (or, more likely, resulted from) defense research. The ARPAnet became the ideal conduit for information exchange in the event of nuclear war.

Big Blue also played a role in the emergence of e-mail. IBM introduced its Network Job Entry protocols back in the 70s. IBM also adapted the S&F paradigm to provide e-mail and enable workers to transfer files and records throughout the giant computer company.

Today, e-mail's popularity can be attributed to the new software interfaces that make sending and receiving electronic messages easy. Its popularity also has a great deal to do with the ease with which you can now operate your personal computers, install and configure (or not configure, courtesy of Plug and Play, *PnP*) modems, and connect to the hosts that provide the store-and-forward functions or mailboxes. Price and access also are contributing factors to connecting the masses to the world of e-mail. Just as everyone has a physical mailbox at their home or business, everyone should have an e-mail mailbox.

Anyone who owns a personal computer will find it a cinch to compose, send, and receive e-mail. Compare this to the days when telex was the only form of electronic mail that an office could afford. The operator needed special training to learn how to feed punched ticker tape through a reader to transmit messages. Information moved at a much slower pace (50 bps). If you ask older but still 30-something reporters (like me) whether they remember filing stories via telex or scanning the Associated Press or Reuters ticker in the newsroom, their fond and wild memories will come flooding back.

Most of your current e-mail experience, however, comes from being connected to the office LAN (local area network). The client/server LAN provides the best example of e-mail in action. The mail host computer is usually a LAN server where a *post office* is installed. When you log in from your workstation, the post office tells you whether you have mail, and then you can read it by opening your mailbox. LAN e-mail software comes with loads of features to make this form of communication easy. You can sort mail according to a variety of criteria, you can broadcast your message, you can store mail in specialized folders, and more. The e-mail application's user interface includes icons that you can use to manage your messages. For example, most e-mail user interfaces enable you to drag an old message and drop it into a wastebasket.

E-mail is great for interoffice communications, but can you use the same user-friendly e-mail software to communicate with business associates, customers, and remote offices around the world? What a great idea if you can receive an on-line letter from a customer with a problem and reply immediately, knowing that the customer will receive the solution in minutes. This method would represent great cost and time savings, not to mention that it would provide customer convenience and enhance your enterprise's professional image (CSI).

This point is where the Internet enters. Because the global, "mother-of-all" networks now spans the world and links millions of computers and sub-networks, e-mail is now possible on a colossal scale. The Internet enables anyone (with access) to send e-mail to anyone, anywhere. Specialized hardware (telephone interface boards, modems, and routers) and software (gateways) allow LANs to send e-mail to other LANs.

Commercial on-line services, such as CompuServe, Prodigy, America Online (AOL), and GEnie, were once closed networks where subscribers could only send mail to other subscribers. The Internet connection now enables their subscribers to send e-mail to each other through Internet gateways. For example, a CompuServe member can send mail to an AOL member because both are connected to the Internet. Because e-mail traverses not only interoffice but also enterprise and geographical boundaries, it deserves to be called the critical service.

Hundreds of millions of computers are installed (many more than fax machines and operational telex machines), and modem prices have dropped so much that PCs include them as a standard component for "free"; many PCs also come with on-line accounts that you can sign up for. Modems operate at terrific speeds (28,800 bps) and make the sending and receiving of e-mail a pleasure when compared to earlier interfaces. Another factor to consider is that the Integrated Services Digital Network (ISDN) is now within the financial reach of the small office/home office user (see Part III), offering super high speeds for accessing the Internet.

So, where is e-mail heading? To a future where it will dominate the world of message-based communications. The desktop computer is at the center of this world — it only makes sense that users communicate right from the desktop. This reason is why fax modems have outsold fax machines three-to-one.

Most major operating systems now have e-mail capabilities embedded in them. Applications will use e-mail to run remote procedures and other applications on distant machines — the new mail transmission standards and protocols that provide this capability are under development. Currently, e-mail software developers are addressing an issue which they paid little attention to in the past: security. Privacy enhanced mail (PEM) is underway for deployment on the Internet. Smarter mail has arrived, such as MIME and SMIME (Multipurpose Internet Mail Extensions and its secure descendant), which enables you to attach multimedia binary data to the SMTP message. (SMTP stands for Simple Mail Transport Protocol, which is the standard message format of the 7-bit Internet.)

As you can see, strenuous efforts and a great deal of money are being invested to make the Internet strong enough to become the chief means by which businesses communicate with other businesses around the world.

THE DOWNSIDE OF E-MAIL

But what about security? What about the horde of cyberthugs lurking in "Net Alley" waiting to read your mail? Until you can adequately secure e-mail (which is not far off), all other forms of communications will — conceptually — be safer. E-mail is not tamper-proof unless you encrypt it. Therefore, you should use it under the assumption that if someone *wants* to intercept your mail, no matter how you send it, they will. You can find out whether someone tampered with your mail, but by then it's usually too late.

One counter-argument is that so much e-mail is flying around the networks that industrial espionage via spying on e-mail is impractical. Cops and hackers may have technology that "listens" to the mail for tidbits of content suggesting contraband, pornography, or other leads, but a commercial spy would be better off to bug your room rather than to try spying on your e-mail. Often, spies do not know what they are looking for, so the costs of e-mail espionage may be greater than the rewards.

Fax *is* more secure, but it is only safe when expensive encryption/decryption devices are installed at both sides of the telephone line. Voice encryption needs the same technology (ironically, it may be more secure and cheaper to make your voice call over the Internet). Encrypting an e-mail file costs nothing but a few minutes (seconds, if automated). Even the software is free, thanks to Philip Zimmermann, the creator of the *Pretty Good Privacy* (PGP) cryptography software product. A rule of thumb to follow: If you have something secret that you want to put into e-mail, lock up the file with encryption software.

With e-mail, you can easily retain a copy of what you receive and send. Recording voice conversations, however, is almost considered criminal (or at the least, rude). Fax also provides you with copies of the information; however, the hard copies curl up and die, the ones on your hard-disk take up valuable space, and the ones that you photocopy are mean on the environment.

Despite all its *current* security drawbacks, e-mail may soon be easier to secure than other communication media. Consider the following:

1. Encryption algorithms are available. Several products are already in the works that allow senders to enclose their messages in an electronic "envelope" that takes seconds to "lick" and send. Only the recipient with a software or hardware key (or both) can decode the message. (The growing need to secure on-line payment data — such as credit card numbers and account information — is the driving force behind e-mail privacy.)

2. E-mail encryption costs pennies. Fax and phone encryption is expensive.

3. You can send encrypted e-mail to a wide audience; recipients only need a software key to read the message. Fax and phone encryption requires that the recipients have a similar encryption device. Only a very small percentage of businesses can afford these encryption devices.

4. The Internet's Simple Mail Transport Protocol (STMP) is being upgraded and enhanced to ensure privacy.

5. The user now has encryption available at the presentation layer in the graphical user interface, making it easier to encrypt and decrypt mail.

E-mail can get lost, however. If a computer holding e-mail crashes, any mail that made it to the connection will be stuck on the hard disk until the server is brought back to life. Voice and fax mail suffer from a similar weakness. The chance of this happening to you, however, is very small, and other communication methods have additional weaknesses. Faxes also get lost or become unreadable because of poor telephone line connections. When the machine runs out of paper, you lose the message, or the paper gets stuck, leaving you high-and-dry again. How many times have you had a fax come through as a line of thin dashes? How many times have you incurred a connection charge for a fax that stayed connected for 10 or 15 minutes, only to have the other party call to tell you that nothing came through? When you consider the problems that other communication methods have, e-mail begins to look even better as an alternative.

If you want to make sure that your e-mail reaches its destination, add a "p.s." at the bottom of the message, asking the reader to confirm its receipt. *Don't call,* as many people did when faxes first made their debut. E-mail can take a few minutes to go from sender to receiver in the U.S. and a little longer when going abroad (don't forget to factor in the time zones), although I now witness e-mail arriving seconds after sending it. If you don't hear anything within a certain amount of time, try sending the e-mail again. New e-mail software packages often include a feature that automatically confirms whether your message was received, just like registering a letter.

Many experts predict that e-mail will supersede the fax machine in the same fashion that faxing replaced telex and teletext communications. Some go as far as to say that fax machines will become obsolete within a few years. Fax machines replaced telex machines because they were easier to use and you could send facsimiles of the original documents — signature, logo, and all (including the staples) very easily. Believe it or not, telex is still used in spite of this. But working habits have changed.

E-MAIL VERSUS FAX COMMUNICATION

As a method of real-time, confirmed, hard-copy communication, the fax machine (or fax-card in the PC) will be around for many years. Its use as an information exchange tool, however, will dwindle in the next few years as users embrace open systems paradigms and interoperability and move beyond fax technology.

In many respects, the fax machine is a dinosaur like the mainframe. Although it was a critical form of communication, faxing capabilities are difficult to integrate with an enterprise's information systems because you have to convert its medium. Even when you install it in a PC, fax is another technology island. As an information exchange (search and retrieve) tool, its user interface is very limited.

Will e-mail replace fax communication? Yes and no. Eventually, yes — but because the fax method is evolving, it will not disappear for some time. Remember when fax machines made their debut? Boy, did they cost a bundle. But most of us still dumped the telex machine. Telex cost much more, and it took too long to prepare and send a few lines of information (the limitation of the transmission technology). You also needed special training to use it. With a fax machine, you just type up a letter, print it, and the machine scans it. The contents of a faxed letter are digitally shredded into thousand of bits of data, and the receiving fax machine puts it all back together.

But faxing also has drawbacks and limitations which e-mail improves on, as discussed earlier. In the same fashion that fax replaced telex, e-mail will eventually replace fax communication.

Fax technology *has* improved greatly since it was first introduced. With the advent of the fax modem for desktop PCs and LAN servers, you no longer need to get up and walk to the fax machine to send a fax. You can fire off a fax right from the word processor, and fax-on-demand enables callers to "down-fax" their information. Still, many factors indicate that fax offers diminishing returns as time goes on and new technologies emerge. The two most significant are cost and convenience.

THE DIMINISHING RETURNS OF FAX

Fax is not as cheap as it seemed in the teletext heyday. Fax can cost a bundle, especially if your recipient is located a few thousand miles from you. You still need to open a direct connection to the receiving fax machine or the fax-on-demand server, or the caller has to make a direct connection to you. You pay heavily for the benefit (see Chapter 10) in terms of time that it actually takes to send the information. It's tantamount to leasing the line for the five or ten minutes needed to transmit or retrieve a couple of documents.

Business still reels under the costs of long-distance calls even with the competition between the long-distance carriers. In third world countries, the cost of replying to a fax may be three to six times greater than the sender's cost. Remember that this is a global marketplace and that you are the anywhere, anytime enterprise.

E-mail and the means by which it is transmitted is much cheaper. Consider the following:

✦ Four-page fax: New York to Hong Kong = $2.00 to $4.00

✦ Four-page e-mail: New York to Hong Kong = FREE (Well, almost. You still pay for your connection to the Internet.)

✦ Four-page fax: Hong Kong to New York = $4.00 to $6.00

✦ Four-page e-mail: Hong Kong to New York = FREE

Although time may be less of a factor for cost, it is something to factor into convenience. I have debated with many people the lack of benefits that fax mail offers, in that it's slower than e-mail and more difficult to learn (see Chapters 10 and 12). Many faxes lie buried for hours, days, and weeks in reception trays or in LAN in-boxes, waiting to be sifted, filtered, collected, collated, or routed to network mailboxes.

You need expensive software, hardware, and human routers to make sure that a fax gets to a desktop on a LAN. You also need special telephony features (see Chapters 10 and 12). Fax mail was supposed to eliminate the inconvenience of collecting and distributing faxes that arrive at one point in the enterprise. Even if you are a one-person show, receiving a fax can be a less than pleasant experience. Those curly thermals that you have to photocopy (doubling the effort) can be a nuisance and a waste of time. Plain-paper fax machines are even more wasteful and costly.

Even faxing into a network (which degrades LAN and especially desktop performance) still requires a human to spend time distributing the "mail." It's a marvelous idea to send people faxes that end up in mailboxes on their desks, but LAN software cannot easily read addresses on faxes, as opposed to e-mail addresses.

Time also is a factor unless the parties coordinate when they intend to send and receive faxes. Negotiating or reconciling contracts provides a good example. Parties send versions of a legal document to each other until the final version is agreed upon and signed. Unless the faxing is coordinated, e-mail gets to the desktop faster. What about fax mail, you ask? You can fire off a fax right from the word processor, but it may not go directly to your recipient. Fax mail also is both difficult to receive and send in comparison to e-mail.

E-mail is as easy to receive as to send. And you don't need to use OCR (optical character recognition) to be able to edit the document or insert it into a database. Although progress is being made in OCR also, I believe that by the time OCR can scan a fax and stick the words into a standard text file without further fuss, we won't need the technology for this purpose. Training people to use fax mail is another problem: In my experience, I've found that your people will not make the effort to learn the process. At best, only a few individuals with very specific security needs will use fax mail.

When a fax journeys across the oceans, its trip is not so immediate anymore. The Internet is booming in the Far East, Pacific Rim, and far off emerging industrial economies like South Africa (I get mail from readers in about 45 countries). These countries need Internet access to survive in the exporting market for the U.S. or the European Economic Community — because while they are working, the gigantic U.S. market sleeps. Foreign businesses know that as much as 85 percent of the faxes they send will not be read until the next day, so unless a fax is extremely urgent, an enterprise in another time zone may wait up to three days or more to reply to a fax. If the fax goes to an office of more than five people, the chance of that fax getting lost is much higher than that for e-mail — and by the time the sender realizes that the fax needs to be resent, the info on it may have become extremely urgent.

For example, in a recent discussion with Eric Lee, the Internet champion of Kibbutz Ein Dor in Israel (home of Teldor Wires & Cables Ltd), he told me that his company now communicates with its field managers around the world almost entirely with e-mail: "We have substituted e-mail for fax as a means of staying in touch."

Here comes the e-mail right hook to fax (and voice mail). I had been expecting this statement for some time — I just did not expect it to come from a very strategically placed person in the CT industry (so I won't name him). I was doing some fact checking, and this person suggested I talk to a certain person about CT standards. The person I was talking to said "Why don't you send e-mail to Priscilla at her Internet address? She takes longer to respond to her faxes and voice mail, but she always reads her e-mail and responds fast."

This statement is all too true. Why waste time on the telephone or with a fax for a simple piece of advice when I do not need an immediate answer? E-mail gets a fast response, and the reason behind this fact is simple: You just click on a reply button and bye-bye. You've responded. You just cannot do this with voice and fax mail.

While writing this chapter, I received a message from Sheila Danzig, a successful marketer in Ft. Lauderdale, Florida, who has made over $20 million selling information. We began our negotiations over the Internet and concluded our arrangements over the Internet. Only once in four exchanges did we have cause to talk on the telephone. It was a quick "Hi Jeff, are we still on for lunch?" When we could not agree to a venue over the phone, I told her that I would confirm the restaurant via e-mail. We didn't leave voice messages for each other, and we completely eliminated telephone tag by exchanging e-mail. Voice mail was supposed to do this, but instead people play telephone tag with their voice mail. Sheila is an extremely busy soul, but wherever she goes, she can access her e-mail. Sheila has started circulating a business card that only has an e-mail address — no voice means of reaching her. One of the benefits of gaining citizenship of cyberspace is that you become omni-present and don't need to be physically attached to the telephone.

In my office, the rule now emerging is this: Only use the fax for urgent facsimiles of legal negotiations (not just information); use e-mail for everything else.

SUMMARY

That wraps up the chapter on messaging. I really had to cram a great deal of information into this chapter, so it may appear a little overwhelming. The messaging subject is diverse and has wide implications for the enterprise. That voice mail has harsh critics only reinforces how critical a service it is.

The challenge ahead now lies in adopting the concepts discussed here and working them into your IT services. Although products that offer integrated mailboxes are available, not too much is on the market in the way of universal mailbox services. The reason is that the technology to support the concept is still very new. Expect and plan for the universal mailbox to take hold towards the end of 1996 and the first half of 1997. These products should be mature around the end of 1997 or early 1998.

Part III

COMPUTER
TELEPHONY STRATEGIES

"Roger is witty, charming, handsome, considerate, intelligent, successful, gentle and the most perfect man I ever met. But we had to break up— he's Windows and I'm Mac."

IN THIS CHAPTER

✦ What is on-hold?

✦ The on-hold problem in perspective

✦ How to reduce or eliminate on-hold time

✦ On-hold devices

✦ Sources for on-hold material

"If you'd like to listen to the entire 4-CD box set of
Barbra Streisand's Greatest Hits while you're on hold, press 1..."

CHAPTER 14

STRATEGIES FOR ATTENDING TO CALLERS ON HOLD

In the preceding chapter, I spoke at length about voice mail, its problems, and the new era of unified messaging and global access. Putting customers on hold excessively, like unanswered voice mail, is yet another reason for customers to view your firm as a repulsive enterprise. Even if you create a good first impression by answering the phone quickly and professionally, employing wise PR strategies, and making a good product that people love, you're throwing it all away when you desert your callers to on-hold hell.

A few years ago, I met the CEO and principal of a school that trained people in telephone skills and manners. She earned more than a million dollars a year teaching people how to answer the telephone and talk to people over the telephone and how to develop good telephone habits. I told her that with the arrival of computer telephony, her business only had a few years left; computers soon would do most of the talking and image-building on the phone.

"Oh, there are many profitable years left," she said. "People will buy your voice-mail technology, but that won't change the way they do business much."

She challenged me to extend her preaching to the computer telephony industry. This person was very outspoken about technologies that created more problems than they solved. "I don't trust voice mail," she once told a reporter. "I have clients who have such bad reputations for not returning calls that their customers now refuse to leave messages. So they hold, and while waiting for you to get off the phone, even more damage is done. It's one disaster following another."

After having trained more than a thousand people in computers and computer telephony, I realize now how right she was.

Enterprises put millions of people on hold every day. Putting people on hold unnecessarily results in congested (blocked) lines, ports, and extensions and puts strain on the enterprise's human and technological resources. Putting people on hold accounts for millions of hours in wasted time. So why do firms do so little to alleviate this problem?

One key strategy for alleviating the on-hold malady lies in using computer telephony, but you also have to change the way you conduct business and service people. Although I made light of this chapter's topic with copious use of Randy's cartoons, in reality, the situation is rather sad. (I was glad to find another person tackling this issue as passionately as I.) This chapter deals with the on-hold problem as a human failing, not a technological one.

Before you can fix your image, you first have to understand what's wrong. You must remember to use computer telephony to streamline your enterprise and make it more productive, to empower it for competitive advantages. Employing computer telephony as a cure-all for all your problems is like treating the symptoms and not the cause of a disease. What your enterprise may need is a change of heart.

WHAT IS *ON-HOLD*?

The on-hold scenario has two perspectives: that of the tortured and the torturers. Enterprises torture their callers when they (inadvertently or blatantly) lie to them with lines such as "Just hold a moment," and "We'll be with you shortly." They never keep that promise — dictionaries define a *moment* as a tiny portion of time, and that certainly equals less than a second. Instead, firms send callers to the on-hold torture chamber in the telecosmos, where they are force-fed garbage or kept in silence for much longer than a moment. Who are these on-hold victims?

These callers are the valuable customers who buy your products, pay your salaries, and keep you in business. The practice I just described is notoriously widespread (see Figure 14-1). How — and more importantly, why — do firms do this?

THE PBX HOLDING AND QUEUING FACILITY

Let's deal with the *how* part of the question first: Thinking back to the first chapter, imagine the PBX switching matrix as a train station again. The station master has an inbound train on Track 1 that is scheduled to stop at Platform 14. He or she must keep the train stationary on Track 1 until the present train at Platform 14 leaves or until the train can be switched from Track 1 to the track that runs to Platform 14.

The same principal exists in the PBX (see Chapters 7 and 4). The call is transferred back to the switch where the PBX can hold it at the entry port or simply park it somewhere. You have to hold the caller on the line while you determine the correct station to which you want to transfer the call. Without this capability, the PBX would be unable to switch calls to the correct extensions.

Figure 14-1: Some companies keep people on hold for so long they forget who or why they called.

The computer telephony system uses the PBX switching and hold features to transfer callers to the correct extensions by using callers' responses to menu choices and prompts. When the caller selects an extension or a menu option mapped to an extension, the voice-processing card calls the PBX and (through the telephony interface on the voice-processing card) requests the on-hold/park service. The caller is then put on hold while the card calls the correct extension to complete the service. The speed of this process and the amount of time the caller is on hold depend on the CTI link, as described in Chapters 5 and 8. The caller is not on hold long enough to cause concern unless the computer telephony system has been set up to handle a large number of extensions.

THE MAKING OF A MONSTER

The capability to keep callers waiting on inbound lines without connecting them to extensions is what often leads to on-hold problems. These problems basically result from abusing a fundamental feature of the switch. To solve them, many modern PBXs have a time-out period on the hold feature, often referred to as *recall on-hold*. If the caller has not been serviced or transferred within a set amount of time, the PBX reconnects the call to the extension that requested the on-hold service.

One of my clients asked the PBX technician to remove the capability to put callers on hold from extensions, or at least to reduce the number of callers that could be on hold at the same time (many PBXs limit the number of callers that can be on hold at any time to nine). The technician explained that this task was not possible and that even if he could do it, the workers would be unable to transfer callers to other extensions.

As an alternative solution, my client asked the technician to reduce the time-out period of the on-hold function, so that workers could not abandon callers for longer than the few seconds needed to make a transfer. To do this task, the technician used a so-called *software patch* because the time-out was hard-coded. This means that the configuration software did not have a setting for the user to change the on-hold time-out, so the software engineer had to reduce the time-out in the code and then recompile the software that drives the PBX.

However, I believe that the PBX and its on-hold technology or features were not to blame for the client's problems — that's like saying your television is broken, yet you haven't turned it on. Rather, the problems stemmed from the people using the technology: their disciplines and their habits and behavior.

THE ON-HOLD PROBLEM IN PERSPECTIVE

If you study several on-hold problem scenarios (as I have), you see two basic routes that lead to the problem:

1. The firm is unable to service callers immediately, so it has the PBX hold the connections until workers can get their acts together.

2. The firm receives too many calls during certain times of the day and does not have enough people to take the calls.

As a result, callers are placed in a *call-queue,* the "virtual line" where they wait and experience group torture.

Here is where you find the simple answer to the question "Why do firms do this to people when they try so hard to be conscious of the CSI (customer satisfaction index)?": They are not prepared — or they do not care — to handle the call or the volume of callers.

I can never understand why the 1-800-PHONESEX and 1-800-4PSYCHIC services are the only ones that seem to have the on-hold beast under control (and why your chances of getting busy or RNA lines are so slim). Do they try harder? Is it because each call is worth a few bucks, or a hundred, or a thousand? Do they employ smarter switching and routing technology and computer telephony? I'm sure that the $3.95 a minute or more that every call earns has something to do with the reason why you never are put on hold.

If you placed such a dollar amount on every call, you wouldn't let things get so repulsive either. This strategy applies in any call-processing situation. Take the following example: My partner, Karl Slatner — the finest marketing and CSI guru I have ever met — recently completed a CSI research project for a large, high-tech company. For more than a week, I could hear him interviewing people on the telephone and pounding the information into his trusted Mac. After several weeks, he finally sent a hefty CSI report to the CEO. One of the first items on the report marked urgent was that when callers pressed zero, they got the message "invalid entry." Karl advised the company to end the callers' distress by fixing the problem immediately.

But months have gone by and still the client has done nothing about the problem. Karl asked me what it takes to fix such a problem: "Is it possible they have to reverse-engineer the software to find the reason?" he half-joked. I don't know what sort of system the firm has, so I cannot give you details, but I can tell you this: There isn't a commercial computer telephony system sold today in which a similar problem cannot be fixed in under a minute.

The above company must be losing thousands of dollars a day, but apparently no one there sees it that way. Perhaps if we presented all callers at a value of $100 from the moment they connect and then deducted dollars for every minute of frustration callers endure while sitting on hold, someone like a shareholder may pay more attention to the problem.

You should adopt the same principles and employ the same (or at least similar) strategies to get rid of the apathy that pervades so many enterprises. Try using the following illustration, which places a $100 value on the head of each caller. This amount is not unreasonable for a company that tries to survive in a fiercely competitive market, like commercial software reselling. You deduct the entire amount for every caller that abandons in frustration:

> Number of calls received each day = 1,000
>
> Dollar value of each call = $100
>
> Calls abandoned or not serviced (per day) = 25
>
> Lost business = $2,500
>
> Annual loss to the enterprise = $375,000

I arrived at the total of $375K by assuming the company in question was fully operational for 30 weeks a year, and then multiplied that by $2,500. Even if you reduce the dollar value of each call by 75 percent, you're still flushing dollars down the toilet. That's quite a chunk of change lost, don't you agree?

Every time I walk down Sixth Avenue in Manhattan, I stare up at a huge LED counter-display just north of 42nd Street that continuously calculates the national deficit. A well known long-distance company now has a similar display above Broadway and 48th, showing how much money you could save by using its long-distance service. Every call center has such a display showing how many callers are on hold and the average hold time. You can use those numbers to build your own on-hold cost scenario.

But getting back to the on-hold problem, the ideal situation is when you do not put anybody on hold other than to switch the call to another extension. This situation *is* possible to duplicate in your regular business environment. By using the right technologies, software, and hardware and by getting your enterprise information network to cater to the on-hold problem better, you can dramatically lessen (even eliminate) on-hold problems altogether.

One way to do this would be to eliminate telephone access to your organization; of course, this solution is rather absurd unless you're striving to be the complete cyber-corporation, like CD-Now, Inc., a corporation that sells most of its products (thousands of music CDs) over the Internet. However, remember that the telephone will be the chief means of communicating with your customers for many years to come. Meanwhile, you need computer telephony to handle the fluctuations in your call flow and fix your on-hold problems.

New communication technologies also will greatly improve the on-hold situation when they emerge: Less people will be calling in this era, but when they do, they will be able to have lucid telephone conversations with computers, even when asking for help. Until this day arrives, however, you'll need to put people on hold. You thus have two objectives in dealing with this dilemma:

1. Strive to keep less callers on hold for less time.

2. Put any on-hold time to good use for the caller, making the wait as painless and damage-free as possible.

REDUCING OR ELIMINATING ON-HOLD TIME

The tools that you need to alleviate or prevent the on-hold problem include management skills, public relations strategies, an enterprise information network or intranet (and its knowledge servers), help-desk software, and — of course — computer telephony. Here are some strategies to help you get a grip on the on-hold fallout.

LOGISTICS

Few enterprises anticipate and prepare for the volume of callers that they receive, resulting in callers being placed on hold while agents and attendants scramble around for the correct information, transfer callers around the enterprise like cattle at the market, or dive behind voice mail, never again to resurface.

If you're about to announce a super glue so strong that you can stick two planets together, you're bound to get calls from people who need to get unstuck; make sure, then, that the related information can be accessed from the desktop by workers trained to answer questions from the public. When you get a call for help, the help desk and the enterprise information network should enable representatives to get the information to the caller without needing to put the person on hold.

You should never need to say to a caller "I don't know." Even the so-so CSI experts will tell you that's the worst line you can use. However, these experts say that the better line is "Good question; may I put you on hold while I find out?" An IT savvy CSI guru knows a better response: "That's a good question. I'm sure we have the answer right here. It will just take a few seconds to look it up."

Remember that every call into a call center was made for a good reason: Callers may want to transact new business with you, close a deal, or may require after-sales support and service. The sale is not concluded until the customer is happy, even after he or she has the product or service. For that reason, you want to anticipate the calls and have the information available at the desktop.

Make sure that you take care of this problem in advance — I have abandoned many software packages because of the inability of the developers to get me up, running, and happy in a short amount of time. Your customers will have similar reactions if the documentation you provided was terrible and the technical support lines kept them on hold well into the night. This strategy becomes *very* important if you sell products on a 30-day, money-back guarantee or offer a free-trial period. If you cannot satisfy the customers, you will never get the chance to bill them.

Frequently, organizations shell out millions of dollars on prime-time ad campaigns without anticipating the stuff that people will check on. Here's a good example: My wife noticed an ad promoting an interesting exercise machine on TV one night. Because Kim is my "personal welfare manager," she grabbed for the phone (as I'm sure thousands of viewers did when the toll-free number appeared). The first question she asked was "Do you have a preview video we can get?" It was a patently obvious question but apparently not an anticipated one. The agent's reply went something like this: "Gee, I don't know. I'll have to put you on hold and find out." Finally, as Kim was entering her fourth minute on hold, the agent came back and said a promotional video was available but that she could not process this request. The agent transferred my wife to another agent who took the order for the free tape. I am sure this company lost some calls (and potential sales) because of this lack of forethought. The moral of this story? Don't let this situation happen to you.

To summarize:

✦ Anticipate, as accurately as possible, the number of calls to expect for any given campaign.

✦ Have information that callers need ready and accessible from every desktop.

✦ Anticipate and prepare for the type of support you may have to give customers to get a product up and running. According to the media, Microsoft ran out of help-desk and technical support people in the first few weeks after the launch of Windows 95. Having possibly more telephone lines than the Pentagon (which is rumored to have 30,000 lines), Microsoft was switching the callers all over the planet in a dire need to get the software running.

✦ Using research, you should draw up a list of all the reasons why people call your enterprise. Couple this information with the call-processing and accounting data that the PBX and computer telephony systems give you. You can then consider ways to improve your on-hold situation. This data will be vital for your new product launch.

FORMULATE WISE HELP-DESK STRATEGIES

Although logistics is a big part of a help-desk strategy, another objective that you should follow is to alleviate your on-hold problems; you can do this by deploying wise help-desk strategies.

The central purpose of every help desk is solving your customers' problems: You want to help customers get your product working as quickly as possible and at the least cost to the enterprise. Apply the following suggestions to process help-desk calls faster while enhancing the image of the enterprise and maintaining (or improving) the customer satisfaction index.

◆ Understand your callers' needs and wants and formulate the help-desk budget around them. By following a good help-desk strategy, you will have fewer people on hold. When it comes to budget, keep in mind that a poor help desk (such as one with poor call-processing software, insufficient information, and attendants with insufficient skills) will impact the callers and dump problems into the laps of the other computer telephony services. The worst thing you can do to callers is force them into voice messaging because the help desk is disabled or weak on features. You'll not only receive complaints from callers, but you'll likely end up with a war between the IT people delegated to each respective service.

◆ Invest in help-desk software tools to empower your help-desk personnel. The enterprise information network and database management system (DBMS) should be geared toward helping your people service callers as quickly as possible. The primary function of help-desk software is to retrieve answers and solutions to problems. Computer telephony features should be a secondary consideration because you can address these needs just by adding plug-ins and modules from vendors who specialize in CTI.

The most basic feature is the capability to type in a key word and bring up a list of possible solutions already on file. Depending on your product, you may need to perform sophisticated searches using a variety of search algorithms and routines, such as artificial intelligence and fuzzy logic.

Some software packages have built-in expert systems to assist help-desk personnel with arriving at possible solutions. The Windows 95 help software is an example of an expert system in action. Instead of typing a key word and then selecting from a list of possible hits, the users work their way through various yes/no and multiple-choice selections to arrive at answers to problems.

◆ Employ a smart tracking strategy. Your help-desk software should have tracking features that can track callers by customer and by case. To do this, you should provide every caller who is serviced with a tracking number. Many help desks call these numbers *ticket* or *case numbers*. If the caller has to call back for a solution or if the problem is holding up other callers, the ticket or case number provides a tie to the customer and a means of keeping track of the problem and solutions.

You can smartly integrate tracking with computer telephony software. You should allow callers to enter their ticket numbers when the computer telephony system answers the call. This number can be the transfer mechanism your system uses to get the callers to an ACD gate, move callers up in the on-hold queue, or even play a message that provides the solution, further instructions, or other options.

✦ Another important strategy is to enable the helper to update the information and knowledge database so that current information is available to everyone in the enterprise. This can be best achieved by putting computer telephony software onto the workstation desktop. Using, for example, NetWare Telephony Services or Windows Telephony Services enables you to pop up data entry screens for the help-desk agent to work with just as the call arrives (see Chapters 4 and 5). If the call arrives at the desktop with Caller ID information or information gleaned by the voice-processing system, you can even bring up information relating to a previous problem.

✦ The quicker you get a person helped and on his or her merry way, the less wait time other on-hold callers have to suffer. Help-desk managers will tell you that nothing is worse than having help-desk personnel so involved in trying to solve a problem or find an answer that the manager or another representative has to intervene. If this happens, help-desk personnel should ask the caller if it's okay to end the call while the help-desk gurus tackle the problem and call back (or send e-mail) as soon as they find a solution. Don't ask callers to call back, but anticipate that they will by giving the caller the direct extension number of the person to contact so that they can "camp" at the extension. You want to avoid having the same caller end up on hold again. The ticket/case number described earlier helps facilitate this process.

✦ Determine the skills sets needed by your people working the help desk, and take the necessary actions to help them acquire these skills. These skills include being able to attend to callers' needs without putting them on hold first.

✦ Employ smart human-resource management practices. Keep help-desk personnel on the phone for no more than five hours a day. When they are off the phone, have your people check their messages and e-mail so that they can do the away-from-desk preparations needed to get back to people in the morning or before they go back on the help desk. Start a daily rotation system, and get help-desk personnel out of the call center and into the field at regular intervals during the month.

✦ Integrate the help desk into the enterprise information network, and link the information to it to assist the process of routing calls intelligently.

START A HELP DESK IN CYBERSPACE

You may want to consider exposing your enterprise to the world of Internet e-mail (if you haven't already). You can send information in response to your customer's cries for help as e-mail enclosures or attachments. Everyone will soon have e-mail (95 percent of all business by 1999); more than likely, lots of your customers already have e-mail and are using it.

Product/service support and CSI can be handled by e-mail; I can personally vouch for this. I'm the editor for a free electronic newsletter called *Online Business Today,* a weekly publication that has thousands of subscribers in more than 55 countries. We've never received a call from a subscriber and thus never have put anyone on hold. All the technical support contact goes through e-mail, whether answering a question on how to print a document or receiving binary attachments. The publication itself is only available via e-mail, sent to subscribers over the Internet as text, uuencoded attachments, or MIME attachments of the Adobe Acrobat PDF format. Although our help desk does not assist readers in real time, we constantly get letters praising the speed and effectiveness of our support.

Every time I call someone for information, I ask if he or she has an e-mail address. Many firms publish these addresses on all enterprise stationery (as they should), so I assume that they can e-mail me the information I need. I have yet to find an organization that has invested some time and a little money into converting its paper documents to a form that can be easily e-mailed. (I suspect that these firms have not given much thought to setting up a *cyberhelp desk.*) I even called a company that specializes in developing e-mail software and was told that it can only fax or mail me its literature. The sales guy said, "Even if we did have this stuff in e-mail, I would not know how to e-mail it to you."

The World Wide Web (see Chapter 12) is an ideal platform on which to implement wise help-desk strategies. You should set up your intranet as a WWW server that can be used to provide hypertext services to customer-satisfaction and support staff. When a consumer logs in with a problem, the help-desk staff should be able to launch a graphical HTML browser and perform speedy searches of the information or knowledge base.

You can make the same information and search capability available on the WWW via a gateway to your intranet. Then users looking for support online can search and retrieve solutions and information without having to make a voice call. This goes a long way toward reducing the number of callers to your help desk. The Microsoft Network (MSN) and Microsoft's WWW site (MSN.COM) are good examples of a company investing a great deal of money to reduce the customer's dependence on the support call. You can access the site and search for information and perhaps never have to make a voice call.

Another option is the fax-on-demand service described in Chapter 10. You should try to help customers by trying to anticipate their needs before they reach for the phone to call you. Converting your extension lists and enterprise information to fax format is relatively simple — any fax software will do this conversion for you. Also, you can use the same list you compiled for posting to the Internet on the fax servers, if you store the information in HTML format. (See Chapters 10 and 12.) At the least, the faxable extension or service list helps reduce the risk of the caller choosing the wrong extensions.

Help desks and the software they use are critical factors in the general computer telephony picture, particularly in terms of solving your on-hold problems. Wise help-desk strategies reduce the time that callers spend on hold and in call queues. You may want to re-read this section with this objective in mind.

GET CALLERS ROUTED CORRECTLY

Routing callers to the right services the moment they call is extremely important. For example, whenever I call the Internal Revenue Service (IRS) — for one reason or another — I never manage to get off hold in less than 30 minutes. As soon as the IRS opens for business for the morning, they have thousands of people holding and waiting in queues (see Figure 14-2). (I'm convinced that some of these callers have been camping on the line from the day before.) Unfortunately, Uncle Sam is the one "enterprise" many people hate to call, yet often they have no choice.

"...**If you'd like to pass the time by speaking to someone else who's on hold, press 4.**"

Figure 14-2: At the IRS, an on-hold time of more than one hour is not uncommon.

The IRS uses computer telephony to route callers into ACD groups where they sit in queues and wait for "the next available *assistor*," but this service does not help much. The problem that causes the on-hold situation here is the same problem a visitor of the physical office has: The enterprise is so vast that the first place you stop is at the information kiosk. Once there, you stand in line for 30 minutes or more to get the information that directs you to the correct line. Then you stand in the correct line (you hope) for another 30 minutes.

If your call center has a similar problem, you need to arm callers with adequate information *before* they call. You cannot expect a computer telephony system that offers 400 menu items to work well as a solution; rather, callers will be on the line another hour just to go through the menu list.

So where does your caller get this information? Your caller gets this information through the CT services described in Part II. If the information is not available in print (or even if it is), you can have callers access a fax-on-demand system (see Chapter 10), the World Wide Web, or a bulletin board system (Chapter 12) that provides a complete list of all the available service options.

Audiotext works for this situation only if you offer a small number of options. Some enterprises, however, have so many information bits that audiotext would keep people on the phone too long, which compounds the problem.

The Web is a perfect choice for callers who have a PC in front of them when they need to call, and most people (especially software users who need help) fit this description. With Internet access as easy as it is now, you can post a list of all possible services and any extension numbers in a hypertext document that can be linked with thousands of other documents. The customer can scroll through the list; establish the correct telephone numbers, menu options, and extensions; and then make the call. You can even put real-time information on your Web site that tells the caller how many people a given service has on hold and the expected hold time for new callers. This information enables customers to call later if they cannot afford to be on hold for any length of time.

Another Internet practice worth pursuing is placing a button or hot spot on the Web page that prompts the caller to "click here to speak with a human." You can pop up a dialog box in response to a click that prompts the caller for the best telephone number where a customer satisfaction representative can reach the caller. You also can prompt the client for a few lines describing his or her need or problem.

INSTALL UNIFIED MESSAGING

One of the biggest gripes about voice mail is that you cannot see your messages but have to access them serially over the telephone instead. If you get many messages, you may end up on the telephone for more time than you care to spend. Another problem is that while you are listening to your messages, you cannot take calls. Anyone wanting to talk to you during this time has to sit on hold and wait.

Unified messaging changes this problem because you see your voice messages in the mail in-box that caters to e-mail and fax. This format enables you to access the messages marked urgent or the ones that you can easily identify without picking up the phone. You also can choose to play the messages over the PC speaker or an ear piece connected to a sound card.

Not only should you install unified messaging (if it's available to you), but you should make sure that the voice messages can be transferred to a laptop or notebook computer, so that you can access and respond to them from a remote location.

SPEND LESS TIME ON THE TELEPHONE

I probably don't need to convince anyone that most people prefer not to spend more time on the telephone than they have to. But the fact is that we do spend too much time on the telephone when we don't manage our lives and enterprises efficiently.

A simple solution is to try to conduct as much business as you can without using the telephone. The new-era technologies, such as e-mail and fax, can help you achieve this goal. I discussed achieving this goal by changing voice mail to unified messaging earlier, but what about when you want to leave voice mail for someone? How do you help keep the communication off the phone, reducing your call load? The voice message practices described in Chapter 13 can go a long way to keeping you off the phone and available as part of the support team.

When you leave someone a voice message, make sure that the person you call gets the full story from you. If the contact or subject is important, back up the voice message with a fax or e-mail address. You want to avoid requiring the other party to call you because your needs or instructions were unclear in the message.

INVESTIGATE WIDE-AREA SWITCHING SERVICES

If your enterprise is large enough, or if you can justify using several call centers spread out across the country or world, then you should be able to switch your callers to any free attendant in the entire group of call centers. This option is a much better one than putting people on hold. In some cases, it may even pay to transfer a call to a foreign-based call center with a free attendant, if that's what's required to take the call and close the sale.

Do your logistics homework and figure out, as best you can, how much call capacity you need. Chapter 7 has more on call-center strategies.

WHEN CALLERS GO ON HOLD

What if you have no choice but to put people on hold or queue them? Perhaps your enterprise provides a service that generates a great deal of calls for billing information; maybe your organization is a giant utility company. Whatever your situation, you first should try everything already suggested and more to eliminate or reduce the on-hold time for your callers. If that doesn't take care of the problem, then you have to deal with the inevitable.

NEVER, BUT NEVER, GO SILENT

I've seen an astonishing number of situations where a company installs a computer telephony system and then leaves callers dangling in silence while on hold. Herein lies the problem: The vast majority of callers who get put on hold by a human and then hear silence will abandon the call in disgust after the first three to four minutes. If a *computer telephony system* puts them on hold and the caller gets silence, however, almost all will abandon the call after the first 30 seconds, thinking the system has disconnected them. (In the U.S., the telephone company usually alerts the caller when he or she has been disconnected, but many countries do not have this feature.) As you should already know, if the caller abandons the call, you run the risk of losing the customer to the competition.

An important rule then is to always play something that tells callers that they are on hold and not floating in orbit like David Bowie's Star Man. (Some European PBX manufacturers refer to the park facility as "orbit." I even found some documentation that read "How to throw a caller into orbit.") Some PBXs default to a periodic beep when the on-hold service disconnects or is unavailable. This irritating noise is *still* better than silence. If your PBX offers no alternative to silence, then you need to supply a simple recording to reassure callers of their status. Your callers should at least be aware that they are not disconnected, although it's better if they know that *you* are also aware of their situation. Any reasonable sound will do until you get a better recording or receive your on-hold material.

RADIO

Many telephony managers or IT people simply opt to play the radio for on-hold material. There are several reasons to avoid this practice:

✦ Radio material is copyright; so no matter where you are in the world, you need rebroadcast rights for the material, especially for the songs. The penalty can be expensive if your company is sued after a covert monitoring of your on-hold service. Several years ago, a company in South Africa was almost forced to close for violating rebroadcast rules in this way.

✦ You have no guarantee that the radio station will not play your competitor's advertisements. You could lose business if callers hear such material. In one incident I know about, the competition targeted the company using the radio for on-hold material just to market to their customers. Its radio advertisement even said: "We won't keep you holding like they do."

✦ Generally speaking, the radio does not do much to make the callers' on-hold time palatable, so don't assume that some soothing radio music will pacify callers with a bone to pick. You also run the risk of not knowing how callers will react to what they hear on the radio. I once abandoned a call because I hated the song playing, so I'm sure that others have, too. And one time, I became so consumed by the lead story on the radio's news that, when my turn came up, I abandoned the call and switched on my own radio to hear the end of the story.

✦ Radio stations also frequently report the time, and it may not be wise to remind the caller of how much time he or she is wasting on hold. You never really know what can happen: For example, one talk show host phoned several companies specifically to evaluate on-hold time, such as caller treatment and length of hold time. The third company that the host called was playing the radio for on-hold callers, and — you guessed it — it was tuned to the talk show's station.

PROMOTION ON HOLD

This basic premise behind this material (also called *promo* or *promoh,* for *promo*tion on *hold*) is to promote your products to your captive audience and maybe sell something while the callers are on hold. I don't really see anything wrong with using promos if you use them wisely; however, the material, the nature and the intent of your promotion, and the timing of it are important. Make sure that hard selling is appropriate for the type of callers you get and the average length of on-hold time. Putting the wrong material on the wrong lines can do serious damage to an enterprise.

If you decide to use promotion on hold, remember that you are taking the time that belongs to your callers to promote your services or products. If your callers have to call you for service or support of the products they bought from you already, the last thing you want to do is try to sell them something else (or even worse, the product that they are currently fighting with). Otherwise, you risk making your callers bitter; some customers complain that this practice is akin to getting pulled over for a speeding ticket and then having the same officer ask you to buy a ticket to the Traffic Department cook-out.

In the best-case scenario, the callers abandon the call, return the product for a refund, or cancel the order. In the worst-case scenario, you get sued. And sue is exactly what one customer did to a client of mine. Although the parties settled the matter out of court, the customer was so furious that she was prepared to go the whole way, even if she lost the case. She believed her hold time had been prolonged so that she could hear the entire promotional message. Although that wasn't the case, the on-hold material sure gave this impression.

If you keep technical support and help-desk lines separate from sales lines, you can more easily control what gets played on what line. The problem is not always what you play, but playing the right thing on the right line.

Unfortunately, most PBX on-hold facilities do not enable you to play different content for different lines — everyone on hold hears the same material. To avoid this problem, you have a few possible options:

✦ You may have enough sales or order lines to justify a separate PBX or ACD with a separate on-hold facility. Then you can use different on-hold material on the different PBXs.

✦ You may be able to justify call-sequencing equipment for the sales lines that have on-hold message facilities.

✦ You may want to consider installing a system that enables callers to select information without abandoning their position in the call sequencer (see Chapter 7).

Whatever you do, the cardinal rule here is that you cannot assume all your callers will be happy to hear your promotions or sales pitches while on hold.

The on-hold system of one of my recent clients, a computer reseller in Miami, illustrates this point. The customers who called to order products and were then put on hold felt that the on-hold material successfully alerted them to new products, special offers, and new prices. Some callers even abandoned their calls when the on-hold message gave them the information they needed. Callers who were waiting for technical support, however, lost patience with the on-hold material. One caller said this: "The material is not telling it like it is. I have had nothing but problems with this product, and when I heard the promotion, it really irked me. I was put on hold several times because the technician could not figure out the problem. Every time I went back on hold, I would hear the promotion again and felt that I was being lied to and cheated."

You also need to make sure that the promotional information you use is accurate and does not conflict with other corporate information. In one case, a caller who had sent in a mail order discovered that the same item was being offered at a reduced price over the phone. That's reason enough for anyone to cancel an order.

As always, your top priorities are the CSI (customer satisfaction index) and creating or maintaining your alluring image. Don't shirk from trying to improve the on-hold situation because it offers you the so-called "opportunity" to sell products to holding callers. Investing heavily in four-, six-, or eight-minute sell messages is absurd by my customer satisfaction standards. After all, what's the point in striving to eliminate the problem and then creating a script of sales messages that makes your customers think you're trying to preserve the status quo?

Thus, the best material to use for on-hold situations where all callers will hear the same messages is information about their call status.

INFORMATION ON HOLD

The difference between information on hold and promoh is that you are not really trying to sell anything to your callers or drum up sales leads; rather, you are trying to inform them. Image, and even direct sales, is the payoff here, but it's not the primary objective. The primary objective is to provide the callers with information that can help their situations and make their on-hold time more palatable. Information ɑ also should be used to keep the callers on the phone for less time, both while ta to agents and waiting on hold.

You should not ignore this opportunity to get a message to your customers. Many large enterprises find that their on-hold audience totals as many as one million peo a year. If you need to convey important information to callers, the minute or two yo give them while on hold may be a better choice than using print media.

The audience is captive. While waiting on hold, often you have the caller's full attention, as they cannot be seriously committed to any other task. This medium's content and presentation may help them tune in to the message better than they would via another medium because the callers are mentally focused on your enterprise and the service or product that you provide.

A good example are the utility companies who spend millions of dollars a year in corporate ID advertising on television and radio. They also buy large quantities of print media. Their objective is to convey to users how best to conserve energy, save money, and, most importantly, how to stay out of harm's way. Many of their ads discuss preventing exposure to electrical current, how to better insulate your wiring, staying away from power lines, and more.

Many people have been exposed to these ads, but few can recall the exact message unless the same ad is repeated frequently. This fact presents several problems: First, this format costs a fortune, and someone has to pay for all the air-time. Secondly, the ads are competing for attention in the chaotic world of publicity and prime-time broadcasting. The attention of the callers is divided between cooking, feeding and watching the kids, eating dinner, and flaking out after a hard day at the office. When the commercials appear, many get up to raid the refrigerator, go to the rest room, or jump to another channel.

I can go on ad nauseam with these viewer statistics. Callers on hold, however, are not as distracted. You have complete control over at least what's going in one ear. Chances are the caller's brain has diverted all attention to the phone-listening process because it's monitoring for the point in the queue when the call will be serviced.

Doing the arithmetic as I describe in Chapter 4, you arrive at a scenario in which you have a captive audience of over a million people. Don't blow the opportunity to convey at least a minute's worth of valuable information to them. Dollar for dollar, this is the cheapest and most powerful medium you will ever buy.

Here are some examples of what I would call information on hold:

✦ Providing answers to Frequently Asked Questions (FAQs). The more FAQs you answer, the better. As long as they apply to the service, every caller you have on hold is likely to benefit from the answers you provide to the FAQs. Callers also will benefit from listening to the same FAQs again, although you certainly can use a 15- or 20-minute-long file so that you reduce the chances of callers hearing the same FAQ again. In other words, by staying away from

…e point of entry and exit from the on-hold content is …nario contrasts sharply with the promoh scenario, in which …ant to play a voice file of longer than four minutes.

…s what's expected of them before you take their calls. If people …quire about bills, statements, account information, status of orders, …on and you cannot process them with an IVR system, use the time on …o tell them what to have ready and handy. If your agents need account …bers before file numbers, tell them this. If callers can reduce the time …gents need to process a query, use the time on hold to cater to this purpose. Preparing callers who need to reconcile financial situations such as arranging bill payments is a good example. If the caller just needs to know the location of the closest office where he or she can pay the bill, the IVR system can handle this; if the caller needs to discuss payment plans or options, you can have the caller retrieve or provide the information needed to help the agent process the call faster and thus reduce the amount of time other callers spend in the queue (see Chapters 7 and 8).

✦ Breaking from the information to reaffirm to customers that you don't want to keep them on hold and are doing everything possible to speed up the calls.

✦ Providing information to help them better use your service or product. While some may construe this as selling, you can win over your customer's attention with intelligent scripting. Be careful not to patronize callers with lines like "Product X, rated by *No-Brainer* magazine as the best widget of '95, is ABC's new XYZ and does KLM." Not all callers might agree, especially if it does not work. If you must include such a line, at least leave out the "rated" bit or only use this information on the order lines. Callers who want to be sold will make their buy call after reviewing the product literature or sell sheets that your company produces. Better lines would be something like "The new version of Product X now allows you to do XYZ; ask your agent for a free upgrade now."

✦ Keeping information fresh. I have called some companies whose on-hold information is great, but it's five years old. Eventually, callers tire of listening to the same information, and this sends callers image signals you don't want to convey.

✦ Employing the services of public relations and corporate identity specialists for your on-hold information files. By getting these professionals to clear and script your on-hold information before it goes to the on-hold recording specialists, you can feel more secure when wondering whether you're portraying the right image to your callers on hold (or within the bounds of broadcast laws).

✦ Providing callers with real-time information about their expected hold time. Many larger corporations are now adopting this practice. You can use a human attendant to broadcast the ACD wait states and the call sequencer queues to the callers. By providing the estimated hold time remaining, you're already servicing callers by telling them — as accurately as possible — how much longer they can expect to wait for live service.

ON-HOLD DEVICES

All on-hold devices connect to the external audio source of the modern PBX or key system. The on-hold devices of yesteryear were just analog cassette tape players using circular or endless-loop tapes. Because of all their moving parts, these old devices tended to break down. Today's on-hold devices typically are digital, stand-alone bolt-ons that store audio material in EEPROM (Electronically Erasable Programmable Read Only Memory) chips. To change the audio material in these devices, you simply flush the chip and record the new material electronically with the EEPROM recorder or you have your audio material vendor replace the chip. The software simply repeats the message on the chip.

Many people advocate using the DSP voice-processing card as an on-hold audio source. With this method, you store audio segments on the computer's hard disk and change them as often as needed. Using DSP cards for this task makes a lot of sense, considering that the average voice-processing card sells for approximately $500 in the U.S., whereas the digital on-hold "announcers" can cost as much as $1,000 for a single port device (playing one audio file at a time). The DSP card typically has four ports, and you can designate one for the on-hold function. Then you can add the remaining three ports to the computer telephony pool.

If your computer telephony software supports audiotext, this service will probably work perfectly well for your on-hold audio needs and still enable you to run computer telephony software in the same computer.

SOURCES FOR ON-HOLD MATERIAL

You have the proper equipment, but where do you get the material to play on it? Your best sources for on-hold material are the scripting and recording consultants you use to create the great sounding, high-quality prompts and menus for the computer telephony system. These specialists have access to commercially usable material that does not violate any copyrights or which includes the correct licenses. Chapter 9 outlines some strategies for creating quality recordings and scripts that are just as valid here. You can also turn to the your local Yellow Pages.

SUMMARY

I discussed the reasons for the on-hold situation. You also learned that you can turn this problem into a means of providing callers with information. But I want to stress that the primary objective in dealing with the on-hold dilemma is to reduce the time that callers spend on hold — and if possible, to eliminate it. Although you shouldn't ignore the opportunity to communicate with callers, don't use it as an excuse to avoid fixing the on-hold problem. Harry Newton, the publisher of *Computer Telephony Magazine,* says the reason his industry is growing so rapidly is because "we waste so much time on the telephone." Remember that on-hold time does not belong to you — it belongs only to your callers.

IN THIS CHAPTER

♦ Achieving strategic synergy between the key management, IT, and IS entities in the computer telephony integration process

♦ Achieving a common vision for requisitioning and integrating computer telephony (integration group one)

♦ Determining the applications you need and deploying systems (integration group two)

♦ Paving the way for integrating computer telephony into the enterprise information network (integration group three)

♦ Assessing the need and paving the way for integrating with enterprise telephony systems: PBXs, telephones, and telecommunications (integration group four)

"We installed little monitors because they make all of our problems seem smaller."

COMPUTER TELEPHONY AND THE INTEGRATED ENTERPRISE

In this chapter, I discuss strategies for achieving synergy among key management, IT, and IS entities, thus paving the way for computer telephony integration in the enterprise. Like all IT projects, a computer telephony project can end up like a safari gone wrong — and you don't want to end up confronting a 1,000-pound gorilla. This chapter provides you with a starting point for your strategic computer telephony plan.

Figure 15-1 depicts the key factors you need to consider for the integration of computer telephony into the enterprise; this diagram will help you focus on the elements that you need for a painless and smart integration process.

ACHIEVING SYNERGY BETWEEN MANAGEMENT, IT, AND IS

When planning to integrate computer telephony with your existing network, you need to think beyond the idea that you can simply plug in the computer telephony system and be done with it. That attitude is a recipe for disaster!

Instead, you should consider how this system will affect the enterprise's people (employees and customers), the existing information systems, the setup and processes of the IT department, and more. You must take into account all the factors at a particular site or any situation that will influence the project. Note both the positive and negative factors.

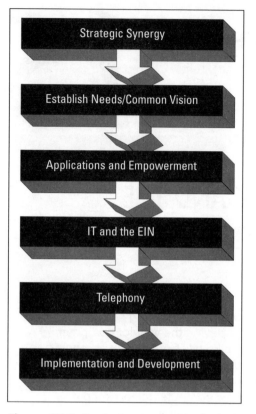

Figure 15-1: Key factors to consider in the integration of computer telephony technology.

Computer telephony is applicable in every area of the world. Telephones are everywhere people are — and frequently, where people are *not.* For this reason, the computer telephony, integrated-office concept applies as much to a country that has only one main telephone exchange (such as Swaziland) as it does to the most computer-literate, integrated office in Manhattan. Computer telephony also deals with enabling people to access your information systems from outside your enterprise's walls.

Many enterprises and consultants think of computer telephony only in terms of what the computer and software can do and how the technology meets application-specific objectives. Many people fail to consider other important factors, such as existing IT infrastructures and management entities.

When consulting, I first survey a site and make a list of factors in the environment, both internal and external, that could positively or negatively influence the computer telephony project. I then whip up a report and hand this to the people who hired me.

Sometimes — even though I hate to do it — I tell my clients to forget about installing computer telephony, to abandon the idea for now. Sure, they may have the money and be great people to work with, but after studying the firm's environment, I know that the project is doomed by factors the enterprise cannot quickly change. If management insists on moving forward with a computer telephony project, I make sure that they understand why I recommended against it — that they will run into implementation difficulties and problems with support (rather than with the telephony product itself).

In some cases, I may tell them to find another consultant rather than get involved with such a project. In other cases, a computer telephony project is commissioned with the knowledge and understanding that it will be long term. Perhaps the PBX was bad, and installing a new one would be too much trouble; perhaps the IT department was weak; perhaps the office PCs are all XT-class machines running DOS 2.0. The bottom line is that computer telephony is not just about fancy software and powerful hardware (although it takes a great deal of processing power). Just the telephony component and the human component (such as dealing with workers that object to anything new in the company) on their own can be the project-killing forces that prevent an otherwise-prepared enterprise from transforming into a computer-telephony-enabled object of envy.

The power of the human component

By human component, I mean the culture, strategy, commitment, vision, relationships, behavior, and so on of the workers. Even the layout of the offices and the software that workers use reveal things about a company.

When you consult for hundreds of companies, you quickly pick up on an atmosphere that tells you whether or not the people like working for the enterprise. I remember walking into an office with a colleague of mine to find fish tanks and goldfish bowls all over the place. Workers at this firm took turns feeding the fish and had posted a duty roster for this task and others, such as making coffee, backing up data, performing security tasks, buying groceries, jogging with the president, checking the general mailbox, and more. These were sure signs that worker satisfaction with the job was high.

This component is an important one because when the workers are happy, the project's chances for a smooth, successful integration increase. Consultants or systems integrators like to see a happy work environment because it gives them confidence that the project will go well and that they will get paid at the end of the project.

Here's an example of human component problems that can help bring down a computer telephony project:

✦ The PBX engineer complains that the computer telephony system is bringing down the PBX. For some reason, the $300,000 switch restarts and cuts off callers whenever the computer telephony system gets busy.

✦ The LAN manager calls you up and accuses your voice-mail system of crashing the network. He tells you that since the company invested in the computer telephony system, his life has been a mess.

✦ The human telephonist tells the CEO that the new IVR system is to blame for the company losing customers. She says that the system must be thrown out or the company will go bankrupt. She cites examples: When callers hit the 0 (zero) key to transfer to the operator, the system mysteriously routes them to a person at another company.

✦ A senior staff member threatens to sue the voice-mail company because the system lost important messages containing a million dollars worth of orders. When the technicians and engineers arrive to fix the problem, the CEO storms out, cursing and threatening to "kill someone." As a result, the CT engineers and the PBX technicians walk out, leaving the corporation in chaos.

✦ Another user discovers a manager's voice message that contains the user's recording of a conversation with a client. The user sends the recording to labor attorneys, who threaten the company with litigation for spying on its staff.

These scenarios are not made up. Similar situations happen and will continue to happen because some firms install CT systems without considering how they fit into the general business plan, without striving to achieve strategic synergy between all information and IT systems, and without involving key management staff (and the people under them) in the decision-making process. No matter what size your business is, you must include IT in the general business plan (see Chapter 16 for a more detailed discussion).

To achieve strategic synergy between all the processes — and to increase the odds for successful integration — you should place all telephony and computer telephony systems under direct IS/IT authority (the person in charge is usually called the Chief Information Officer, or CIO). Following this strategy from the outset is important even if another department originally determined the need for computer telephony in your enterprise (typically, human telephonists suggest this need before anyone else). The IT/IS authority then needs to involve all the appropriate players in the decision-making process of the computer telephony project.

Most importantly, the motivation for investing in computer telephony should stem from the general business plan as a means to empower workers, not as an afterthought to save money. If your general business plan doesn't include IT (and computer telephony in particular), you ought to place it there now. I make a habit of asking to look at the general business plan (or at least the section that deals with IT), and I worry when management hasn't included IT and computer telephony strategies there. (I get *really* anxious if no general business plan exists or if it's out of date.)

When you consider or propose implementing computer telephony, keep in mind that the enterprise information network (remember that the EIN consists of all your LANs, WANs, intranets, and telephone networks) and systems are in a constant state of flux — especially when the enterprise is gradually divesting or downsizing from old-era legacy systems. (A global, multitrillion-dollar installed base of legacy hardware and software still exists that enterprises cannot simply switch off and replace.) Although the new frontier of IT holds great promise (see Chapter 3), it also introduces new management problems — the most challenging of them being to keep abreast of new technological developments and still achieve integration goals.

In today's market, corporations with large software investments typically wait six months or more before upgrading existing equipment. As a result, you need to carefully consider your investment decisions to make sure that you're making the right ones. You don't want to be left behind by new technologies that emerge soon after your enterprise commits to an expensive system or product.

For example, the critical emergence of the Internet caught many companies off-guard. One rumor going the rounds in cyberspace says that Microsoft did not see the Internet coming. (I have worked with Microsoft, and they seem to know about everything that's coming — or going.) Many IT consultants admit that they are constantly caught off-guard while predicting or advising on a technology's coming-of-age date and cost-justification. However, the blistering pace in the new frontier in information technology is such that you cannot afford to be caught off-guard. Gone are the days when enterprises purchased upgrades of a software product just to stay current with existing capabilities.

I recently watched several expensive, interactive voice response (IVR) projects fall apart after IT personnel suddenly realized that a Web site on the Internet was the better way to go. Others who had planned to use fax-on-demand (FOD) systems had to shelve their projects to set up an Internet site (for good reasons too, but mostly because of a lack of foresight — see Chapters 11 and 12).

Upgrading decisions are even more risky in computer telephony because these upgrades touch the external environment and can directly influence a customer's perception of the enterprise. A poorly chosen upgrade can have frightening repercussions. Because of this fact, no enterprise can afford to install a computer telephony system without involving all of its IS and IT specialists, including consultants and engineers from the PBX service providers and LAN providers.

The IT person or CIO needs to keep the interoperability of all systems foremost in his or her mind and should work toward establishing a common vision for choosing and implementing a system. That vision should include a continuous learning plan and adaptation process for the staff (I discuss this in depth in Chapter 16).

To do this, the computer telephony consultant or the IT person charged with the responsibility must consider four distinct integration groups — in a divide-and-conquer process — when planning to introduce or enhance computer telephony systems.

✦ The *People* group (integration group one)

✦ The *Applications* group (integration group two)

✦ The *Enterprise Information Network* group (integration group three)

✦ The *Telephony Component* group (integration group four)

Each group presents challenges to the project that you must deal with from a holistic point of view.

You may be surprised to see the People group listed as the most important group. When formulating this grouping process over the past few years, I tended to concentrate on the information network group (IT) first and the People group last. But I changed my views after I realized — through bitter experience — that the key to a successful project also lies in ensuring that all the workers of an enterprise share a common vision of the project and how they fit into it.

Without this common vision, you may have to deal with some tough issues in the information technology and telephony groups, which mainly have to do with training people and coaxing them to use the systems. Some experts may disagree with me on this point, but, as I mentioned earlier, I have seen too many systems fall apart because of unplanned issues regarding the first group. (I talk further about this topic later on in this chapter.)

Computer telephony projects can and do fail. The CT guru cannot guarantee success based on the wonder of the technology alone. The guru only can bring the new technology to the planning table and then advise you on how best to integrate computer telephony with existing systems and use the services. The enterprise often brings the telephony portion to the project because more than likely the client already has a PBX, a telephony VAR (interconnect company, see the Lexicon), and a PBX company (unless you're dealing with a small business guru who installs the phones, sets up the networks, hires the people, and typically works 20 hours a day).

Many companies don't care how the CT gurus succeed, just as long as they do. The company may bring the required management skills to the table or it may ask the consultant to deliver them. Either way, you need to be prepared. So, if you're an independent consultant or the person in the enterprise charged with computer telephony integration, it's a good idea to lug around a clipboard and legal pad — you'll need them to take extensive notes regarding the four groups. Oh, and don't forget the antacids.

Here's a good field example. In 1994, I left my comfortable, technological haven in southern Florida and flew to South Africa to wrap up some consulting work for Voicematrix, the leading computer telephony vendor and solutions provider for Africa. One of Voicematrix's clients was a branch of ESCOM, the massive Electronic Supply

Commission, which supplies power to almost all of Africa. The mission: To investigate the feasibility of an automated attendant, call queuing, and a voice-messaging system for the ESCOM branch.

To get to the site, I had to take a two-hour ride west of Johannesburg. I took it in a good mood, thinking that the experience would be a great case study for a book (from the streets of Miami to Africa — both jungles, in many respects). Halfway to the client's site, I got lost and searched for a phone that worked (Gil Caplan, the CEO of Voicematrix, had the cellular phone and had rushed off to another site). Finally I found a booth that — despite being chopped up for firewood — contained a working telephone. As I listened to the familiar click, click, click of the old rotary exchange, I said to myself, "Integration nightmare number one: rotary phones. Gee, this is going to be fun."

Getting lost, however, proved to be a valuable information-gathering experience for the project. Before heading out to the site again, I whipped out my clipboard and turned to my notes for the last of the four groups (telephony); there I noted that most callers would probably use rotary/pulse-dial telephones to call the branch. These notes led to more ideas and follow-up notes for the other groups. The experience gave me important insights on the computer telephony project that may have been easier to overlook otherwise.

Now let's take a time-out from my African computer telephony safari and move on to strategies for achieving the CT-integrated office.

INTEGRATION GROUP ONE: PEOPLE

Justifying and deploying computer telephony is no longer a top-down decision. Instead, it's a process of deploying learning systems throughout the enterprise to create a common vision of a project by allowing experienced workers to evolve and adapt the system. Less than a decade ago, the CEO would have been in charge of commissioning a computer telephony project and deciding how the enterprise would use it; after all, most people felt that if the CEO could merrily manage a voice mail system, then the entire company would do it, too. After management green-lighted a technology, users would be *"sold-in"* and the system would be deployed; however, this seldom turned out to be the case. The following example is a case in point.

My colleague, Michael Edwards, and I agreed that the MVIS project (introduced in Chapter 1) met its end in the People group, long before we could address the switching or network integration issues. Although the project was under direct IT staff authority and involved the telephonists from the start, the IT staff and the CEO did not share the purpose, integration methods, and objective of the CT project with the entire personnel spectrum. As a result, we discovered (too late) that the only senior staff member behind the project was the CEO.

Let's look at this situation in detail. The CIO at MVIS established the need for computer telephony and got the human telephonists to side with him on the project (which was the easy part because the human telephonists worked under extreme pressure with the existing system). When MVIS went live with the voice-response service, it took the load off the telephonists — at first. But in the following weeks, calls began bouncing back to the telephonists because the MVIS employees were not servicing the calls. Although voice mail was available to them, the vast majority of the company was either unwilling or unable to use it.

Many workers rebelled against the system. Although the CEO had approved the system on the recommendations of IT personnel and the telephonists, an employee backlash erupted. Some senior executives even confronted the CEO about it. MVIS had a serious problem that really had nothing to do with computer telephony. The big problem? Management was split over the computer telephony issue, and the split had not been resolved — something that I now look for and encourage my clients to fix before launching a project.

To avoid this situation in your enterprise, you must — first and foremost — make it very clear what the project objectives are and understand where the system can work or fail for the enterprise. The computer telephony guru sets the groundwork for IT in this respect. This guru should set up learning sessions and evaluation meetings with the workers who will be using the technology. From these sessions, you can get valuable insight on the project feasibility and worker attitude regarding the technology. It also gives you the opportunity to remind workers (and management) that the technology is supposed to empower them, not replace them or force a new discipline on them that they do not understand.

To quote business sage Peter Drucker from his legendary book, *Management in Turbulent Times,* "It is simply not true, as most managers assume, that they always understand how best to lay out routine work, whether machine-paced or clerical. Whenever we have asked: 'What do we do that helps you in your work, and what do we do that hampers you?' we have found that there are a great many things that hamper and too few things that help." I will deal with the human learning processes as they relate to computer telephony in more detail in Chapter 16.

For starters, you have to get your people involved in the project. To do this, IT must involve the leaders of *key management entities* (KMEs) in charge of human resources. (KMEs are the company divisions involved in plotting the company's course and making its products/services . . . essentially, mapping out what the company does.) This group includes personnel managers and human resource managers as the key members, followed by representatives of worker unions, employee representative groups, work groups, and committees. These people inform their fellow coworkers about the requirements and features of the proposed CT system after they feel comfortable with the project's objectives and share in the common vision (the learning process starts at this point, which I discuss further in Chapter 16).

Where does the computer telephony guru fit into this part? The guru provides the IT manager and the KME leaders with the factors that they need to consider for deploying the new system. The guru should assist management in establishing that common vision among all the workers in the organization. I found that IT fails to understand this even in very sophisticated and computer-savvy enterprises.

The computer telephony consultant may find it difficult to dictate IT strategy to stubborn IT people, which he or she shouldn't have to do. However, consultants need to be assertive. I have consulted for enterprises where the integration of the computer telephony system failed (I was called in to clean up the mess) because the IT people were too stubborn to listen to the consultant or the enterprise lacked a common and strategic IT objective. In this case, the only thing you can do is take up the problems with the CEO. Usually, these problems can be avoided by placing computer telephony and telephony under the direct authority of IT. Typically, any project leadership problems that the IT executive runs into are human resource problems, not technology ones.

The computer telephony version of David versus Goliath

Here's my IT hero: About a year ago, the CIO of a Fortune 500 company told me that the CEO was vehemently opposed to voice messaging because of what he'd heard about voice mail; as a result, he was going to move to kill the computer telephony project. Because the chairman owned the majority of stock in this billion-dollar enterprise and was feared more than respected by his employees, I asked the CIO what he was going to do.

The CIO decided that he could do only one thing: argue that it was a technology that the employees wanted, not a pet project forced on them by a senior manager or IT person (we had the data to support our arguments). The subject was on the board's meeting agenda, and the CIO planned to attend in order to counter the chairman's resistance. I stood by in case I was needed to support the CIO's arguments.

During the meeting, the CIO told the chairman that the decision to install the voice-messaging system was one that the workers, represented by their departments heads, had voted for. Those workers who did not want to use it or for whom voice messaging was not appropriate would not be required to use it. The CIO then explained the workers' specific reasons for voting to make the purchase. The CIO reminded the chairman that the decision was on the same scale as when the staff had opted for e-mail (which the chairman also had resisted).

As the tension increased, I witnessed an astounding display of conviction by the CIO, who then advised the chairman: "I proposed the voice-messaging system because it's what the staff needs, and they voted for it. You pay me $500K a year to make these decisions. If the board declines the request that the enterprise — not IT — has made as a common objective, it would be better for me to terminate my employment with this company."

His tactic worked — he eventually won over the chairman's support for the project. (How this company later achieved its common vision and enterprise-wide utilization of the computer telephony project is the subject of Chapter 16.)

Integration group one should represent the first chapter in your integration strategy. Here, you assess training possibilities, employee acceptance, employee technology savvy, and computer literacy when considering a computer telephony project. The abilities of employees will differ with each business and project. The discipline and cooperation that employees offer you also will be key factors for a successful project. You need to watch for and identify the factors that could lead your project astray as early as possible.

One type of company is not inherently a better candidate for computer telephony than another. A computer telephony project may go smoothly at an accounting firm, whereas a similar project has hard times at a computer hardware reseller, distributor, or software company. (My software clients were always trying to reverse-engineer the products I was selling, just to see if they could do a better job.)

INTEGRATION GROUP TWO: APPLICATIONS

Chapter 2 already outlined computer telephony applications, and Part II is devoted to application strategies. However, at this stage of evaluating and certifying the integration qualifications of an enterprise, you also want to make notes about the applications and their potential for success and failure. By the time you've made it this far in the evaluation, you should have a pretty accurate picture of computer telephony potential.

Let's return to the "lost safari" example of the ESCOM project to demonstate the sort of things you'll want to take into consideration for this group.

The branch was situated in one of the largest townships west of Johannesburg and served several smaller townships surrounding it. Located right in the middle of the gold-mining belt and the lightning capital of the world, the western areas experienced frequent power outages. Whenever the lights went out somewhere in the branch's service area, calls would start pouring in — not in the hundreds, not in the thousands, but in the tens of thousands. ESCOM wanted Voicematix to call computer telephony to the rescue.

The ESCOM office had only about 20 people working in it; of these staff members, only one person was responsible for answering the main number and routing the calls. When the power was on and pumping volts into the townships, the workload was comfortable for the lean complement, and the telephonist had an easy life.

I had more or less written off any idea of using messaging because of the nature of the calls, the outflow of information from the enterprise, and the urgency of the required information. The fact that the majority of callers used pulse-dial phones created another problem because I would not recommend pulse detection services even in the best of cases (see Chapters 4 and 8 for more details). At best, pulse detection is unreliable. Additionally, in many countries that use microwave links on the PSTN (public-switched telephone network; the network of telephone companies and central offices that contain the switching equipment and telephone exchanges), the transmission equipment filters out the pulses from the voice channels as soon as it establishes a connection to the called party.

Audiotext was a more feasible solution (it usually is) because all the company needed was a way to tell the caller why power is down and when ESCOM expects to resume service (see Chapter 9). The telephony system did not need to interrogate the caller for information. You need to be aware of all the factors that will influence a CT project in the future.

INTEGRATION GROUP THREE: THE ENTERPRISE INFORMATION NETWORK

In the old era of computer-telephone integration, the desktop was not as much a factor as it is today. Previously, users interacted with voice-mail systems exclusively from the telephone because desktop computers did not provide an interface for it.

Today, however, things are different. Computer telephony is an enterprise-wide phenomenon that is becoming as pervasive as word processing. Computer telephony systems must be integrated into the enterprise information network, which requires that they must interoperate with existing systems.

Figure 15-2 depicts the most important factors to consider when evaluating computer telephony products (from the buyer's point of view) and integrating them with the customer's existing equipment (from the consultant's point of view). There are, of course, more things to think about, but these factors are some of the most important.

INTEGRATION AND INTERCONNECTION

Both the computer telephony environment and the existing information and IT systems should support seamless (if possible) integration and interconnection. Your enterprise cannot afford to invest in "islands of technology," stand-alone products, or bolt-ons. This philosophy is as important for the telephony systems (PBXs, ACDs, and telephones) as it is for computer telephony products. The fact that manufacturers can achieve interoperability among computer telephony products in the mid-1990s is a technological wonder made possible by the cooperation of different product and service providers on standards and specifications (to avoid the mess described in Chapter 3).

Manufacturers achieved seamless integration among their products by providing wide support for network protocols (NetBEUI, IPX, TCP/IP, and others); applications programming interfaces (APIs) such as the messaging API from Microsoft (MAPI, the heart and soul of Microsoft's Exchange), the telephony API from Microsoft and Intel (TAPI), and the telephony services API from Novell (TSAPI); operating systems such as Microsoft Windows, the so-called universal client; network operating systems and their various layers; and server platforms such as UNIX, Windows NT, OS/2, and so on.

It is vitally important not to forget the telephony service providers either. The PBX product or vendor you choose should be committed to the same seamless integration and interconnection philosophies promoted for enterprise networking and information systems.

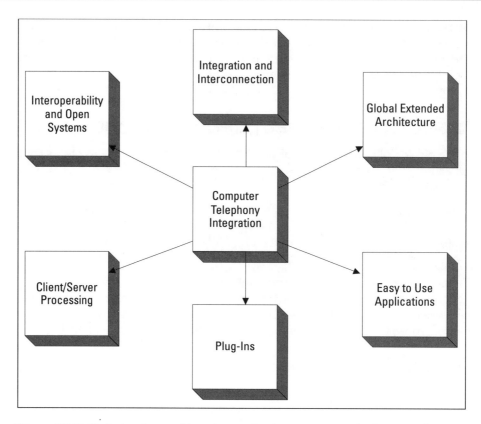

Figure 15-2: Six factors to consider when evaluating computer telephony products.

The manufacturers who do not support standards or provide service provider interfaces (SPIs) and drivers are following short-sighted principles. Integration and interconnection is a wildfire notion. Although you can use smart integration techniques with these products to get a "poor man's" integrated CT system from them, such products will rapidly lose market share in the long run.

INTEROPERABILITY AND OPEN SYSTEMS

With the advent of the new IT era, firms are rapidly moving away from proprietary systems that operate in closed environments. Often an enterprise needs specialized staff to upgrade, test, and debug these systems; so adding new features to these dinosaurs is expensive. And without interoperability, integrating computer telephony with your systems is a painful — if not impossible — exercise.

Take my company's bank, for example. It invested huge sums in legacy closed systems (much to my dismay). As a result, providing a limited, shaky e-mail system (only capable of sending telex-type, uppercase text messages) recently cost the bank six figures in programming fees (assembler). How the bank hopes to integrate anything else with its current systems is a mystery to me.

In banking, you can easily spot the corporations that have shifted over to interoperable and open systems. The banks on the World Wide Web offer home banking services (using personal computer software such as Intuit's Quicken) and voice-response systems that act as information-only ATMs, thus positioning themselves to become truly global operations. No matter what interface you use to view the data, all information is updated in real time.

Such openness enables the enterprise to be global, friendly, and alluring to its people (customers and employees). This setup also enables the staff to work remotely. In an open system, for example, you can move customers from a Manhattan office to a Seattle office to complete electronic transactions without the customer noticing any changes.

You need portable information and software that can work with the systems and platforms that the enterprise uses. A good example is the ability of customers to send an e-mail message from their home office computers directly to the desktops of their account executives or business peers. Today, messages can travel over several networks and move between various computer platforms and software without running into any glitches between point A and point B.

Perhaps one of the most significant movements in achieving interoperability and integration aims (with regard to computer telephony) comes from an organization called *versit*. Apple, AT&T, IBM, and Siemens-Rolm founded this brainchild, which is essentially a quasi-standards committee, in November 1994 to pool their efforts and open up their technology. Thus, versit's aim is to "address this need." The following is taken from the founding charter:

> We are on the threshold of the convergence of the communications and computing worlds.

> This convergence is creating a diversity of new products and services that combine communication and information capabilities. In addition, we are also experiencing a variety of products and services within the traditional domains of communications and computing.

> As communications and computing converge, people want to take advantage of these innovative technologies while leveraging their substantial infrastructure investments.

> Innovations always start as "islands," but their practical use requires that the new products and services work together with existing and emerging products. Users expect diverse products offered by *competing* vendors to work together — that is, to interoperate.

> versit is focused on helping people obtain maximum value from the exciting opportunities created by the convergence of communications and computing. The versit participants believe that great potential exists to significantly improve this environment.

In order to unleash this potential — for business and individuals alike — versit's objective is to jointly develop and support open specifications that enable diverse communications and computing devices, applications, and services from competing vendors to interoperate. This gives customers choice and interoperability and protects their investment.

versit believes this approach not only supports the implementation of practical solutions to today's problems, but also accelerates the availability of innovative new products. This approach is expected to result in a diversity of competing products and services that will greatly facilitate how people communicate and work together.

The versit initiative is a cooperation for diversity which will help promote the growth of emerging markets and will give customers a choice of products and services.

IBM released this statement at the same time:

As one of the founding partners [of versit], IBM is playing an important role by contributing skills and technology to the development of versit specifications and supporting specifications in IBM products.

versit is aimed at identifying, developing, and promoting open technical specifications to advance the compatible exchange of information among a wide variety of devices, such as personal computers, Personal Digital Assistants (PDAs), and telephones. versit specifications will help break down the barriers between the worlds of telecommunications and computing by enabling these devices to "speak the same language." This will make it easier for people at work, at home, or on the road to exchange information and communicate, no matter what device they may be using.

Although computer telephony had been around for years, a lack of interoperability stymied its growth and limited its potential for a long time.

Take the words of Ellen M. Hancock, IBM senior vice president and group executive: "The revolution promised by the convergence of telecommunications and computing will not reach its full potential unless our industries agree to open, interpretable standards that make using a PDA, telephone, and notebook computer together as easy as turning on the different components of a stereo system." (Refer to Chapter 5 for a more detailed discussion of standards and APIs with respect to CTI.)

CLIENT/SERVER PROCESSING

For many years, computer aficionados have heatedly debated the pros and cons of client/server computing, including what it is and what it achieves. Since the aftermath of the downsizing revolution, it's now universally accepted that the most effective way to use microprocessor technology (as opposed to the older technology of mainframes and dumb terminals) is to divide the application and information processing between computers designated as *clients* and *servers*. The degree of split depends on the applications, platforms, and objectives. Client/server (C/S) systems enable enterprises to effectively distribute resources and processing power. (Chapter 11 also discusses C/S technology.)

E-mail systems are good examples of client/server systems. The server machines (typically known as the mail servers) handle the routing, serving, and storing of messages. The client (or front end) handles the requests to read, send, and reply to messages. Typically, the clients do not need a great deal of processing power because the servers handle the task of managing the information.

The biggest client/server network is the World Wide Web. Millions of Web servers process information, data, and transactions and then serve the fruits of their processing labor to tens of millions of clients around the world.

Computer telephony products should — no, *must* — employ client/server architecture to integrate effectively into the enterprise information network. Years ago, I predicted that unless the computer telephony industry shifted to client/server platforms and architecture, the products would be caught on uneven footing when IT managers demanded integration into their existing client/server systems. My company developed one of the first client/server telephony engines, which is now the core of a commercially available product (unfortunately, I cannot mention it by name — I had to sign an agreement promising not to). As a result, interconnected servers that handle mail, data, information, files, documents, communications, applications, printing, maintenance, archiving, and — don't forget — telephony have become a familiar sight.

Using this architecture, client-based computer telephony software (that is, the applications running on the desktop PCs) request services and information from their server siblings. The back-end servers connect to the PBX and process requests to the telephony equipment, such as transferring calls or playing messages over the telephone. Computer telephony hardware, such as voice-processing and voice-recognition cards, operates in the servers.

At the minimum, your computer telephony server will need high-end 486 class machines driven by robust operating systems such as UNIX, OS/2, and Windows NT. Client PCs are where the real fun lies; the new models support integrated or unified messaging and desktop call processing and call control.

In addition, the users' client machines need to be at least 486-class machines; their machines should run Windows 3.11 or higher, and the client machines must be networked. Also, you'll need to equip the computers with color VGA screens and a mouse, the essential tool for managing calls and messages on your system.

I've walked into some very profitable and progressively minded companies in Miami and Ft. Lauderdale, only to find them running unnetworked systems equipped with just one 486-class computer in a sea of XT machines. (Never mind that these guys can't use the old machines for computer telephony — I want to know how they're able to use the XTs for anything at all!) Not much in the way of critical application software is available today that can run on these old boxes.

My client (ESCOM) in South Africa surprised me in this area. When I checked to see what its users had on their desks, I was happy to find 486-class machines, all running the latest versions of Windows and set up with gobs of RAM. The client's machines were connected together by a well-planned Novell LAN, and ESCOM had all the necessary servers in place for computer telephony. The telephony group (integration group four) may not have been ready for CT, but the computer and software group (integration group three) certainly was.

OFF-THE-SHELF COMPONENTS (PLUG-INS)

Object-oriented design and programming in software manufacturing, computer-aided software engineering (CASE), rapid application prototyping (testing of a concept or idea for a software application), and rapid application development (RAD) — which cuts down on the so-called number of man-hours to bring software to market — brought forth a new era of software (and system) modularity. In this era, you can plug together different software and hardware components to create a system that best meets your business objectives. Enterprises that follow this doctrine are often said to have a "plug-in" mentality in the IT shop. This doctrine is not a bad practice to follow; rather, it's a very good concept (although the component industry has yet to mature into full capability).

Why is it a good practice to follow? To develop effective, long-term strategies for computer telephony integration and deployment, you need to invest in a system that has an architecture capable of evolving with the times. In the past, enterprises relied on a single computer telephony system to handle their telecommunications needs, seldom investing in turnkey products from a number of different vendors (because the old turnkey products were stand-alone islands of technology). Thus, if a particular service or key component of the system did not serve the enterprise's needs, the enterprise had little choice but to dump the system and try something else. Often, enterprises had to try several different systems before finding one that worked and committing to any one product.

As you may have guessed, this situation had a big impact on the strategic common vision the enterprise wanted to achieve in the People group. Many enterprises tried various products and ended up without a real solution because users witnessed system after system coming and going. (This situation was not just a problem with computer telephony systems; the same situation applied when testing other types of systems, too.)

If the products that you buy conform to common APIs and standards and are interoperable with other systems, you reduce the risk of failure. Although following these guidelines may make finding a system more difficult, you'll be grateful that you went to the extra effort in the long run.

You want products that work with popular database management systems (such as SQL servers and client/server databases); you want products that work with your network protocols; you want products that are accessible (you can plug into them or extend them) and open (you can build applications in-house that work with them); and you want products that run on popular operating systems and hardware platforms.

Computer telephony products that meet the accessibility criteria are ideal candidates for module-based systems (in other words, systems from the same manufacturer to which you add new modules, or systems that you can "plug into" to extend the functionality of the original purchase). These systems facilitate the ideal of off-the-shelf purchasing. For example: PBX companies sell call-accounting packages that consist of little more than a printer connected to the data port of the PBX. Instead of a picture of your call-processing expenses, all you get is two miles of data which you cannot make heads or tails of.

With the CTI link now provided by NetWare Telephony Services or Windows Telephony Services, you can channel data from the CTI-link into a database application, and link it to a financial package or a spreadsheet. Not only will you be able to manipulate the data in a fashion that is more meaningful, but you can pipe the data directly into budgets, reports, and business plans. In other words, you are not "locked-in" to a solution you cannot extend or enhance. Cheap computer telephony solutions that lend themselves to plug-in strategies are now available.

You also can, for example, use a call-control system based on NetWare Telephony Services with an off-the-shelf, voice-messaging product (based on Windows Telephony Services) supplied by a different vendor. You can then plug this messaging product into the LAN and use a separate server machine to deploy it to the Novell telephony server, even if the enterprise backbone and server technology supports Windows NT or UNIX platforms.

Why would you want to do this as opposed to using an all-in-one system from one vendor? Well, perhaps the messaging features of one product are better than the product that came with a system you chose for its prowess in call processing situations. The pay-off is a dynamic computer telephony environment that you can regularly improve and enhance.

EASE OF USE

Whatever products you choose to integrate with your system, make sure that they are easy to learn and simple to use. These features have a big impact on the speed with which your staff learns and accepts the changes. For example, I find it strange and unacceptable that many voice-messaging products tout client/sever features and boast pretty, Windows-based applications for managing voice mail. Even if the applications are Windows GUI-based, you do not want to force users to work with more applications than the ones they already use when managing multiple message types.

With 30 million-plus popular e-mail clients in use worldwide, I fail to understand why manufacturers did not already integrate voice and fax messages into their environments (see Chapter 13). They could have (and should have) provided these services, given the capabilities that are built into open APIs, such as dynamic data exchange (DDE) and object-oriented programming technology.

By ensuring that your systems are easy to use, you help bring about the common vision of which I spoke earlier. This attribute also helps the enterprise build and maintain an alluring image from both the staff's and customers' points of view. You want to follow a similar practice with the telephone user interface (TUI), because making sure that the TUI (which in the past has been the only window the user has had to the voice mail system) is easy for users and customers to use is just as important. If you install a difficult, confusing voice-response system, you may as well be answering the phone with this message: "Get lost — we don't want your business."

GLOBAL AND EXTENDED ARCHITECTURE

The open, alluring enterprise is one that its employees can access anywhere and at any time. Therefore, the enterprise information network needs to include servers that enable users to remotely access information in a variety of simple ways. The remote access server (RAS) is a vitally important component in larger organizations in that users can access the network as if they were directly connected to the LAN in the office.

With standardization of platforms and software, users can dial in (via modem communications) or connect to the LAN in a variety of seamless routes (such as via the Internet) to gain access to critical information, especially their multimedia array of messages (voice mail, e-mail, fax mail, and so on).

INTEGRATION GROUP FOUR: PBXS, TELEPHONES, AND THE PSTN

Although I saved this section for last, this information is by *no* means the least important that I talk about. Without decent telephony, you do not have a project. When I say, "How are we doing on the telephony side?" I'm asking about the features that you have on the PBX and the environment you have to deal with outside the world of the PTT (post, telephony, and telegraph administrations), telcos (telephone companies), and the PSTN.

Let's take another look at the ESCOM case. ESCOM's external environment was *not* unique in that a majority of its callers used old, mechanical rotary exchanges — interaction nightmare number one. This situation is the case in many parts of Europe and the United Kingdom. (Rotary detection does not work. If you disagree, stop reading now, and go call a computer telephony system —if you can find one — that understands the clicks. Spend 15 minutes trying to make headway with passwords and ID numbers, and then come back and talk to me.) Thus, when considering integration group four, list the sub-headings depicted in Figure 15-3 on your legal pad.

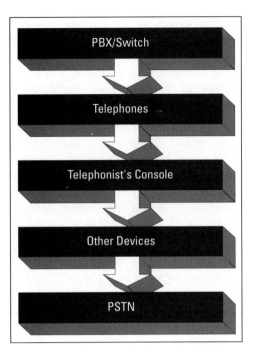

Figure 15-3: Integration group four.

THE PBX (OR OTHER VOICE/DATA SWITCHING DEVICE)

The first place that I visit when I'm at a site is the PBX closet (or room — it depends on the size of the company). Without a decent PBX, many computer telephony services will not work, or at least will be very limited. If, like me, you've worked with many different makes and manufacturers of PBXs, you'll know the limitations and features of each system on sight. It's important to know these limitations up front because with closed systems from the old IT era, you're at the mercy of your switch and the people who created and maintain it. The fact that Siemans joined versit (thanks in part to its love affair with IBM) is, in itself, something of a marvel, given that PBX companies have been so secretive in the past.

When I'm on a site, the first question that I usually ask is this: "How long have you had your PBX (or PABX in the ESCOM case, for African PBX)?" The answer I received from a senior ESCOM telephonist was not one that I like to hear: "About two months."

Why do I say this, you ask? Because nine times out of ten, the IT people have far-fetched ideas about computer telephony regarding the equipment needed, the existing technology in place, and — of course — the budget. If I know that an enterprise has recently shelled out some major bucks to buy equipment, I hate being the one who says "It's impossible to do that with your new PBX (the one you just blew the IT budget on)."

In my view, the longer the PBX has been around, the better; it will be less likely to suit your purpose and therefore make your decision to upgrade and junk your old box easier. ESCOM had a good PBX, although it was limited in terms of its CTI capacity. It had a Siemens 601, a PBX model that was adopted from equipment in the Siemens/Rolm line and sold only in South Africa (other users of this PBX are Microsoft and KLM Airlines, both heavy users of computer telephony applications).

This PBX had several features that made integration easier (including the capability to perform repeat dialing, an in-band integration feature that I addressed in Chapter 5). But this box does not have gobs of memory, nor does it have great software, and several of the call-processing systems I installed brought this box crashing to a halt. Without going into too much detail on PBXs and switching systems, just know that you should hold off making that new PBX purchase until you fully understand what's needed for computer telephony integration.

PBX systems are not as cheap as computers. A PBX system for a small business (servicing 30 to 100 people) can easily cost as much as $10,000 in the United States and $50,000 in Europe, Africa, and Australia (some PBXs may even go for a million bucks). Many of my clients opt to lease their equipment. Just be careful if you go this route — once you're locked into a lease, it's not that easy to get unlocked, and upgrading the lease or selling the box can be an expensive exercise (adding a dent to your strategic plans — see Chapters 16 and 17).

Now, if you take out your legal pad, you can jot down some notes about the PBX and its capabilities (and limitations) as they relate to computer telephony services that you want to provide. These points are discussed more fully in Chapters 4 and 7; by the end of the book, you will have formulated your own checklist that you can use to help you decide what you need. ESCOM provided a piece of equipment that could be worked with reasonably well (it was not the ideal CTI partner, but it was doable).

TELEPHONES

Now it's time to move on to the next item on the telephony checklist: the telephones that sit on the desks of the service or knowledge workers. You may think that the telephones you have now will work fine, but I have consulted for several companies where its telephones were less than ideal for integration with computer telephony.

One large client had recently changed its environment (both internal and external) over to a digital PBX that used both DTMF (dual-tone, multifrequency tones; better known as touch tone) and digital dialing, but several hundred of the organization's phones were still pulse-dial telephones. The cost of upgrading all these phones was staggering.

Because many keypad-type phones still dial using the pulse system, the best way to determine DTMF phones at a glance is to check for the star key (*) and the pound key (#). Don't look for a tone/pulse switch. (In Europe, the pound key is also known as the hash key — this does not mean the PBX smokes hashish or marijuana.)

Why is DTMF so important? Because this method is still the chief means by which users interact with a CT system. In the ESCOM safari case, all the telephones in the organization had DTMF dial capabilities, but callers were saddled with the old, pulse-dial technology which made it harder to deal with (voice mail was not much of an option).

Another important feature to check is whether your organization has digital or analog (POT or 2500 port instruments) telephones. I see a great deal of digital telephones installed at my clients' organizations nowadays. Many organizations have invested heavily in these instruments. Digital telephones can cost as much as $1,000 a set. Although digital phonesets are great, they cause problems on the CT side. Almost all the major CT products still integrate with the PBX via the analog ports; user interaction with the CT system is still analog.

One of my New York clients, an investment firm, had recently installed a fancy PBX before I was called in to consult for it. "No can do," I said. "Your entire office is on digital telephones, and the CT systems you want to buy talk analog. We have no analog ports that we can hang the system on." This client had three options: spend tons of money on the CT side and throw out the $100-a-shot digital sets; load the PCs with desktop CT solutions (which would not help the analog-centric CT server); or do without.

Fortunately, the PBX company provided us with a fourth option: It traded the digital phones for analog sets and put the credit into extension cards and more PBX capacity. (See Chapters 4 and 5 for more on analog and digital phones.)

TELEPHONIST'S CONSOLE

This area requires careful consideration. The PBX console that the human telephonist or operator uses to route and manage calls is a digital device that connects directly to the PBX. As a result, the telephonist cannot interact with the CT system; before the advent of desktop computer telephony, the telephonist needed a second (analog) instrument to interact with the CT server (see Chapters 4 and 5).

The consoles should provide a clear indication of which extensions are calling the console and be sophisticated enough to alert the telephonist to the nature of the calls flying in (such as, "Returned from camp on extension 223"). The Philips line of PBX systems uses a console that has a huge liquid-crystal display the size of a small notebook computer screen. It can be programmed to describe the extension or service calling the console (such as "Call from voice mail port" or "Coverage — extension 200"). Otherwise, consoles cannot tell the telephonist that the CT system diverted the incoming call to the operator's console because the caller was pounding away at the 0 key. Thus, when the telephonist answers the call, the caller becomes even more frustrated when he or she hears the telephonist recite the company greeting for the umpteenth time.

OTHER DEVICES

You may have to consider other telephony devices attached to the EIN during your computer telephony integration project. You will want to make sure that they do not run or bump into computer telephony objectives. This includes Internet servers (especially Internet telephony servers), fax-servers and fax machines (on dedicated lines or as extensions off the switch), modems, and remote access servers. Many large enterprises connect their offices in one private data network. Others use electronic data interchange (EDI) services.

THE PUBLIC-SWITCHED TELEPHONE NETWORK

Until you can have a lucid conversation with a computer over the telephone without the need to send and receive DTMF (with reliable speech and voice recognition), the PSTN and the telephone companies will be important partners in the CT picture. Whether your enterprise resides in safari country, the United States, Africa, or Asia, you will be hampered by the limitations of old mechanical exchanges and the level of touch-tone dialing penetration. You also need to consider the technology and services your local telephone company can offer before you rush into setting up a call center or extensive computer telephony service.

Your checklist of services to consider should contain items like Caller ID, Centrex services, DNIS, ISDN, fiber optics, and more. You'd be surprised what the telephone company can offer you.

In Chapter 2, I introduced the Philips competition example. You may recall that so many callers dialed in to the competition line that all the circuits maxed out. During one session, a whole exchange came to a halt. When I called the telephone company to find out what had happened, the engineers informed me that the equipment was not equipped to handle 30,000 calls an hour. Thus, you need to make sure that if you're planning a massive campaign, the telephone company will be able to handle the traffic and your requests. It's like working on publishing a book and then, at the last minute, the printer tells you he or she can't print color or that his or her machine won't print the page size you need.

The telephone company makes big money from your service: If you are planning a big campaign, make an appointment to go and see their business services division. Have your gurus meet theirs to discuss, among other things, if the telco switch has both the hardware and software to meet your needs. Again, I should remind you that the telco switch is just a huge switch that works like your PBX. Most PBX manufacturers, like Northern Telecom, AT&T, Siemens, Alcatel, and Plessey, supply equipment for use in the central office.

So how did my lost safari case (ESCOM) turn out? Pretty well, actually. (The only "lost" component of this case was me after I mislaid my directions to the site.) During a crisis, we would easily route calls to other stations to prevent the hour-glass syndrome from happening, so everyone in the company could become a telephonist. An audiotext system was also proposed for after-hours situations, providing a single message box where customers could optionally record messages.

Few customers were actually stuck with pulse-dial technology, even though the area exchange required pulse dialing. Callers could switch to touch-tone dialing after making a connection by hitting the star (*) key. I also discovered that many of the residents had cellular phones (GSM standard) and that the telephone company did not plan to make any significant upgrades to the ground-based exchange facility because of the high rate of cable theft for the area.

SUMMARY

This chapter discussed strategies for the requisition and integration of computer telephony. You may want to take a look at the chapters in Part I before proceeding further. Those chapters defined computer telephony and looked at how the new frontier in information technology affects it. Those chapters also discussed the elements, or service domains, of computer telephony (call processing, messaging, interactive telecommunications, information exchange, and communications) and explored enterprise readiness for computer telephony applications. Where do you need to go next?

✦ If you are planning a new business, telemarketing campaigns, product launches, or a new division or department or if you are generally considering a means of empowering your service and knowledge workers, then I recommend reading Chapter 16.

✦ If you're ready to bring in some expertise, I urge you to read Chapter 17.

IN THIS CHAPTER

✦ IT and business planning: The old way

✦ IT and business planning: The new way

✦ Computer telephony and the new business: Small office or home office

✦ Commissioning champions and educating them

"Technology has made my job much easier!
I begin each morning by listening to all my
voice mail and when I'm done with that
it's time to go home!"

COMPUTER TELEPHONY AND BUSINESS PLANNING

Much has been written on the subject of what it takes to keep a customer. Today, a satisfied installed base or customer base is the most important asset of almost any modern enterprise. Keeping and reselling to a customer is far easier and less expensive than trying to capture and sell to new people or businesses. My friend and partner, Karl Slatner (who authored *How to Boom Your Business with Customer Satisfaction*), will tell you that one of the best business situations to be in is the one in which you never have to make a cold call again: "A million satisfied customers equals $50 million in the bank."

Customers like to be loyal; they don't like to shop around if they don't have to. If they've been happy with you before, they'll keep coming back. Your cost of selling to them will drop as long as you keep making new and exciting products or offer new and exciting services that people want — and as long as you keep them satisfied. Keeping customers satisfied means making sure that they can set up and use your product successfully; when they have a problem, they should be able to find you available to listen, 24 hours a day. (Refer to Chapter 2 for more on customer satisfaction.)

The biggest mistake businesses make today is ignoring — intentionally or unintentionally — the fact that its best sales prospect is its existing, *satisfied* customer base. You can use computer telephony to achieve these customer satisfaction goals by helping your firm be more productive when it comes to using the telephone. For this reason, it's now more important than ever to include computer telephony and IT on the business plan. Business owners and planners should be aware of the enabling power of information technology, the competitive advantage it provides, and the various technology domains (such as computer telephony) that spring forth from it.

Before you can explore deployment of computer telephony further, you have to get your business plans in order. Figure 16-1 depicts three steps to take in bringing the IT and business management entities together at the business plan level.

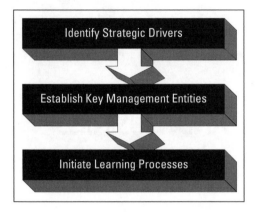

Figure 16-1: The three steps to bringing IT and business planning together.

I stress in Part I how important it is to make computer telephony considerations part of the overall business strategy of the enterprise. Although the subject of this book is computer telephony and computer-telephone integration, this business strategy applies to all IT systems. This subject should be part of all university courses in business and information technology administration — but sadly, it isn't.

This book does not make the same mistake; I know of many cases where a systems integration project wouldn't work because the enterprise still viewed information technology and business strategies as separate issues. Computer telephony requisition must be part and parcel of business strategy. I've seen many situations where the introduction of a new system — some much less complex than computer telephony — failed for no reason other than a lack of common vision for using it throughout the enterprise. The chief factor behind this lack of common vision — whether the company was based in Europe, Africa, the Middle East, or North America — was the self-imposed separation that existed between business planners/owners and their IT departments.

I don't want this to happen to you. Nothing is more frustrating than going through all the pain and expense of an integration project that later fails for a simple reason like a lack of common vision in the enterprise.

IT AND BUSINESS PLANNING: THE OLD WAY

If you were following the old business plan, you would establish the business purposes and methods and then describe what the business does. After that task was completed, IT would be called in to ensure that the necessary architectures and supporting systems were put in place. The users of the systems had little say (and frequently no say) in these matters. This setup alienated the IT department from the enterprise.

I'm not saying that the information technology executives should not plan and manage their own departments and develop strategy; rather, I'm saying that IT must be involved from the first step as part of this process. Such a job is a perfect task for a Chief Information Officer (CIO) with a business administration background, an individual who also appreciates what IT means in terms of competitive advantage for the enterprise.

I was privy to some of Microsoft's business strategies for setting up subsidiaries in foreign countries. When the software giant set up its South African company, I was impressed by the methods of the implementation team—how they included both the business planners for the new offices and the IT executive. Every business function was shadowed by the consequences it would have on enabling IT systems and structures. Microsoft explored the computer telephony needs long before it signed the office lease or hired a single telephonist.

With the focus more on business planning and how IT can empower and enable the enterprise and workers, implementation has a better chance of working, especially for computer telephony. The business owners and the IT department will not have to work as hard to "sell" the new systems to an ambivalent staff. Why? Because at the business plan level, the department heads have the opportunity — under the guidance of IT and the CIO — to determine their own IT needs.

IT *can* initiate the need for computer telephony if no one else sees it, but the business planners should insist that the direction, scope, needs, capacity, and so on come from the workers. After all, they are the ones who must use the system the most; they should be able to indicate which tools they need. A carpenter decides what chisels he needs; a chef decides what spices or condiments she needs — so why not let service and knowledge workers determine their needs?

If your business plan is an enterprise-wide working document for establishing IT needs, you'll help minimize negative canteen discussions among employees about what "management wants us to use." Instead, their discussions may go something like this: "Jill's department installed voice mail, and they love it. We need to talk to the VP to get the system installed in our section."

Warning: Do not confuse this strategy with one in which you give departments, subsidiaries, and associate companies complete control over their IT architecture — especially purchasing control. If you follow that strategy, you'll end up with matzo pudding for an IT infrastructure, where your company's network becomes crippled because different parts of it are using incompatible systems and software.

Believe it or not, this situation has happened before. One such situation occurred at the South African Breweries, one of the largest breweries in the world. The head office discovered that its numerous branches had become so different in IT make-up (different operating systems, different applications, different networks, different topologies, and so on) that in order to implement an enterprise-wide computer telephony and call management architecture, it had to completely overhaul the IT infrastructure, bringing all maverick departments under the umbrella of a central IT authority.

A similar case cropped up at the giant Electricity Supply Commission (ESCOM), which had no less that five different voice-messaging systems installed at various branches, each purchased from different vendors. And in one memorable visit to the highly sophisticated help desk of the South African postal service, I saw a new, state-of-the-art computer telephony system (worth $100,000) sitting on a desk, gathering dust. No one had a clue how to use it or even why it was purchased.

As a result, the days when smart computer scientists suddenly discover the need for computer telephony, get approval for purchase, and then proceed to install a system with no more than three or four people knowing about it are over in many corporations.

IT AND BUSINESS PLANNING: THE NEW WAY

Today, businesses can achieve very little without the power of IT systems. Just how empowered an enterprise can become if it integrates IT systems with the telephone network is becoming more and more apparent. The flow of and access to information is just as important to the modern enterprise as the blood flowing through veins is to humans. Yet it still baffles me why so many businesses fail to see IT's importance. To be competitive, every business must now have access to the Internet, a fact that has many managers realizing that they are under-equipped to enter the new age of electronic commerce and on-line business. In many cases, whole industrial centers are sitting in the dark when it comes to the Internet and intranets.

IDENTIFY STRATEGIC DRIVERS

People associated with a failed business will make many excuses about why it failed; some of the more popular ones are "Times have changed," "People don't use what we make anymore," "The opposition imports a product that the makers use slave labor to build," and so on. These aren't really the reasons. Sure, some of these statements may be true, but forethought and good business planning can keep an enterprise going and profitable, even if its wares today are nowhere close to the services or products it offered 10 or 20 years ago.

Whatever happens in the world, individual business managers, planners, and entrepreneurs have little control over the events that may bring new forces and needs to bear on business. Take AT&T for example: It was one of the world's largest companies, monopolizing the U.S. telephone business for more than 100 years, until the government finally forced it to divest in 1983. In 1995, it underwent a further self-imposed divestiture, splitting up so that each smaller unit could concentrate on its core business and survive in a more competitive market. AT&T may not closely resemble the giant it once was, but to Americans, the name is still synonymous with its former self.

More than just new technology can change the way you do business; politics is another factor that few businesses can control. For example, thousands of businesses in South Africa involved in the foreign currency dealings for imports and exports folded in the mid-1980s when Chase Manhattan Bank led all U.S. banks in withdrawing investments from South Africa to protest Apartheid. Who do you blame, Chase or Apartheid, for the business failures and the loss of jobs? Well, that's another story.

Don Tapscott and Art Caston, in their marvelous book, *Paradigm Shift,* call such factors *strategic drivers.* In other words, then, you need to identify the strategic drivers that may impact the enterprise. These drivers could be new laws, new discoveries, law suits, labor disputes, new technology, and much, *much* more. Business owners should delegate this task (identifying the strategic drivers) to a senior member of the staff or to themselves. Otherwise, they should invest in the services of an enterprise analyst, such as my late friend, Dr. Michael Edwards.

Michael would often say to me, "I make my money just by looking at a company and telling the owners what their business really is. Often, they don't have a clue." Naturally, he didn't mean that what he did was tell the telephone company that it should be in the food business (for example). Rather, he meant that he told the local telephone company that it makes money by keeping its subscribers satisfied and happy, not by diverting its attention to, say, a computer manufacturing venture that it might be considering.

A good example of a strategic driver, perhaps one that is being felt by every business in America today, is the critical advent of the Internet. I brought up this topic with a new client of mine in southern Florida, a $25-million firm that ranks third in its field of 10 competitors around the world but is at least $200 million in annual revenue behind the second-highest competitor and approximately $1 billion behind the industry leader. This company asked me to name a strategic driver that could positively affect the company's rank, and I said that the Internet could play an important part in narrowing the distance between it and the leading competitors. Why? Because the Internet is the greatest leveler of business playing fields since the invention of money.

But the management team works slow in this company, so they may take a year to make up their minds about their plan of action, which equals four technology years in my book. That's *too* slow when it takes so little money and time to just put an e-mail address and domain name on everyone's business card.

Thanks to the rapid pace of change, you can buy computer equipment that is state-of-the-art now and, six months later, the machine is passé. Although many owners blame business failure on external circumstances, the real reasons are often internal, due to a lack of planning anticipation and foresight (logistics): Bad decisions equal bad business.

A human's sixth sense of common sense and logic must play a role in determining some of these drivers. (This stuff is not the material of which the *X-Files* are made.) If you set up a Web site on the Internet and fail to install sufficient security, and a hacker sucks out the insides of your information base, who's to blame — the hacker or you? Now the entire company's secrets end up floating in cyberspace for everyone to pick at. You may contend that "the business failed because it was robbed." You probably won't see that you failed to recognize strategic drivers and could have prevented the theft.

Say Tapscott and Caston: "The productivity of service and knowledge workers, in addition to production workers, is a key driver for most organizations, whether in the private or public sector." This point is where IT and CT in particular come in.

ESTABLISH THE KEY MANAGEMENT ENTITIES (KMES)

Business planners should sufficiently understand the role that IT plays in the daily operations of the enterprise, in terms of both the competitive threat (them) and advantage (us), and plan accordingly. After planners establish the key management entities (KMEs) of the enterprise, IT and its various service domains need to be addressed in the business plan as they relate to individual KMEs.

KMEs are the management or service components of a business that describe what the business does. KMEs do not appear on any organizational chart, but they are best represented on a matrix of the business. Each KME represents an area of responsibility that must be measured and evaluated. KMEs give you the opportunity to expose costs and benefits.

After you establish these KMEs, you need to develop and implement IT architectures and systems for them, such as computer telephony or workgroup software. These KMEs need not be actual, physical groups — they can be logically dispersed between several departments in the enterprise and even across several workgroups.

After you identify these KMEs, you can also describe them on the business plan. Business managers, owners, or administrators are responsible for this task, not IT. After that task is completed, these same individuals can establish how IT (and more specifically, CT) can improve efficiency in these entities. Does this mean the business professionals should learn about the competitive advantages and threats of IT? Yes, it does. If a general wants to win the war, he or she has to know which weapons to use and when to use them.

INITIATE LEARNING PROCESSES

The next step, as illustrated by Figure 16-1, is to initiate learning processes. I am convinced that the reason Motor Vehicle Insurance Services, Inc.'s computer telephony project failed was because the firm took the traditional approach to implementing the system. The IT executive and the CEO determined the need for computer telephony (rather than the users), commissioned the project, had the system installed, and then had to "sell" the system to its intended users (see Chapter 1).

This approach is outmoded, outdated, and doesn't work — certainly not for computer telephony and its service domains, like voice messaging. I'm not basing this statement on the failure of one project alone. Many companies I have worked with used the traditional approach; not all failed, but even where the systems are still being used, users are generally under-utilizing the services even years after the project was completed.

So, what should you do? Using a strategy described earlier, the IT executive should gather up the heads of the various departments — those responsible for the key management entities like marketing, fulfillment, technical support, customer training, and so on — to initiate learning processes.

These management heads should know which service domains of computer telephony will benefit their departments, based on input from their workers. These groups of personnel should get together with the CIO or IT director and then volunteer members of their workgroups to assist with analyzing a new system. In large organizations, including pockets of users among the key management entities is a good idea.

After you've gathered together the necessary people, the training begins. First, you give a handful of people in the group some lessons in how to use the systems. Whatever teaching methods and materials you prefer are up to you. The trainer can work with three or four people in a group and show them, for example, how to access voice mail over the telephone.

The training should cover more than how to use the system in general; it also should cover how to use it more productively. The trainer should be cognizant of the reasons each group has for wanting the technology. That way, he or she can tailor the IT directives so that the training empowers users to meet the specific goals and objectives set out in the business plan.

After the small pockets of users begin to use and appreciate the enabling effects of the technology, they will explore more advanced ways to use the systems on their own. They also will begin to show others in the group how to use the system; gradually, a common vision will take hold.

As the workers learn to use the technology to make their lives easier, other users in the organization will get wind of the results and suddenly management will be faced with requests to commission more sample user groups. Using this strategy, a learning process begins on its own. Rather than rebelling against the new system, I have found that the opposite starts to happen. Users begin to take the initiative to learn how to use the system themselves.

In my earlier training projects, I had to battle to get users together for training sessions. After my partners and I learned to involve the users in the planning stages of a project, however, we typically became inundated with requests to learn how to use the system for later projects. We would have to turn away users who wanted to learn the new system, too, or who felt that the users to be trained were part of an elite, select group that they wanted to be part of.

What really impressed me was when some groups of users determined that certain services or features were not right for them and should be removed or shielded from the system. Other groups asked to have certain features enabled so that they could achieve particular goals. As you can tell in these cases, project leaders no longer had to sell the system to the users. Instead, management found that the users were driving the project.

COMPUTER TELEPHONY AND THE NEW BUSINESS, SMALL OFFICE, OR HOME OFFICE

The philosophy just described applies equally to the new or small business. New businesses have both a disadvantage and an advantage: The disadvantage is that everything they do is untried for their situation, and (typically) everyone is nervous. After all, the new owners have everything to lose — they've raised the money, sold the farms, and liquidated heirlooms by the time they're ready to go.

Whatever the nature of the business, not a single enterprise in the world exists today that can function (that is, be ready, empowered, and enabled) without the aid of IT systems. Be it a one-person beauty parlor or an individual who plans to raise billions with a stock offering within a year — the day and age we live in dictates the need for the aid of computers. Not so long ago, only the larger business could afford the technology, but this situation is no longer the case.

Many people may disagree with me. I have an associate in southern Florida who works as an endodontist. "What do I really need a computer for?" he challenged me. "It's just me and the assistant in the office."

"Did you participate in the endodontics conference last week?" I asked.

He said he'd been too busy, but I told him he could have gone there and back for 30 minutes every evening. He looked at me as if I had finally lost my mind, but my answer was this: "The conference was covered in a Usenet group on the Internet, but, of course, you don't have a computer."

Similar to my associate, the biggest mistake a new business can make today is underestimating its needs for IT. Every business can be empowered with a database, every business can be empowered with a spreadsheet (if only as a catalyst for your imagination); whatever you plan to do, whether it's selling potatoes or finding the cure for the common cold, you need to determine your needs for information technology and place them on your business plan.

For starters, the first and most important investment is a computer—not a fancy MIPS workstation, but a fast notebook. Why a notebook, you ask, when they cost almost twice as much as a standard computer? Because the one problem you will have with the desktop computer is that you can't take it just anywhere on short notice. In today's world, you need to take the computer with you. Perhaps you need to work at home; perhaps you need to take the kids to baseball or perhaps you need to demonstrate something to the investor, banker, or customer. Regardless of the task you put to it, the notebook is the perfect machine for the job. After you have a notebook computer, install the necessary computer telephony components that were discussed earlier.

Every business can function with more power and gain a competitive advantage by connecting to an enterprise information network of some sort, even if that network consists of your sole computer connected to the largest of networks (the Internet) or to a smaller sub-network (like one of the commercial services, such as CompuServe or America Online). This connection is vital because you need to be able to find and send information over it. Even just having an e-mail address is important. IT gives you an even footing on which to compete against big, corporate giants.

The problem is that few businesses anticipate their needs and the minimum investment required for IT systems and technology. A desktop publisher tight for funds will take on a graphics-intensive newsletter by using an Intel 386-class machine instead of a Pentium. Because doing the layout on this machine takes ages and wastes time (such as when the person has to sit and stare at the screen while it takes more than a minute to redraw), the minutes eventually translate into hours, and jobs back up, deadlines go bust, and the customers go somewhere else.

If you don't have the funds to acquire the computers or the credit to lease them, then scale down the work you plan to take on or change your assumptions in the business plan. If you have budget constraints, then purchase the computers you can afford, and if the computers are not adequate for fancy color layouts, then (using the previous example) start small with simple, text newsletters. When you have more money in the bank eight months later, the business may either have the cash or credit required to buy that fancy workstation, which will enable you to take on the color layouts.

You should follow a similar practice with computer telephony systems (see the next chapter). If your business depends on the telephone (as do all) to achieve certain goals and objectives, then you need to invest in technology to enable workers to use the telephone more sensibly and be more productive. For example, if the business plan calls for a great deal of telephone calling, you will need a contact manager to keep track of names and phones numbers integrated with a dialer. Today, you no longer have the excuse that the technology you need has not yet been invented. Even the simplest TAPI dialer will make you more productive, as discussed earlier.

One of my smaller clients is a four-person travel agency within a 3,000-branch, publicly owned travel enterprise. The enterprise set up the division to take advantage of the big discounts that the airlines were willing to give them to fill up seats that remain vacant a week or less before scheduled departures. As such, the business plan called for a small ACD and call sequencer, working with a voice-messaging and computer-telephonist system, to cater to the expected barrage of calls that would arrive when advertisements hit the streets.

I looked at the business plan and made sure that its IT systems were sufficiently upgraded to do business. At one of the meetings, I said, "I don't see you achieving this level of sales without decent headsets." The more calls that came in, the more the attendants would need to have both hands free at all times during the day.

SUMMARY

Parts I and II of this book gave you an idea of the computer technology that's available to you and how it can increase productivity, help you better serve and satisfy customers, stay open for business all the time, and more. But you need to make sure that you plan adequately for the IT needs of your business and that the business planning people — or you — bring these needs to the business plan.

I discuss this subject from the perspective of deploying computer telephony systems in Chapter 17.

IN THIS CHAPTER

- ✦ How to determine the number of ports

- ✦ Cost justification and return on investment

- ✦ Requisition and purchasing decisions

- ✦ Up and running

"I found the problem. This unit was manufactured on February 20th, so it's a Pisces. You can network a Pisces with a Scorpio or Aquarius, but *never* with a Taurus or Capricorn!"

17

DEPLOYING COMPUTER TELEPHONY

T he world of Information Technology, computing, and telephony has become so explosive that often you may find yourself drowning in all those "bits" and "bytes." In contradiction to the new promises of IT, you can lose sight of your objectives and visions once you get down to integration and installation. I discuss at length phased implementation and testing in Chapter 8. This chapter, however, provides some strategies for deployment.

FINDING YOUR ERLANGS

No, this chapter is not a lesson in physiology. This chapter is a crash course in call-traffic engineering and management. An *Erlang* is a measurement of telephone traffic in hours and was named after Danish telephone engineer A. K. Erlang, whose forte — you guessed it — was call-traffic engineering. Why do you have to find your Erlangs? Well, one of the goals of this chapter is to help solve one of the biggest puzzles that any fledgling CT project or call center campaign has — determining the number of ports you need. (More information on this subject is available in the Lexicon, Appendix A.)

But why do you need to determine the number of ports? Why should you even care? The reason is that this information can help you when performing the following tasks:

✦ Establishing needs

✦ Determining number of ports for the service

✦ Determining how much the system will cost

✦ Justifying the cost

+ Predicting amortization and establishing a return on investment

+ Preparing equipment purchases

+ Formulating budget and ordering necessary hardware and software

+ Extending or expanding existing systems (such as the PBX)

+ Ordering more telephone lines

All these factors are important decisions that you have to make when deploying and purchasing computer telephony equipment. To make the correct decisions, you need data, and you need data that you can trust.

The process to get that data is not unlike the effort that road-traffic engineers go through to determine how much traffic a stretch of highway can handle or what its peak hour is. The road-traffic engineers lay a cable across the road, and every time that a vehicle drives over it, a counter records the event. The engineers can then compare the data acquired on one road to the data acquired from other routes and plan roadway needs accordingly.

In computer telephony, you use various tools to do the same thing with call traffic. You also try to predict calling patterns, which is a lot tougher than counting calls. This chapter tells you how to acquire this data and how to use the data when buying and deploying CT systems.

Before discussing the tasks that you need this data for, as listed earlier, I'll get into some background information, have you do a quick exercise to determine some Erlang values, and, thereby, determine the number of ports needed for your computer telephony services. Before you can ask me for my definition of a port, here it is (as it relates to a computer telephony system and this exercise).

Many telephony or telecommunications gurus argue about the proper definitions for channels, ports, lines, trunks, conferencing, and so on, but within the scope of this book, you can basically view a port as the number of "electronic doorways" that you need to make your enterprise or service accessible to a caller. The ports on your PBX or switching service are the entrances via the telco lines or telephone extensions. Ports also include the telephone entrances to the voice-processing system, the fax server, the call sequencer, or the ACD unit. Other ports include the entrances to your popular Web server that 100 million Netizens are trying to "hit."

Although you have ports on all telephony devices in the enterprise, the number of callers who can connect to your service or services depends on the number of lines that come into your facility. For example, you may have 100 telephone lines entering your PBX and several hundred extensions, of which you've dedicated 24 to the voice-processing system.

But let's get back to call-traffic engineering: I learned an Erlang-forecasting technique for determining Erlang values from the telephony and PBX community and then successfully used it for computer telephony. This procedure is often used to forecast the number of PBX ports and lines needed by the enterprise, based on call information provided by the central office or telephone exchange.

I'll get into the specifics of this forecasting method later in this chapter, but here's basically how it works: The telephone company monitors call traffic on your group of telephone lines and determines an Erlang value for the group. Your call traffic is measured in *Erlangs per hour*. In other words, if your group of 20 lines carries 15.55 Erlangs per hour, you're using just over 15 of your lines during your peak calling hour.

This type of call-traffic engineering is as critical for telemarketing campaigns and call centers as it is for the telephone company. New technologies are making call-traffic engineering a little easier to perform. One school of thought is that computer simulation should be applied to telecommunications traffic management. Computer simulation is very expensive, however: One of the best simulation suites you can get costs a fortune, and the actual simulation would cost more than the system it imitates.

Many believe that applying logistics — doing the math; using common sense, sixth sense, and reason; and drawing on experience — still works best. Many consultants try to monitor lines by using an assortment of electronic equipment, such as current-detection devices, but this method is just not practical for forecasting call traffic for a large installation where call patterns may vary widely.

Determining the number of ports you need is an important task that you must perform for all of the CT service domains. As such, although the consultant or vendor can help you determine your needs, you, the IT executive or enterprise CT engineer, should be familiar with the analysis and needs procedure in order to plan accordingly.

By first understanding what Erlang set out to accomplish, you will discover why this section is one of the most important technical considerations in this book — cost. At the dawn of the twentieth century, when telephone traffic started to go ballistic, Erlang used his engineering skills to determine how to deploy telephone exchanges. The dilemma he set his sights on was figuring out a way to predict the hardware necessary to handle the widely fluctuating call traffic; if not enough ports were available to switch lines, callers would be *blocked* from obtaining service.

Blocking is another telephony term you need to know about (from the deployment angle), as it applies to several concepts. A call is blocked when the caller gets a busy tone — or, as they say in Europe, an engaged signal. Essentially, the service you were trying to reach is unavailable because someone else got there before you — or so you think. What you don't know is that back at the telephone company, the engineers are getting ulcers because their subscribers, who expect to hear a dial tone when they lift their handsets or press 9 to get service from the PBX, cannot be serviced because all possible call paths to connect them are in use.

In small telephone exchanges, it's not uncommon for subscribers to receive an "exchange busy" signal. Even the big exchanges can max out. Remember the San Francisco and Los Angeles earthquakes? California calls were blocked for many hours afterward.

In Chapters 4 and 7, I discuss the similarities between the PBX catering to 100 extensions and a telephone exchange catering to tens of thousands of subscribers. Computer telephony software also has to take call blocking into consideration. A system trying to seize a line to deliver a message or make a call may be blocked because every outbound telephone line is in use. The CT software has to cater to two scenarios: The system being blocked because all internal lines are in use (indicated by service unavailable or reorder tone 1) or because the exchange itself is unable to provide the PBX with dial tone (indicated by service unavailable or reorder tone 2).

Call blocking also refers to the incapability to make a call (which has nothing to do with a busy service). For example: A person who tries to make a long-distance call from the enterprise or a hotel may be *blocked* from incurring long-distance charges. The term *blocked* also refers to the caller who receives a polite "take a hike" message from someone who uses Caller ID. (By the way, Caller ID is great for blocking unwanted calls from in-laws.) Finally, the term applies to digital PBX systems. As discussed in Chapter 7, non-blocking refers to the routing of voice and data through a digital PBX.

You can view the exercise that you'll perform later from another angle: how much you need to spend. Ports usually come on the interface cards to the PBX or CT system, and, nowadays, you pay by the card. The more ports you have, the less risk you run of blocking callers and ruining that alluring image you want to protect, especially if you provide the computer telephonist, automated attendant services, or voice mail facilities described in Part II.

For example, I recently called on a large public company in New Jersey that was having a problem with its voice mail system. They use a few human telephonists to route calls manually, and the calls then divert to voice mail if the party is unavailable. As it turned out, I didn't have to visit the site to determine the problem. The telephonist told me that the system works at certain times of the day but not during the peak calling periods.

"The voice mail refuses to take the calls, including the ones I transfer directly, and then they return to the console," she said. "We have recommended to the CIO that he throw out the system because there is obviously a bug in the software."

The telephonist and her coworkers were wrong in their assessments, however; what was really happening was that the callers were being blocked from leaving messages at busy times because the firm did not have enough voice mail ports to handle the voice mail traffic. The PBX engineer correctly catered to this possibility by diverting the unserviced subscribers back to the telephonist consoles, rather than letting the calls ring endlessly at the voice mail ports or get busy signals. Nothing was wrong with the software; the firm just had not anticipated or planned for the increase in traffic.

Be that as it may, you do not want to invest in equipment that "maxes out" for only a short while and then stands idle for the rest of the day. This situation is exactly the type of problem that you can avoid by applying Erlang's theories.

The following exercise will help you understand your telephone line requirements when dealing with the telephone companies. This list represents the steps that you take in the port-forecasting process:

1. Forecast the number of calls in the peak hour.

2. Determine the average call length.

3. Determine the Erlang value.

4. Determine the blocking tolerance level (the acceptable percentage of people who won't be able to connect to your service).

5. Determine the number of ports.

Let's perform a quick exercise in port forecasting so that you get the idea. (Then I'll discuss some factors that illustrate that this science is not exact but rather an exercise in educated guessing.)

Consider the math: In telephone-traffic engineering, one Erlang, the known value, is equal to one hour of telephone conversation. Multiply 60 minutes by 60 seconds to get a value that you can apply to an equation.

1 Erlang = 3,600 seconds of telephone conversation

Thus, if you can establish the number of calls on a network, multiply this by the average length of a call and then divide this product by one Erlang, you arrive at the number of Erlangs carried by the network in an hour. The equation looks like this:

$(a \times b) / 3,600 = x$

where a = number of calls, b = average length of call (in seconds), and x = number of Erlangs.

Say that you have a trunk group (a collection of telephone lines) and have established that the number of peak-hour calls to the service is 1,000. After some further analysis, you also determine that the average call time is 120 seconds (two minutes). Now back to the equation:

$(1,000 \times 120) / 3,600 = 35.27$ Erlangs

Thus, your group of lines is carrying 35.27 Erlangs. Translated into lay terms, this means that for the busiest hour, 35 lines in the trunk group were carrying conversations.

Does this mean you now need to have no less than 35 ports (or at least 50) to make sure that every caller is serviced by the equipment? No, you are not that far yet. You have to take blocking into account. This part of the forecasting method is known as Erlang B theory.

Erlang B is the probability theory developed by Erlang to estimate the number of lines needed to carry telephone traffic, assuming that callers will abandon the call if they are not serviced quickly. (There are many other factors to consider, especially if you bring sequencing and hold facilities into the picture. If you want to study this further, a number of books are available that you can consult. The bibliography at the back of this book is a good place to start your search.)

No two enterprises are the same; as such, no two call-processing campaigns or computer telephony projects are the same. Just how many blocked or unserviced calls you feel are tolerable depends on the situation and the application — and the business plan.

For example, if you are planning a sales campaign that incorporates some very costly publicity, you may feel one blocked call in a thousand is the limit, or .1 percent. Alternatively, the sales room manager would freak out if one out of every ten calls to the enterprise is blocked, because he or she may have sales agents waiting for calls and no one can get through. (One Connecticut financial services firm hired a consultant to find out why its blocked-call levels were going through the roof. It was later discovered that the IT department gave staff access to the World Wide Web and someone had found a link to a very graphic home page at Amsterdam's Red Light district.) If your application is not as critical as a sales campaign, however, then one blocked call in ten, or 10 percent, may be acceptable.

With the call-blocking tolerance in percentage terms in hand and armed with the Erlang value you calculated in the preceding exercise, you need to reference the Erlang B Carried-Traffic Table shown in Appendix A, the Computer Telephony Lexicon.

From the table, you can determine that a blocking tolerance of 1 percent requires at least 47 telephone lines for an Erlang value of 35.27 and at least 37 ports for a tolerance of 10 percent. A campaign manager in a call center might opt to install 45 ports just to be "on the safe side." Keep in mind, however, that being on the safe side can be costly.

Now let's discuss some variables.

FORECASTING THE NUMBER OF CALLS IN THE PEAK HOUR

This task is no easy matter, especially when you are not experienced in it, are starting a new campaign for which you have very little data, or are setting up a new voice-processing or voice-response system. Enterprises throughout the world engage the services of their telephone companies, which can provide such data. The telco can keep tabs on the inbound call traffic and the blocking levels on your group of lines.

Often, however, this service does not come cheap, and many telcos do not have the staff or equipment to provide you with more advanced data, such as peak hours and calling patterns. Some companies may also refuse such requests from small businesses. In many parts of the world, this data is unavailable, period. This last problem was the case in South Africa before the telephone department was privatized.

In telemarketing campaigns or call-center applications, the number of calls per hour varies according to factors such as extent of paid-for publicity, media coverage, nature of the product being offered, application, and so on. In voice-processing or voice-response applications, forecasting the number of calls per hour is even more difficult because so many unknown factors can influence the calling patterns.

Trying to pinpoint the peak hour so that you can count the calls manually is no cinch, either — believe me, I know. I have analyzed informal call centers where the hour after the doors open in the morning is the busiest period. Other organizations experience their busiest hour after 2 p.m. International or national call centers may experience their busiest hour as late as midnight or in the early hours of the morning, depending on the location of the site.

In voice mail applications, I have found the busiest hours for the voice-processing ports are when staff are least likely to be at their desks. (Makes sense, right?) Often that includes just before and just after the enterprise opens for business, when workers are either standing in line at the coffee machines, in meetings, or settling down for the day ahead; during the lunch break; just before and just after close of business; late at night; between 10 a.m. and 11 a.m.; and between 2:30 p.m. and 3:30 p.m. (usually the busiest period). Again, these busy periods naturally vary from enterprise to enterprise; you also have to factor in that IVR systems vary from application to application.

In South Africa, as you learned earlier, during a thunderstorm, calls disappear like a pack of baboons under a leopard attack. Calls return with a vengeance when the clouds clear. In southern Florida, the lightning capital of America, I expected the same phenomenon. But the storms do not last as long. While doing a needs analysis for a huge shoe manufacturer, we found it easy to pin down the busiest hour of the month. After paychecks were handed out, callers would flock to the phones and dial up Accounting to clarify their deductions.

Trying to influence calling patterns also achieves mixed results. My travel agent client, Jan, advertises her special offers in the newspapers on Friday afternoons and Saturday mornings. In her ad, she advises people to call between 8 and 10 a.m. on Saturday morning. Do you think we could determine which hour or hours would be the busiest? Not so. The busiest hour was after 7 p.m. on Friday evening. People don't always read the whole ad, and others hope that they will catch an agent in the office "on the off-chance."

For the sake of this exercise, let's pretend that you received 1,000 calls during the busiest hour.

DETERMINING THE AVERAGE CALL LENGTH

Don't despair. This part of the exercise is a little easier than forecasting the number of calls in the peak hour. Call center and telemarketing campaign planners work with scripts that require them to know the average length of a call. Inbound sales calls — say, those in response to an ad on TV — can be pretty uniform. Agents have scripts and software to help them complete a call within predetermined parameters.

Voice-processing, automated attendant, IVR, and audiotext services are a little harder to determine the average call length for, but you at least have something to work with: the predetermined call paths and human-computer interaction. You know how long it takes to enter an extension number or listen to voice mail or enter a password, so you can do a little caller simulation.

Let's take computer telephonist and automated attendant services as an example. First, we list the most common types of callers in groups. These might be the following:

1 = Calls abandoned at the company greeting

2 = Calls abandoned after dialing an extension and receiving voice mail

3 = Calls that go through filtering and routing menus

4 = Calls that access the company directory

5 = Calls in which you leave a voice message

6 = Calls to retrieve voice mail (including message delivery)

Now you need to apply an average call length to each group. This task is the easy part. You'll need a stopwatch or regular watch with a second hand (and a little time). Call the CT system and time each call group to determine its average call length.

At this point, you may ask yourself, how this can be done for a company that has no computer telephony system? The answer is that the consultant or vendor will usually do this with you, and they do this with a demo system or during the trial or evaluation period before you buy the hardware. The following list represents the average call length, measured in seconds, for each type of call:

1 = 5	4 = 300
2 = 45	5 = 200
3 = 300	6 = 300

Now you need to forecast the number of callers that each group will have. Some estimates will be wild guesses; other estimates will be more educated. Sometimes there's just no way to predict what ends up happening. For example, I remember installing my first voice mail system and computer telephonist. The client was Comprehensive Property Services, and the systems were two of the first systems ever installed in South Africa. After planning for weeks, we finally went live. On the first day, every caller abandoned the call at the greeting, much to my embarrassment. I had believed the callers would take to the system like fleas to dogs. (I never assumed how callers would react again.)

To illustrate a similar situation, in the example that follows, you deal with a typical installation in technology-savvy but often impatient New York City. The sample size is 100 calls. The following list shows how that sample broke down into the call groups listed previously:

1 =	3 callers	4 =	5 callers
2 =	25 callers	5 =	40 callers
3 =	15 callers	6 =	12 callers

Now, follow these steps to figure out the parameters of the system that will meet your needs.

1. Determine the average call length. The following list shows the average call length for each group. From this list, you then total the results for each group and divide by the sample call size.

Group	Calls	Length	Total (seconds)
1	3	5	15
2	25	45	1,125
3	15	300	4,500
4	5	300	1,500
5	5	200	1,000
6	12	300	3,600

Total call duration = **11,740**

Average call length = **117 seconds**

2. Using these values, you can now determine the Erlang value:

$$(1,000 \times 117) / 3,600 = 32.50 \text{ Erlangs}$$

3. Next, determine the blocking tolerance level (people who don't connect). Because this is New York City, a tolerance level of 10 percent should be acceptable.

4. Determine the number of ports. Using the Erlang B table again in Appendix A, a tolerance of 10 percent against an Erlang value of 32.36 (the closest value) indicates that you need a 32-port CT system. If the tolerance value was 1 percent, you would need 44 ports.

You may have noticed that in determining the call types, the calls to retrieve voice mail are included in these groups. Sometime back, when I knew less about CT than I do now, I estimated the number of inbound ports needed and then added four or eight ports for delivering messages. Using this method, frequently an extra board stood idle all day. When measuring Erlangs, all you need to do is lump all message retrievals into one group and possibly increase the average length of this call to compensate for tying up the port when dialing and performing call-progress analysis (see Chapter 4).

A word of advice about the sample lists provided in the preceding example: Applications vary from site to site, city to city, and country to country, so you need to draw up lists that apply to *your* situation and conditions, not mine or someone else's. You may find that average call lengths double in your country due to factors that, for example, do not exist in the U.S. Here's a short list that elaborates on how factors can vary.

✦ **Rotary detection.** Boy, does this task chew up ports. As discussed earlier, the systems have to listen to the clicks (pulses-per-second) and work much harder to detect the digit than with tone detection. Pulse-to-tone converters do not help much either.

✦ **Voice recognition.** Voice recognition calls may vary in length from person to person and nation to nation (see Chapter 6).

✦ **Computer telephony hardware and software (poor products, discussed later in this chapter).** Some systems on the market do not do such a good job of detecting touch tone, cutting though prompts, and integrating with the PBX. The hang-up detection factor is so important that it earns a section on its own in the next section of this chapter.

✦ **Telephony conditions in the external environment.** One factor is noisy telephone circuits (which lowers the success rate of detecting touch tones). Many others exist, such as weather conditions and so on.

✦ **User's culture, behavior, and acceptance.** Some cultures may find that human-computer dialog still goes against their grain, and users will take a long time to accept and work with voice mail features. In situations where most of the staff has never used voice mail, the average call length might be tenfold that of the company across the street.

HANG-UP DETECTION

Many computer telephony buyers get lost in the jungle of features and options and seldom consider *hang-up detection*. Hang-up detection is one of the most important factors to be aware of when deploying computer telephony systems. The rule of thumb to follow is that a computer telephony system, upon getting a signal from the PBX or the exchange (either as loop-current drop or a hang-up signal), must reset the line to provide access to another call within five seconds. Anything longer will push your port requirements through the roof and squeeze your wallet.

I am fanatical about hang-up detection. When I design computer telephony software, I make sure that the software engineers really put a great deal of effort into this feature. In countries like South Africa, the telephone company typically does not provide you with a loop-current off/on transition (a drop). In this case, the CT system relies on a hang-up signal.

At first, a basic algorithm using the Rhetorex DSP cards and its patented AccuCall technology had us resetting lines in less than five seconds. Eventually we got it down to three seconds. But that time was still not good enough when compared to the rapid reset that you can achieve in the U.S. when the loop-current status changes. Eventually, one of our smart engineers came up with a formula to detect the hang-up signal and reset the line in under a second. Often, it took less time to detect the signal, analyze it, confirm it as a hang-up, and reset the line.

When upgrading a blocked 16-port system with the new "blitz-reset" software, however, we were stunned to see the port requirements drop to 12 ports. During the slower periods, port requirements further dropped to 8 ports. The real advantage was in the financial area: This decrease represented between a $5,000 and $10,000 savings in hardware and software license fees. The savings could be even more with custom-made IVR software.

Hang-up detection and line reset should be an instant and automatic function of your computer telephony system. An exchange or PBX that provides loop-current drop after a call is abandoned can make this capability happen. Often, as mentioned in Chapter 4, you don't get a loop-current transition or other signal, just silence. The CT software then has to switch to a time-out function, which, as discussed in Chapters 4 and 5, cannot be set to less time than it takes for two humans to enjoy some silence in their conversation.

Keeping that fact in mind, this situation is a less-than-happy one. The CTI-link between NetWare or Windows Telephony Services (TSAPI and TAPI) and the PBX, however, changes things for the better because the PBX can alert the telephony server at the exact moment when a caller abandons the call.

Never invest in a system that requires the caller to enter a terminating digit in order to reset the port. I have never encountered any person, and I don't think I ever will, who has the time to press the star or pound sign at the end of a call. After a caller is done, he or she just drops the line.

The best place to look for evidence of a user-affected terminating digit is the flow-chart documentation. Go through the documentation of the proposed system and check for such a requirement. If it exists, make sure that this form of hang-up detection is not the only type employed. A time-out function should be located somewhere in the picture.

COST JUSTIFICATION

Let's talk about cost justification, return-on-investment, and amortization. In the 1,000-call per hour scenario described earlier, you determined the need for a 32-port system. Do you think that sounds right? After all, 32 ports is a rather big system. It may require two workstations; big hard disks; double the components; and at least eight analog, voice-processing cards or two expensive, digital, voice-processing cards (as well as their very expensive interface cards). And don't forget to add software costs and the consultant's fee.

The big investment here could be at least $20,000 in software alone. Add hardware costs, and you have at least another $10,000. Depending on the country, this system is proving to be an expensive one. On the foreign currency U.S. dollar exchange rate, this financial burden could equal as much as $100,000!

But wait; there's more. We spoke of 1,000 calls in the peak hour. I've managed a number of systems in which 1,000 calls in the peak hour extrapolated out to at least 5,000 calls a day. That's a heck of a load. A thousand calls in an hour, need I tell you, is about 16 callers every minute. That type of call traffic requires at least five human telephonists in the peak hour, just taking calls. The following is a description of what it takes to gainfully employ five telephonists:

First, you need a manager who can be used to switch calls during a low complement period. This person's job includes commissioning telephonists; managing their worksheets and duty roster; acting as a liaison with IT, PBX technicians, sales agents, computer telephony consultants, and telephone companies; taking complaints; counseling highly pressured telephonists; keeping switch rooms well-stocked with coffee, tea, cookies (U.S.), and biscuits (U.K.); getting involved in training, strategic vision, and learning processes; and more.

Do not plan on loading down this person with menial office work, such as running off some photocopies. This guy or gal will be a high-powered executive. To manage five telephonists, his or her salary burden could be between $36,000 and $50,000 for a medium to large firm, perhaps even more with the big public companies.

Next, you need to employ five telephonists to occupy your workstations and consume huge volumes of coffee every day. The costs involved here all add up to a great deal of cash and time (you can work out the salary and staff burden yourself). Then you have to factor in other expenses, like telephone equipment (such as consoles), worker's compensation, fatigue, and the general health of the employees. When does the system pay for itself? In two months, three, maybe four?

Right now, you may be thinking, "Now, just wait a minute, Jeff. Right at the very outset, you told us that computer telephony is not to be used to cut staff." That's right. This tenet is one I have repeated often. The most important rule to follow in the new frontiers of IT and CT is that you should never fire staff just to replace them with machines. So what's this about salary burdens and so on?

Well, I am not going to launch into the subject of personnel or resource management. But I will cover bases here and add that a well thought-out retirement program, reassignment, or internal placement or recruitment program, or other preferred form of compensation must be introduced if you want to provide your system with backup (and you'll need to).

Finally, consider again what I have discussed in the earlier chapters about investing in systems that bring enterprise-wide gains in productivity, competitive advantages, and tools to resist the total onslaught from the opposition. Do you need any more convincing from me? I didn't think so.

ENGAGING THE SUPPORT OF THE TELEPHONISTS

Though you may no longer need five telephonists, you still need back-up, perhaps even just one individual who has turned what was once a full-time job into an "area of responsibility." This individual needs careful induction and training in the new computer telephony system. No other individual in the enterprise will appreciate more the power and increase in productivity and harmony that computer telephony can bring to the chaotic life of the telephonist. But if the system fouls up, you're in trouble.

Remember the anecdote of the telephonist whose life was bliss until the voice mail stopped working? She wanted to have the product thrown out when all that was wrong was that the system lacked the necessary number of ports to handle the call traffic. The vendor who installed the system and the IT staff who manages it now had an enemy in their camp.

I have experienced this unpleasant situation on a number of occasions. In the beginning, the telephonist stands by your side, acting as your lieutenant by supplying the motivation for purchasing CT equipment or by helping to create an enterprise-wide strategy for using the CT system. But when CT systems begin to quiver and quake, this person is the first one to feel the tremors. Thus, I believe that the telephonist needs to understand the technology more than he or she currently does and join with IT in achieving system objectives.

When the other IT systems go down, such as when the network crashes, or the application or print server goes off-line, the IT department feels the impact and bears the brunt of the fall-out. But when computer telephony systems don't work, the call load comes pouring down on the telephonists.

As a result, these valuable members need to be involved more in the CT systems and should, if qualified, contribute to the business-planning sessions. They'll have important input for logistics and planning.

Seeking the input of the telephonists at every level of a computer telephony project also is important. These individuals need to understand the reasons behind project decisions; they should have selective access to the business plan components that deal with the key management entities and the supporting IT systems.

More than that, the telephonist can be part of the team that assists members of the enterprise with a configuration or feature problem when IT gurus are unavailable. For example, a telephonist should know how to access voice messaging, use the e-mail or GUI-based messaging packages, transfer calls, set up conferencing, and more.

If your telephonists do not understand the objectives, appreciate the technology, or are kept in the dark, telephonists can become your worst enemy. Instead, the telephonists should be your best friends, even your champions of computer telephony. They also can give you more needed feedback, because often users feel more comfortable talking to them about the system. You need to make sure that you have telephonists on your side.

COMMISSIONING CHAMPIONS AND EDUCATING THEM

An important strategy in successful computer-telephone integration is commissioning *champions* and educating them. As with all IT systems, you need to designate people within the IT ranks to take on the responsibility of maintaining and managing computer telephony systems in the enterprise. A large enterprise should have several people trained on computer telephony technology.

IT departments take on computer-science degree earners, engineers, and data- and information-processing experts. During their tenures, you probably have sent them out for vocational or continued training, such as how to implement and manage networks, servers, routers, workstations, security, and more. You now have to do this for computer telephone integration.

Consider the alternative. Over the years, CTI and system management has been exclusively delegated to value-added resellers and external experts and suppliers, such as PBX companies or voice mail sellers, often to the detriment of the enterprise. If you use these entities as your CT champions, often under hefty service contracts that do not get renewed, and the systems you install fall into disrepute or are put out of commission, the VAR will not return to keep your project alive. Instead, you'll finally end up with a situation similar to the one Rubber Pencils found itself in. This legal firm determined the need for a voice mail system and contracted us for consulting. But we discovered a voice mail system already sitting in its basement, where it had remained unused for several years.

Another reason to have an in-house CT champion is that computer telephony systems are no longer islands of technology that users try out as an afterthought. Rather, these systems are integrated with the enterprise information network and are intrinsically part of all work processes. Computer telephony systems run on operating systems like NetWare and Windows NT. You have to integrate computer telephony systems with other servers on the network, with users' workstations, with applications, with mainframes and legacy systems, and more.

As a result, the new wave of computer telephony requires a new breed of IT engineers. These people have to learn about telephony, switching, voice processing, call processing, and more, and, at the same time, have a wealth of knowledge that covers general networking.

UP AND RUNNING

Many debates have been raging in the media about the reliability of the new models of computer telephony, particularly the ones that involve large LAN integrations (see Chapter 5). Implementing a CT system that requires a LAN integration can be a daunting task, but not installing the system places added pressure on the private telephone system, so despite its complexity, the task is worth the effort. The difficulty of such an implementation has led many IT executives and LAN managers to take a step back to observe what others are doing and the levels of success they are enjoying with LAN integration. Nevertheless, I believe that some computer telephony is far

better than no computer telephony. To successfully commission a computer telephony system, I suggest the following strategies (this list is by no means complete; it's
just food for thought):

✦ Hire experts.

✦ Invest in proven computer telephony products.

✦ Make sure your PBX is up to it.

✦ If shy, try.

✦ Have a recovery plan.

✦ Install redundant systems.

HIRE EXPERTS

Computer telephony systems are complex. Rather than learn the hard way, it makes
sense to commission the services of an expert consultant or vendor who can bring
knowledge and expertise to the people charged with computer telephony systems in
the enterprise. Once decisions have been made with this person (or group of people)
as to which products to acquire, this person can help with installation, implementation, commission training, and learning processes.

Hiring an independent consultant is a good idea because many systems are on the
market. They have many features, and they all have their particular strengths and
weaknesses. Based on a knowledge of your needs (as a result of needs synthesis or
requirements analysis), a consultant can act as a buffer between the enterprise and
eager salespeople trying to get their products chosen for the project.

But how do you know that you have an expert CT consultant in the first place? The
following list is a starting point in your search for the ideal consultant (I am not going
to talk about degrees and formal education; only experience counts when dealing with
mission-critical applications):

1. Hire a person with a knowledge of software engineering. The consultant does
   not have to be a programmer, but he or she should be able to spot poor
   products (no matter what the operating system) or those rushed to market.
   With the GUI featuring more and more in the computer telephony picture, a
   well-designed application for the desktop is as important as the telephone
   user interface. With a good knowledge of software engineering, setup, and
   support, the consultant will be able to help and train people in the installation
   and CTI process.

2. Hire a person with a knowledge of networking (LAN integration and engineering). Again, you do not have to go overboard here and retain a $1,000-per-
   hour guru. But the consultant should have a broader knowledge of LAN

protocols, network hardware, network operating systems, and more than your average CNE. For example, it may seem like a trivial matter to remember to prevent the earlier versions of NetWare from sending messages to remote clients. When a computer telephony system is attached to the network as a client, a single message sent to the machine can bring down the system and wipe out 12 to 24 callers in the process. Try explaining that to the CEO. It's a small detail, but only the consultant, one with bitter experience, knows about such problems.

3. Make sure that the consultant has a more than cursory knowledge of telephony. He or she should know about in-band and out-of-band signaling, loop current and telephones, and PBX systems and ACD units. Although not essential, it pays to have a consultant who has rapport with PBX and telephony technicians, engineers, and telecommunications authorities.

4. Get references . . . and check them. If the consultant has a good list of clients and comes recommended by known companies, you will feel only that much more secure in your hiring or retainer plans.

5. Hire a person with leadership qualities. He or she should be in a position to instantly take charge of a situation that may be going wrong (if required to do so by the IT executive). A good consultant should be trusted to make important decisions when IT staff, still green with the new technology, call. Nothing is worse than a consultant who gets a call from the CEO about a major problem with the system and then says "Switch it off for now, and I will check with the vendor." No system should have to be switched off because the consultant was clueless as to the problem or was incapable of making a decision to keep things running smoothly.

6. Hire a person who is assertive and authoritative. You cannot afford to have a computer telephony product go sour because the consultant let "small things" slide. There are no "small things" in computer telephony. A small software patch that *should have been installed* can mean the difference between life and death of the system. The CT consultant must make sure that the vendor has taken care of everything. If a problem occurs with a port, action must be taken immediately. If the vendor says "Give us a week to get you another voice board," I say "Sorry, my client's business depends on this system. I want a service replacement within 24 hours."

7. The consultant should be available 24 hours a day, 7 days a week. If the consultant cannot be available in person, the consulting firm should hire its own technical staff so that it can send out someone day or night to help fix a problem. A computer telephony problem cannot wait until morning. The CEO may be trying to get voice mail from two continents away, and it is frustrating and damaging to call the system and hear ring-no-answer (RNA).

INVEST IN PROVEN COMPUTER TELEPHONY PRODUCTS

Many products are available, so why take chances on a new product that has no track record? This is a difficult statement for me to make because I know, as the head of a software company, how difficult it is to build an installed base. However, because of the mission-critical nature of computer telephony projects, a new kid on the block will find it difficult to establish an installed base, even if the product is great.

Check with the vendors and the manufacturers about their installed base and existing users. Then call the users, and see how they feel about the product. Call their system and get a feel for it from the telephone user interface. Try to go over to the company and ask if you can see the system in action. Talk to the telephonists at this company. The consultant will usually have clients that won't mind you coming over. The vendors can arrange this also. Then talk to the existing user's IT staff.

Several people have asked me for my opinion on developing computer telephony applications in-house, as opposed to investing in turnkey systems or commercially available products. One large company I consult for employs about five software engineers, and they, too, asked this question. The advice I give you here is the advice of both a computer telephony consultant/reseller and the head of a company involved in computer telephony, telecommunications and office automation software development for several years.

Recent years have seen a number of visual development tools that cater to the new era of computer telephony. The market leader is Visual Voice, a telephony software development toolkit produced by Stylus Innovation out of Cambridge, Massachusetts. (Stylus is a division of LAN product giant Artisoft, Inc.) Stylus produces a collection of computer telephony software components for applications that run on the Windows operating systems. Of particular note is its collection of 32-bit ActiveX components that "embody" the core computer telephony functionality of Microsoft's TAPI code, and the interface code to the functionality of the key computer-telephony hardware components, such as Dialogic Corporation's voice-processing boards. David Krupinksy, Marketing Director for Visual Voice, has kept me "fed" with components for some time to provide hands-on visual development for this book.

The undeniable strengths of toolkits such as Visual Voice are the rapid applications development and the rapid prototyping that you can achieve with them. The time it takes to get applications to market or deploy computer telephony software has been reduced, in some cases, from years to months and even to weeks. The toolkits are also extendible. The Visual Voice toolkit works with the C/ C++, Visual C++, Delphi and Visual Basic development environments . . . any development environment that supports Microsoft's ActiveX (Microsoft's nerds say the "X" is silent) technology.

The Visual Voice tools do not need a plug from me — this product has several awards. No computer telephony software developer should be without it. You can connect with Stylus on the World Wide Web at http://www.stylus.com or http://www.artisoft.com or point your browser to my computer telephony "lounge" at http://www.wizzkids.com/ctlounge.

If you have a large, internal programming department and need to do some tailored computer telephony software development, then these toolkits are the place to start. However, telephony and computer-telephone integration, no matter what type of development platform, toolkits, visual development environment, or API you use, remains highly complex fields. The best computer telephony software has taken years to evolve into the feature-rich and reliable products that they are.

I view these tools as more for the computer telephony development industry than as tools for the corporate developer. Developing computer telephony systems and writing code that caters to mission-critical situations and support highly complex telephony and telecom environments is not trivial software engineering. The learning curve and resources required to create a full-featured call- and voice-processing system would be too expensive for most corporations, and the company would lose the benefits and empowering capabilities of computer telephony while internal software developers struggled to test, debug, and prove applications.

Most importantly, you have to remember that the computer telephony system is your electronic doorway into the enterprise. You want to be sure it has strong hinges and was constructed by an experienced carpenter.

As such, I recommend leaving mission-critical computer telephony applications — such as voice-processing, computer telephonists, IVR, and audiotext systems — to established, proven products that have installed bases (some as many as 30,000 sites). You wouldn't write an operating system to replace Windows NT, NetWare, or OS/2, would you? The same goes for CT software.

Computer telephony software, however, also has entered the new era of Lego-like software, and it can be extended through programming interfaces and plug-ins. *Computer Telephony* magazine's Publisher and Editor-in-chief, Harry Newton, calls this "Erector-set Computer Telephony" (see Chapter 1). A beneficial strategy is to invest in the core computer telephony server engines (the software that sits atop the DSP voice-processing cards, switching cards, recognition cards, and telephone interface cards) and then build supporting software around these systems. The new era of CTI has opened opportunities for corporations to develop applications for the computer telephony desktop that do not interfere with the essential telephone call services. These opportunities include screen pops (see Chapter 5), dialers, and computer-telephony-enabled database management systems.

MAKE SURE YOUR PBX IS UP TO IT

The PBXs designed to work with computer telephony systems are a new breed. Most of what is currently installed was not built with computer telephony applications in mind. Several thousand calls an hour is a big load for a PBX to take. Add to that several message-waiting lamps being switched on and off by voice-processing ports that think the PBX is a robust ACD switch, as well as a continuous stream of users accessing voice mail — the PBX may just say "enough" and keel over.

You wouldn't think that a PBX could break down and stop working. They are reliable devices. They are designed to take a lot more than they typically get. But the modern PBX is only as good as its software, and the software depends on the CPU and the memory available to it. I have seen several PBXs simply run out of memory and choke when calls to the switch literally double during the installation of a messaging system or computer telephonist.

Computer telephony systems also reflect the flaws in the switching equipment. For example: When you needed to forward a call to a fellow worker, did it ever occur to you how many rings the switch will send to your telephone before diverting? Probably not. But when converting to a voice-processing system, suddenly everyone is counting the rings. I have encountered many switches that sometimes ring three times, perhaps four, and then once in every ten or so calls they seem to just forget that coverage is in place.

You need to talk to your PBX vendor or interconnect company. It will have suggestions for resolving such problems and can put you in touch with other companies who have commissioned computer telephony systems. Refer to Chapter 8 and the phased implementation. Make sure the PBX or switch does what it's supposed to. The PBX manufacturer may advise against certain features when you explain the application, may suggest a new or different switch, or may provide you with parameters and guidelines. The manufacturer also may throw you out of its offices.

IF SHY, TRY

Many popular systems can be installed with as little as two ports. Rather than hold off on a project because it's over-budget, it will pay to install a minimal system and make it available to a select group of workers who will benefit the most from the system. Then you can gradually add more voice-processing hardware, computer components, software modules, and so on. I discussed the concept of plug-ins and modularity. That concept works well in the deployment of new systems. I advise against leap-frogging from demo system to demo system. I have some clients who followed this strategy. Years later, they still have no strategic plan or objective for the integration of computer telephony.

For example, my good friend and leading computer telephony guru Gil Caplan installed a CT system in a bank several years ago as a demo system. I frequently visited this site to help Gil maintain the system and train the more than 1,000 employees in the bank's work force. Despite project support from several departments, the IT manager has never been able to get the chairman to approve purchasing the system. The reason is simple: the chairman hates voice mail, and as long as he runs the show, the bank will "never" buy a computer telephony system.

When it came time to pack up the model system, however, several departments refused to let us tear it down — they were too attached to it. The chairman still refuses to give in, however, so the IT department found a way around it — they've been renting the system from Gil for almost three years now. With the total amount of rent they have paid thus far (which doesn't attract the attention of the chairman or require his approval), this company could have bought three CT systems. I guess the chairman also hates spreadsheet software.

HAVE A RECOVERY PLAN

The recovery plan is something you must formulate long before you go live with a computer telephony system. What if the system crashes? Systems do crash. If a computer fails for some reason, you're going to lose callers. The problem is not whether these people call back. Most are forgiving and may think that the telephone network has something to do with the why they were cut off (although I am not suggesting that it's okay to lose calls). The problems, however, start when callers try to call back and get nothing but RNA.

If the computer telephony system goes down, especially one that is processing callers as a computer telephonist system (auto-attendant), you need to be able to revert to the old way almost instantaneously. This means having to reprogram the switch to pass calls to the telephonist's console or to certain workstations in the enterprise. Fortunately, many PBX systems enable you to recover the calls to the consoles rapidly.

A good plan is to install coverage on the computer telephony extensions that will bring calls to the telephonist's console in the event of failure. Failure of the CT system will result in RNA for about three rings, but calls will at least get answered. Staff will no doubt have to know what to do when this happens because you don't want to ruin things by keeping people on hold indefinitely or cutting people off inadvertently.

If possible, setting all voice-processing ports to on-hook is a good idea. That way, calls to the "sick" system jump directly to the extension set up to take the runover.

Your recovery plan also includes installing real-time monitoring and reporting systems. Why wait for a system to go down or for the CEO to go berserk or for faxes to start rolling in to be notified that the computer telephony system is off-line? By scanning the reports generated by the computer telephony system and routing the data into a monitoring application, you can ensure that you are updated every five minutes, if necessary, that the system is still processing. At least if the computer telephony system goes down, your software can report the delay between two points in time or that no activity has occurred for a certain length of time.

To achieve this feature, I installed a product that automatically alerts my pager should a critical event occur at the computer telephony system. As a result, whenever a client called to report a problem, they were told that "He is already on his way."

INSTALL REDUNDANT SYSTEMS

Large systems, from 12 ports onwards, should be split over two or more computers and commissioned as redundant systems from the word go. It is relatively easy to coordinate and recover hunting lines coming to the dead system from the central exchange or your PBX and then cover them to the "live" system. When the live system maxes out, the overflow can go to the telephonists or to other workers as explained earlier. At least you have 50 percent or more of your system up and running.

Keep in mind that redundancy in computer telephony is much harder to achieve than you might think. For starters, without mirroring (two or more hard disks that are kept identical in content and file allocation), all systems will need to access to a common database and message storehouse. The reason is that you cannot afford to have message files split across two computers. In this situation, a caller will call the live system only to find that his or her message exists on the dead system. If you cannot keep messages and database files on a network server — and often there are good reasons not to — you will need a real-time mirroring process taking place.

It also pays to invest in known and reliable PC components (if the vendor does not supply these). This step can go a long way to ensuring that systems stay up and running. Often, the power supply on the clone PCs is what brings the whole computer house crashing down on you.

SUMMARY

So now you know a little bit more about computer telephony. Perhaps the picture I have painted throughout this book is a little different from the ones you may have been reading about in the popular computer press and even in some IT journals claiming to have expert information. Generally speaking, computer telephony integration is a challenge, even to the most learned of IT gurus and network engineers. But with common sense, it can be fun and rewarding.

Remember, too, that this technology is valuable to any enterprise. It has incredible ability to empower the enterprise, becoming a force that can be successfully employed to ward off competitive threat. In closing, I refer you again to the wise words of Peter Drucker, quoted from *Managing With Results*.

No book will ever make a wise man out of a donkey or a genius out of an incompetent. The foundation in a discipline, however, gives to today's competent physician a capacity to perform well beyond that of the ablest doctor of a century ago, and enables the outstanding physician of today to do what that medical genius of yesterday could hardly have dreamt of. No discipline can lengthen a man's arm. But it can lengthen his reach by hoisting him on the shoulders of his predecessors. Knowledge organized in a discipline does a good deal for the merely competent; it endows him with some effectiveness. It does infinitely more for the truly able; it endows him with excellence.

Part IV

Appendixes

Appendix A: Computer Telephony Lexicon

Appendix B: Recommended Reading
and Bibliography

COMPUTER TELEPHONY LEXICON

This Lexicon is by no means complete. There are thousands of terms, acronyms, definitions, and so on in the telecommunications industry, and it would be difficult (if not impossible) to list all of them. The entries that follow here are, however, the ones you most likely will come across in the computer telephony industry. For a much more complete reference, I refer you to Newton's Telecom Dictionary.

ADPCM — Adaptive Differential Pulse Code Modulation. ADPCM is a method of compressing data. It calculates the difference between two consecutive speech samples in PCM-coded voice signals (see also *PCM*).

AGC — Automatic Gain Control. This is a voice-processing algorithm that normalizes the volume level of recorded data to –6dBm. In telephony, it refers to the technique of automatically raising and lowering a transmitted signal to keep volume levels in a conversation even.

Analog — Analog comes from the word analogous, which means "similar to." To understand the term better, think of an analog watch; the hands that turn clockwise represent, or are "similar to," the passing of time. The digital time-piece does not represent a comparison for the passing of time; it is a counter of seconds, minutes, and hours.

Analog Transmission — Analog transmission means that the amplitude of the transmitted signal varies over a continuous range. It also refers to the transmission of analog signals without regard to the content. In other words, although the signal may be amplified, there is no immediate attempt to extract data from the signal.

ASI — Analog Station Interface. The circuitry that interfaces with an analog telephony station.

ATI — Analog Trunk Interface. The circuitry that interfaces with an analog telephone trunk.

Audio Frequencies — This term refers to the range of frequencies that can be heard by the human ear (see Chapters 4 and 5).

Audio Messaging Interchange Specification (AMIS) — AMIS is a set of standards that address the problem of how different voice-messaging systems from various vendors can network or internetwork. AMIS enables these systems to share messages. An AMIS-compliant computer telephony system will thus enable you to install systems in a number of locations and conduct message interchange between the systems.

Auto-attendant — This refers to a computer telephony service or system (short for automated attendant) that stands in for a live telephonist. The term is problematic for me in Europe and elsewhere outside North America. In Israel, for example, I did some consulting for the King Solomon Hotel in Eilat. When I explained to the concierge (in my limited Hebrew) what I needed to look at in the PABX room, he brought me the valet. In the U.S., I find that many clients of mine also get confused with the term and thus use "voice mail" as a generic term for all computer telephony systems and services, especially when referring to the automated attendant (and even if it doesn't take voice mail). I thus used the term computer telephonist throughout the book.

Automatic Speech Recognition (ASR) — Automatic speech recognition (ASR) technology reliably recognizes certain human speech, such as discrete numbers and short commands, or continuous strings of numbers, such as a spoken credit-card number. Speaker-independent ASR can recognize a limited group of words (usually numbers and short commands) from any caller. Speaker-dependent ASR can identify a large vocabulary of commands from a specific speaker. Speaker-dependent ASR is popular in password-controlled systems and hands-free work environments (see also *SIR* and *Voice Recognition* below).

BABT — British Approvals Board for Telecommunications. This is the British agency that approves telecommunications equipment.

Basic Rate Interface — BRI. One of two interfaces for ISDNs that refers to the two 64 Kbps B-channels and the 16 Kbps data or D-channel.

Busy — Busy means that a telephone service is in use. You get two busies in telephony. Normal busy refers to the off-hook state of a telephone, which signifies that a connection has been set up between subscriber and the CO. Fast busy refers to the "blocked" state of a network (see Chapters 4, 5, and 17).

Cadence — A repeating cycle. In computer telephony, it refers to the cycle of tones and silence intervals in the audio signal. In the U.S., a ringing tone cadence is typically one second of tone followed by three seconds of silence.

Call Progress Tone — The call progress tone is an audible tone that indicates the progress of a telephone call. Call progress tones include busy tones and ring tone. (See Chapters 4 and 5.)

CCITT — *Cimite Consultatif Internationale de Telegraphique et Telephonique,* or the International Telephone and Telegraph Consultative Committee. This committee sets the international standards for data communications.

CEPT — Conference on European Posts & Telecommunications. This committee sets worldwide standards for data communications.

Channel — In computer telephony (voice processing), a channel is a logical path that is used for voice processing (see also entries for *Port* and *Line* to avoid confusion).

CO — CO stands for central office. This is the telephone company location that houses switching gear and other services for local telephone subscribers. Outside North America, the equivalent term is telephone exchange (or local telephone exchange).

CO Lines — CO Lines are the telephone lines that connect CPE to the telephone company.

Codec — The codec is a device that converts an analog signal into a digital signal and vice versa.

Compression — Compression means reducing the representation of information but not the information itself. Voice data that is recorded and stored at high resolution is referred to as linear and is thus uncompressed. Compression saves transmission time and storage space. For voice-processing purposes, data has to be compressed to PCM or ADPCM (see also *Linear* below).

Conference — The ability to join three or more people in a telephone call. Certain privileges may apply to a conference call. For example, callers may be allowed to listen to the conference but not speak.

CPE — Customer-Premises Equipment or Customer Premise Equipment. CPE is any piece of telecommunications equipment that is not owned by the CO. A PBX or ACD unit is CPE. The telephone set or telephone devices are also CPE.

CSID — CSID means customer subscriber indentification — the remote devices telephone number.

Device — The device is a hardware or logical entity referred to in software engineering or computer telephony language. DOS and Windows view each board as a device, an entity, that can be attached to the computer.

Device Driver — The device driver is a collection of subroutines and data that provides an interface between the operating system and the application that needs to make use of the device or drive it.

Dial Tone — Dial tone is the sound you hear upon lifting the receiver (not when you lift the telephone). The signal usually is transmitted in the frequency range 300Hz to 450Hz. It signifies the "all clear" to dial a number (see Chapter 4).

DID — DID is the capability to directly dial into a company extension without going through a computer telephonist (automated attendant) or a live telephonist.

Digitization — Digitization is the process of converting analog signals into digital representations of that signal.

Digits — Telephony digits:

✦ 0 through 9

✦ A though D

✦ (star)

✦ # ("pound," also known as "hash")

DTMF — DTMF means dual-tone multifrequency. It refers to the tone used in dialing (also known as *touch tone*). When you depress the key or button on the telephony set or click on the button on your "soft-dialer," you are transmitting not one tone but two. This combination of tones is where the term *dual* comes in. Figure A-1 illustrates the frequencies used on the world's touch-tone telephones.

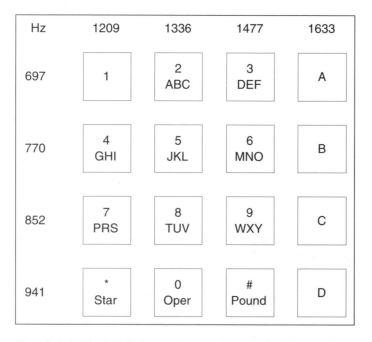

Figure A-1: The DTMF frequencies used on the world's touch-tone telephones. The A, B, C, and D tones are not usually found on common telephone sets.

DTMF Cut-Through — Cut-through refers to the capability of voice processing systems to detect and act on touch tones during the playing of a voice. The tone can either suspend the playing of a file or be used to replay or forward to portions of it. Not only can the digit be detected, but the information can be passed to software control in order to execute a new event, such as transferring to a telephonist.

DTMF-On Time — The length of DTMF tone.

EIN — Enterprise information network. Many IT specialists refer to the enterprise network, which refers to the LAN. In recent years, the flow of enterprise information now traverses interconnecting corporate networks, wide-area networks, secure data links between offices and associated companies, public networks (such as the Internet), and the telephone network. I thus use the term *EIN* to refer to all telecommunications networks used by the enterprise to manage and provide access to information.

Erlang B Carried-Traffic Table — A table used to determine port requirements for telephony and computer telephony services. You need to first determine your Erlang value for the specific group of telephone lines coming into your service (see Chapter 17). A Ports Requirements software suite, which automates the establishment of values through simulation of traffic and usage patterns and automatically calculates port requirements, is available from the author at no charge (see Introduction). See Table A-1 for these Erlang values.

FCC — Federal Communications Commission. The FCC is the U.S. government agency that regulates telecommunications.

Full Duplex — Full duplex is simultaneous, bidirectional communication.

Gain — The volume level of voice files in computer telephony systems.

Glare — Glare is a condition that occurs when both the CPE and CO equipment try to make an outbound call on a line at the same time.

Hook State — Hook state is the state of the telephone line (closed or open) at the CPE.

Hunt/Hunt Group — When you order more than one telephone line from your local provider, an inbound call needs to know which line to call on if the first line is in use. This searching process continues until a free line is found. This process is known as a hunt. If the first line is busy, the call will try a second line; if that's busy, it hunts for a third. The hunt group is a collection of lines that are organized in a fashion required by the enterprise. Hunting and hunt-group management is important in computer telephony because you need to route the inbound calls to the computer telephony ports. Hunt groups can collapse; thus you may think that business is quiet because several ports on the computer telephony system are inactive when really several lines in the hunt group are lost.

Intranet — Enterprise information network (LAN and WANs) technology blended with Internet technology, such as World Wide Web browsers.

ISA — ISA means Industry Standard Architecture (see Chapter 4). It is the standard of IBM's PC bus architecture.

ISDN — Integrated Services Digital Network. This is the international standard for digital telephone sevices.

ISO — The International Standard Organization which sets standards for international data communications.

Isochronous — The term *isochronous* comes from the Greek words "iso" for equal and "chronous" for time and has to do with the time-sensitive transmission of data. Voice and video transmission equipment need isochronous transmission because this method enables the communication to happen in real time. Isochronous transmission delivers voice and video data without detracting from the natural style of conversation taking place between several parties.

KSU — Key Service Unit refers to the switching electronics of a PBX or key system.

Line — The electrical path between the CO and CPE.

Linear Data — Linear data refers to voice data that has been recorded at high resolution.

Line Status — The status of the line at the CO.

Loop Current — Loop current is the current that flows through the analog line from the telephone switch when the telephone is off-hook. Loop current on the digital line means that the CO is off-hook.

Loop Drop — Loop drop is the transition from loop current on to loop current off.

Loop Reversal — Loop reversal refers to the reversal of current flow to provide signaling information to the CPE.

Loop Start — Loop start is a telephone protocol (see Chapter 4).

MF — Multi-Frequency. MF is a type of tone consisting of the ten tones that can be generated by the keypad.

Micro Channel — Micro Channel is the proprietary bus developed by IBM for its PS/2 family of computers.

m-Law — The PCM coding, compression, and expansion standard used in Japan and North America.

MVIP — MVIP refers to a communications standard (hardware and software) that enables the printed circuit boards from different vendors or manufacturers to communicate with each other and exchange information in a PC. The boards communicate over a ribbon bus that connects one card to another card. The MVIP standard was defined by Natural MicroSystems and Mitel with significant input from voice-processing companies such as Rhetorex. Hundreds of companies support the MVIP standard now, and they offer voice-processing cards, switching cards, voice-recognition cards, and fax cards.

Off-Hook — The state of a closed telephone line, which means that current is flowing.

On-/Off-Hook Transition — The transition from on-hook to off-hook status.

PABX — A PBX (private branch exchange) that is automated.

PCM — Pulse Code Modulation. A method of compressing data in which a signal is sampled, and the magnitude of each sample is quantitized and converted into digital code.

PCPM — Programmable Call Progress Monitoring (see Chapters 4 and 5). This refers to the capability of a computer telephony system to monitor the progress of a call under software control. The tones received during PCPM are matched against a table of tones loaded into memory during the normal functioning of a computer telephony system.

Port — In computer telephony and telephony, a port is where you plug in devices.

PPS — Pulses Per Second. The number of pulses transmitted or received in a second (ranges mostly from 9 to 22 in various parts of the world).

PVC — Positive Voice Control. An algorithm (Rhetorex, Inc.) that distinguishes between voice, data, call-progress tones, noise, and silence.

SCSA — Signal Computing System Architecture (SCSA). This is a comprehensive open architecture for providing multiple-user computer telephony services in a client-server environment. An SCSA server offers call control capabilities, such as the capability to make calls, answer calls, route calls, monitor calls, conference calls, and manipulate information (affect the content of calls) over the telephone network. SCSA servers also offer the capability to process various types of media (for example, voice, fax, text, and e-mail) and make conversions between those types of media in order to present the information in a more useful form.

SCSA is composed of a hardware model and a software model. The SCSA Hardware Model defines the interfaces and protocols for a real-time communication bus and a flexible, high capacity, distributed switching fabric.

The SCSA Telephony Application Objects Framework™ (TAO) defines a standard set of software interfaces, protocols, and services that constitute the software model. These interfaces are open, object-oriented, and hardware-independent.

The SCSA TAO Framework contains a standard set of APIs that lets multiple-client applications share a common server and the call control and media-processing resources within the server. Below the API level, the SCSA TAO Framework consists of a service provider framework that includes a standard set of services that manage the server without requiring any application involvement. It also consists of a standard protocol that allows for communications within the server.

Together, these models are designed to offer tight interoperability and extensive functionality, not only for today's computer telephony systems, but also for tomorrow's more complex systems and new technology.

SIR — Speaker independent recognition. SIR refers to the recognition of a vocabulary by a computer telephony system, albeit limited. The speaker can be any caller to the system (see also *Voice Recognition* below).

Spike — A temporary and unexpected signal on the telephone line.

Station — The station (in computer telephony) is the communications equipment at the end of the telephone line. It also refers to the physical connection or integration of this equipment with the PC. The PC as a communications device thus comprises the station.

Talk-Off — Related to cut-through, talk-off occurs when the human voice produces what sounds like a tone-tone digit. This can happen during a recording; the system will recognize the tone and terminate the event.

Telematics — Essentially information exchange (see Chapters 7–12). It refers to information transmission services such as fax and telex.

Telephone Network Interface — The telephone network interface enables computer telephony systems to communicate with specific telephone networks. Calls arriving from telephone networks can be carried on a variety of lines, from analog loop start and DID (DDI) lines to digital T-1, E-1, and primary rate Integrated Services Digital Network (ISDN) lines. Network interfaces also interpret signaling coming across the telephone line, provide data buffering, and include surge protection circuitry.

Telephonist — A species of human (*homo telephono*) that has evolved from the now highly endangered species that only handled the answering, routing process, and message-taking functions of the enterprise-wide telephone service. Since the advent of the voice-processing board and the era of computer telephony, the duties of the telephonist include business administration, word- and data-processing, telephone management, call accounting, PBX maintenance and management, user training, public relations, press liaison, computer telephony scripting, voice recording, data back-up and information archiving, executive assistance, and much more. The earlier species that did nothing more than answering, routing, and message taking will likely be extinct by the end of the decade. Although there are very few left in the world, conservation authorities have no inclination to preserve this animal.

Terminating Tone — A call-progress tone that indicates the termination of a connection. Terminating tones are received with remote CPE, or callers end the communication.

Text-to-Speech — Also known as TTS, the technology for converting text (ASCII) into a synthetic speech. TTS is used in computer telephony, especially interactive voice response, to read the values and information in database tables to callers. TTS is an economical way of giving customers telephone access to information that would be too expensive or impractical to record using voice technology.

TTS also is used to read text in a direct human-computer dialog. A computer can, for example, read a book to a blind person; it also is used to help people who cannot speak.

Tone Detection — Tone detection and processing includes the capability to receive, recognize, and generate specific telephone and network tones. This capability enables a computer telephony application to place a call and monitor its progress. Tones that are processed include busy tones, ringing, dial tones, fax machine tones, modem tones, and MF tones.

Voice Processing — Voice is the fundamental technology at the core of most computer telephony systems. It encompasses both the processing and the manipulation of audio signals in a computer telephony system. Tasks include filtering, analyzing, recording, digitizing, compressing, storing, expanding, and replaying signals.

Voice Recognition — Voice recognition is the technology that enables a computer telephony system to recognize and understand the human voice. Voice-recognition systems require training and are becoming outmoded in favor of speech recognition technology that enables any speaker to have a conversation with a computer (see *ASR*).

VoiceView — VoiceView, a protocol developed by Radish Communications, enables switching between voice and visual data in very rapid sequence during the same call. It is supported by Microsoft Windows 95.

Table A-1   The Erlang B Carried-Traffic Table

Ports	10%	5%	2%	1%	.5%	.1%	Ports	10%	5%	2%	1%	.5%	.1%
4	2.05	1.52	1.09	0.87	0.70	0.44	29	27.05	23.83	21.04	19.49	18.22	15.93
5	2.88	2.22	1.66	1.36	1.13	0.76	30	28.11	24.80	21.93	20.34	19.04	16.58
6	3.76	2.96	2.28	1.91	1.62	1.15	31	29.17	25.77	22.83	21.19	19.86	17.44
7	4.67	3.74	2.94	2.50	2.16	1.58	32	30.23	26.75	23.73	22.05	20.68	18.20
8	5.60	4.54	3.63	3.13	2.73	2.05	33	31.30	27.72	24.63	22.91	21.51	18.97
9	6.55	5.37	4.34	3.78	3.33	2.56	34	32.36	28.70	25.53	23.77	22.34	19.74
10	7.51	6.22	5.08	4.46	3.96	3.09	35	33.43	29.68	26.43	24.64	23.17	20.52
11	8.49	7.08	5.84	5.16	4.61	3.65	36	34.50	30.66	27.34	25.51	24.01	21.30
12	9.47	7.95	6.62	5.88	5.28	4.23	37	35.57	31.64	28.25	26.38	24.85	22.09
13	10.47	8.83	7.41	6.61	5.96	4.83	38	36.64	32.63	29.17	27.25	25.69	22.86
14	11.47	9.73	8.20	7.35	6.66	5.45	39	37.71	33.61	33.08	28.13	26.54	23.65
15	12.48	10.63	9.01	8.11	7.38	6.08	40	38.79	34.60	31.00	29.01	27.38	24.44
16	13.50	11.54	9.83	8.87	8.10	6.72	41	39.86	35.59	31.92	28.89	28.23	25.24
17	14.52	12.46	10.66	9.65	8.83	7.38	42	40.94	36.58	32.84	30.77	29.08	26.04
18	15.55	13.38	11.49	10.44	9.58	8.05	43	42.01	37.57	33.76	31.66	29.94	26.84
19	16.58	14.31	12.33	11.23	10.33	8.72	44	43.09	38.56	34.58	32.54	30.80	27.64
20	17.61	15.25	13.18	12.03	11.09	9.41	45	44.16	39.55	35.61	33.43	31.66	28.45
21	18.65	16.19	14.04	12.84	11.86	10.11	46	45.24	40.54	36.53	34.32	32.52	29.96
22	19.69	17.13	14.90	13.65	12.64	10.81	47	46.32	41.54	37.46	35.21	33.38	30.07
23	20.74	18.08	15.76	14.47	13.42	11.52	48	47.40	42.54	38.39	36.11	34.25	30.88
24	21.87	19.03	16.63	15.29	14.20	12.24	49	48.48	43.54	39.32	37.00	35.11	31.69
25	22.83	19.99	17.50	16.12	15.00	12.97	50	49.56	44.53	40.25	37.90	35.98	32.51
26	23.88	20.94	18.38	16.96	15.80	13.70	51	50.60	45.50	41.20	38.80	36.85	33.30
27	24.94	21.90	19.26	17.80	16.60	14.44	52	51.70	46.50	42.10	39.70	37.72	34.20
28	26.00	22.87	20.15	18.64	17.41	15.18	53	52.80	47.50	43.10	40.60	38.60	35.00

(continued)

Ports	10%	5%	2%	1%	.5%	.1%	Ports	10%	5%	2%	1%	.5%	.1%
54	53.90	48.50	44.00	41.50	39.47	35.60	79	81.10	73.80	67.70	64.40	61.77	57.00
55	55.00	49.50	44.90	42.40	40.35	36.60	80	82.20	74.80	68.70	65.40	62.67	57.80
56	56.10	50.50	45.50	43.50	41.23	37.50	81	83.30	75.80	69.60	66.30	63.57	58.70
57	57.10	51.50	46.80	44.20	42.11	38.80	82	84.40	76.90	70.60	67.20	64.49	59.50
58	58.20	52.60	47.80	45.10	42.99	39.10	83	85.50	77.90	71.60	68.20	65.39	60.40
59	59.30	53.60	48.70	46.00	43.88	40.00	84	86.60	78.90	72.50	69.10	66.29	61.30
60	60.40	54.60	49.60	46.90	44.76	40.80	85	87.70	79.90	73.50	70.00	67.20	62.10
61	61.50	55.60	50.60	47.90	45.64	41.60	86	88.80	80.90	74.50	70.90	68.11	63.00
62	62.60	56.60	51.50	48.80	46.53	42.50	87	89.90	82.00	75.40	71.90	69.02	63.90
63	63.70	57.60	52.50	49.70	47.42	43.30	88	91.00	83.00	76.40	72.80	69.93	64.70
64	64.80	58.60	53.40	50.60	48.31	44.20	89	92.10	84.00	77.30	73.70	70.85	65.60
65	65.80	59.60	54.40	51.50	49.19	45.00	90	93.10	85.00	78.30	74.70	71.75	66.50
66	66.90	60.60	55.30	52.40	50.09	45.80	91	94.20	86.00	79.30	75.60	72.67	67.40
67	68.00	61.60	56.30	53.30	50.98	46.70	92	95.30	87.10	80.20	76.20	73.58	68.20
68	69.10	62.60	57.20	54.30	51.87	47.50	93	96.40	88.10	81.20	77.50	74.49	69.10
69	70.20	63.70	58.20	55.20	52.77	48.40	94	97.50	89.10	82.20	78.40	75.41	70.00
70	71.30	64.70	59.10	56.10	53.66	49.20	95	98.60	90.10	83.10	79.40	76.33	70.90
71	72.40	65.70	60.10	57.00	54.56	50.10	96	99.70	91.90	84.10	80.30	77.24	71.70
72	73.50	66.70	61.00	58.00	55.46	50.90	97	100.8	92.90	85.10	81.20	78.16	72.60
73	74.60	67.70	62.00	58.90	56.35	51.80	98	101.90	93.20	86.00	82.20	79.07	73.50
74	75.60	68.70	62.90	59.80	57.25	52.70	99	103.0	94.20	87.00	83.10	79.99	74.40
75	76.70	69.70	63.90	60.70	58.15	53.50	100	104.1	95.20	88.00	84.10	80.91	75.20
76	77.80	70.80	64.90	61.70	59.05	54.40							
77	78.90	71.80	65.80	62.60	59.96	55.20							
78	80.00	72.80	66.80	63.50	60.86	56.10							

APPENDIX B

RECOMMENDED READING AND BIBLIOGRAPHY

Dialogic Corporation, *Computer Telephony Resource Directory, 1995 Ed.* New Jersey, 1995.

Drucker, Peter F., *Managing For Results,* Pan Books Ltd./William Heinemann Ltd., 1980.

Drucker, Peter F., *Managing in Turbulent Times,* Pan Books Ltd./William Heinemann Ltd., 1980.

Edgar, Bob, *PC Telephony,* Flatiron Publishing, New York, 1995.

Gunton, Tony, *Inside Information Technology: A Practical Guide to Management Issues,* Prentice Hall, New Jersey, 1990.

Inmon, William H., *Managing End User Computing in Information Organizations,* Dow Jones-Irwin, 1986.

Kauffman, Maury, *Computer Based Fax Processing: The Complete Guide to Designing and Building Fax Applications,* Flatiron Publishing, New York, 1994.

Martin, James, *Information Engineering, Book I: Introduction and Principles,* Prentice-Hall, New Jersey, 1989.

Martin, James, *Information Engineering, Book 2: Planning and Analysis,* Prentice-Hall, New Jersey, 1989.

Martin, James, *Information Engineering, Book 3: Design and Construction,* Prentice-Hall, New Jersey, 1989.

Martin, James, *Telecommunications and the Computer, 3rd Ed.* Prentice Hall, New Jersey, 1990.

Newton, Harry, *Newton's Telecom Dictionary, 9th Ed.* Flatiron Publishing, New York, 1995.

Roszak, Theodore, *The Cult of Information,* Pantheon Books, New York, 1986.

Senge, Peter M., *The Fifth Discipline: The Art and Practice of the Learning Organization,* Doubleday, New York, 1990.

Stallings, William, *Data and Computer Communications, 3rd Ed.* Macmillan Publishing Company, New York, 1991.

Tapscott, Don and Caston, Art, *Paradigm Shift: The New Promise of Information Technology,* McGraw-Hill, 1993.

Walton, Richard E., *Up and Running: Integrating Information Technology and the Organization,* Harvard Business School Press, Boston, 1989.

INDEX

NUMBERS

A

(continued)

(continued)

D

S

T

W

NOTES

NOTES

NOTES

NOTES

NOTES

The Fun & Easy Way™ to learn about computers and more!

Windows® 3.11 For Dummies,® 3rd Edition
by Andy Rathbone

ISBN: 1-56884-370-4
$16.95 USA/
$22.95 Canada

Mutual Funds For Dummies™
by Eric Tyson

ISBN: 1-56884-226-0
$16.99 USA/
$22.99 Canada

DOS For Dummies,® 2nd Edition
by Dan Gookin

ISBN: 1-878058-75-4
$16.95 USA/
$22.95 Canada

The Internet For Dummies,® 2nd Edition
by John Levine & Carol Baroudi

ISBN: 1-56884-222-8
$19.99 USA/
$26.99 Canada

Personal Finance For Dummies™
by Eric Tyson

ISBN: 1-56884-150-7
$16.95 USA/
$22.95 Canada

PCs For Dummies,® 3rd Edition
by Dan Gookin & Andy Rathbone

ISBN: 1-56884-904-4
$16.99 USA/
$22.99 Canada

Macs® For Dummies,® 3rd Edition
by David Pogue

ISBN: 1-56884-239-2
$19.99 USA/
$26.99 Canada

The SAT® I For Dummies™
by Suzee Vlk

ISBN: 1-56884-213-9
$14.99 USA/
$20.99 Canada

Here's a complete listing of IDG Books' ...For Dummies® titles

Title	Author	ISBN	Price
DATABASE			
Access 2 For Dummies®	by Scott Palmer	ISBN: 1-56884-090-X	$19.95 USA/$26.95 Canada
Access Programming For Dummies®	by Rob Krumm	ISBN: 1-56884-091-8	$19.95 USA/$26.95 Canada
Approach 3 For Windows® For Dummies®	by Doug Lowe	ISBN: 1-56884-233-3	$19.99 USA/$26.99 Canada
dBASE For DOS For Dummies®	by Scott Palmer & Michael Stabler	ISBN: 1-56884-188-4	$19.95 USA/$26.95 Canada
dBASE For Windows® For Dummies®	by Scott Palmer	ISBN: 1-56884-179-5	$19.95 USA/$26.95 Canada
dBASE 5 For Windows® Programming For Dummies®	by Ted Coombs & Jason Coombs	ISBN: 1-56884-215-5	$19.99 USA/$26.99 Canada
FoxPro 2.6 For Windows® For Dummies®	by John Kaufeld	ISBN: 1-56884-187-6	$19.95 USA/$26.95 Canada
Paradox 5 For Windows® For Dummies®	by John Kaufeld	ISBN: 1-56884-185-X	$19.95 USA/$26.95 Canada
DESKTOP PUBLISHING/ILLUSTRATION/GRAPHICS			
CorelDRAW! 5 For Dummies®	by Deke McClelland	ISBN: 1-56884-157-4	$19.95 USA/$26.95 Canada
CorelDRAW! For Dummies®	by Deke McClelland	ISBN: 1-56884-042-X	$19.95 USA/$26.95 Canada
Desktop Publishing & Design For Dummies®	by Roger C. Parker	ISBN: 1-56884-234-1	$19.99 USA/$26.99 Canada
Harvard Graphics 2 For Windows® For Dummies®	by Roger C. Parker	ISBN: 1-56884-092-6	$19.95 USA/$26.95 Canada
PageMaker 5 For Macs® For Dummies®	by Galen Gruman & Deke McClelland	ISBN: 1-56884-178-7	$19.95 USA/$26.95 Canada
PageMaker 5 For Windows® For Dummies®	by Deke McClelland & Galen Gruman	ISBN: 1-56884-160-4	$19.95 USA/$26.95 Canada
Photoshop 3 For Macs® For Dummies®	by Deke McClelland	ISBN: 1-56884-208-2	$19.99 USA/$26.99 Canada
QuarkXPress 3.3 For Dummies®	by Galen Gruman & Barbara Assadi	ISBN: 1-56884-217-1	$19.99 USA/$26.99 Canada
FINANCE/PERSONAL FINANCE/TEST TAKING REFERENCE			
Everyday Math For Dummies™	by Charles Seiter	ISBN: 1-56884-248-1	$14.99 USA/$22.99 Canada
Personal Finance For Dummies™ For Canadians	by Eric Tyson & Tony Martin	ISBN: 1-56884-378-X	$18.99 USA/$24.99 Canada
QuickBooks 3 For Dummies®	by Stephen L. Nelson	ISBN: 1-56884-227-9	$19.99 USA/$26.99 Canada
Quicken 8 For DOS For Dummies,® 2nd Edition	by Stephen L. Nelson	ISBN: 1-56884-210-4	$19.95 USA/$26.95 Canada
Quicken 5 For Macs® For Dummies®	by Stephen L. Nelson	ISBN: 1-56884-211-2	$19.95 USA/$26.95 Canada
Quicken 4 For Windows® For Dummies,® 2nd Edition	by Stephen L. Nelson	ISBN: 1-56884-209-0	$19.95 USA/$26.95 Canada
Taxes For Dummies,™ 1995 Edition	by Eric Tyson & David J. Silverman	ISBN: 1-56884-220-1	$14.99 USA/$20.99 Canada
The GMAT® For Dummies™	by Suzee Vlk, Series Editor	ISBN: 1-56884-376-3	$14.99 USA/$20.99 Canada
The GRE® For Dummies™	by Suzee Vlk, Series Editor	ISBN: 1-56884-375-5	$14.99 USA/$20.99 Canada
Time Management For Dummies™	by Jeffrey J. Mayer	ISBN: 1-56884-360-7	$16.99 USA/$22.99 Canada
TurboTax For Windows® For Dummies®	by Gail A. Helsel, CPA	ISBN: 1-56884-228-7	$19.99 USA/$26.99 Canada
GROUPWARE/INTEGRATED			
ClarisWorks For Macs® For Dummies®	by Frank Higgins	ISBN: 1-56884-363-1	$19.99 USA/$26.99 Canada
Lotus Notes For Dummies®	by Pat Freeland & Stephen Londergan	ISBN: 1-56884-212-0	$19.95 USA/$26.95 Canada
Microsoft® Office 4 For Windows® For Dummies®	by Roger C. Parker	ISBN: 1-56884-183-3	$19.95 USA/$26.95 Canada
Microsoft® Works 3 For Windows® For Dummies®	by David C. Kay	ISBN: 1-56884-214-7	$19.99 USA/$26.99 Canada
SmartSuite 3 For Dummies®	by Jan Weingarten & John Weingarten	ISBN: 1-56884-367-4	$19.99 USA/$26.99 Canada
INTERNET/COMMUNICATIONS/NETWORKING			
America Online® For Dummies,® 2nd Edition	by John Kaufeld	ISBN: 1-56884-933-8	$19.99 USA/$26.99 Canada
CompuServe For Dummies,® 2nd Edition	by Wallace Wang	ISBN: 1-56884-937-0	$19.99 USA/$26.99 Canada
Modems For Dummies,® 2nd Edition	by Tina Rathbone	ISBN: 1-56884-223-6	$19.99 USA/$26.99 Canada
MORE Internet For Dummies®	by John R. Levine & Margaret Levine Young	ISBN: 1-56884-164-7	$19.95 USA/$26.95 Canada
MORE Modems & On-line Services For Dummies®	by Tina Rathbone	ISBN: 1-56884-365-8	$19.99 USA/$26.99 Canada
Mosaic For Dummies,® Windows Edition	by David Angell & Brent Heslop	ISBN: 1-56884-242-2	$19.99 USA/$26.99 Canada
NetWare For Dummies,® 2nd Edition	by Ed Tittel, Deni Connor & Earl Follis	ISBN: 1-56884-369-0	$19.99 USA/$26.99 Canada
Networking For Dummies®	by Doug Lowe	ISBN: 1-56884-079-9	$19.95 USA/$26.95 Canada
PROCOMM PLUS 2 For Windows® For Dummies®	by Wallace Wang	ISBN: 1-56884-219-8	$19.99 USA/$26.99 Canada
TCP/IP For Dummies®	by Marshall Wilensky & Candace Leiden	ISBN: 1-56884-241-4	$19.99 USA/$26.99 Canada

For scholastic requests & educational orders please call Educational Sales at 1. 800. 434. 2086

FOR MORE INFO OR TO ORDER, PLEASE CALL ▶ 800 762 2974

For volume discounts & special orders please call Tony Real, Special Sales, at 415. 655. 3048

Title	Author	ISBN	Price
The Internet For Macs® For Dummies® 2nd Edition	by Charles Seiter	ISBN: 1-56884-371-2	$19.99 USA/$26.99 Canada
The Internet For Macs® For Dummies® Starter Kit	by Charles Seiter	ISBN: 1-56884-244-9	$29.99 USA/$39.99 Canada
The Internet For Macs® For Dummies® Starter Kit Bestseller Edition	by Charles Seiter	ISBN: 1-56884-245-7	$39.99 USA/$54.99 Canada
The Internet For Windows® For Dummies® Starter Kit	by John R. Levine & Margaret Levine Young	ISBN: 1-56884-237-6	$34.99 USA/$44.99 Canada
The Internet For Windows® For Dummies® Starter Kit, Bestseller Edition	by John R. Levine & Margaret Levine Young	ISBN: 1-56884-246-5	$39.99 USA/$54.99 Canada

MACINTOSH

Title	Author	ISBN	Price
Mac® Programming For Dummies®	by Dan Parks Sydow	ISBN: 1-56884-173-6	$19.95 USA/$26.95 Canada
Macintosh® System 7.5 For Dummies®	by Bob LeVitus	ISBN: 1-56884-197-3	$19.95 USA/$26.95 Canada
MORE Macs® For Dummies®	by David Pogue	ISBN: 1-56884-087-X	$19.95 USA/$26.95 Canada
PageMaker 5 For Macs® For Dummies®	by Galen Gruman & Deke McClelland	ISBN: 1-56884-178-7	$19.95 USA/$26.95 Canada
QuarkXPress 3.3 For Dummies®	by Galen Gruman & Barbara Assadi	ISBN: 1-56884-217-1	$19.99 USA/$26.99 Canada
Upgrading and Fixing Macs® For Dummies®	by Kearney Rietmann & Frank Higgins	ISBN: 1-56884-189-2	$19.95 USA/$26.95 Canada

MULTIMEDIA

Title	Author	ISBN	Price
Multimedia & CD-ROMs For Dummies® 2nd Edition	by Andy Rathbone	ISBN: 1-56884-907-9	$19.99 USA/$26.99 Canada
Multimedia & CD-ROMs For Dummies® Interactive Multimedia Value Pack, 2nd Edition	by Andy Rathbone	ISBN: 1-56884-909-5	$29.99 USA/$39.99 Canada

OPERATING SYSTEMS:

DOS

Title	Author	ISBN	Price
MORE DOS For Dummies®	by Dan Gookin	ISBN: 1-56884-046-2	$19.95 USA/$26.95 Canada
OS/2® Warp For Dummies® 2nd Edition	by Andy Rathbone	ISBN: 1-56884-205-8	$19.99 USA/$26.99 Canada

UNIX

Title	Author	ISBN	Price
MORE UNIX® For Dummies®	by John R. Levine & Margaret Levine Young	ISBN: 1-56884-361-5	$19.99 USA/$26.99 Canada
UNIX® For Dummies®	by John R. Levine & Margaret Levine Young	ISBN: 1-878058-58-4	$19.95 USA/$26.95 Canada

WINDOWS

Title	Author	ISBN	Price
MORE Windows® For Dummies® 2nd Edition	by Andy Rathbone	ISBN: 1-56884-048-9	$19.95 USA/$26.95 Canada
Windows® 95 For Dummies®	by Andy Rathbone	ISBN: 1-56884-240-6	$19.99 USA/$26.99 Canada

PCS/HARDWARE

Title	Author	ISBN	Price
Illustrated Computer Dictionary For Dummies® 2nd Edition	by Dan Gookin & Wallace Wang	ISBN: 1-56884-218-X	$12.95 USA/$16.95 Canada
Upgrading and Fixing PCs For Dummies® 2nd Edition	by Andy Rathbone	ISBN: 1-56884-903-6	$19.99 USA/$26.99 Canada

PRESENTATION/AUTOCAD

Title	Author	ISBN	Price
AutoCAD For Dummies®	by Bud Smith	ISBN: 1-56884-191-4	$19.95 USA/$26.95 Canada
PowerPoint 4 For Windows® For Dummies®	by Doug Lowe	ISBN: 1-56884-161-2	$16.99 USA/$22.99 Canada

PROGRAMMING

Title	Author	ISBN	Price
Borland C++ For Dummies®	by Michael Hyman	ISBN: 1-56884-162-0	$19.95 USA/$26.95 Canada
C For Dummies® Volume 1	by Dan Gookin	ISBN: 1-878058-78-9	$19.95 USA/$26.95 Canada
C++ For Dummies®	by Stephen R. Davis	ISBN: 1-56884-163-9	$19.95 USA/$26.95 Canada
Delphi Programming For Dummies®	by Neil Rubenking	ISBN: 1-56884-200-7	$19.99 USA/$26.99 Canada
Mac® Programming For Dummies®	by Dan Parks Sydow	ISBN: 1-56884-173-6	$19.95 USA/$26.95 Canada
PowerBuilder 4 Programming For Dummies®	by Ted Coombs & Jason Coombs	ISBN: 1-56884-325-9	$19.99 USA/$26.99 Canada
QBasic Programming For Dummies®	by Douglas Hergert	ISBN: 1-56884-093-4	$19.95 USA/$26.95 Canada
Visual Basic 3 For Dummies®	by Wallace Wang	ISBN: 1-56884-076-4	$19.95 USA/$26.95 Canada
Visual Basic "X" For Dummies®	by Wallace Wang	ISBN: 1-56884-230-9	$19.99 USA/$26.99 Canada
Visual C++ 2 For Dummies®	by Michael Hyman & Bob Arnson	ISBN: 1-56884-328-3	$19.99 USA/$26.99 Canada
Windows® 95 Programming For Dummies®	by S. Randy Davis	ISBN: 1-56884-327-5	$19.99 USA/$26.99 Canada

SPREADSHEET

Title	Author	ISBN	Price
1-2-3 For Dummies®	by Greg Harvey	ISBN: 1-878058-60-6	$16.95 USA/$22.95 Canada
1-2-3 For Windows® 5 For Dummies® 2nd Edition	by John Walkenbach	ISBN: 1-56884-216-3	$16.95 USA/$22.95 Canada
Excel 5 For Macs® For Dummies®	by Greg Harvey	ISBN: 1-56884-186-8	$19.95 USA/$26.95 Canada
Excel For Dummies® 2nd Edition	by Greg Harvey	ISBN: 1-56884-050-0	$16.95 USA/$22.95 Canada
MORE 1-2-3 For DOS For Dummies®	by John Weingarten	ISBN: 1-56884-224-4	$19.99 USA/$26.99 Canada
MORE Excel 5 For Windows® For Dummies®	by Greg Harvey	ISBN: 1-56884-207-4	$19.95 USA/$26.95 Canada
Quattro Pro 6 For Windows® For Dummies®	by John Walkenbach	ISBN: 1-56884-174-4	$19.95 USA/$26.95 Canada
Quattro Pro For DOS For Dummies®	by John Walkenbach	ISBN: 1-56884-023-3	$16.95 USA/$22.95 Canada

UTILITIES

Title	Author	ISBN	Price
Norton Utilities 8 For Dummies®	by Beth Slick	ISBN: 1-56884-166-3	$19.95 USA/$26.95 Canada

VCRS/CAMCORDERS

Title	Author	ISBN	Price
VCRs & Camcorders For Dummies™	by Gordon McComb & Andy Rathbone	ISBN: 1-56884-229-5	$14.99 USA/$20.99 Canada

WORD PROCESSING

Title	Author	ISBN	Price
Ami Pro For Dummies®	by Jim Meade	ISBN: 1-56884-049-7	$19.95 USA/$26.95 Canada
MORE Word For Windows® 6 For Dummies®	by Doug Lowe	ISBN: 1-56884-165-5	$19.95 USA/$26.95 Canada
MORE WordPerfect® 6 For Windows® For Dummies®	by Margaret Levine Young & David C. Kay	ISBN: 1-56884-206-6	$19.95 USA/$26.95 Canada
MORE WordPerfect® 6 For DOS For Dummies®	by Wallace Wang, edited by Dan Gookin	ISBN: 1-56884-047-0	$19.95 USA/$26.95 Canada
Word 6 For Macs® For Dummies®	by Dan Gookin	ISBN: 1-56884-190-6	$19.95 USA/$26.95 Canada
Word For Windows® 6 For Dummies®	by Dan Gookin	ISBN: 1-56884-075-6	$16.95 USA/$22.95 Canada
Word For Windows® For Dummies®	by Dan Gookin & Ray Werner	ISBN: 1-878058-86-X	$16.95 USA/$22.95 Canada
WordPerfect® 6 For DOS For Dummies®	by Dan Gookin	ISBN: 1-878058-77-0	$16.95 USA/$22.95 Canada
WordPerfect® 6.1 For Windows® For Dummies® 2nd Edition	by Margaret Levine Young & David Kay	ISBN: 1-56884-243-0	$16.95 USA/$22.95 Canada
WordPerfect® For Dummies®	by Dan Gookin	ISBN: 1-878058-52-5	$16.95 USA/$22.95 Canada

Fun, Fast, & Cheap!™

The Internet For Macs® For Dummies® Quick Reference
by Charles Seiter

ISBN:1-56884-967-2
$9.99 USA/$12.99 Canada

Windows® 95 For Dummies® Quick Reference
by Greg Harvey

ISBN: 1-56884-964-8
$9.99 USA/$12.99 Canada

Photoshop 3 For Macs® For Dummies® Quick Reference
by Deke McClelland

ISBN: 1-56884-968-0
$9.99 USA/$12.99 Canada

WordPerfect® For DOS For Dummies® Quick Reference
by Greg Harvey

ISBN: 1-56884-009-8
$8.95 USA/$12.95 Canada

Title	Author	ISBN	Price
DATABASE			
Access 2 For Dummies® Quick Reference	by Stuart J. Stuple	ISBN: 1-56884-167-1	$8.95 USA/$11.95 Canada
dBASE 5 For DOS For Dummies® Quick Reference	by Barrie Sosinsky	ISBN: 1-56884-954-0	$9.99 USA/$12.99 Canada
dBASE 5 For Windows® For Dummies® Quick Reference	by Stuart J. Stuple	ISBN: 1-56884-953-2	$9.99 USA/$12.99 Canada
Paradox 5 For Windows® For Dummies® Quick Reference	by Scott Palmer	ISBN: 1-56884-960-5	$9.99 USA/$12.99 Canada
DESKTOP PUBLISHING/ILLUSTRATION/GRAPHICS			
CorelDRAW! 5 For Dummies® Quick Reference	by Raymond E. Werner	ISBN: 1-56884-952-4	$9.99 USA/$12.99 Canada
Harvard Graphics For Windows® For Dummies® Quick Reference	by Raymond E. Werner	ISBN: 1-56884-962-1	$9.99 USA/$12.99 Canada
Photoshop 3 For Macs® For Dummies® Quick Reference	by Deke McClelland	ISBN: 1-56884-968-0	$9.99 USA/$12.99 Canada
FINANCE/PERSONAL FINANCE			
Quicken 4 For Windows® For Dummies® Quick Reference	by Stephen L. Nelson	ISBN: 1-56884-950-8	$9.95 USA/$12.95 Canada
GROUPWARE/INTEGRATED			
Microsoft® Office 4 For Windows® For Dummies® Quick Reference	by Doug Lowe	ISBN: 1-56884-958-3	$9.99 USA/$12.99 Canada
Microsoft® Works 3 For Windows® For Dummies® Quick Reference	by Michael Partington	ISBN: 1-56884-959-1	$9.99 USA/$12.99 Canada
INTERNET/COMMUNICATIONS/NETWORKING			
The Internet For Dummies® Quick Reference	by John R. Levine & Margaret Levine Young	ISBN: 1-56884-168-X	$8.95 USA/$11.95 Canada
MACINTOSH			
Macintosh® System 7.5 For Dummies® Quick Reference	by Stuart J. Stuple	ISBN: 1-56884-956-7	$9.99 USA/$12.99 Canada
OPERATING SYSTEMS:			
DOS			
DOS For Dummies® Quick Reference	by Greg Harvey	ISBN: 1-56884-007-1	$8.95 USA/$11.95 Canada
UNIX			
UNIX® For Dummies® Quick Reference	by John R. Levine & Margaret Levine Young	ISBN: 1-56884-094-2	$8.95 USA/$11.95 Canada
WINDOWS			
Windows® 3.1 For Dummies® Quick Reference, 2nd Edition	by Greg Harvey	ISBN: 1-56884-951-6	$8.95 USA/$11.95 Canada
PCs/HARDWARE			
Memory Management For Dummies® Quick Reference	by Doug Lowe	ISBN: 1-56884-362-3	$9.99 USA/$12.99 Canada
PRESENTATION/AUTOCAD			
AutoCAD For Dummies® Quick Reference	by Ellen Finkelstein	ISBN: 1-56884-198-1	$9.95 USA/$12.95 Canada
SPREADSHEET			
1-2-3 For Dummies® Quick Reference	by John Walkenbach	ISBN: 1-56884-027-6	$8.95 USA/$11.95 Canada
1-2-3 For Windows® 5 For Dummies® Quick Reference	by John Walkenbach	ISBN: 1-56884-957-5	$9.95 USA/$12.95 Canada
Excel For Windows® For Dummies® Quick Reference, 2nd Edition	by John Walkenbach	ISBN: 1-56884-096-9	$8.95 USA/$11.95 Canada
Quattro Pro 6 For Windows® For Dummies® Quick Reference	by Stuart J. Stuple	ISBN: 1-56884-172-8	$9.95 USA/$12.95 Canada
WORD PROCESSING			
Word For Windows® 6 For Dummies® Quick Reference	by George Lynch	ISBN: 1-56884-095-0	$8.95 USA/$11.95 Canada
Word For Windows® For Dummies® Quick Reference	by George Lynch	ISBN: 1-56884-029-2	$8.95 USA/$11.95 Canada
WordPerfect® 6.1 For Windows® For Dummies® Quick Reference, 2nd Edition	by Greg Harvey	ISBN: 1-56884-966-4	$9.99 USA/$12.99/Canada

For scholastic requests & educational orders please call Educational Sales at 1. 800. 434. 2086

FOR MORE INFO OR TO ORDER, PLEASE CALL ▶ 800. 762. 2974

For volume discounts & special orders please call Tony Real, Special Sales, at 415. 655. 3048

Macworld® Mac® & Power Mac SECRETS, 2nd Edition
by David Pogue & Joseph Schorr

This is the definitive Mac reference for those who want to become power users! Includes three disks with 9MB of software!

HOT!

WINNERS 1994-95
TECHNICAL PUBLICATIONS AND ART COMPETITIONS OF THE SOCIETY FOR TECHNICAL COMMUNICATION

ISBN: 1-56884-175-2
$39.95 USA/$54.95 Canada

Includes 3 disks chock full of software.

NEWBRIDGE BOOK CLUB SELECTION

Macworld® Mac® FAQs
by David Pogue

HOT!

Written by the hottest Macintosh author around, David Pogue, *Macworld Mac FAQs* gives users the ultimate Mac reference. Hundreds of Mac questions and answers side-by-side, right at your fingertips, and organized into six easy-to-reference sections with lots of sidebars and diagrams.

ISBN: 1-56884-480-8
$19.99 USA/$26.99 Canada

Macworld® System 7.5 Bible, 3rd Edition
by Lon Poole

ISBN: 1-56884-098-5
$29.95 USA/$39.95 Canada

NATIONAL BESTSELLER!

Macworld® ClarisWorks 3.0 Companion, 3rd Edition
by Steven A. Schwartz

ISBN: 1-56884-481-6
$24.99 USA/$34.99 Canada

NATIONAL BESTSELLER!

Macworld® Complete Mac® Handbook Plus Interactive CD, 3rd Edition
by Jim Heid

BMUG
SPRING 1995 CHOICE PRODUCT

ISBN: 1-56884-192-2
$39.95 USA/$54.95 Canada

Includes an interactive CD-ROM.

NEWBRIDGE BOOK CLUB SELECTION

Macworld® Ultimate Mac® CD-ROM
by Jim Heid

ISBN: 1-56884-477-8
$19.99 USA/$26.99 Canada

CD-ROM includes version 2.0 of QuickTime, and over 65 MB of the best shareware, freeware, fonts, sounds, and more!

Macworld® Networking Bible, 2nd Edition
by Dave Kosiur & Joel M. Snyder

ISBN: 1-56884-194-9
$29.95 USA/$39.95 Canada

Macworld® Photoshop 3 Bible, 2nd Edition
by Deke McClelland

ISBN: 1-56884-158-2
$39.95 USA/$54.95 Canada

Includes stunning CD-ROM with add-ons, digitized photos and more.

WINNERS 1994-95
TECHNICAL PUBLICATIONS AND ART COMPETITIONS OF THE SOCIETY FOR TECHNICAL COMMUNICATION

NEW!

Macworld® Photoshop 2.5 Bible
by Deke McClelland

ISBN: 1-56884-022-5
$29.95 USA/$39.95 Canada

NATIONAL BESTSELLER!

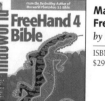

Macworld® FreeHand 4 Bible
by Deke McClelland

ISBN: 1-56884-170-1
$29.95 USA/$39.95 Canada

Macworld® Illustrator 5.0/5.5 Bible
by Ted Alspach

ISBN: 1-56884-097-7
$39.95 USA/$54.95 Canada

Includes CD-ROM with QuickTime tutorials.

Mac is a registered trademark of Apple Computer. Macworld is a registered trademark of International Data Group, Inc. ----SECRETS, and ----FAQs are trademarks under exclusive license to IDG Books Worldwide, Inc., from International Data Group, Inc.

For scholastic requests & educational orders please call Educational Sales, at 1. 800. 434. 2086

FOR MORE INFO OR TO ORDER, PLEASE CALL ▶ 800. 762. 2974

For volume discounts & special orders please call Tony Real, Special Sales, at 415. 655. 3048

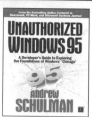

IDG BOOKS WORLDWIDE ™

Order Center: **(800) 762-2974** (8 a.m.–6 p.m., EST, weekdays)

3/26/9

Quantity	ISBN	Title	Price	Total

Shipping & Handling Charges

	Description	First book	Each additional book	Total
Domestic	Normal	$4.50	$1.50	$
	Two Day Air	$8.50	$2.50	$
	Overnight	$18.00	$3.00	$
International	Surface	$8.00	$8.00	$
	Airmail	$16.00	$16.00	$
	DHL Air	$17.00	$17.00	$

*For large quantities call for shipping & handling charges.
**Prices are subject to change without notice.

Ship to:

Name _____

Company _____

Address _____

City/State/Zip _____

Daytime Phone _____

Payment: ☐ Check to IDG Books Worldwide (US Funds Only)

☐ VISA   ☐ MasterCard   ☐ American Express

Card # _____ Expires _____

Signature _____

Subtotal _____

CA residents add
applicable sales tax _____

IN, MA, and MD
residents add
5% sales tax _____

IL residents add
6.25% sales tax _____

RI residents add
7% sales tax _____

TX residents add
8.25% sales tax _____

Shipping _____

Total _____

Please send this order form to:

IDG Books Worldwide, Inc.
Attn: Order Entry Dept.
7260 Shadeland Station, Suite 100
Indianapolis, IN 46256

Allow up to 3 weeks for delivery.
Thank you!

IDG BOOKS WORLDWIDE REGISTRATION CARD

RETURN THIS REGISTRATION CARD FOR FREE CATALOG

Title of this book: **Computer Telephony Strategies**™

My overall rating of this book: ❑ Very good [1] ❑ Good [2] ❑ Satisfactory [3] ❑ Fair [4] ❑ Poor [5]

How I first heard about this book:

❑ Found in bookstore; name: [6]

❑ Advertisement: [8]

❑ Word of mouth; heard about book from friend, co-worker, etc.: [10]

❑ Book review: [7]

❑ Catalog: [9]

❑ Other: [11]

What I liked most about this book:

What I would change, add, delete, etc., in future editions of this book:

Other comments:

Number of computer books I purchase in a year: ❑ 1 [12] ❑ 2-5 [13] ❑ 6-10 [14] ❑ More than 10 [15]

I would characterize my computer skills as: ❑ Beginner [16] ❑ Intermediate [17] ❑ Advanced [18] ❑ Professional [19]

I use ❑ DOS [20] ❑ Windows [21] ❑ OS/2 [22] ❑ Unix [23] ❑ Macintosh [24] ❑ Other: [25]_____
(please specify)

I would be interested in new books on the following subjects:
(please check all that apply, and use the spaces provided to identify specific software)

❑ Word processing: [26]

❑ Data bases: [28]

❑ File Utilities: [30]

❑ Networking: [32]

❑ Other: [34]

❑ Spreadsheets: [27]

❑ Desktop publishing: [29]

❑ Money management: [31]

❑ Programming languages: [33]

I use a PC at (please check all that apply): ❑ home [35] ❑ work [36] ❑ school [37] ❑ other: [38] _____

The disks I prefer to use are ❑ 5.25 [39] ❑ 3.5 [40] ❑ other: [41]_____

I have a CD ROM: ❑ yes [42] ❑ no [43]

I plan to buy or upgrade computer hardware this year: ❑ yes [44] ❑ no [45]

I plan to buy or upgrade computer software this year: ❑ yes [46] ❑ no [47]

Name: _____ Business title: [48] _____ Type of Business: [49] _____

Address (❑ home [50] ❑ work [51] /Company name: _____)

Street/Suite# _____

City [52] /State [53] /Zipcode [54]: _____ Country [55] _____

❑ **I liked this book!** You may quote me by name in future
IDG Books Worldwide promotional materials.

My daytime phone number is _____

IDG BOOKS
®

THE WORLD OF COMPUTER KNOWLEDGE

❏ YES!

Please keep me informed about IDG's World of Computer Knowledge.
Send me the latest IDG Books catalog.